THURGOOD MARSHALL

Also by Roger Goldman

Federal Criminal Trial Evidence
With J. O'Brien

Individual Rights: The Universal Challenge
By Roger Goldman

Also by David Gallen

Malcolm X: The FBI File
Introduction by Spike Lee
Commentary by Clayborne Carson
Edited by David Gallen

The Baseball Chronicles
Edited by David Gallen

Malcolm X: As They Knew Him
By David Gallen

THURGOOD MARSHALL
JUSTICE FOR ALL

Roger Goldman with David Gallen

Carroll & Graf Publishers, Inc.
New York

First Carroll & Graf edition 1992

Carroll & Graf Publishers, Inc.
260 Fifth Avenue
New York, NY 10001

Library of Congress Cataloging-in-Publication Data

Goldman, Roger L.
    Thurgood Marshall: justice for all/by Roger Goldman with David Gallen. —1st
Carroll & Graf ed.
        p.   cm.
    Includes bibliographical references and index.
    ISBN 0-88184-805-0 : $24.95
    1. Marshall, Thurgood, 1908–   . 2. Judicial opinions—United States.   I. Mar-
shall, Thurgood, 1908–   .   II. Gallen, David.   III. Title.
    KF8745.M34A4   1992
    347.73′2634—dc20
    [B]
    [347.3073534]
    [B]   92-5400
                                                                           CIP

Interior Design by Terry McCabe

Manufactured in the United States of America

Acknowledgments

Without the inspiration many years ago of my professors at the University of Pennsylvania Law School, particularly Paul Mishkin and Tony Amsterdam, I would not have undertaken this project.

I am also indebted to Joyce Armstrong and Fred Epstein, both non-lawyers, whose many years of work for the American Civil Liberties Union of Eastern Missouri serve as a constant reminder of the importance of keeping alive the words and hopes of Thurgood Marshall.

Finally, I am grateful to my wife, Stephanie, and two sons, Josh and Sam, for their willingness to discuss Justice Marshall's views on civil rights and civil liberties around the dinner table.

—Roger Goldman

I wish to thank Marty Eskenazi for helping me read through so many of Justice Marshall's Supreme Court opinions and his research help. I also thank Kate Jetmore, NYU's finest acting student, for typing the manuscript.

I am also grateful to the entire staff of Gallen Sports Productions, particularly Jon Gallen, Mike Bertolini and Michael Hisler; they were always willing to share their keen insights on Thurgood Marshall with me.

—David Gallen

Permissions

The publisher gratefully acknowledges permission to reprint the following:

Dr. Randall Bland for chapters 1–4 of *Private Pressure on Public Law,* Kennikat Press, 1973.

Justice William Brennan, Jr. and the *Harvard Law Review* for November 1991 tribute to Thurgood Marshall, pp. 23–33.

Judge Robert Carter and the *Harvard Law Review* for November 1991 tribute to Thurgood Marshall, pp. 33–42.

Stephen L. Carter, "Living Without the Judge." Reprinted by permission of Stephen L. Carter, The Yale Law Journal Company and Fred B. Rothman & Company from *The Yale Law Journal,* vol. 101, pp. 1–6. © copyright Stephen L. Carter.

Glen Darbyshire, Esq. and the *American Bar Association Journal* for September 1991 essay, "Clerking for Justice Marshall."

Paul Gewirtz, "Thurgood Marshall." Reprinted by permission of The Yale Law Journal Company and Fred B. Rothman & Company from *The Yale Law Journal,* vol. 101, pp. 13–18.

Professor Martha Minow and the *Harvard Law Review* for November 1991 tribute to Thurgood Marshall, pp. 66–76.

Constance Baker Motley, "My Personal Debt to Thurgood Marshall." Reprinted by permission of The Yale Law Journal Company and Fred B. Rothman & Company from *The Yale Law Journal,* vol. 101, pp. 19–24.

Juan Williams and the *Washington Post* for January 7, 1990 feature on Thurgood Marshall.

Contents

Preface

CREATING A BOOK ON THURGOOD MARSHALL IS NO EASY TASK. FOR ONE thing, Marshall is a fiercely private person who shuns interviews and the press. For another, Justices with whom Marshall worked on the Supreme Court are reluctant to speak of the cases over which they presided. For a third, Marshall's law clerks are, for the most part, also hesitant to discuss either Marshall's career as an Associate Supreme Court Justice or his colorful personality. Finally, many of Marshall's childhood friends and constituents in the NAACP are no longer alive. In light of such problems, the best way to present a complete picture of Thurgood Marshall, it seems to me, is to offer a selection of essays that provide insights into the unique professional and personal qualities that have made Thurgood Marshall a justice for all.

The first section of the book focuses on Marshall the man. It includes nine pieces, seven of them by people who were closely associated with Marshall in some phase of his long career. Professor Martha Minow of Harvard University, Professors Paul Gewirtz and Stephen L. Carter of Yale University Law School, and attorney Glen Darbyshire were law clerks to Justice Marshall, while Judge Robert Carter and Judge Constance Baker Motley worked daily with Marshall during their tenure at the NAACP. Former Associate Justice William Brennan sat on the Supreme Court with Marshall for twenty-three years and shared with him a professional compassion for the disenfranchised of our society. In addition, a feature story by *Washington Post* correspondent Juan Williams is included, along with four chapters from Randall Bland's study of Marshall's life and career up to 1973. Bland's biography remains, in my opinion, the best treatment published to date on Marshall's early life and career.

An essay written by Constitutional Law Professor Roger Goldman comprises the second section of the book. Analyzing Marshall's jurisprudence as an associate Supreme Court Justice, Goldman illuminates Marshall's decisions on such topics as First Amendment and Fourth Amendment issues, civil rights cases, education, poverty, equal protection and the death penalty. The essay portrays Marshall as a caring, deeply intelligent man who continually fought to protect the rights of all citizens.

The third section of the book reprints the opinions that Marshall himself wrote as Associate Supreme Court Justice. The fifteen opinions have been carefully chosen from over nine hundred cases to illustrate Marshall's compassion, intensity and fair-mindedness.

I

Recollections of Thurgood Marshall

*Justice William Brennan, Jr., worked closely with Thurgood Mar-
shall as an Associate Justice of the Supreme Court for twenty-three
years. More than any other justice, William Brennan, Jr., shared
Marshall's passionate commitment to the civil rights of the less privileged. In this tribute to Marshall, originally published in the* Harvard
Law Review *(November 1991), Brennan reminisces about his old
friend and his contributions to American law.*

A TRIBUTE TO JUSTICE THURGOOD MARSHALL

William J. Brennan, Jr.

IT IS A GREAT PLEASURE TO JOIN IN THE *HARVARD LAW REVIEW*'S TRIBUTE
to Justice Marshall, but the task is daunting. Thurgood is one of our
century's legal giants; one cannot take his full measure within the compass of an essay, and even a summary is difficult. One can begin, of
course, by noting that in his twenty-four terms on the Supreme Court,
Justice Marshall played a crucial role in enforcing the constitutional
protections that distinguish our democracy. Indeed, he leaves behind
an enviable record of opinions supporting the rights of the less powerful and less fortunate. One can then add that, for more than twenty-five
years before he joined the judiciary, Thurgood Marshall was probably
the most important advocate in America, one who used his formidable
legal skills to end the evils of discrimination. Thurgood would be the
first to remind us that he was supported by a host of other talented
lawyers, beginning with his mentor Charles Houston. But it was
Thurgood who took the lead, and it was his presentations, in case after
case and in court after court, that helped bring about a society in which
"equal protection of the laws" could be a reality and not merely a legal
phrase.

Yet these profiles of Thurgood Marshall as Justice and as counsel
leave the picture incomplete. Those who know him well recognize that

a portrait of Thurgood must also reflect the dedication, the courage, the humanity, and the warm humor of the man. Perhaps, then, the only way to begin this tribute is to say that I have had the privilege of serving on the Supreme Court with twenty-two Justices and that my dear friend Thurgood was unique among them. His departure from the Court brings a richly deserved retirement for him but, regrettably for the country, signals the twilight of a remarkable public career. Of no other lawyer can it so truly be said that *all* Americans owe him an enormous debt of gratitude.

What made Thurgood Marshall unique as a Justice? Above all, it was the special voice that he added to the Court's deliberations and decisions. His was a voice of authority: he spoke from firsthand knowledge of the law's failure to fulfill its promised protections for so many Americans. It was also the voice of reason, for Justice Marshall had spent half a lifetime using the tools of legal argument to close the gap between constitutional ideal and reality. And it was a voice with an unwavering message: that the Constitution's protections must not be denied to anyone and that the Court must give its constitutional doctrine the scope and the sensitivity needed to assure that result. Justice Marshall's voice was often persuasive, but whether or not he prevailed in a given instance, he always had an impact. Even in dissent, he spoke for those who might otherwise be forgotten—when, for example, he chided the Court for doubting that a fifty-dollar bankruptcy fee was a burden for the "over 800,000 families in the Nation [who] had . . . incomes of less than . . . $19.23 a week" or when he chastised his colleagues for concluding that a juvenile in police custody could invoke his *Miranda* rights only by requesting a lawyer, not a probation officer or when he reminded the majority that "many families do not conform to th[e] ideal" and that parental notification requirements may therefore result in "physical or emotional abuse, [or] withdrawal of financial support" for minors seeking abortions.

I joined the Court the year after its second decision in *Brown* v. *Board of Education (Brown II),* and so I did not hear that urgent voice until the desegregation cases that followed in *Brown's* wake. I particularly remember the argument in *Cooper* v. *Aaron* the case involving Arkansas's armed resistance to federal court desegregation orders in Little Rock. Although the issues before us in that case were largely procedural, Thurgood's forceful presentation helped influence the Court's unprecedented and decisive response: we reinstated the deseg-

RECOLLECTIONS / 15

regation order on the day after oral argument and our subsequent opinion was signed by all nine Justices.

The Court addressed the most serious episodes of *Brown*'s enforcement a decade later, after Thurgood joined our bench. Beginning in 1968, the Court issued three crucial decisions reaffirming the commitment to desegregation. The Court overturned one school district's "freedom of choice" plan and then affirmed a court-imposed pupil reassignment plan in another district after finding failure to comply with *Brown* in both cases. In the third case, the Court found that proof of de jure segregation in a substantial portion of a school district could support a finding of a dual system of schools throughout the whole district. Although Justice Marshall did not write in these cases, his strong statements during the Court's conferences—drawing on his familiarity with the problems—sharpened the Court's resolve to strive for unanimous decisions.

Eventually, of course, the Court's consensus disintegrated in *Milliken* v. *Bradley*, the 5–4 decision that overturned a multidistrict desegregation plan approved by a federal judge in Detroit. Justice Marshall filed a compelling dissent decrying the majority's holding that the remedy for decades of official segregation in Detroit could not extend beyond the city itself, even though two-thirds of that city's students were now Afro-American. As Justice Marshall observed, a remedy thus confined "simply d[id] not promise to achieve actual desegregation at all," and he warned that "unless our children begin to learn together, there is little hope that our people will ever learn to live together."

Justice Marshall's dissent may well have made the Court more responsive to the plight of Detroit's schoolchildren when the case returned before us in *Milliken* v. *Bradley (Milliken II)*. On that occasion, the Court unanimously upheld a desegregation plan that, although limited to Detroit, broke new ground by requiring remedial education programs as part of the plan to redress discrimination. And Justice Marshall's influence was felt again two years later when the Court inferred de jure segregation from a series of administrative decisions in Columbus, Ohio, that could not "reasonably be explained without reference to racial concerns." In sum, Justice Marshall's persuasive voice made all of us more sensitive to the legacy of discrimination. As President Johnson predicted at the time of his nomination, placing Thurgood Marshall on the Court was "the right thing to do, the right time to do it, the right man and the right place." This was true not only in the desegregation era, but also in later years, when questions such as affirmative action reached the Court.

Justice Marshall was the "right man" in countless other ways, of course, ranging far beyond cases involving racial equality. His constitutional vision, like his courtroom experience, was broad, and so were his insights. To me, three crucial areas of his constitutional vision stand out: the First Amendment, the rights of criminal defendants, and the death penalty.

In his first Term on the Court, Justice Marshall wrote the majority opinion in *Amalgamated Food Employees Union Local 590* v. *Logan Valley Plaza, Inc.,* which significantly expanded the "public forum" doctrine. The issue in that case was whether owners of a large shopping mall could invoke private property rights to exclude picketers. Justice Marshall recognized shopping centers as the suburban counterparts of central business districts and concluded that picketing and other protected expression could not be prohibited.

Logan Valley Plaza was soon followed by Thurgood's opinion in another landmark case: *Stanley* v. *Georgia.* The defendant there had been convicted of possessing obscene material after officers who were searching his home for evidence of bookmaking came upon an allegedly obscene film. In claiming that this arrest violated the First Amendment, the defendant had to overcome the Court's established view— reiterated in an opinion that I had recently written—that obscene material was not protected by the Constitution. Justice Marshall properly limited such prior holdings to cases involving some public activity; mere private possession of obscene materials, he concluded, could not be subject to prosecution. "If the First Amendment means anything," he wrote, "it means that a State has no business telling a man, sitting alone in his own house, what books he may read or what films he may watch."

Three years later, Justice Marshall authored an equal protection decision that significantly curtailed content-based limitations on speech. In *Police Department* v. *Mosley,* a black postal worker was prevented from protesting discriminatory policies on a sidewalk adjacent to a high school. The pertinent ordinance barred such demonstrations during school hours but exempted labor picketers from the restriction. Justice Marshall found this preference for certain picketers unconstitutional. He observed that government "may not select which issues are worth discussing or debating in public facilities. . . . There is an 'equality of status in the field of ideas.' " Justice Marshall extended this finding fifteen years later when he invalidated a sales tax that exempted certain journals such as religious and sports publications.

Underlying each of these advances in First Amendment doctrine was a personal awareness of the First Amendment's central meaning. More than any other Justice on the Court, Thurgood Marshall knew what it was like to stand up for unpopular ideas. The voice of experience echoes in his reminder that "equal protection . . . is closely intertwined with First Amendment interests" and in his remark that restrictions on free speech might exclude not only the labor picketers arrested in *Logan Valley Plaza* but also "consumers protesting . . . overpriced merchandise, and minority groups seeking nondiscriminatory hiring policies."

Thurgood also knew what it was like to stand up for unpopular clients. He often defended men and women who had no other lawyer. These experiences gave him a special appreciation for the constitutional rights of those accused of crimes. He viewed the Bill of Rights' key protections for the accused as magnificent but fragile creations— magnificent because they seek to shield individuals from the overweening power of the state; fragile because such shields can easily crumble if courts create exceptions or narrow their scope. More than any other recent member of the Court, Justice Marshall leaves a legacy of powerful dissents protesting the curtailment of defendants' rights—dissents with a vision of fairness and order that is stirring in its clarity.

In *Rawlings* v. *Kentucky,* for example, Justice Marshall protested the Court's retrenchment in its Fourth Amendment doctrine. Rawlings was convicted of possessing contraband that had been seized in a search of a friend's purse. The purse search was concededly illegal, but the majority held that the defendant had no "subjective expectation" of privacy in the other person's purse and therefore lacked standing to challenge the seizure of items he himself owned. In dissent, Justice Marshall noted that "[t]he history of the Fourth Amendment," as well as the Court's prior enforcement of it, "shows that it was designed to protect property interests as well as privacy interests." The Fourth Amendment's text, Justice Marshall reminded us, assures " '[t]he right of the people to be secure *in* their persons . . . and effects *against* unreasonable searches and seizures,' " and thus, if "property was seized as the result of an unreasonable search, the seizure cannot be other than unreasonable."

Justice Marshall's essential point in *Rawlings* was that we should not adjust constitutional doctrine to enhance "the government's ability to obtain criminal convictions," because the proper "balance" between governmental interests and individual liberty was chosen long ago by those who framed the Bill of Rights. This important insight recurred often in Thurgood's writings. A few years later, in *New York* v. *Quarles,* he denounced a similar sacrifice of Fifth Amendment rights to the perceived needs of law enforcement. The *Quarles* Court created a "public safety" exception to the requirement that defendants in police custody be informed of their right to remain silent before interrogation. "Though the majority's opinion is cloaked in the beguiling language of utilitarianism," Justice Marshall warned, "the Court has sanctioned *sub silentio* criminal prosecutions based on compelled self-incriminating statements."

Justice Marshall's most eloquent defense of constitutional protections, however, was likely his dissent in *United States* v. *Salerno.* In that case, the Court approved the potentially unlimited detention of indicted defendants based on a showing of future dangerousness that need not satisfy the "beyond a reasonable doubt" standard. Justice Marshall denounced the detention law for violating the presumption of innocence and the protection against excessive bail. "Such statutes," Marshall wrote, "[which are] consistent with the usages of tyranny and the excesses of what bitter experience teaches us to call the police state, have long been thought incompatible with the fundamental human rights protected by our Constitution." The closing paragraph of the *Salerno* dissent captured in somber tones Justice Marshall's sense of judicial duty toward the rights of the accused:

> Throughout the world today there are men, women, and children interned indefinitely, awaiting trials . . . because their governments believe them to be 'dangerous.' Our Constitution, whose construction began two centuries ago, can shelter us forever from the evils of such unchecked power. Over 200 years it has slowly, through our efforts, grown more durable, more expansive, and more just. But it cannot protect us if we lack the courage, and the self-restraint, to protect ourselves.

The number and quality of Justice Marshall's dissents should not obscure his important successes in the realm of defendants' rights. Chief among these was his campaign to eradicate discrimination from jury selection procedures. In an opinion written during his fourth Term on the Court, *Peters* v. *Kiff,* Justice Marshall upheld a white defendant's claim that his due process rights were violated by the systematic exclusion of blacks from grand and petit juries. He argued that, even if race was not an issue in the trial, such juror exclusions could render the trial unfair by narrowing the range of juror backgrounds. Notwithstanding the difficulty of proving such unfairness, Justice Marshall believed the very risk of its existence offended due process. Only two other Justices joined his plurality opinion. It seems fair to say, however, that his view has ultimately prevailed. This past Term, in *Powers* v. *Ohio*, the Court upheld by a decisive margin a white defendant's claim that a prosecutor's discriminatory use of peremptory challenges against black potential jurors entitled him to a new trial. Although the focus in *Powers* upon the rights of excluded jurors differed somewhat from Justice Marshall's analysis in *Peters*, the decision clearly reflected his original concern, because it acknowledged that "discrimination in the selection of jurors . . . places the fairness of a criminal proceeding in doubt."

Justice Marshall's opinion in *Bounds* v. *Smith* has had a comparable impact on the rights of prisoners. *Bounds* required that prisoners be provided law libraries or legal assistance to preserve their right of access to federal courts. Justice Marshall's opinion for the Court bespoke a familiarity with the plight of unschooled litigants. A pro se prisoner, he noted, has as much need as any lawyer to "research[] such issues as jurisdiction, venue, standing, exhaustion of remedies, proper parties plaintiff and defendant, and types of relief available." No one familiar with today's federal court dockets could fail to appreciate the impact of *Bounds,* for it has enabled prisoners not only to challenge unfair convictions, but also to place before the courts claims of prison mistreatment and unconstitutional conditions.

Because I have emphasized the effect that Thurgood's experiences in his early years had on his opinions, I should perhaps explain how I have come to know the details of his early life. The chief and surely the most enjoyable source of such knowledge has been Thurgood himself; he is simply unsurpassed as a raconteur. On many occasions, some fact or event will remind him of an earlier episode in his richly varied life. When that moment arrives, a flicker of recollected amusement passes over his face, the magic words "You *know* . . ." signal the onset of another tale, and soon Thurgood has plunged his audience into a different world. The locales are varied—from dusty courtrooms in the Deep South, to a confrontation with General MacArthur in the Far East, to the drafting sessions for the Kenyan Constitution. They are brought to life by all the tricks of the storyteller's art: the fluid voice, the mobile eyebrows, the sidelong glance, the pregnant pause, and the wry smile.

The stories are never self-aggrandizing; indeed, they often focus upon someone else. They have provided many with amusement, but they have also given all of Thurgood's colleagues remarkable glimpses of his experiences—of the time when he was run down by hostile sheriffs who tried to frame him on a drunk driving charge, or when a preacher with whom he was working came within a few minutes of being lynched at the riverside, or when a young defendant facing the death penalty asserted his innocence and refused to accept a plea bargain of life imprisonment, or when the Ku Klux Klan warned him not to stay in town during trial (and the word went out in the black community that men were needed "to sit up with a sick relative" at the house where Thurgood stayed), or when a long-shot lawsuit unexpectedly created the Tuskeegee Airmen, or of countless other episodes, in and out of the courtroom.

What prompts these stories? Justice Marshall thoroughly enjoys good (and even bad) jokes, of course, and the stories are peppered with them, even in the midst of grimmer narratives. But, as I have suggested, the anecdotes serve a deeper purpose. In some cases, I think, they are his way of preserving the past while purging it of its bleakest moments, for Marshall has clearly confronted a great deal of ugliness in his life. But they are also a form of education for the rest of us. Surely Justice Marshall recognized that the stories made us—his colleagues—confront walks of life we had never known. That, too, has been part of the voice that Thurgood Marshall brought to the Court.

I have left for last my comments on one other aspect of Justice Marshall's jurisprudence: his views on the death penalty. Thurgood and I, of course, were alone on the Court in believing that capital punishment was in all cases barred as "cruel and unusual punishment" under the Eighth Amendment. In his sixty-page concurrence in *Furman* v. *Georgia*, Justice Marshall canvassed a vast array of historical and social science materials to demonstrate that punishments are deemed "cruel" if excessive and that, when judged by any acceptable theory of punishment, the death penalty is excessive. Justice Marshall held to that view, even when four years later the rest of the Court again permitted death penalties. But he never became complacent in his opposition. Rather, as one scholar has pointed out, he challenged the majority view on its own terms by arguing that there were insufficient safeguards to ensure the "reliability" of capital sentencing—safeguards that several other justices found constitutionally *necessary.* Justice Marshall's dedication to this task has been remarkable. Perhaps few outside the Court realize that, quite apart from his general opposition to all executions, Thurgood has filed more than 150 dissents from "denial of certiorari" in capital cases. These dissents called his colleagues' attention to particular problems, often involving procedural unfairness, in the imposition of individual death sentences that he thought warranted review.

In cases that the Court did review, Justice Marshall succeeded in implementing some crucial reforms. In *Ake* v. *Oklahoma,* his majority opinion held that an indigent defendant was entitled to have a psychiatrist present his insanity defense to a murder charge and respond to the prosecutor's claim (in seeking the death penalty) regarding the defendant's future dangerousness. And in *Ford* v. *Wainwright,* Justice Marshall persuaded a majority that the execution of insane prisoners violated the Eighth Amendment; in his opinion, he noted "the natural abhorrence civilized societies feel at killing one who has no capacity to come to grips with his own conscience."

Decisions like *Ake* and *Ford* mark substantial advances in the law, yet they also underscore the continuing wrong of capital punishment. Justice Marshall would not want us to forget that. Ten years ago, at the unveiling of a statue honoring him in his home city of Baltimore, Thurgood warned the assembled guests: "I just want to be sure that when you see this statue, you won't think that's the end of it. I won't have it that way. There's too much work to be done." It was typical of Thurgood to eschew complacency even at that moment. He has never stopped challenging us to make the Constitution fulfill its promises for all Americans; he has never stopped calling upon (in Lincoln's words) "the better angels of our nature." One can only hope that his voice will continue to resonate in the future work of the Court.

This examination of Marshall's career prior to his Supreme Court tenure originally appeared in the dissertation Private Pressure on Public Law, *written by Randall Bland at Notre Dame in 1973. First published by Kennikat Press and scheduled for reissue this year it remains, in my opinion, the most thorough and enlightening treatment of Marshall's early career. The first four chapters of this work follow.*

1

The Making of an Advocate

THURGOOD MARSHALL WAS BORN ON THE LOWER SIDE OF BALTIMORE, Maryland, on July 2, 1908, the younger of two sons born to William Canfield and Norma A. Marshall. The Marshalls were mulattoes; both William and Norma were calculated to be at least half white. (Indeed, the census taker did not know whether to record Thurgood's paternal grandmother as Negro or white. All Mrs. Marshall knew was that she had been raised as a Negro in her home in Virginia.) The Marshalls taught their children to be proud of their ancestry, which they traced to a nineteenth-century Congolese slave who caused so much trouble for his master that he was set free. Even today Marshall enjoys telling the story of this remarkable man, who had been brought as a slave to the Eastern shore of Maryland by a big-game hunter who had captured him in Africa:

> His polite descendants like to think he came from the cultured tribes in Sierra Leone . . . but we all know that he really came from the toughest part of the Congo. Wherever he came from, the fellow made his objections to slavery so widely known that the master called him in one day and told him: "Look, I brought you here so I guess I can't very well shoot you—as you deserve. On the

other hand, I can't, with a clear conscience, sell anyone as vicious as you to another slave holder. So, I'm going to set you free—on one condition. Get the hell out of this country and never come back." And that . . . is the only time Massuh didn't get an argument from the old boy.

Marshall's paternal grandfather was a freeman of Maryland who enlisted in the Union Army during the Civil War. He took the name "Thoroughgood" in order to satisfy Army regulations that "every volunteer have both a first and last name for the records," but "as a youth, Thurgood . . . got tired of laboriously spelling out Thoroughgood in grammar school.

Looking back, the Associate Justice remembers his early home life as warm and secure. Marshall's parents were intelligent and strongly antisegregationist. His father was an amateur writer who held down a well-paying job as a Pullman-car waiter. It was a signal advance when he was appointed steward at the exclusive Gibson Island Club on Chesapeake Bay.

Marshall's mother was an elementary schoolteacher who tried her best to convince her younger son that dentistry was "a safe and relatively lucrative career for a Baltimore Negro." Granted, young Thurgood made an attempt at studying dentistry during his first two years in college, but the subject failed to hold his interest. His parents encouraged him to get the best education possible, and his mother sold her engagement ring to help pay for Thurgood's college expenses. As it turned out, it was the paternal influence that ultimately determined Marshall's choice of a career. The senior Marshall had great faith in facts and devoted much of his free time to assembling data which he used to challenge the logic of even the most commonly accepted concepts. Nothing was taken for granted. This tendency to disputation, as well as his oratorical talents, manifested itself in his younger son. As Thurgood was to recall later, "He never told me to become a lawyer, but he turned me into one. He did it by teaching me to argue, by challenging my logic on every point, by making me prove every statement I made."

As a young boy living in Baltimore in the early twentieth century, Thurgood was forced to endure the usual treatment that went with being a Negro. But, as a friend has pointed out, "A James Baldwin he was not." He experienced no great racial trauma that forever changed his life, even though his parents urged him to become involved in the civil-rights movement. Although Marshall was "not at all pugnacious on the subject of civil rights . . . his legal ability made him a formidable advocate of them." Even today, Marshall likes to tell of his days as a youth in the old neighborhood:

> We lived on a respectable street, but behind us there were back alleys where the roughnecks and the tough kids hung out. When it was time for dinner, my mother used to go to the front door and call my older brother. Then she'd go to the *back* door and call me.

Marshall's drive for an education did not begin on a very promising note. His father was convinced that shiftlessness was a direct cause of crime and poverty and that improvidence could be acquired at any time. Accordingly, Thurgood was sent to the school where his mother taught to enable her to maintain surveillance over him. After attending elementary and high schools in Baltimore, however, his prospects seemed "no better than those of his Negro classmates, many of whom failed to finish high school." When the time came for choosing a college, it was decided that Thurgood should select a nearby institution. In September 1925 he enrolled at Lincoln University, a Negro institution in Pennsylvania, with a growing reputation that caused it to be referred to as the "black Princeton," since its founder had been a man of old Nassau. Lincoln used the same colors as Princeton, and its white staff was for the most part composed of Princetonians. The student body included a wide geographic and sociological spectrum: both Asians and Africans, as well as members of every economic class from working poor to wealthy aristocrat. Lincoln men were aware that they constituted a potential black elite, and the University encouraged the development of a sense of dedication because

> beneath the selfish ambitions projected in their boastful dreams blazed a furious zeal for the concept of racial equality, burned a bitter hatred of injustice, smoldered a lava flow of race consciousness, that alternately anguished and exalted them.

In his sophomore year Marshall was temporarily expelled for hazing freshmen; as he put it, "I got the horsin' around out of my system." It was at this time that he met his future wife, Vivian Burney, who became a stabilizing influence on his activities. On September 4, 1929, before he started his junior year, they were married. (The marriage lasted for twenty-five years, until Vivian's death of cancer in February 1955. Marshall subsequently married Cecilia Suyat.) Vivian Marshall helped "turn him around" and inspired in him an academic zeal. He worked at a number of jobs during this period to finance his education: as a bellhop, a dining-car waiter, and even as a pinochle player. Thurgood Marshall finally abandoned his idea of a career in dentistry and now set his sights on law school. He began to find his own identity and slowly matured. He was impressed by the accomplishments of fellow Negroes in the "new age" of the 1920s: Paul Robeson, the singer and actor; Florence Mills, the musical-comedy star; and others. He engaged in an extensive reading program, absorbing any books that were of or by Negroes. He was challenged by Carter Woodson's the *Negro in American History, The American Negro* by Jerome Dowd, and the works of W. E. B. DuBois. In his senior year at Lincoln he starred as a debater in the Forensic Society, and in June of 1930 he received his A.B. degree with honors in the humanities.

Marshall's first choice of law schools was the University of Maryland, but when his application was turned down by the all-white school, he decided to enter the law school at Howard University in Washington, D.C. The Negro university was going through a period of transition. Mordecai Johnson, the university's first black president, was attempting to change the image of the institution from one of social glamor to that of social consciousness. A man of tremendous insight, Johnson believed that "an institution of learning, while it protected the good and valuable in older traditions, must at the same time encourage that 'higher individualism' that constantly makes for new and greater values."

He brought to Howard instructors who held similar ideals and who were destined to become renowned in their respective areas of competence: Charles Burch and Sterling Brown in literature; Alain Locke in philosophy; Franklin Frazer in sociology; Rayford Logan in history; E. E. Just in the natural sciences; Ralph Bunche in government and politics; and Charles Houston, William Hastie, and James Nabrit, Jr., in law. During his first year at Howard, Marshall came in contact with Dr. Charles Hamilton Houston, Vice-Dean of the Law School. Houston, a brilliant lawyer who had been a Phi Beta Kappa at Amherst, had obtained his law degree from Harvard. He taught at Howard for fifteen years and was a practicing attorney for six. A dedicated worker and activist in the newly mobilized civil-rights movement, the dean was also a member of the NAACP. Houston felt that Negro lawyers should be social engineers, and he attempted to make Howard the production center for the new breed of Negro lawyer. He sponsored such teachers as William Hastie, a former editor of the *Harvard Law Review,* and devoted his efforts to students with the most potential. In 1930 his most promising student was Thurgood Marshall.

Houston was Marshall's mentor in law school. He taught his protégé the strategy of using existing laws to defeat racial discrimination. Moreover, Houston encouraged his student to know the law thoroughly. "I heard lawbooks were to dig in," said Marshall of this period, "so I dug, way deep." Houston, Hastie, and Nabrit represented the NAACP in a number of cases and in so doing, made the law school a kind of legal laboratory in which Association leaders met with faculty and students to debate courtroom strategy. It was at this time that one of the students attracted the attention of Walter White, Executive Secretary of the NAACP. Later, White was to describe Thurgood Marshall as:

> a lanky, brash young senior law student who was always present. I used to wonder at his presence and sometimes was amazed at his assertiveness in challenging positions [taken] by Charlie [Houston] and the other lawyers. But I soon learned of his great value to the case in doing everything he was asked, from research on obscure legal opinions to foraging for coffee and sandwiches.

Marshall did so well academically under Houston's tutelage that he led his class in all three years and was graduated as valedictorian in 1933.

Dean Houston had a tremendous impact on the career of Thurgood Marshall. Their close association continued for many years after Marshall's graduation from law school. After his many legal victories before the Supreme Court, the future Director-Counsel of the Legal Defense and Educational Fund never failed to give credit to Charles H. Houston for any of his accomplishments in the courtroom.

Of the Man and the Law

Marshall's manner and personality have remained consistent over the years. It has been said that he has a natural-born way. "I intend to wear life like a very loose garment and never worry about nothin'!" he told Sidney Zion. He is a member of the Episcopalian Church and is a 33d Degree Mason. He has been glorified by leading Negroes for his legal accomplishments; Charles S. Johnson called him the "Cyrano de Bergerac of the Constitution," the Negro press has nicknamed him

"Mr. Civil Rights," and to many others he is known as "Mr. Desegregation." Many of his race consider him a modern folk hero:

> To Negroes of the rank and file he represents what folk heroes have represented immemorially: the ability to outwit, outscore, and eventually overcome forces of entrenched and organized oppression. What is also essential in this role, of course, is that he has accomplished this without becoming pompous or thinking himself too important.

In 1933 Marshall and his wife moved back to Baltimore. He was admitted to the Maryland bar and set up private practice. His legal education at Howard had been general, but in his final year Marshall had concentrated on corporation aspects of the law. Reflecting on his first three years of private practice, Marshall recalls that it "was a complete general practice, ranging from representing business corporations, building associations, negligence cases, criminal cases, probate cases, and so forth—the general practice of law in the State and Federal Courts in Maryland." In fact, he started his career as a labor and antitrust lawyer, but the Depression helped make such profitable cases few and far between. These were the first of many years that Marshall was to spend in trial courts on behalf of defendants.

His early years in Baltimore were arduous and discouraging. Clients were hard to find, and fees a rarity. Marshall did not expect to become wealthy in private practice, but he certainly thought that he would maintain a modest income; however, even a "modest income" was impossible during this period. As Marshall reminisced: "One day, I'd bring two lunches and the next day my secretary would bring two lunches and sometimes we'd be the only two people in that office for weeks at a time." He represented numerous defendants without charging a fee, purely for the experience:

> It was all those freebees that finally sent me to the NAACP . . . but I did have one paying client. The fellow used to get picked up quite a bit and the only thing he ever said to the cops was "I want to see my lawyer." That was the extent of his interrogation-room vocabulary.
>
> So then I'd come into the station and he'd say, "Lawyer, how much they got on me?" I'm not saying he got off all the time but one thing was sure—he didn't hurt himself any by keeping quiet, and that's his right. No doubt about it, it's everybody's right.

Marshall began to develop his style and some normative concepts of the law and its application. Normally a person who speaks in italics, Marshall, once in a courtroom, has been described by his associates as a persuader who has often taken the opposition off guard and, in Langston Hughes' words, "has moved many a judge to search his conscience and come up with decisions he probably did not know he had in him." After observing Marshall's skillful court-room tactics, Francis X. Beytagh, Jr., who worked under Marshall during his tenure as Solicitor General, commented: "He doesn't purport to be a legal scholar, but he is an effective lawyer because he has common sense and a good instinct for facts." Apparently Marshall had come to believe that the success of litigation depends greatly on the amount of preparatory work done before the case is brought to court. Marshall spent countless weeks and months in research, evaluating precedents, consulting with witnesses, and writing and rewriting briefs. Later on, he and his associates in the Legal Defense and Educational Fund put this lesson to work in the years before the *Brown* case.

Having spent most of his time in the trial courts as a criminal lawyer, Marshall developed some strong convictions about the rights of the accused. Prior to the *Miranda* doctrine, he expressed his feelings on the right of counsel in an interview with Sidney Zion which appeared in *The New York Times Magazine* on August 22, 1965:

> As of today and for many years the Courts have held that you can't plead guilty without counsel by your side. But you can, without a lawyer, make a confession. Now why is that?
>
> You know when they take you into that precinct and start marching you up those stairs you keep getting further and further away from everybody. Now up in that room they take you to, it's not the same as a courtroom. Why should it be different? Why should your rights change depending on whether you're in the station house or in Court? Now that's the problem. That's the issue.

Marshall advocated further research and review by the courts in the area of confessions, and went on to dispute the concept of a balancing test when dealing with civil liberties:

> A lot of people talk in terms of balancing. You know, balance the public interest against the individual's rights. Well, I don't see

this as a balancing problem. I get into trouble every time I try to balance something.

My original position has been that constitutionally protected rights take precedence, and that is still my position. Of course, in confessions what you've got to face up to is that the guy is guilty, nearly all who confess are guilty. Now nobody writes that, but you see it all the time. Still the guilty guy's rights are just as important. Everybody writes that, but how many believe it? Well, I believe it.

Of equal importance to Marshall is the role of lawyers in society. In lecturing on the obligations of lawyers to the public, at the Washington University School of Law in 1967, Marshall said:

The lawyer has often been seen by minorities, including the poor, as part of the oppressors in society. Landlords, loan sharks, businessmen specializing in shady installment credit schemes—all are represented by counsel on a fairly permanent basis. But who represents and speaks for tenants, borrowers, and consumers? Many special-interest groups have permanent associations with retained counsel. Who speaks for the substantial segment of the populace that such legislation might disadvantage? Outside of the political processes, I think the answer is clear. Lawyers have a duty in addition to that of representing their clients; they have a duty to represent the public, to be social reformers in however small a way.

In addition, Marshall pointed out that lawyers through their usage of the law are often able to shape the forces affecting society:

Some . . . may undoubtedly disagree with some of the recent changes in social patterns and in the law. Well-considered dissent is, of course, an intimate part of the process of society. But I am sure . . . all agree that the force of law—its capacity to initiate change and its flexibility to accept and mold change—is a major force in society, a force which lawyers are most often called upon to shape. From the early days in this country's history, it has been the traditional task of lawyers to mediate between principle and practice, between man's heritage and his hopes—that is the message of law and the quest for equality—and that task and message we must never forget.

In 1934 Marshall began his long association with the NAACP when he volunteered his services to the local branch in Baltimore. At this time the NAACP had turned its attention to segregated public schools and was beginning to file suits in the lower state courts. The first case had been filed on March 15, 1933, on behalf of a young Negro seeking admission to the University of North Carolina; the case was lost on a technicality, however.

The National Association was growing at an accelerating pace. The American Fund for Public Service made a grant to the NAACP which enabled it to draw up a long-range program to attack racial discrimination in education. Nathan Margold, a brilliant advocate who later became Solicitor General of the United States, composed the guidelines for national action. On October 26, 1934, the national office in New York hired Charles Houston to direct the campaign.

Obviously the appointment of Houston was to have a monumental effect on Marshall's career, since the dean planned to gather his more able students around him. The strategy that Houston employed was aimed at what he called "the soft underbelly" of Jim Crow—the graduate schools. In 1935 Houston was appointed Special Counsel for the NAACP, and in this capacity he began filing a series of taxpayer suits aimed at segregated graduate schools. His strategy was based on the hope that segregated education would prove to be prohibitively expensive. In the same year that his former mentor became Special Counsel, Marshall won his first case for the NAACP. He convinced the Maryland Court of Appeals to order the University of Maryland Law School (the same institution that had refused to admit him five years earlier) to admit its first Negro applicant—Donald Murray. "What's at stake here is more than the rights of my clients," he argued, "it's the moral commitment stated in our country's creed." Redding has noted that Marshall had come to realize, if not yet to articulate, that "the test of democracy, no less than the moral power of justice, lay in the people's will to accept the equal appreciation of the laws," and was beginning to see his race's role as "the catalyst in the slow-working moral chemistry of America." An Amherst graduate, Murray later received his law degree, established private practice in Baltimore, and volunteered his services to the NAACP throughout his career.

Although education was the primary target of the NAACP during the 1930s, it was not the only one. On the national front the NAACP aimed its sights at discrimination in employment as well. One of the most obvious inequities was the disparity between white and black teachers' salaries. The first teachers' pay case, against the Board of Education in Montgomery County, Maryland, was filed on behalf of

William Gibbs, an acting principal in the county at a salary of $612 per year, while the average salary of a white principal at this time was $1,475. The decision of the Maryland Court of Appeals, which ordered the equalization of salaries within the county, established a guideline to be followed throughout the state by the NAACP in future cases. The case, which was filed on December 8, 1936, and was not legally closed until two years later, represented a significant victory for the NAACP. The cumulative pay won for Negro teachers in nine counties exceeded $100,000. In a number of southern and border states, the NAACP won fifty cases dealing with the equalization of teachers' salaries, which put over $3 million into the pockets of Negro teachers over a fifteen-year span.

By 1936 the national office of the NAACP had taken notice of the young lawyer. Charles Houston called Marshall to New York and convinced the organization to appoint him Assistant Special Counsel. From this time on, Houston, Marshall, and William Hastie began plotting the long series of legal battles that would ultimately call on the Supreme Court to overrule the "separate but equal" concept which, since 1896, had been accepted as law by both Negroes and whites.

The next two years were extremely busy ones for Marshall:

Between 1936 and 1938, I commuted practically between Baltimore and New York, and there was considerable practice in that period. . . . I was based in New York, but I maintained an office in my mother's home in Baltimore, and I would come back to take care of the clients that really needed me until they adjusted over to new lawyers.

His appointment as Assistant Special Counsel was a milestone in his legal career and began a rewarding chapter in his life.

2

The NAACP and the Struggle for Legal Equality: 1915–1944

FOLLOWING THE CIVIL WAR THE NEWLY FREED SLAVE IN THE UNITED States found himself at a disadvantage in a social structure not of his own making. During the Reconstruction period the Southern Negro found himself in an environment almost as hostile as slavery. The Ku Klux Klan employed terror and violence to keep him at the lowest level of society. Southern landowners manipulated Negro workers in a peonage system that was little better than slavery itself, while mobs drove Negro voters from the polls, and "lynchings increased to extraordinary numbers," as Marshall himself noted. Deep concern over human dignity, self-preservation, and civil rights led the American Negro to seek collective action.

Although several early attempts at organizing had transpired outside the South, the only Negro structure that possessed a lasting quality in the South was the church. The slaves had adopted the white man's religion, primarily the Baptist and Methodist denominations, and this tradition was maintained after the Civil War. Negro ministers provided leadership and were respected uniformly by the entire Negro community. After numerous unsuccessful attempts, the first national organization to have lasting quality was the National Association for the Advancement of Colored People (NAACP), founded in 1909.

The NAACP has employed two basic methods in its protest movement—the legal approach and public education. As one noted historian has pointed out:

> The roles of the lawyer and the public relations man are paramount. The NAACP and other groups like it that are seeking social reform operate on the assumption that an informed public and the traditional channels of judicial appeal are all that are

necessary to bring about the desired social change. It is in this sense that the NAACP protest is typically "American."

Moreover, during its first thirty years, "the militant protest organization of a small number of intellectuals" was transformed into "a large nationwide association with an elaborate bureaucracy" which had "achieved a certain degree of acceptance and middle-class respectability."

The NAACP and the Law

During its first years the NAACP was concerned principally with the urgent problems of mob violence and lynching and with appealing to the American conscience for law with justice. In 1914 Arthur B. Spingarn—a devoted white liberal—was appointed to supervise the legal program of the organization. As chairman of legal defense Spingarn was able to persuade a number of prominent lawyers throughout the United States to volunteer their services to the Association; Moorfield Storey of Boston, Louis Marshall of New York, and Clarence Darrow of Chicago were among them.

Between 1915 and 1936, until Thurgood Marshall joined the national office in New York, the NAACP had participated in ten cases brought before the Supreme Court, not counting some which involved a denial of certiorari. The main thrust of these cases was in four major areas: Negro suffrage, residential segregation ordinances, restrictive covenants, and due process and equal protection for Negroes accused of crimes. Ironically, the Association was not involved, either directly or indirectly, with a single education decision before the Supreme Court in this period.

The first case in which the NAACP participated was *Guinn* v. *United States,* in 1915. In an earlier decision—*Williams* v. *Mississippi,* (1898)—the Supreme Court had directly approved Mississippi's Constitution of 1890, which was written with many devices barring the Negro from the ballot box. This decision led to a flurry of activity on the part of southern legislatures to imitate these practices. The "Grandfather Clause" of the 1910 Oklahoma Constitution prevented Negroes from voting on the grounds that their ancestors did not have the franchise. After the case was appealed to the Supreme Court, Moorfield Storey, the lawyer who had begun his career as secretary to Charles Sumner, filed an amicus curiae brief for the NAACP, on the grounds that the "Grandfather Clause" was a clear-cut violation of the Fifteenth Amendment. In an 8–0 decision, the Supreme Court agreed with Storey's contention and invalidated the clause. Speaking for the majority, Chief Justice Edward White held that, while the Fifteenth Amendment "gives no right of suffrage, it was long recognized that in operation its prohibition might measurably have that effect." To hold otherwise, he maintained, would make the amendment "inapplicable by mere forms of expression embodying no exercise of judgment and resting on no discernible reason other than the purpose to disregard" its restriction. The *Guinn* decision was a political victory for Negroes that was to be reflected in two other cases brought before the Supreme Court during this period; both were concerned with the laws of Texas which excluded Negroes from participating in the Democratic primary.

Texas law, as determined in *Nixon* v. *Herndon,* stipulated that "in no event shall a Negro be eligible to participate in a Democratic Party election." Having been denied the right to vote in the primary, a Negro resident of El Paso, Dr. L. A. Nixon, sued the election judges for damages. Nixon lost in a series of lower court decisions, but his attorneys, Arthur Spingarn and Fred C. Knollenberg of the NAACP, won appeal to the Supreme Court. On March 7, 1927, speaking for the majority, Justice Oliver Wendell Holmes held the "white primary" law to be invalid as a violation of the "equal protection" clause of the Fourteenth Amendment: "We find it unnecessary to consider the Fifteenth Amendment, because it seems to us hard to imagine a more direct and obvious infringement of the Fourteenth." Following quickly on the heels of the Court's decision, a special session of the Texas legislature was called to draw up a more ingenious plan. Patently the Court had prohibited the state legislature from enacting laws denying Negroes participation in the party primary, but what about a law that authorized the Democratic State Committee to make its own rulings on voter eligibility? Consequently the executive committee of the party resolved that only *white* Democrats could vote in the Democratic primary. Once again, Dr. Nixon with the support of the Association brought suit, lost in the lower courts, and finally won appeal to the Supreme Court. Arthur Spingarn argued the case before the Court. In a 5–4 decision delivered on May 2, 1932, the Court held that this device constituted a delegation of state power to the party's executive committee, that the committee's discriminatory act was de facto state action, and as such was prohibited by the guarantee of "equal protection of the laws" of the Fourteenth Amendment.

Another legal area in which the Association met with some measure of success was that of racial zoning laws. At the outset an attempt was made to eliminate racial discrimination in housing through publicizing the evils of such practices. In its first year the NAACP familiarized its membership with the practice of writing letters to the press and magazines regarding any and all matters where the rights of Blacks were at issue. However, as more and more city councils enacted segregation ordinances, it became clear to the Association leaders "that a city ordinance could not be stopped by a letter to the editor." The first case brought by the NAACP before the Supreme Court dealt with the state-enforced segregation ordinance of Louisville, Kentucky. In November 1917 the Court in a unanimous decision *(Buchanan* v. *Warley)* invalidated the Louisville ordinance because it interfered with the rights of an owner to dispose of his property "in direct violation of the fundamental law enacted in the Fourteenth Amendment of the Constitution."

Despite the fact that new segregation ordinances were still appearing throughout the country, the *Buchanan* rule made it possible to overturn these devices by way of litigation. In 1927, when Louisiana courts upheld the zoning ordinance of New Orleans in spite of the objections of local NAACP members, the Association's legal staff was again able to take the matter to the Supreme Court of the United States, in *Harmon* v. *Tyler.* The Court, by invalidating the ordinance on the grounds that it violated the Fourteenth Amendment, adhered to the Buchanan decision. Three years later the NAACP brought before the Court another case—*City of Richmond* v. *Deans*—which involved a Richmond zoning ordinance that based its segregation on the prohibition of intermarriage rather than on color or race. The Supreme Court was not fooled by the disguise and agreed with the pronouncement of a lower federal court in concluding that the legal prohibition of intermarriage is itself based on race and, as such, violates the Fourteenth Amendment. So successful was the NAACP's effort against racial zoning laws that "since 1929, segregation by ordinance has been a rarity of no consequence." This same measure of success was not accorded the legal committee of the Association in combating private agreements that provided for residential segregation.

The first attempt by the NAACP to overturn the enforcement of restrictive covenants before the Supreme Court occurred in 1926 in *Corrigan* v. *Buckley.* Association lawyers Louis Marshall and Moorfield Storey contended in their brief that "the decrees of the courts below constitute a violation of the Fifth and Fourteenth Amendments to the

Constitution, in that they deprive the appellants of their liberty and property without due process of law." In a unanimous decision the Supreme Court dismissed the appeal of the Association lawyers. Speaking for the Court, Justice Sanford noted that the contention that the restrictive covenant violated the Constitution was "entirely lacking in substance or color of merit." The Thirteenth, Fourteenth, and Fifth Amendment, he continued, did not have as their object private individuals, nor do the Amendments prohibit them "from entering into contracts respecting the control and disposition of their own property."

The final area of legal activity in which the NAACP played an important part prior to Thurgood Marshall's arrival in 1936 was the protection of civil liberties of Negroes accused of crime. A notorious example of injustice emanated from the mob action which took place in Elaine, Phillips County, Arkansas, in October 1919 that led to the case of *Moore* v. *Dempsey,* (1923). Negro sharecroppers and farmers in Elaine had been harassed by their white landlords for years. They were refused itemized bills for the amounts on supplies owed to their landlords, and they were unable to obtain an accounting of weights and prices for their crops. In desperation, the Negroes hired a white lawyer to make their claims. Fearing a possible conviction for peonage, the landlords made an attack with firearms on a meeting of Negro farmers in a church. In the exchange of fire that ensued, several Negroes and one white man were killed. Hours later, enraged mobs of white residents killed over two hundred Negroes. Over a thousand Negro men and women were placed in a large stockade and were tried by a kangaroo court of their overseers. Within five days twelve Negroes received the death penalty and sixty-seven others were sentenced to long prison terms, after a trial that lasted only forty-five minutes. The legal arm of the NAACP fought for four years in ensuing litigation through the lower courts. Finally the case reached the Supreme Court, and in February 1923 it was decided that a new trial must be held for all the defendants. Such a trial, said Justice Holmes for the majority, held in a hostile atmosphere of fear and hate, was inherently unfair and resulted in a denial of due process of law as protected by the Fourteenth Amendment. By 1925 all seventy-nine defendants were released without additional prosecution.

The Association also challenged the arbitrary exclusion of Negroes from petit and grand juries. The first such case brought by the NAACP before the Supreme Court—*Hollins* v. *Oklahoma*—was decided in 1935. The litigation had originated four years earlier when Jess Hollins, a resident of Sapulpa, Oklahoma, was convicted of rape and sentenced to death. He could not afford counsel, and one was not provided for him by the court. Qualified Negroes had been systematically excluded from the jury that sentenced him. In a memorandum opinion the Supreme Court established the principle, reiterated in a number of subsequent decisions, that

> the trial and conviction of a Negro by a jury of whites, upon an indictment found and returned by a grand jury of white persons, from both of which all qualified Negroes have been excluded solely on account of race or color is a denial of the equal protection of the laws guaranteed by the Fourteenth Amendment to the Constitution.

Although at this time the states were not required to provide a trial by jury for accused persons, if a jury were employed, it would have to be essentially fair and the trial kept free from the intimidation of the mob as well as from the subtleties of systematic racial exclusion.

Finally, the Association fought against convictions of Negroes that were based on confessions admittedly obtained under torture. It first confronted the Supreme Court with this matter in February 1936, in the case of *Brown* v. *Mississippi.* In 1934 Ed Brown, Henry Shields, and Yank Ellington, Negro farm workers in DeKalb County, Mississippi, were convicted of murder solely on the basis of confessions obtained by force. Moreover, none of the men who participated in the torture denied beating the defendants. The Supreme Court of Mississippi affirmed the conviction, whereupon the Association's legal staff petitioned for certiorari to the highest federal court. The Supreme Court reversed the convictions and granted a new trial. In the majority opinion Chief Justice Hughes noted that the use of confessions obtained in such a manner violated the Fourteenth Amendment's guarantee of "due process of law," and that the "complaint is not of the commission of mere error, but of a wrong so fundamental that it made the whole proceeding a mere pretense of a trial and rendered the conviction and sentence wholly void."

In the years prior to Marshall's joining the national office, the NAACP had participated in ten cases before the Supreme Court and had suffered only one defeat—the decision in which the Court had upheld the validity of restrictive covenants. Of the legal accomplishments of the Association during this period Marshall later wrote:

These decisions have served as guideposts in a sustained fight for full citizenship for Negroes. They have broadened the scope of protection guaranteed by the Thirteenth, Fourteenth and Fifteenth Amendments . . . in the fields of the right to register and vote, equal justice before the law, Negroes on juries, segregation. . . .

In addition, they broaden the interpretation of constitutional rights for all citizens and extend civil liberties for whites as well as Negroes.

The activity of lawyers acting for the NAACP has added to the body of law on civil rights for all Americans. The Association, by pressing these cases, has brought nearer to realization the ideal embodied in the quotation engraved over the Supreme Court building in Washington, D.C.: "Equal Justice Under Law."

The record of the NAACP before the Supreme Court in its first twenty-five years seemed to reaffirm his faith in the legal structure of the United States, despite the fact that progress for the American Negro under the law was stymied by procrastination:

While it may be true that laws and constitutions do not act to right wrong and overturn established folkways overnight, it is also true that the reaffirmation of these principles of democracy builds a body of public opinion in which rights and privileges of citizenship may be enjoyed, and in which the more brazen as well as the more sophisticated attempts at deprivation may be halted.

Unlike Marshall, not all Negro leaders, even within the NAACP, were satisfied with its accomplishments. In 1934 W. E. B. DuBois, editor of *The Crisis,* the official publication of the organization, maintained that efforts thus far had been futile. In fact, he added, there was more discrimination and actual segregation at this time than had existed when the Association was formed. Joel Spingarn, Executive Secretary Walter White, and other Association officials were shocked by this unexpected attack from their director of publicity and research. In defense of NAACP policies, the official leadership of the organization retaliated with a bitter attack against DuBois, until DuBois was forced to resign and return to his teaching career at Atlanta University. But the criticisms that DuBois had leveled could not be quieted so easily. His attack had been only one of many against the Association. Indeed, the situation was worsening; segregation was on the increase and the

NAACP was so poor that it could not afford to sustain the struggle. In response to its critics, the organization appointed a Committee on Future Plans and Programs, headed by Abram Harris. The Committee's proposal, released at the annual convention of the NAACP in St. Louis in 1935, called for "vigorous economic action and unification of black and white workers" and "the organization of classes in workers' education, the creation of industrial and agricultural councils, and the setting up of workers' councils." As late as 1940 Ralph Bunche added his voice to the growing criticism of the NAACP by accusing its leaders of having "a narrow vision of leadership." Bunche, whose critique of the Association was used by Gunnar Myrdal in his landmark work *An American Dilemma,* concluded: "In an era in which the Negro finds himself hanging ever more precariously from the bottom rung of a national economic ladder that is itself in a condition of not too animated suspension, the Association clings to its traditional faith, hope and politics." The future did not seem bright for the NAACP in the mid-1930s.

The Director-Counsel

Often a relatively insignificant and unnoticed event can change the entire course of history. Such an incident took place in 1930, when a young white man, Charles Garland, refused to accept an inheritance in excess of a million dollars. Garland simply wished that the money be donated "as quickly as possible . . . to 'unpopular' causes, without regard to race, creed or color." He attached no conditions to this gesture; he simply did not want the money. Subsequently the inheritance was used to create the American Fund for Public Service, which distributed grants to a number of groups including the Urban League, the Brotherhood of Sleeping Car Porters, and the NAACP. Loren Miller writes that, upon receiving the grant, Executive Secretary Walter White convinced the leaders of the Association that they should emphasize the legal approach and initiate a

large-scale, widespread, dramatic campaign to give the Southern Negro his constitutional rights, his political and civil equality . . . and to give the Negroes equal rights in the public schools, in the voting booths, on the railroads and on juries in every state where they are at present denied them, and the right to own and occupy real property.

The objectives of this proposal were in no way novel, but the method—a major dependence on the orderly process of litigation—was certainly a unique suggestion. The NAACP chose Nathan Margold to plan and implement the program.

The decision to utilize the courts as a major tool to bring about full legal equality for the American Negro was almost a mandatory one. No other avenue lay open: Southern Democrats controlled Congress through the seniority system, which led to the conclusion that the possibility of any remedial civil-rights legislation was impossible; moreover, a Democratic president—even Franklin Roosevelt—would not risk racial reform in the face of Southern opposition from his own party, since his whole program of reform would be placed in jeopardy. The only hope of Negro leaders therefore rested on the argument that "the struggle for full citizenship rights can be speeded by enforcement of existing statutory provisions protecting . . . civil rights." However, the new legal program was not meant to imply that the Association would abandon its other activities. There was still political power to be won in the cities outside the South, and reform still to be obtained in statutes and ordinances. Propaganda was also to remain a formidable weapon in the campaign for racial equality.

The Supreme Court was at this time under consistent attack from liberal and reform leaders who sympathized with objectives of the Negro movement; this was an additional factor favoring the new reliance on the courts. The Court was criticized for being composed of conservatives who were outdated and outmoded. NAACP leaders felt that if a true reforming spirit were imprinted on the Supreme Court, the American Negro could hope to be only one of its beneficiaries. In 1933 Nathan Margold resigned his position to become the solicitor for the Department of Labor. The Association searched for a man with the ingenuity and ability to fill the shoes of its first special counsel. On October 26, 1934, it named Charles Houston, then Vice-Dean of the Law School at Howard University. Houston left the law school in the capable hands of William Hastie, who soon joined him in the national office, and invited Marshall to become his assistant.

Houston worked to expand and improve Margold's original plans for legal activity. He recruited a number of capable Negro lawyers from all parts of the country. For Marshall the job of Assistant Special Counsel meant a regular though meager income. Moreover, Houston made clear to his new assistant that he would often be frustrated, discouraged, and possibly in danger of his life.

The first brief that the new assistant prepared was of great importance to the legal arm of the NAACP because it was employed in the first case involving education brought before the Supreme Court by the Association. In 1936 Lloyd Gaines, an otherwise qualified Negro student, applied for admission to the Law School at the University of Missouri. Gaines was rejected on the grounds that Missouri, having no separate Negro law school, provided financial assistance in the graduate and professional training of Negroes in schools *outside the state* as was consistent with the "separate but equal" doctrine. A series of lower-court decisions upheld the contention of the state that it was "contrary to the constitution, laws, and public policy of the State to admit a Negro as a student in the University of Missouri." Association lawyers—Charles Houston, Sidney R. Redmond, and Leon A. Ransom—brought the case before the Supreme Court two years later as *Missouri ex rel. Gaines* v. *Canada* (1938). Relying heavily on Marshall's brief, the lawyers based their argument solely on section one of the Fourteenth Amendment, which forbids a state to "deny to any person within its jurisdiction the equal protection of the laws." Since Missouri had no separate and equal law school for the Negroes of its community, and having admitted that Gaines was otherwise eligible for admission, acceptance was requisite by the force of the Constitution:

> Even if it be considered that under any circumstance a money grant could constitute the equal protection of the laws under the Fourteenth Amendment . . . to a Negro citizen forced by the State to go outside the state solely because of race or color to study courses offered to all other students in the state university within the state border, nevertheless there is an irreconcilable conflict in the statutes of the scholarship law as to size of grant, elements of compensation and other conditions which leaves the question in confusion and great uncertainty. There is no Federal precedent establishing whether a scholarship grant can constitute the equal protection of the laws; and if so, what the standard of equal protection should be. A decision in this case will go far towards establishing a standard of conduct for the States under the equal protection clause of the Fourteenth Amendment.

On December 12, 1938, the Court held that Gaines must be allowed to attend the Law School of the state in the absence of a comparable Negro institution. In a 7–2 decision in which Justices McReynolds and

Butler dissented, Mr. Chief Justice Hughes nullified Missouri's out-of-state plan:

> Here, petitioner's right was a personal one. It was as an individual that he was entitled to the equal protection of the laws, and the State was bound to furnish him within its borders, facilities for legal education substantially equal to those which the State there afforded for persons of the white race, whether or not other Negroes sought the same opportunity.

Although the decision reaffirmed the doctrine that separate educational facilities are legal only if the facilities are intrinsically equal, it did open the floodgates of litigation to force the equalization of tangible facilities already in existence. Many Negro leaders felt that the time was ripe for asking the courts to invalidate the "separate but equal" doctrine altogether, but Marshall favored a more conservative approach. He was of the opinion that the struggle had only just begun; that the decision of *Plessy* v. *Ferguson*, (1896), reached by the Supreme Court some forty-two years earlier, would have to be legally assaulted again and again. For the time being, the best that Marshall and his legal staff could do was to make the expense of providing equal facilities prohibitive to the states and thereby attempt to weaken their resistance.

The immediate effects of the *Gaines* case were not readily apparent. Missouri wasted no time in opening a separate law school for Negroes and classifying it as equal to that of the state university. In addition, Charles Houston, who had argued the case, resigned his position because of ill health shortly after the decision. Marshall succeeded him as Special Counsel.

In his new position Marshall argued that the *Gaines* decision was a significant victory in that it broadened educational opportunities for future Negro students, provided that legal support was available to pry open the doors of white institutions. Naturally, such support required an expansion of the NAACP legal staff and more revenue than the Association's treasury could provide. It was agreed that a legal and educational fund be established, separate from the other resources of the NAACP. On October 11, 1939, the NAACP Legal Defense and Educational Fund, Inc., was created as a membership corporation in accordance with the laws of the State of New York. The purposes of the fund were succinctly listed in the charter:

To render free legal aid to Negroes who suffer legal injustice because of their race or color and cannot afford to employ legal assistance; To seek and promote educational opportunities denied to Negroes because of their race or color; To conduct research and publish information on educational facilities and inequalities furnished for Negroes out of public funds and on the status of the Negro in American life.

The charter went on to distinguish the functions of the new body from those of the NAACP by stating that the Fund was not a pressure group, nor would it engage in any lobbying activity:

The corporation shall not engage in any activities for the purpose of carrying on propaganda, or otherwise attempt to influence legislation, and shall operate without pecuniary benefits to its members.

It should be pointed out that, while the charter stipulated that the Fund would not engage in propaganda "or otherwise attempt to influence legislation," this was, in reality, obiter scriptum. The Fund lawyers fully intended to use the courts as a "forum for the purpose of educating the public" on any form of discrimination. While speaking on discrimination in housing, Thurgood Marshall admitted that "the only method of counteracting this vicious practice is by means of educating the general public, from which juries are chosen, to the plight of the Negro." Needless to say, an aroused and informed public can also, if even indirectly, influence the flow of legislation.

During the next several years Marshall continued his predecessor's attempts at gathering the best possible legal talent, Negro and white, willing to devote itself to the purposes of the Fund. A permanent staff of six lawyers was established, in addition to a large number of volunteer workers, most of whom later became prominent in legal and academic circles. In addition to the permanent staff, four lawyers were employed on a retainer basis—one in the District of Columbia; one in Richmond; one in Dallas; and the other in Los Angeles.

By 1958 the staff of the Fund had won thirty-six of the forty-one cases it had brought before the Supreme Court. If those cases handled jointly under a single title are included, the figure is even more remarkable: forty-six out of fifty-one decisions. Attorneys general and lawyers who spoke for segregation, particularly in the South, found themselves pitted against capable and dedicated opponents. Loren Miller, who has occasionally acted as counsel for the NAACP, holds that a significant portion of the success of the NAACP legal staff must be attributed to the ability of Marshall and his colleagues to perceive the changes in social climate and the resultant change of judicial attitudes in the decades following the 1930s, since legal experience and skill is not sufficient to win decisions in controversial areas in "an unchanged climate or in a closed society."

In 1940 the position of Director-Counsel was created and Thurgood Marshall was selected for the job. As the top legal officer of the Legal Defense and Educational Fund, the Director-Counsel is responsible for planning the strategy to be used in the courts and for coordinating the entire legal program. According to the charter of the Fund, Marshall was charged with the duty of carrying out the policies established by the Board of Directors. He had under his direction a legal research staff of six full-time lawyers who lived in New York but who could be assigned to places outside of the state. In explaining his duties, Marshall stated: "the board charges me with the responsibility of keeping the work within the policy adopted by the board moving along, with general supervisory powers over the staff and the other people working for us." In the same statement he explained the methods of the Legal Defense Fund in executing its legal program:

We get either a letter or a telephone call or telegram from either a person or a lawyer saying that they have got a problem involving discrimination on the part of race or color and it appears to be a legal problem. Then the question is as to whether or not we will help. If it is a worthwhile problem, we look into it. . . . If the investigation conducted either from the New York office or through one of our local lawyers reveals that there is discrimination because of race or color and legal assistance is needed, we furnish that legal assistance in the form of either helping in payment of the costs or helping in the payment of lawyers' fees, and mostly it is legal research in the preparation of briefs and materials.

Marshall served in this capacity for twenty-one years. Most major cases in the field of civil rights were handled by the Fund during this period, and the Director-Counsel was to a large degree responsible for its successes and failures.

According to the *United States Reports,* the official publication of Supreme Court decisions, Marshall argued thirty-two cases and assisted in preparing the briefs in eleven others brought before the Court. Of the cases he argued, four were lost, one was dismissed for lack of a substantial federal question, and twenty-seven were substantive victories. Obviously these accomplishments were not the result of a singular effort on Marshall's part—he argued only six cases without the support of his staff; rather, the success was based on the work of many. In the early 1940s the position of Director-Counsel became an increasingly demanding one. The United States was once again preparing to go to war abroad, while failing, in the minds of many Negroes, to ensure the rights of many of its citizens at home. When white men were available, most of the nation's industries, including steel mills, aviation plants, munitions factories, and other vital concerns, refused to hire Negroes except for traditional menial tasks. These industries had been awarded large government contracts to be paid by Negro and white taxpayers, and the situation therefore led to a demand for action by Negro leaders. In 1941 A. Phillip Randolph, head of the Brotherhood of Sleeping Car Porters and Maids, put forth the idea of a massive march on Washington to demand the right of Negroes to work in the country's defense plants. One authority has noted: "In electrical equipment plants, out of 1,066 applicants hired in a three-month period that year, only 5 were Negro. Of 8,000 people added to the payroll in aviation plants, only 13 were Negroes. In machine and tool shops, only 245 out of 35,000 new employees were Negroes." The date for the march was set for July 1, 1941, but before it could take place President Franklin Roosevelt acted under pressure. On June 25 he issued Executive Order 8802 which declared: "There shall be no discrimination in the employment of workers in defense industries and in government because of race, creed, color, or national origin. . . . And it is the duty of employers and labor organizations . . . to provide for the full and equitable participation of all workers." In addition, the Fair Employment Practices Committee was established in the Executive Department.

The matter of discriminatory hiring on grounds of race did not come to an end in American defense plants, particularly in the southern states; however, in many areas of the North industries began to drop the color bar altogether, thus relieving the frustrations of thousands of discontented Negroes.

During World War II American Negroes were required to serve in segregated units of the armed forces, as they had since the Civil War. Negro servicemen were often killed, maimed, or otherwise injured by their more prejudiced white comrades. Ironically, white German prisoners of war ate openly on American trains and in restaurants, while their Negro guards either ate at separate tables or, if none were provided, did not eat at all. In addition, race riots broke out in a number of cities including Los Angeles, Harlem, Philadelphia, Beaumont, and Houston. The worst racial agitation occurred in early 1942 in Detroit, where thirty-four persons were killed and hundreds were wounded. Of this number, twenty-five were Negroes. Thurgood Marshall was called on by the Detroit chapter of the NAACP to help establish a relief headquarters for the injured and homeless. In examining the interiors of a number of Negro apartments riddled with bullets by state police, Marshall stated that they "resembled a battlefield."

Between 1940 and 1945 Marshall and his staff aimed their sights at two major areas of Negro frustration—racial injustice in court procedure and discrimination in the voting process. A principal point of concern was the question of involuntary and forced confessions. In 1936 the Supreme Court of the United States had held in *Brown* v. *Mississippi,* that a confession obtained by overt force and violence would be inadmissible in court. But what of confessions extracted through mental duress and exhaustive questioning? The NAACP Legal Defense Fund brought this question up to the Supreme Court in its very first case.

Four Negroes—Irish (Bill) Chambers, Jack Williamson, Charles Davis, and Walter Woodward—were found guilty of murdering a white fish peddler in Pompano, Florida. The confessions used to convict the defendants were obtained only after five days of continuous questioning and grilling by the police, in the absence of friends or counsel. Two juries, in trial and retrial, found that since no force was employed, the confessions were both voluntary and admissible as evidence in court. After the Florida Supreme Court had upheld the conviction, NAACP lawyers Leon A. Ransom and S. D. McGill petitioned the Supreme Court for a grant of certiorari on behalf of the Negro defendants. Certiorari was granted and the case was brought before the Court in 1940 as *Chambers* v. *Florida.* In the preliminary legal brief, prepared by Marshall, it was argued that these "sunrise confessions" extracted at a point of extreme mental duress and fatigue, in the absence of friends, counsel, relatives, or anyone sympathetically inclined to the plight of the defendants, were just as involuntary as if they had been secured at the point of a gun. The guarantee of "due process of law" provided by the Fourteenth Amendment against state interference, he concluded, had been denied by admitting these confessions into court.

Associate Justice Black, speaking for a majority of the Court, agreed that the defendants were placed "under circumstances calculated to break the strongest nerves and the strongest resistance." Moreover, he continued, it seemed that "they who have suffered most from secret and dictatorial proceedings have almost always been the poor, the ignorant, the numerically weak, the friendless and the powerless." No one can be punished for a crime, Black maintained, without "a charge fairly made and fairly tried in a public tribunal free of prejudice, passion, excitement, and tyrannical power."

Marshall's staff sought to take advantage of the Court's decision in *Chambers* in three separate cases argued by lawyers Leon Ransom and Carter Wesley. In all three, Negro defendants had been convicted on the basis of involuntary confessions, and in each, the Supreme Court overturned the convictions on the basis of its ruling in the *Chambers* case. In a fourth case involving the use of two separate confessions against an accused Negro—the first admittedly involuntary and the second claimed to be freely given—the Fund did not fare as well.

The small town of Hugo, Oklahoma, was seething with racial tension in 1941 when Thurgood Marshall arrived to defend a Negro accused of murder. An odd-jobs man named Lyons had been accused of murdering a white family of four and of setting their home on fire to cover up the crime. The Negroes of the town were convinced that all available evidence pointed to the guilt of others, and they informed the NAACP that Lyons was being framed. The Director-Counsel himself decided to defend him.

So intense was the racial animosity stirred up by the case that many Negroes smuggled weapons into the town from Oklahoma City and Tulsa. Elaborate precautions were taken for Marshall's safety, to the extent that he was to sleep at a different well-guarded home every night.

When the trial began, everyone in the town knew who the Director-Counsel was and what he was attempting to do. The small courtroom was packed with a crowd that was as curious as it was hostile. In his defense of Lyons, Marshall contended that the accused had been beaten and intimidated by the police. He made local law enforcement officers admit that they had stacked the charred and bloody bones of the victims on the defendant's body in order to extract the original confession. Moreover, he continued, it was fear of more of such "sadism" and "police brutality" that led to the second "voluntary" confession which provided material evidence used to support a conviction.

Throughout the ordeal Marshall never lost faith in human nature. Later he reflected that "even in the most prejudiced communities, the majority of the people have some respect for truth and some sense of justice, no matter how deeply hidden it is at times."

The trial court found Lyons guilty and sentenced him to life imprisonment. Marshall petitioned the Supreme Court and was granted certiorari two years later. In oral argument before the Court in *Lyons* v. *Oklahoma,* (1944), Marshall emphasized the means of force used to extract the original confession and pointed out that even the state recognized its involuntary nature. The procedures used to obtain the first confession, he contended, had a direct bearing on the admissibility of the second. State action in this case, Marshall concluded, had denied the accused "due process of law" as guaranteed by the Fourteenth Amendment.

In a 6–3 decision in which Justices Black, Rutledge, and Murphy dissented, the Supreme Court handed Marshall his first defeat before that body. Speaking for the majority, Mr. Justice Reed explained:

The Fourteenth Amendment does not protect one who admitted his guilt because of forbidden inducements against the use at trial of his subsequent confessions under all possible circumstances. The admissibility of the later confession depends upon the same test—is it voluntary.

For the first time in his career Marshall had lost a major decision involving the rights of a Negro defendant. The *Lyons* case was the third one he had argued before the Supreme Court in four years as Director-Counsel of the Fund.

The first case Marshall argued before the Supreme Court for the NAACP arose in 1942. Three Negro soldiers were convicted in federal district court for the Western District of Louisiana under a federal assimilating statute on the charge of rape. The alleged crime took place on a military base—Camp Claiborne, Louisiana—to which the federal government had acquired title at the time of the offense. The case turned on the question of whether the military camp was actually at the time of the crime within federal criminal jurisdiction according to the language of the Federal Act of 1940. The legal arm of the NAACP took up the cause, only to have the convictions upheld in the U.S. Court of Appeals. Eventually the case was certified to the Supreme Court. In oral argument before the Court, Marshall, with W. Robert Ming, Jr., on the brief, pleaded for a dismissal of the convictions on narrow technical grounds. Under the terms of the assimilating statute, the federal government must file a notice with the governor of Louisiana in order to have either "exclusive or partial" jurisdiction over crimes committed on the military base; this, Marshall maintained, the government had failed to do before the alleged offense took place. In a unanimous decision, Justice Hugo Black agreed with Marshall's contention and reversed the convictions.

The second major target of the Fund in its infancy was racial discrimination in the political process. In the year the Fund was established, the NAACP won a follow-up victory to an earlier decision by the Supreme Court in *Guinn* v. *United States*. In that 1915 decision the Court had invalidated Oklahoma's "Grandfather Clause." In order to circumvent the decree of the Court, Oklahoma passed a law that required all eligible voters to register within a twelve-day period or otherwise be declared ineligible. Moreover, the Oklahoma statute provided that all persons who had voted under the "Grandfather Clause" in 1914 were automatically registered, thereby continuing the policy of racial disfranchisement. The NAACP challenged the statute before the Supreme Court in *Lane* v. *Wilson* (1939). On May 22, 1939, Justice Felix Frankfurter spoke for the Court in holding that the act violated the Fifteenth Amendment:

> The Amendment nullifies sophisticated as well as simple-minded modes of discrimination. It hits onerous procedural requirements which effectively handicap exercise of the franchise by the colored race, although the abstract right to vote may remain unrestricted as to race.

Although the "Grandfather Clause" and its variations had been overthrown by the Court, the right of Negroes to vote in the South remained, indeed, abstract. In June 1940 Negro leaders who attempted a voting-registration drive in Brownsville, Tennessee, were openly terrorized by whites. The body of one, Elbert Williams, was found in the river, while the president of the local branch of the NAACP was run out of town along with seven other Negroes. Two years later, Columbia, South Carolina, enacted a law which, in effect, required Negroes to be eighty-seven years of age or older in order to vote. Finally, in September 1942, Thurgood Marshall officially presented to the Justice Department the sworn statements of more than twenty Southern Negroes who had paid their poll tax but were prohibited from voting.

Another form of political discrimination was exemplified in the systematic exclusion of Negroes from serving on juries. In 1940 a Negro physician residing in Dallas received and complied with a summons to jury duty. In attempting to exercise his civil right, he was kicked down the courthouse steps by a group of whites. Informed of the incident, Marshall flew to Texas. He realized that he had a good case for assault, but the Director-Counsel was prepared to stalk bigger game. Armed with all the details of the case, Marshall set out for the governor's office in Austin. Though James Allred, a controversial and liberal Southern governor, was somewhat taken aback by Marshall's unannounced protest, the Director-Counsel's plea obviously had a decided effect on the Governor. That same day Allred ordered the Texas Rangers to protect the right of Negroes to serve on juries.

Undoubtedly it was in the area of political rights that the Fund enjoyed its most successful undertakings in its first four years. Moreover, the victory was to be personal one for Thurgood Marshall—the defeat of the "white primary."

The use of the primary as a means of nomination did not become a permanent fixture of Southern politics until the mid-1880s. Obviously in Texas, as in all of the one-party states in the South, nomination in the Democratic party primary was tantamount to victory in the general election. Attempts at excluding the Negro from participating in the party primary by way of statutory authorization on the part of the state legislatures, were held to be a denial of "equal protection of the laws" of the Fourteenth Amendment. In reaction to these reversals at the hands of the Supreme Court of the United States, the Texas Democratic Convention adopted a significant resolution on May 24, 1932: "Be it resolved, that all white citizens of the State of Texas who are qualified to vote under the constitution and laws of the state shall be eligible to membership in the Democratic party and as such entitled to participate in its deliberations." A Negro resident of Houston, R. R. Grovey, brought suit for damages against the county clerk of Harris County who denied him an absentee ballot. The case was carried all the way to the Supreme Court and became the Third Texas White Primary case. Nine years before Marshall was able to have the white primary declared legally dead, the Court handed the Negro voters a setback. As Marshall later wrote about the case:

the members of the court "blinded themselves as judges to what they knew as men" and unanimously held that the Democratic primary was a private matter and that Grovey had not been discriminated against pursuant to any state law nor had he been denied any right guaranteed under the Fourteenth and Fifteenth Amendments.

However, the *Grovey* decision did not long remain a road block, for in 1941 the Supreme Court stripped away the façade of the Democratic party as a private club immune from federal law. In *United States* v. *Classic,* Justice Stone, speaking for the majority in a case involving fraudulent activities of election officials in Louisiana, held "that a primary election which involves a necessary step in the choice of candidates for election as representatives in Congress, and which in the circumstances of this case controls that choice, is an election . . . and is subject to congressional regulation as to the manner of holding it," thereby overruling their 1921 decision in *Newberry* v. *United States.* "Because it was not a white primary case, *Classic,* of course, did not go behind the law and ferret out the trickery," Marshall wrote, but "it paved the way to the next milestone on the long road toward political equality—the Fourth Texas White Primary case."

About the same time the *Classic* decision was announced, another white-primary case was being appealed from the lower courts in Texas; it was withdrawn, however, so that the new case could be drawn up along the lines of *Classic.* The suit was brought by Lonnie E. Smith, a Negro citizen of Houston, against S. E. Allwright, election judge, and his associate, James E. Liuzza, both of whom refused to permit him to vote in the Democratic primary election of 1940. The lower federal courts again dismissed the new case, relying on the rationale of *Grovey* that the State Democratic party was indeed a private organization and therefore not subject to the restrictions of the Fourteenth and Fifteenth Amendments. This class-action suit, on behalf of Smith and all other Negroes similarly situated, was argued in the state courts by W. J. Durham, a member of the NAACP from Sherman, Texas. After losing a move for a declaratory judgment in the U.S. Circuit Court of Appeals, the Legal Defense Fund joined the battle and in 1944 won an order of certiorari to have the case reviewed by the Supreme Court of the United States; the legal team assisting Durham in *Smith* v. *Allwright,* included such legal specialists as William Hastie, Leon Ransom, Carter Wesley, W. Robert Ming, Jr., George M. Johnson, and the director of the operation, Thurgood Marshall.

Marshall and Durham were primarily responsible for writing the brief, which was greatly reflected in oral argument before the Court.

The major issue was identical in both: the Court must apply the rationale of the *Classic* decision to the case now to be decided. In the brief itself the following points were emphasized:

> The Constitution and laws of the United States as construed in *United States* v. *Classic* prohibit interference by respondents with petitioner's right to vote in Texas Democratic primaries. . . .
>
> There is no essential difference between primary elections in Louisiana and Texas. A comparison . . . demonstrates that in Texas, as in Louisiana, "the state law has made the primary an integral part of the procedure of choice [and that] . . . in fact the primary effectively controls the choice" of Senators and Representatives. . . . The legal consequence of this, under the *Classic* case, is that the right to vote in Texas primary elections is secured by the Constitution.

Marshall and his Texas colleague continued this line of argument by directly connecting the legal duties of the election judges with the sovereign authority of the state. The election judges were required by Texas law, "to administer oaths, to preserve order, and to appoint special officers to assist in the maintenance of order." These major "police powers" of primary election judges were and are "derived solely from and exercised under the sovereign authority of the State of Texas." Of special importance was the fact that the respondents were required to take the exact same oath required of officials in general elections. The advocates for the petitioner continued:

> With their offices thus created by the State and with their duty to receive and count ballots imposed by statute, respondents so exercised their official function under the laws of Texas as to deny petitioner the right to vote. Thus, the action . . . comes squarely with the test of action under color of state law as formulated in *United States* v. *Classic*. . . . Controlling effect should be given here as in the *Classic* case, to the relationship of the State to the enterprise in which primary judges are engaged. Once the state's relationship to the enterprise in which the offending persons are engaged is established, it is immaterial what sanction, if any, is claimed for a particular act done in performing an official function. Indeed, if the matter of such sanction were controlling, the Court would necessarily have concluded in the *Classic* case that

the alleged election frauds were not "under color of state law" because they were not authorized by the State.

In bringing their argument to a conclusion, Marshall and Durham demanded that the Supreme Court clarify the existing contradictions between the rationale of *Classic* and that of the *Grovey* decision, which considered the conduct of primary election judges to be private rather than state action.

On April 3, 1944, Justice Stanley Reed, speaking for a majority of the Court, with only Mr. Justice Roberts dissenting, completely embraced the argument made by the Legal Defense lawyers. In overruling *Grovey* v. *Townsend,* Justice Reed noted:

When primaries become a part of the machinery for choosing officials, state and national, as they have here, the same tests to determine the character of discrimination or abridgement should be applied to the primary as are applied to the general election. If the state requires a certain electoral procedure, prescribes a general election ballot made up of party nominees so chosen and limits the choice of the electorate in general elections for state offices, practically speaking, to those whose names appear on such a ballot, it endorses, adopts and enforces the discrimination against Negroes, practiced by a party entrusted by Texas law with the determination of the qualifications of participants in the primary. This is state action within the meaning of the Fifteenth Amendment.

Attempts were made by several Southern states, including Texas, to circumvent the ruling of the Court in *Smith* v. *Allwright.* Within a year of the *Smith* decision the South Carolina legislature repealed in excess of 1,000 voting statutes in order to leave racial discrimination in the hands of local registrars. In a case argued by Thurgood Marshall, a federal district court invalidated this procedure and enjoined local registrars from denying to qualified Negroes the right to vote in democratic primaries. At the same time Alabama adopted the "Boswell Amendment," which required voters to "read and write, understand and explain any article of the Constitution of the United States to the satisfaction of the registrars." The Alabama Federal Court struck down the amendment as unconstitutional, and the Supreme Court affirmed, in *Davis* v. *Schnell.* In 1953, some fourteen years after the *Smith* case, the Supreme Court in *Terry* v. *Adams* nullified the activities of the Jaybird Party, or the Jaybird Democratic Association, which excluded

Negroes from participating in Democratic primaries in Fort Bend County, Texas. These "private clubs," which had been in existence since 1899, were found to be in violation of the Fifteenth Amendment as had been the white primary in the *Smith* decision. The fact nevertheless remains that the "white primary" was effectively destroyed as a means of racial discrimination in the political process. Moreover, it seemed to some Negro leaders that the attitude of the Supreme Court in rendering the *Smith* decision was only an indication of things to come. As Marshall confided later: "the story of the struggle to overcome this barrier is particularly meaningful. . . . For, if nothing else, it indicates the fate which awaits the 'legal means' which some of the Southern states have drafted to preserve segregated schools."

In his first ten years with the NAACP, and then with the Legal Defense and Educational Fund, Marshall had seen vast improvements in the life of the American Negro. Nevertheless, he continued to believe—then and throughout his career—that as an advocate for civil rights he must be both cautious and patient in utilizing the judicial process. He later admitted to a colleague in the Department of Justice

> that he and those working with him [on the NAACP legal staff] carefully selected the cases they brought to appeal to the courts and the Supreme Court in those areas where the likelihood of success would appear the greatest.

On July 13, 1944, the Director-Counsel delivered an address to the NAACP Wartime Conference in which he reaffirmed his belief that the best method of increasing Negro rights was the usage of the American court system. Though far from satisfied with the progress made thus far, Marshall insisted that the NAACP must continue to make use of existing laws and to push for the enactment of new legislation. "In its broadest sense," he declared, "the term civil rights includes those rights which are the outgrowth of civilization, the existence and exercise of which necessarily follow from the rights that repose in the subjects of a country exercising self-government." He emphasized that these rights will be preserved against state interference *only* if Negroes avail themselves of the protection afforded by the United States Constitution and statutes. In acknowledging the victory obtained through the action of the NAACP in the *Smith* case, Marshall continued to assign responsibility for law enforcement to the individual Negro and the federal government:

It is up to us to see that these officials of the Department of Justice are called upon to act again and again wherever there are violations of these civil rights statutes. Unfortunately, there are plenty of such cases. It is equally unfortunate that there are not enough individuals and groups presenting these cases and demanding action.

In concluding his address the Director-Counsel summarized the legal strategy of the NAACP's Legal Defense Fund and called for more immediate and aggressive participation from all interested parties:

We must not be delayed by people who say "the time is not ripe," nor should we proceed with caution for fear of destroying the "status quo." Persons who deny to us our civil rights should be brought to justice now. Many people believe the time is always "ripe" to discriminate against Negroes. All right then—the time is always "ripe" to bring them to justice. The responsibility for the enforcement of these statutes rests with every American citizen regardless of race or color. However, the real job has to be done by the Negro population with whatever friends of the other races are willing to join in.

It should be noted that in this very aggressive address—aggressive for 1944—Marshall attacked segregation in housing, transportation, jobs, and public facilities. Ironically, he mentioned discrimination in public education only once and seemed to give it only passing attention. The reason for this apparent playing down of segregated educational facilities is obvious enough—as of 1944 the Negro leadership, including Marshall, had not adopted a positive strategy to deal with the problem, as it had with other areas of discrimination. In short, NAACP leaders had not yet decided whether to continue emphasizing the term "equal" in "separate but equal educational facilities," or to challenge head-on a concept embodied in American social and legal systems for nearly half a century.

Less than a year later they made this fateful decision and, consequently, initiated a ten-year period in which the federal courts were asked to bring about sweeping changes in American education.

3

A Decade of Decision: 1945–1955

BEGINNING WITH THE CONCLUSION OF THE SECOND WORLD WAR AND ending with the second *Brown* v. *Board of Education* decision, history witnessed a number of significant developments that were to have a lasting effect on civil rights litigation: new pleas for humanitarianism after witnessing the atrocities of war both on the battlefield and in the concentration camp; a fear of communist ideology and expansion, replaced by a period of reactionary "McCarthyism" at the expense of individual freedoms; and in 1953, a dramatic change in the leadership of the Supreme Court of the United States from a rather ineffective Chief Justice Fred M. Vinson to the more dynamic Earl Warren.

During this period the legal arm of the NAACP, under Marshall's direction, extracted from the federal courts in general—and the Supreme Court in particular—a number of decisions with great constitutional importance, especially in the field of education. Although the Legal Defense Fund made considerable gains by having nullified discrimination in transportation, exclusion from primary elections, state enforcement of restriction covenants, and segregation of tax-supported recreation facilities, its greatest victory came with the tearing down of the wall of segregation in public schools. Beginning with *Sipuel* v. *University of Oklahoma,* (1948), and ending with *Brown* v. *Board of Education,* (1955), the legal staff of the NAACP brought eight education cases before the Supreme Court. Eventually they found the Court willing, not only to end segregation in state colleges and upper-level institutions, but to declare the "separate but equal" concept unconstitutional in elementary education as well.

The Initial Decision

With the end of the war in Europe, there seemed to be a rising tide of renewed humanitarianism in the United States. The terrors of mechanized warfare, and the near genocide of some six million Jews in such extermination centers as Buchenwald and Auschwitz, had shocked the conscience of the American people. Now Negro leaders began to ask how it was possible to condemn these crimes brought about by a madman in the name of racial superiority on the one hand and still cling to the notion of white supremacy on the other.

The year 1945 was symbolic of the awakened yearnings for humanity and civility. It was the year in which the U.S. Army took on the task of integration, assuring it in the future of the other armed services. It was the year in which the United Nations was organized for the pacific settlement of international disputes; the year in which two states, New York and Massachusetts—later to be followed by Oregon and Wisconsin—created Fair Employment Practices agencies; the year A. Philip Randolph, head of the Brotherhood of Sleeping Car Porters and Maids, was selected to serve as a vice president of an international union in the CIO; and the year that a member of the NAACP's Legal Defense and Educational Fund, William H. Hastie, was first mentioned for and several months thereafter selected to be governor of the Virgin Islands.

Few civil-rights leaders welcomed these developments with greater anticipation than did Thurgood Marshall and Walter White, the executive secretary of the NAACP. Seizing the opportunity given them, Marshall and White promulgated a novel and daring concept: segregation of the races, whether in public facilities or in education, is an abjuration of the notion of democracy. To establish this concept as a principle of law loomed as a difficult task in the light of opposing legal precedent.

Though no one was more cognizant of the legal complications involved than Marshall, he believed that the NAACP ought to take the risk. In late 1945, at a closed meeting in Manhattan, Marshall, White, and Hastie made the decision that the time had come for a direct attack on racial segregation. No longer should the Association be satisfied with the strategy of attacking the inequality of separate facilities; rather, it should demand fully integrated facilities. The courts must be forced to commit the doctrine of "separate but equal" to the realm of forgotten ideas. On that day they had decided, as Marshall later admitted, to "go for the whole hog."

Victory did not come overnight. The period 1945–1950 was one of extensive preparation. Comprehensive work had to be done in the courts, ranging from frontal attacks on discrimination in criminal cases and the exercise of suffrage to housing, the armed forces, and higher education. Periodic meetings with scholars and experts who wished to participate in the cause became an increasingly popular innovation. Leaders in the fields of education, social science, psychology, history, and law were called together time and again to examine all case aspects which Marshall and his colleagues adjudged might be raised in the courtroom. In the days just prior to each case, it became standard for Marshall's staff to test its argument before a moot court in the Howard Law School Library, members of the faculty participating as judges. As the Director-Counsel used to say about the opposition: "They're going to try everything in the book . . . our job is to stay ahead of them."

Besides planning the strategy that would inevitably bring down the wall of segregation in education, Marshall was engaged in a number of other ventures during this five-year span. The "new humanitarianism" seemed to be reflected in an apparently well-founded and growing concern for the civil liberties of all persons.

In the first three years after World War II the Soviet Union moved to expand its control over Eastern Europe, thereby creating what Winston Churchill called "an Iron Curtain." The United States considered its security threatened by the aggressive Soviet attitude and by the spread of communist ideology. America's psychological reaction to these events, and to others, is probably best described by John W. Spanier:

> Whenever the nation is threatened from the outside, the public becomes fearful of internal disloyalty. It is one of the great ironies of America's society that, although Americans possess . . . unity of shared beliefs to a greater degree than any other people, their apprehension of external danger leads them, first, to insist upon a general and somewhat dogmatic reaffirmation of loyalty to the "American way of life," and then to a hunt for internal groups or forces that might betray this way of life. Disagreement tends to become suspect as disloyalty; men are accused of "un-American" thinking and behavior, and labeled "loyalty or security risks."

Leading civil libertarians fought this "reaction of fear" as symbolized by a number of congressional statutes dealing with "subversive activities" and by a series of investigations carried on by the House Un-American Activities Committee (HUAC). Marshall committed himself to the struggle by making speeches, sending letters and telegrams, and joining organizations which attacked supposed governmental encroachments on individual freedoms. In 1947, Marshall sent a telegram to

New York congressmen asking them to oppose the contempt citations by HUAC in the "Hollywood Ten" case. Two years later, in addressing a public forum in Washington for the National Lawyers Guild, he lashed out at President Truman's Federal Loyalty Program on the ground that it was blatantly unconstitutional.

During the mid-1940s the Director-Counsel grew impatient and began to demand greater enforcement of existing civil-rights statutes by the federal government. One incident typical of the situation occurred when Marshall and several members of his staff were arrested on trumped-up charges of drunken driving outside of Columbia, Tennessee. The lawyers had gone to Columbia to represent a number of Negro defendants arrested as a result of racial violence in that city in February, 1946. The morning after his arrest, Marshall sent the following telegram to the Attorney General of the United States, Tom Clark:

Last night after leaving Columbia, Tennessee, where we secured acquittal of one of two Negroes charged with crimes growing out of February disturbances three lawyers, including myself, were stopped . . . in the night by three carloads of officers including deputy sheriff, constables and highway patrolmen. Alleged purpose was to search car for whisky. When no whisky was found we were stopped by same officials two more times and on last occasion I was placed under arrest for driving while drunk and returned to Columbia. Magistrate refused to place me in jail after examining me and finding I was extremely sober. This type of intimidation of defending persons charged with crime cannot go unnoticed. Therefore, demand immediate investigation.

Interstate Transportation

In 1946, the Director-Counsel brought the first case involving segregation in interstate transportation presented by the NAACP before the Supreme Court of the United States—*Morgan* v. *Virginia*. Four cases dealing with state laws either requiring or forbidding racial segregation on vehicles engaged in interstate commerce had preceded the *Morgan* decision to the Supreme Court. In *Hall* v. *De Cuir*, (1878), the Supreme Court held invalid a Louisiana statute which forbade racial segregation on steamboats traveling on the interstate channel of the Mississippi River. Strictly relying on the "Cooley Doctrine," the Court held that in this case the Louisiana statute placed an unreasonable burden on interstate commerce and that such questions as segregation of the races, if they were to be dealt with at all, required congressional attention. The second case to reach the Court on this question, was the landmark case of *Plessy* v. *Ferguson,* (1896). In 1890, twenty-eight years after the adoption of the Fourteenth Amendment forbidding the states to deny to persons within their jurisdiction the "equal protection of the laws," the all-white Louisiana legislature passed a statute which provided "that all railway companies carrying passengers in their coaches in this state shall provide equal but separate accommodations for the white and colored races, by providing two or more passenger coaches for each passenger train, or by dividing the passenger coaches by a partition so as to secure separate accommodations." Plessy, a mulatto, refused to move from the white section of a railway car and as a result was placed under arrest. The Supreme Court upheld the statute on essentially the same grounds that the Court had earlier declared invalid the Civil Rights Act of 1875 in *Civil Rights Cases* (1883).

Citing separate public schools for white and Negro children, the Court noted that the Fourteenth Amendment can be applied neither to the discriminatory acts of private persons nor to state statutes dealing with *social* activity, as long as the separate facilities are intrinsically "equal."

At the start of the twentieth century, the Court emphasized the requirement of equality in separate facilities. In the third case involving interstate transportation—*McCabe* v. *Atchinson,* (1914)—it was held that an Oklahoma statute allowing railroads to haul variously equipped cars for whites only, without providing the same facilities for Negroes, violated the demand for equality in the Fourteenth Amendment.

Finally, in 1937, Arthur W. Mitchell of Chicago, the first Negro Democratic congressman elected in the United States, was ordered by a Rock Island conductor to move from his first-class railway car to the Negro smoking car. After protesting in vain, he finally complied under threat of arrest for violation of state law—the train was passing through Mississippi at the time. Mitchell filed a complaint with the Interstate Commerce Commission, asking it to order the Rock Island to alter its methods of treating Negro passengers. Despite a dissenting vote by five members, the Commission rejected the congressman's plea on the grounds of the earlier decisions of the Supreme Court. After a federal district court held that it had no jurisdiction in the matter, he took his case to the Supreme Court as *Mitchell* v. *United States,* (1940). The ground on which Mitchell had complained to the ICC was a provision of the Interstate Commerce Act (1887) that made it unlawful for a common carrier engaged in interstate commerce "to subject any particular person . . . to any undue or unreasonable prejudice or disadvantage in any respect whatsoever." Mitchell's lawyers extended his plea before the Court, however, to attack the *Plessy* decision. Ten Southern attorneys general quickly filed briefs amici curiae, demanding that the Court uphold the "separate but equal" doctrine. Significantly, the Attorney General of the United States, Frank Murphy, sided with Congressman Mitchell despite the fact that, nominally, the United States was the defendant.

In 1940 the Supreme Court handed down a unanimous decision delivered by Chief Justice Hughes. While it avoided the constitutional implications of the *Plessy* decision, the Court did hold that the Interstate Commerce Commission was in error and that the congressman had been subjected to "unreasonable prejudice or disadvantage" in violation of the Act of 1887. The Chief Justice stated that a denial of equal facilities because of Mitchell's race was "an invasion of a fundamental individual right which is guaranteed by the Fourteenth Amendment."

There the matter stood until a similar incident occurred to Miss Irene Morgan in 1946. Miss Morgan was a passenger on a Greyhound bus traveling from Gloucester County, Virginia, through Washington, D.C., to Baltimore, her point of destination. Virginia law provided for the segregation of the races on buses transversing the state—whether in interstate or intrastate travel—and further stipulated that passengers may be required to move at any time to effectuate this policy. Consequently, when the bus driver ordered Miss Morgan to the back of the bus and she refused, she was placed under arrest and fined ten dollars. The Legal Defense Fund came to her assistance, Thurgood Marshall acting as her counsel.

The Supreme Court of Virginia upheld the statute, declaring that the law applied to all passengers, even if they were in interstate commerce. The court rejected the traditional argument, advanced by Marshall, that such a law was an undue burden on the flow of interstate traffic and that such matters could only be regulated by uniform national treatment in accordance with the *Cooley* rule. On appeal, the case was taken to the Supreme Court of the United States as *Morgan* v. *Virginia*, (1946).

Marshall's argument before the Court ran parallel with his brief entered for the appellant. First the Director-Counsel assaulted the Virginia statute for placing an impossible burden on commerce:

Not only does the statute require a particular arrangement or rear-rangement of interstate passengers while traveling through Virginia, but it accomplishes this result by a criminal sanction the invocation of which completely interrupts the interstate movement. . . . Thus, the very analysis of the incidence and effect of the statute reveals so direct and serious an imposition upon interstate travel as to place upon the State an extremely heavy burden of justification which it is submitted the State has not met and cannot meet.

Marshall concluded his argument with an emotional appeal to justice based to a great extent on humanitarian grounds:

Today, we are just emerging from a war in which all of the people of the United States were joined in a death struggle against the apostles of racism. We have already recognized by solemn sub-scription to the charter of the United Nations . . . our duty, along with our neighbors, to eschew racism in our national life and to promote "universal respect for, and observance of, human rights and fundamental freedoms for all without distinction as to race, sex, language or religion." How much clearer, therefore, must it be today, than it was in 1877, that the national business of interstate commerce is not to be disfigured by local practices bred of racial notions alien to our national ideals, and to the solemn undertakings of the community of civilized nations as well.

The Court agreed with both the sense and the point of Marshall's argument. Justice Jackson took no part in the decision, while Justice Burton dissented on the grounds that separation of races is a matter better left to the discretion of the states. In a 7–1 decision, therefore, Mr. Justice Reed delivered the opinion of the Court:

As no state law can reach beyond its own border nor bar transportation of passengers across its boundaries, diverse seating requirements for the races in interstate journeys result. As there is no federal act dealing with the separation of races in interstate transportation, we must decide the validity of this Virginia statute on the challenge that it interferes with commerce, as a matter of balance between the exercise of the local police power and the need for national uniformity in the regulations for interstate travel. It seems clear to us that seating arrangements for the different races in interstate motor travel require a single, uniform rule to promote and protect national travel. Consequently, we hold the Virginia statute in controversy invalid.

The decision was an important victory for the NAACP, even if it seemed at the time that the Court had merely found the seventy-year-old case of *Hall* v. *De Cuir* controlling. But applying the logic of the *Hall* case, the Court would declare invalid *any* attempt by a state to impose racial requirements upon interstate carriers; it would make no difference if the particular statute required or *forbade* segregation of the races, since either type would result in an unconstitutional burden on commerce. Consequently, the Supreme Court of the United States was put to the test two years later in the case of *Bob-Lo Excursion Co.* v. *Michigan,* (1948).

Bob-Lo (Bois Blanc) Island, located in the Detroit River about fifteen miles from Detroit, is positioned on the Canadian side of the international boundary line. The island is almost entirely owned by the Bob-Lo Excursion Corporation, a Michigan firm. It serves as an amusement park, and the corporation transports patrons to and from the island for a set rate. In 1947 an official of the corporation refused passage on the excursion boat—the only available means of access to the island—to Sarah E. Ray on the ground that she was a Negro. Consequently, the official was convicted of violating the Michigan Civil Rights Act forbidding such racial discrimination. Appeal was won to the Supreme Court of the United States, where the lawyers for the appellant argued that the Michigan law was unconstitutional interference with foreign commerce. In other words, they were asking for a reaffirmation of the *Hall* case along the lines of the Court's decision in *Morgan* v. *Virginia.* Although the NAACP was not directly involved in the case, Marshall did file a joint friend-of-the-court brief in favor of Michigan's position, along with the American Civil Liberties Union and the National Lawyers Guild.

Marshall attacked the appellant's reliance on the *De Cuir* and *Morgan* cases and based his defense on the Michigan statute primarily on the *Cooley* doctrine:

The free flow of commerce, which the federal government has an interest to maintain and a right to regulate, can be hampered as well by the discriminatory refusal of a carrier to transport as by physical obstructions. Since the states may, in the absence of federal action, enact laws and authorize the erection of docks, dams, locks and other physical improvements, and may remove obstructions in the form of adverse currents, shallow channels, log jams . . . in aid of interstate and foreign commerce, the state may likewise act "in aid of congress" to remove the obstruction to commerce caused by appellant's absolute refusal to transport Negroes.

The Supreme Court held that the state act forbidding segregation was indeed applicable to the boats, even though they were clearly plying international waters. Mr. Justice Rutledge, in speaking for a majority of the Court, noted that since the *Cooley* doctrine deals with foreign as well as interstate commerce, neither *Hall* nor *Morgan* is controlling in the present case; neither was "involved so completely and locally insulated a segment of foreign or interstate commerce. In none was the business affected merely an adjustment of a single locality or community as in the business here so largely." The apparent change in attitude on the part of his colleagues prompted Justice Jackson in dissent to remark: "The Court admits that the commerce involved in this case is foreign commerce, but subjects it to the state police power on the ground that it is not very foreign."

Even though the *Bob-Lo* decision was more far-reaching, the Court's decision in *Morgan* was viewed as a personal victory for Marshall. As of 1946, he had argued four major cases before the Supreme Court and had won three of them. In the same year the NAACP bestowed on Marshall its highest symbol of appreciation—the Spingarn Medal—for his distinguished legal contributions to the Association.

The Last Primary Case

Concern over Negro participation in the political process did not end with the landmark case of *Smith* v. *Allwright*. Within a year of the Court's decision, a special session of the South Carolina legislature attempted to circumvent the *Smith* decision by repealing over 1,000 of its statutes and constitutional provisions dealing with the subject of primaries. Democratic party officials now contended that the party was a private organization and as such was not subject to the constitutional restrictions applying to the states. In a 1947 class-action case, George Elmore sought injunctive relief to enjoin Clay Rice and other election officials in South Carolina from denying to Negro electors the right to vote in the Democratic primary. Elmore's lawyers were Thurgood Marshall, W. Robert Ming, Jr., and Marion Wynn Perry. In a decision handed down by the federal district court—(1948)—Judge J. Waties Waring enjoined the local registrars, saying in part:

When this country is taking the lead in maintaining the democratic process and attempting to show to the world that the American government and the American way of life is the fairest and the best . . . it is time for South Carolina to rejoin the Union. . . . Racial distinctions cannot exist in the machinery that selects the officers and lawmakers of the United States.

The lawyers for the defendants appealed the case to the Circuit Court of Appeals, Fourth Circuit as *Rice* v. *Elmore* (1947). Here their cause fared no better. In affirming the decision of the district court, Circuit Judge Parker spoke for his colleagues:

An essential feature of our form of government is the right of the citizen to participate in the governmental process. The political philosophy of the Declaration of Independence is that governments derive their just powers from the consent of the governed. . . . The disfranchised can never speak with the same force as those who are able to vote . . . there can be no question that such denial amounts to a denial of the constitutional rights of the Negro and we think it is equally clear that those who participate in the denial are exercising state power to that end, since the primary is used in connection with the general election in the selection of state officers.

Rice petitioned for a grant of certiorari from the Supreme Court of the United States. In a per curiam decision—*Rice* v. *Elmore* (1948)—the Court denied certiorari, thus in effect upholding the prior decisions of the lower federal courts. The fight to end state-enforced voting discrimination was a difficult one for Marshall and his staff; he did not consider it fully won until the passage and enforcement of the Voting Rights Act of 1965.

Rights of Accused Negroes

Another legal area which consistently posed problems for the legal Defense Fund was the providing of "due process" and "equal protection of the laws" for accused Negroes. In dealing with exclusion of Negroes from petit and grand juries in cases where a Negro is on trial, the Supreme Court had been less than unequivocal. In *Norris* v. *Alabama* (1935), and in *Hill* v. *Texas* (1942), the Court had held that planned and systematic exclusion of Negroes from juries resulted in a denial of "equal protection of the laws" required by the Fourteenth

Amendment. Yet in a 1945 decision—*Akins* v. *Texas*—the Court sustained a scheme by the state of Texas which placed only one Negro on such a jury. There the matter stood for two years.

A Negro resident of Mississippi, named Patton, was indicted by an all-white grand jury for murdering a white man. He was subsequently convicted by an exclusively white petit jury despite a motion on the part of Patton's counsel to quash the indictment. A small staff of lawyers from the Legal Defense Fund, headed by the Director-Counsel, joined the case. They succeeded in taking the case before the Supreme Court of the United States by obtaining a grant of certiorari for *Patton* v. *Mississippi* (1947).

Relying on the *Hill* case, Marshall realized that all he need do to have Patton's conviction reversed was to prove that the Mississippi plan systematically excluded Negroes from juries over a period of time. In his Brief for Petitioner, the Director-Counsel laid bare the evidence: The adult population of the county was 34,821, of whom 12,511 were Negroes. Of this number at least 25 qualified Negro male electors were eligible for jury service. Finally, the venues for the term from which the grand and petit juries were selected did not contain the name of a single Negro, and not one Negro had served on either type of criminal jury in the county for the past thirty years. Such purposeful administrative exclusion of qualified persons from jury duty because of race or color, he maintained, was a violation of the Equal Protection Amendment.

In a unanimous decision delivered by Mr. Justice Hugo Black, the Court agreed. In reversing Patton's conviction and remanding the case for further proceeding, Justice Black wrote:

When a jury selection plan, whatever it is, operates in such a way as always to result in the complete and long-continued exclusion of any representative at all from a large group of Negroes, or any other racial group, indictments and verdicts returned against them by juries thus selected cannot stand.

The Court reasoned that it was the "duty of the State to try to justify" the exclusion where it had continued for a number of years; however, in this case, thirty years of determined exclusion was apparently impossible to justify.

Another area of the legal process which seemed to plague Marshall and his colleagues was that of forced confessions. In 1948 the Legal Defense Fund suffered a setback at the hands of the Vinson Court.

Taylor, an Alabaman, had been convicted of raping a white woman, and the trial court sentenced him to death by electrocution. Later Taylor claimed that his confessions and admissions introduced in evidence at the trial had been coerced by local police officers. His lawyers petitioned the Supreme Court of Alabama for permission to file a petition for a writ of error coram nobis in the trial court. Having previously upheld the conviction, the state supreme court denied the petition on the ground that there was no evidence to justify such a grant.

The case was then brought before the Supreme Court of the United States with the assistance of the Legal Defense Fund. Thurgood Marshall argued *Taylor* v. *Alabama* for the defendant. It was his contention that by first upholding the conviction and subsequently denying the petition, the Supreme Court of Alabama had prejudiced the cause of the defendant. Taylor, he concluded, had therefore been denied "due process of law" of the Fourteenth Amendment since defendant's claims of a forced confession, used to convict, had not even been considered.

In a 5–3 decision, in which Justice Jackson took no part and in which Justices Murphy, Douglas, and Rutledge dissented, the Court upheld the decision of the Alabama Court. Speaking for the majority, Justice Burton concluded:

> The Supreme Court of Alabama was acting within its constitutional authority when, in its supervisory capacity over procedure in the criminal trials of that State, it denied to petitioner the right to file this petition for writ of error *coram nobis* and stated that "Upon due consideration we conclude that the averments of the petition are unreasonable and that there is no probability of truth therein, and that the proposed attack upon the judgment is not meritorious," *Ex parte Taylor,* supra.

The *Taylor* decision was the second case involving the rights of accused Negroes that Marshall had lost before the Supreme Court (the other having been *Lyons* v. *Oklahoma).*

The following year Marshall and his staff brought before the Supreme Court a related case involving a police-obtained confession in the absence of counsel. Watts, a Negro laborer, was convicted in an Indiana court of murder and was sentenced to death. The accused was arrested on a Wednesday and held without arraignment until the following Tuesday, when he finally confessed to the crime. During this seven-day period of confinement Watts was without the assistance of counsel or friends and was accorded no advice on his constitutional rights. Moreover, he was held much of the time in solitary confinement in a cell with no place to sit or sleep except the cement floor, and he was questioned by relays of police interrogators, usually way beyond midnight. At his trial the confession was admitted in evidence over his objection, and he was convicted. The NAACP's Legal Defense Fund was called into the case, which was eventually brought before the Supreme Court of the United States. In *Watts* v. *Indiana,* (1949), Robert L. Carter, Franklin H. Williams, and Thurgood Marshall were listed as counsel for petitioner, with Warren M. Brown, Emerson J. Brunner, Willard B. Ransom, and Henry J. Richardson serving of counsel, as listed in the brief. In the brief, Marshall pleaded for a reversal of the conviction on the grounds of the Court's earlier decision in *Chambers* v. *Florida,* (1940). Here, as in *Chambers,* declared Marshall—who had written the *Chambers* brief—is witnessed the use of "third degree" tactics by police officers in the absence of counsel during a period of confinement, the sole purpose of which is to obtain a confession. Such methods, continued counsel for the petitioner, are inconsistent with the requirements of "due process of law" provided by the Fourteenth Amendment.

Exactly one week after the Supreme Court handed down its landmark decision in *Wolf* v. *Colorado,* it delivered its decision in the *Watts* case. Justice Felix Frankfurter announced the unanimous judgment of the court in an opinion in which Justice Murphy and Rutledge joined:

> A confession by which life becomes forfeit must be the expression of free choice. A statement to be voluntary of course need not be volunteered. But if it is the product of sustained pressure by the police it does not issue from a free choice. When a suspect speaks because he is overborne, it is immaterial whether he had been subjected to a physical or mental ordeal. Eventually yielding to questioning under such circumstances is plainly the product of the suction process of interrogation and therefore the reverse of voluntary.

On the same day the Court reversed two other state convictions based on forced confessions; however, as in *Watts,* in neither was there an opinion in which a majority joined. Thus by attempting to secure equal justice for Negro defendants, Marshall felt that he had helped secure justice for all accused persons, regardless of race or color. The decisions of the Court, first in *Chambers* and then in *Watts,* created a temporary barrier between officials working "under the color of state law" and the accused when in the absence of counsel and subjected to such treatment. That barrier was not permanently established by the Court until fifteen years later.

The Restrictive Covenant Cases

In 1926, in *Corrigan* v. *Buckley,* the Supreme Court of the United States had held that neither the Fifth nor the Thirteenth and Fourteenth Amendments "prohibited private individuals from entering into contracts respecting the control and disposition of their own property." Regarding the claim that judicial enforcement of restrictive covenants was, in fact, *state* action, Justice Sanford, speaking for a unanimous Court, concluded that this contention "is likewise lacking in substance." The Court adamantly stuck to this decision for two decades by denying all requests for review of litigation challenging the *Corrigan* rule. A temporary victory came in 1940, when the Chicago Chapter of the NAACP brought before the Supreme Court the case of *Hansberry* v. *Lee.* The restrictive covenant in question required the signatures of 95 percent of the property owners; however, this requirement had not been met. The Supreme Court found that a prior state court had erred in upholding the improperly enforced covenant, thereby siding with the petitioners in the case. Although the decision was not significant in the legal drive against the enforcement of racial covenants, it did have the immediate effect of "opening for purchase and rental to Negroes an entire area of twenty-seven city blocks in Chicago." The process by which the NAACP and a number of other organizations succeeded in persuading the Supreme Court to reconsider this question in the late 1940s, is of both constitutional and practical significance.

With the end of World War II, the enforcement of such racial contracts worked to limit the supply of housing for Negro veterans; consequently the problem was given priority by the NAACP's Legal Defense and Educational Fund. As in the legal approach to education, the year of genesis for the all-out attack against restrictive covenants in the courts was 1945. The NAACP called a national conference on the matter in Chicago on July 9 and 10. The then Governor of the Virgin Islands, William Hastie, presided over the meetings, while Director-Counsel Marshall discussed possible legal strategies. The objective, explained Marshall, was to develop cases by which the constitutionality of the enforcement of racial contracts could be successfully challenged before the Supreme Court of the United States. As Clement Vose pointed out, "The continuing failure of Negroes to convert a major appellate court to their viewpoint in a racial case made it urgent for them to reach the Supreme Court." Every possible aspect of the techniques of attacking restrictive covenants was discussed.

When the two-day conference came to a close, the Director-Counsel announced that the NAACP and the Legal Defense and Educational Fund would place special emphasis on the fight against restrictive covenants. Marshall committed the NAACP to a propaganda crusade against "the evils of segregation and racial restrictive covenants" and recommended that the national office create a staff position devoted to the subject of housing.

A shroud of caution and apprehension had been placed over the conference by a case decided in Washington, D.C., several months earlier. *Mays* v. *Burgess,* involved the enforcement of a restrictive covenant against a federal government employee, Miss Clara I. Mays. Defending her were a number of lawyers associated with the NAACP in Washington, including William Hastie, George E. C. Hayes, and Leon Ransom. Not unsurprisingly, the decision of the federal district court enjoining Miss Mays from occupancy was affirmed by the Court of Appeals for the District of Columbia. Judge Henry Edgerton, however, wrote a stinging dissent which gave some ray of hope to the Negro lawyers. Basing his argument on economic and social data, Edgerton maintained that the shortage of Negro housing was so severe that enforcement of restrictive covenants was in opposition to the public interest. The lawyers for the defendant attempted to get the case reviewed by the Supreme Court, but it denied their petition for a writ of certiorari (1945). The NAACP lawyers were nevertheless encouraged by the fact that Associate Justices Murphy and Rutledge disagreed with the majority and voted to grant the writ. This vote was of particular significance because of the traditional "rule of four," by which the Supreme Court will review any lower-court decision if at least four justices favor granting certiorari. It was clear, therefore, that only two additional votes would be necessary if any later petition to review a restrictive covenant case was to succeed.

With this circumstance in mind, eighteen Negro leaders held a second conference at Howard University on January 26, 1947. Among those present were Marshall; Hastie; Loring Moore; George Vaughn, a Negro lawyer from St. Louis; and Loren Miller.

The decision was made to use sociological and economic support in the fight against restrictive covenants in the next case to be brought before the Supreme Court. They had come to realize, as Clement Vose points out, that "the interpretation of the Negroes' position in American society by sociologists after 1920 placed the race problem in an environmental setting and proved to be potent assistance in the struggle toward a higher status for colored people" and that "the growing political power of Negroes and their increasing effectiveness in pressure politics had to be supported by facts and theories."

The reasons for relying on sociological jurisprudence at this time were compelling. Since 1908, when Louis Brandeis first laid before the Supreme Court of the United States a brief based primarily on sociological, economic, and statistical data rather than on legal argumentation and, by doing so, was able to win approval of Oregon's ten-hour work law for women in *Muller* v. *Oregon,* an increasing number of American scholars and jurists began to accept sociological jurisprudence as a part of constitutional law. By 1921 Roscoe Pound, a leading advocate of the use of sociological data in interpreting the law, was led to write:

> The jurists of today seek to enable and to compel law-making and also the interpretation and application of legal rules, to take more account and more intelligent account, of the social facts upon which law must proceed and to which it is to be applied . . . they strive to make effort more effective in achieving the purposes of law. Such is the spirit of twentieth-century jurisprudence. Such is the spirit in which legal reason is to be employed upon our received jural materials in order to make of them instruments for realizing justice in the world of today.

Because of such political thinkers as Pound, such political activists as Franklin Roosevelt, and such jurists as Holmes, Brandeis, Cardozo, Stone, and Frankfurter, sociological jurisprudence had become the "official doctrine" of the Supreme Court of the United States after 1937.

Marshall and Loring Moore were impressed with the growing number of articles and other publications showing the disastrous sociological and economic effects of not only racially segregated housing but racial segregation per se. Since Marshall was already making use of social theories in two cases involving higher education *(Sipuel* v. *University of Oklahoma,* and *Fisher* v. *Hurst),* he was predisposed to the doctrine. The decision was inevitable: the Legal Defense and Educational Fund of the NAACP would rely on sociological and economic material as its principal point of attack against restrictive covenants before the Supreme Court of the United States. The implications involved were tremendous. If Marshall and his staff could succeed in overturning state-enforced racial covenants with the use of the sociological approach, why not employ it against even more formidable means of state-enforced segregation? If the Court could be convinced of the extralegal effects of state enforcement of racially exclusive contracts in housing, could it resist the logic of such an attack on state-required segregation in public elementary schools, where the "victims" are not adult consumers, but children during their most formative years? Obviously the future of the Fund's overall legal strategy depended greatly on the next restrictive-covenant case to be brought before the Court.

At the time of the Howard Conference, two significant covenant cases were being decided in the lower courts in St. Louis and Detroit— *Shelley* v. *Kraemer,* and *McGhee* v. *Sipes,* respectively. The state courts had upheld the enforcement of the private racially restrictive agreements in both. On April 21, 1947, George Vaughn filed a petition for certiorari with the Supreme Court of the United States in *Shelley* v. *Kraemer.* Accordingly, Marshall and his New York staff filed a petition in *McGhee* v. *Sipes* on May 10. On June 23 the Supreme Court of the United States granted the petitions for writs of certiorari to the Supreme Court of Michigan and Missouri, and on October 20, granted certiorari in two similar cases in Washington, D.C. Although some measure of coordination and consolidation was achieved between the advocates, the lawyers in St. Louis, Detroit and Washington worked on the specifics of their cases differently.

The only case planned solely by the Legal Defense and Educational Fund was *McGhee* v. *Sipes,* although the NAACP made its resources available to the other participants in St. Louis and Washington. Marshall and the other Negro leaders, realizing that legal precedent favored the opposition, planned their strategy accordingly. In addition to showing the social and economic evils resulting from state enforcement of racial contracts in this class-action case, Marshall opted for two other tactics in the case: first, to demonstrate legally, as D. O. McGovney had argued, that enforcement of restrictive agreements by state courts was clearly state action and, as such, violated "equal protection of the laws" protected by the Fourteenth Amendment; and second, to make apparent to the Court the widespread support for the Negro cause by having a large number of interested groups file amicus curiae briefs, and by focusing attention on the problem in journals and law review studies.

Finally group pressure was brought to bear on the administration, particularly on President Truman and the Department of Justice, for the United States to enter a friend-of-the court brief on behalf of the petitioners. In response to a number of racial incidents involving Negro homes in white neighborhoods, representatives of an organization called the National Emergency Committee Against Mob Violence, which represented forty-seven interested groups, called on President Truman in 1946. The group, headed by NAACP leader Walter White, requested that the President create a commission to examine the critical state of race relations in the United States. On December 5, 1946, President Truman issued an executive order establishing the President's Committee on Civil Rights, which was composed of fifteen prominent members. After studying the problem, on October 29, 1947, the committee issued its report, *To Secure These Rights.* Of its forty recommendations, three were concerned with restrictive covenants. Significantly, one of the recommendations called for the Department of Justice to intervene in future litigation aimed at the downfall of state-enforced racial agreements. The response of the Truman administration to the committee's recommendation was immediate. On the day following the release of the committee's findings, Attorney General Tom C. Clark announced at a press conference that the Solicitor General, Phillip B. Perlman, would submit an amicus curiae brief in what now had become known as the Restrictive Covenant Cases. This was, in Marshall's words, "the first amicus curiae brief ever filed, by the United States in private civil rights litigation," and it apparently affected the outcome of the Court's decision.

The legal arm of the NAACP entered its Brief for Petitioners, in *McGhee* v. *Sipes* on November 17, 1947. Listed as counsel for the petitioner were Thurgood Marshall, Loren Miller, Willis Graves, and Francis Dent. The background of the *McGhee* case was quite similar to that of the *Shelley* and *Hurd* litigations.

Mr. and Mrs. Orsel McGhee, Negro citizens of Michigan, purchased residential property in the Seebaldt's Subdivision of the City of Detroit. The persons who sold the land to the McGhees made no conditions on the sale, nor had they signed the restrictive covenant that had been drawn in 1934. The brief quoted the statements of the agreement:

This property shall not be used or occupied by any person or persons except those of the Caucasian race.

It is further agreed that this restriction shall not be effective unless at least eighty percent of the property fronting on both sides of the street in the block where our land is located is subjected to this or a similar restriction.

Owners of property in the same and adjoining subdivisions—including Mr. and Mrs. Benjamin Sipes and Mr. and Mrs. James A. Coon—obtained a decree from the Circuit Court of Wayne County requiring the McGhees to move from their home and restraining them from using or occupying the premises. The Supreme Court of Michigan, on appeal, upheld the decree (1947).

The question presented to the Supreme Court of the United States by Marshall and Miller, both in the brief and in oral argument, was predicated on the facts involved in the case: "Does the enforcement by state courts of an agreement restricting the disposition of land by prohibiting its use and occupancy by members of unpopular minority groups, where neither the willing seller nor the willing purchaser was a party to the agreement imposing the restriction, violate the Fourteenth Amendment and treaty obligations under the United Nations Charter?"

The Negro lawyers developed their argument along six principal points in the brief. First, they maintained that racial compacts restricting occupancy had developed through an uncritical distortion of commonly accepted doctrines concerning valid restrictions on the use of property. Moreover, the historical development of these restrictive devices had almost obliterated the distinction between restrictions on the use of property and those on the occupancy of property by members of unpopular minority groups:

With the urbanization of the population, and the more crowded conditions of modern life, the desire to secure suitable home surroundings led to a demand for real estate limited solely to development for residential purposes. This natural desire of householders has been exploited by land developers and realtors so that the restriction of particular areas of property in or near American cities to residential use is now becoming the rule rather than the exception. The legal machinery to achieve this end has been found in the main not in the ancient rules of easements or covenants enforceable only at law, but in the activities of courts of equity in enforcing restrictions as to use of land where reasonable.

Marshall and Miller continued by pointing out the change in both the intent and the use of restrictive covenants in the early twentieth century:

From its inception until the wave of the last century, the restrictive covenant enforceable in equity was always and only an agent selective of the type of use which might be made of another's land. Neither the history of its development nor the economic or social justifications for its judicial enforcement disclose a basis for its employment as a racially discriminatory device preventive of occupancy. This novel twist in the law was introduced by historical accident, and has survived only because of judicial indifference toward the consequent distortion of fundamental concepts and principles and the economic and social havoc thereby wrought.

The "historical accident" to which the NAACP lawyers referred was a decision handed down by Supreme Court of California in *Los Angeles Investment Co.* v. *Gary,* (1918). Two years after the *Buchanan* case, the state court upheld a racially restrictive covenant, but only because of "restraints on use imposed by way of condition and not to those sought to be imposed by covenant merely." Nevertheless, courts subsequently faced with the racial occupancy covenant followed the lead supplied by this case.

Second, they continued, the right to use and occupy real estate as a home is, in fact, a civil right guaranteed to all persons and is protected by the Constitution and the laws of the United States. They supported their contention by explaining that such was the purport of Congress when it proposed the Fourteenth Amendment and the Civil Rights Bill of 1866.

The third major point expounded by Marshall and his colleague was that under the Fourteenth Amendment no state may deny the right to own and occupy property to any person solely because of his race, color, religion, or national origin. "The decision in the Buchanan case," they pointed out, "disposed of all of the arguments seeking to establish the right of a state to restrict the sale of property by excluding prospective occupants because of race or color." Consequently such a civil right is protected from invasion by any agency of the state including the judiciary:

Both on analysis and authority, it is plain that the acts of state courts are those of the state itself within the meaning of the limitations of the Fourteenth Amendment. Any other conclusion in a common law system would be untenable. For, to the extent that decisions of courts serve as authoritative precepts regulatory of conduct beyond the case in litigation, no logical distinction can be drawn between the acts of the legislature and the decisions of the court. The creative role of the judiciary as a source of law to meet the demands of society by filling the interstices between precedents, and between precedent and legislation has long been recognized.

Fourth, the enforcement of restrictive covenants by the state courts is not only unconstitutional; it also works to the disadvantage of both the restricted group and the white home owners, because it pressurizes the already critical demand for housing.

On the fifth point, Marshall and Miller opened up a heavy barrage of sociological and economic findings to show that it is the Negroes and other minorities who suffer most harm from the enforcement of racial agreements:

> While no state sanctioned discrimination can be consistent with the Fourteenth Amendment, the nation-wide destruction of human and economic values which results from racial residential segregation makes this form of discrimination particularly repugnant. . . .
>
> Judicial enforcement of restrictive covenants has created a uniform pattern of unprecedented overcrowding and congestion in the housing of Negroes and an appalling deterioration of their dwelling conditions. The extension and aggravation of slum conditions have in turn resulted in a serious rise in disease, crime, vice, racial tension and mob violence.

The authors of the brief for the petitioners devoted thirty-eight pages to a discussion of the damaging effects on unpopular minorities because of these agreements. Using data extracted from the Bureau of Census figures and Special Census, Race, Sex by Census Tract, they analyzed the problems of overcrowding and of deteriorated dwellings. They cited such findings as revealed in Britton, "New Light on the Relations of Housing to Health," in the *American Journal of Public Health* (1942); Hyde and Chisholm, "Relations of Mental Disorders to

Race and Nationality" in *New England Journal of Medicine* (1944); Cooper, "The Frustration of Being a Member of a Minority Group" in *Mental Hygiene* 29 (1945); and Farris and Dunham, *Mental Disorders in Urban Areas: An Ecological Study of Schizophrenia and Other Psychoses* (1939). In this way Marshall and Miller attempted to link the unsanitary conditions of the ghetto with ill health. Moreover, they contended, the perpetuation of slum areas amounted to greater costs for the whole community in prejudice, hostility, and racial tension. The Negro lawyers pointed to an argument presented in Gunnar Myrdal's *An American Dilemma,* a recent study of American race relations conducted by a Swedish sociologist, "that in many northern states . . . there is partial segregation aided by the gerrymandering of school districts." Referring to an article by Robert Weaver, the advocates for the petitioners concluded that the inevitable result of such redistricting was to place Negroes in an inferior position:

> As long as Negroes are relegated . . . to physically undesirable areas . . . they are associated with blight. The occupants of the black belt are all believed to be undesirable . . . and their perpetual and universal banishment to the ghetto is defended on the basis of racial characteristics.

In concluding the socioeconomic portion of the brief, the authors discussed the ability of Negroes to pay for and to maintain better housing; again citing Weaver:

> Already there is a body of evidence which indicates that Negroes with steady incomes who are given the opportunity to live in new and decent homes . . . instead of displaying any 'natural' characteristics to destroy better property have, if anything, reacted better towards these new environments than any other groups of a similar income.

The sixth and final point made by the NAACP lawyers was that the enforcement by the state court of the restrictive covenant involved in this case violates the Charter of the United Nations, of which the United States is a member, and, therefore, the covenant is null and void. They based their argument particularly on the pledges to end racial discrimination on the part of the member nations found in Articles 2 (Section 2), 55, and 56.

In conclusion, Marshall and Miller called for an end to the enforcement of racially restrictive agreements for the future development of the individual and of American society itself:

> This case is not a matter of enforcing an isolated private agreement. It is a test as to whether we will have a united nation or a nation divided into areas and ghettos solely on racial or religious lines. To strike down the walls of these state court imposed ghettos will simply allow a flexible way of life to develop in which each individual will be able to live, work and raise his family as a free American.

On May 3, 1948, the Supreme Court handed down a single opinion for the two state cases in *Shelley* v. *Kraemer,* and subsequently, in *Hurd* v. *Hodge,* an opinion in the consolidated cases from the District of Columbia. Speaking for a unanimous six-man court, Chief Justice Vinson confined himself to the strict constitutional issues involved, without any reference to the extralegal materials brought before the Court. First, with regard to the constitutionality of the private agreements per se, the Chief Justice concluded:

> Since the decision of this Court in the Civil Rights cases . . . the principle has become firmly embedded in our constitutional law that the action inhibited by the first section of the Fourteenth Amendment is only such action as may fairly be said to be that of the States. That amendment erects no shield against merely private conduct, however discriminatory or wrongful.
> . . . the restrictive agreements standing alone cannot be regarded as violative of any rights guaranteed to petitioners by the Fourteenth Amendment.

Secondly, Chief Justice Vinson made it clear that the enforcement of such a covenant by state courts was a violation of "equal protection of the laws" under the Fourteenth Amendment:

> We have no doubt that there has been state action in these cases in the full and complete sense of the phrases. The undisputed facts disclose that petitioners were willing purchasers of properties upon which they desired to establish homes. The owners of the properties were willing sellers; and contracts of sale were accordingly consummated. It is clear that but for the active intervention of the state courts, supported by the full panoply of state power,

petitioners would have been free to occupy the properties in question without restraint.

In a separate opinion in *Hurd,* Chief Justice Vinson again spoke for a unanimous Court, with Associate Justice Felix Frankfurter concurring, and struck down enforcements of restrictive covenants by federal district courts in the District of Columbia. Since the limitations of the Fourteenth Amendment do not restrict federal action, the Court could not use the reasoning it applied in the *Shelley* decision. In addition, the Court avoided discussion of whether the "due process of law" clause of the Fifth Amendment could be made applicable to the federal government in this case. Instead, Vinson held that federal enforcement violated the Civil Rights Act of 1866, which guaranteed to all citizens of the United States, in "every State and Territory," the equal right to own and maintain property.

The immediate effect of the Court's decision was gratifying to the petitioners; it seemed more difficult, however, to assess the situation of others similarly situated who would now be attempting to purchase property in white neighborhoods. While many legal scholars favored the Court's ruling and remained essentially optimistic about the future, others noted that Negro purchasers attempting to gain admission to white neighborhoods "still must face onerous difficulties." Marshall believed that the Restrictive Covenant Cases represented the first of many small steps in the right direction taken in 1948:

> In that year, the federal government officially revoked its discriminatory policies and began a slow effort to undo what it had done. The desegregation of the armed forces was undertaken. Discrimination in government hiring was ordered stopped. And FHA reversed its stand on the insurability of homes in mixed neighborhoods.

Technically speaking, one question remained unanswered in the *Shelley* and *Hurd* decisions; it centered on "willing sellers" and "willing buyers." If someone had previously signed a restrictive agreement in good faith and had subsequently sold his property to members of a group expressly prohibited from acquisition by the terms of the covenant, can he be sued for damages by his fellow signers in a state court? The Legal Defense and Educational Fund had occasion to bring such a question before the Supreme Court of the United States in 1953, in *Barrows* v. *Jackson.*

Mrs. Leola Jackson, a white homeowner in Los Angeles, had entered into a covenant with other owners of residential estates in her neighborhood, restricting "the use and occupancy thereof to persons of the white or Caucasian race" and obligating the signers to incorporate this restriction in all transfers of land. When Mrs. Jackson decided to sell her home to Negroes, therefore, Mrs. Olive B. Barrows and other signers brought a suit against her for breach of contract. The California state courts decided in favor of Jackson (1952) on the grounds that the *Shelley* decision invalidated state enforcement of restrictive covenants as violating the Fourteenth Amendment. Barrows received a grant of certiorari to have the case reviewed by the Supreme Court of the United States. Loren Miller argued the cause for the respondent, while Marshall and Franklin H. Williams assisted in preparing the brief. Although the argumentation made in the Brief for Respondent, repeated much of that contributed by Marshall and Miller in the *McGhee* case, it devoted a great deal more discussion to the subject of standing. The Negro lawyers recognized the "unique" position of the respondent under the Court's rule of practice to deny standing to a person not sustaining direct injury to his rights; however, if the Court were to side with the petitioners and allow state participation, it would deny to Negroes the "equal protection of the laws" derived from the Fourteenth Amendment and thus "create precedential substantive law that would have consequences far beyond the outcome of this case."

On June 15, 1953, Associate Justice Minton, speaking for six members of the Court, with Chief Justice Vinson dissenting and Justices Reed and Jackson taking no part, held that a restrictive covenant could not be enforced at law by a suit for damages against one who breaks the covenant. In discussing the rule of standing, Minton allowed:

> We are faced with a unique situation in which it is the action of the state *court* which might result in a denial of constitutional rights and in which it would be difficult if not impossible for the persons whose rights are asserted to present their grievances before any court. Under the peculiar circumstances of this case, we believe reasons which underlie our rule denying standing to raise another's rights, which is only a rule of practice, are outweighed by the need to protect fundamental rights which would be denied by permitting the damages action to be maintained.

Relying on the *Shelley* decision, Justice Minton held that such a suit, if granted, would violate the Fourteenth Amendment, since no individual has a right "to demand action by the state which results in the denial of equal protection of the laws to other individuals."

In his stinging dissent, Chief Justice Vinson, author of the *Shelley* opinion, criticized the majority viewpoint and its decision on the grounds that the respondent had no standing in the case and, further, that the petitioners were entitled to bring a suit for damages. He reasoned that Mrs. Jackson could not base her claim on the rights of "some unnamed person in an amorphous class."

The point was not lost on Marshall and his colleagues: in the future the Chief Justice would be unwilling to apply the restraints of the Fourteenth Amendment to any conduct, "however discriminatory or wrongful," that did not *directly* result from the commands of the state.

Having successfully employed social materials in combating racial discrimination in higher education and housing in *Sipuel* and *McGhee,* Marshall and his legal staff became convinced of its utility as a manipulative tool for future litigation. This conviction was reinforced by two increasingly evident factors. The first was that a majority of the justices on the Supreme Court of the United States accepted sociological jurisprudence as a part of constitutional law and were willing to weigh social theories and data heavily in their considerations. Chief Justice Vinson's warning to his colleagues in the *Barrows* decision, that "we must set aside predilections on social policy and adhere to the settled rules which restrict the exercise of our power of judicial review," was the lone dissenting opinion. Second, the Restrictive Covenant Cases proved to the legal arm of the NAACP that utilization of multigroup support through amici curiae briefs and other forms of group pressure on concerned federal agencies was an invaluable asset. Essential to the success of this strategy in the present cases was the fact that for the first time in a private suit the federal government had submitted a brief friendly to the Negro cause. This lesson was not lost on the Director-Counsel and his colleagues in the public-education cases.

Finally, the success of the Legal Defense and Educational Fund in the Restrictive Covenant Cases supported its long-practiced strategy of lengthy, legal preparations, exposing arguments before moot courts of interested law schools, obtaining sufficient monetary assistance, and soliciting the finest professional talent.

Examining the activities of Thurgood Marshall and his staff in the development of these cases, Clement E. Vose concluded:

Analysis of the Negro victory in the Restrictive Covenant Cases forces the conclusion that this result was an outgrowth of the complex group activity which preceded it. Groups with antagonistic interests appeared before the Supreme Court, just as they do in Congress and other institutions that mold public policy. Because of organization the lawyers for the Negroes were better prepared to do battle through the courts. Without this continuity, money, and talent they would not have freed themselves from the limiting effects of racial residential covenants, notwithstanding the presence of favorable social theories, political circumstances, and the Supreme Court justices.

The Higher Education Cases: Development of NAACP Strategy

The legal staff of the NAACP was engaged on a strategy of attrition against the concept of "separate but equal" facilities in education since 1945. Beginning with an attack on segregated public professional schools and colleges, and working down to the more sensitive area of elementary education, Marshall and his staff attempted to erode the basis of discrimination by pushing for de facto equality not only in tangible facilities, but also in intangible factors. By demonstrating to the Supreme Court of the United States that it is impossible for a state to provide equality in such intangible features as the prestige of an institution, the quality of the faculty, and the reputation of degrees for Negroes in separate schools, they hoped to prove the inconsistency of the "separate but equal" doctrine itself.

As revealed by an examination of NAACP strategy in the Restrictive Covenant Cases, Director-Counsel Marshall and the other Negro lawyers were prepared by 1947 to reinforce their legal arguments against racial discrimination in the courts with favorable social theories. The first case to arise affording them this opportunity was *Sipuel* v. *University of Oklahoma,* (1948); it involved a state law school's denial of admission to an otherwise qualified Negro solely on the grounds of race and color.

In September 1946, Ada Lois Sipuel, a citizen and resident of Oklahoma, applied for admission to the first-year class of the University of Oklahoma School of Law, the only institution in the state offering instruction in law. Recognizing her academic qualifications, the school refused her admittance on the grounds that a "substantially equal" Negro law school was to be established at a future date. Miss Sipuel then applied to the District Court of Cleveland County, Oklahoma, for a writ of mandamus against the Board of Regents to compel her admission. The Legal Defense and Educational Fund, as represented by lawyers Marshall, Amos Hall, Robert Carter, Edward Dudley, Marion Wynn Perry, Frank D. Reeves, and Franklin Williams, joined her cause and appealed the judgment to the Supreme Court of Oklahoma. On April 29, 1947, the state supreme court affirmed the action of the lower court on the ground that a separate Negro law school need not be provided by the state until enough applications warranted its creation. After Sipuel was denied a rehearing by the court, Marshall and his colleagues petitioned and received a grant of certiorari from the Supreme Court of the United States to review the case.

Marshall and Amos Hall, in both the argument before the court and in the Brief for Petitioner, contended that the central question of the case paralleled that of the *Gaines* decision: "Does the Constitution of the United States prohibit the exclusion of a qualified Negro applicant solely because of race from attending the only law school maintained by a state?"

The authors of the brief constructed the outline of their argument on three major points. First, the Oklahoma Supreme Court erred in not ordering the lower court to issue a writ of mandamus to the school to admit petitioner in light of the *Gaines* decision. Consequently, Miss Sipuel had been denied "equal protection of the laws" guaranteed by the Fourteenth Amendment.

The second point was one of historical significance. For the first time in its thirty-three years of operation, the legal staff of the NAACP demanded that the Supreme Court of the United States reexamine the constitutionality of the doctrine of "separate but equal" educational facilities. Reference to this doctrine in the *Gaines* decision, they maintained, had been consistently relied on by state courts to render the thrust of the decision meaningless:

> Petitioner is entitled to admission now to the University of Oklahoma and her right to redress cannot be conditioned upon any prior demand that the state set up a separate facility. The opinion in the *Gaines* case is without meaning unless this court intended that decision to enforce the right of a qualified Negro applicant in a case such as here to admission *instanter* to the only existing state facility. The equal but separate doctrine has no application in cases of this type. The *Gaines* decision must have meant

at least this and should so be clarified. Beyond that petitioner contends that the separate but equal doctrine is basically unsound and unrealistic and in the light of the history of its application should now be repudiated.

In noting the "striking similarity" between the decisions of the state courts in *Gaines* and those in the present case, as well as in the statutes of the two states, the NAACP lawyers led a frontal assault on the rationale of establishing a separate law school for Negroes:

> The "separate but equal" doctrine, based upon this assumption that equality is possible within a segregated system, has been used as the basis for the enforcement of the policy of segregation in public schools. The full extent of the evil inherent in this premise is present in this case where the "separate but equal" doctrine is urged as a complete defense where the State has not ever made the pretense of establishing a separate law school.

Turning from the specific discrimination involved in the present case to racial segregation in general, Marshall and his fellow lawyers employed a line of argument that was to be used in every other education case by the NAACP down to the *Brown* case itself; that is, that the doctrine of "separate but equal" was without legal foundation or social justification:

> Classifications and distinctions based on race or color have no moral or legal validity in our society. They are contrary to our Constitution and laws, and this Court has struck down statutes, ordinances or official policies seeking to establish such classification. In the decisions concerning intrastate transportation and public education, however, this court appears to have adopted a different and antithetical constitutional doctrine under which racial separation is deemed permissible when equality is afforded. An examination of these decisions will recall that the "separate but equal" doctrine is at best a bare constitutional hypothesis postulated in the absence of facts showing the circumstances and consequences of racial segregation and based upon a fallacious evaluation of the purpose and meaning inherent in any policy or theory of enforced racial separation.

Counsel for the petitioner contended that history has proved that segregation of the races connotes inferiority of the Negro group and that the terms "separate" and "equal" are totally inconsistent:

> Segregation in public education helps to preserve a caste system which is based upon race and color. It is designed and intended to perpetuate the slave tradition sought to be destroyed by the Civil War and to prevent Negroes from attaining the equality guaranteed by the Federal Constitution. Racial separation is the aim and motive of paramount importance—an end in itself. Equality, even if the term be limited to a comparison of physical facilities, is and never can be achieved. . . .
>
> The Supreme Court in *Plessy* v. *Ferguson* . . . without any facts before it upon which to make a valid judgment adopted the "separate but equal" doctrine. Subsequent cases have accepted this doctrine as a constitutional axiom, without examination. Hence what was in reality a legal expedient of the Reconstruction Era has until now been accepted as a valid and proven constitutional theory.
>
> Racial segregation in education originated as a device to "keep the Negro in his place," i.e., in a constantly inferior position . . . the terms "separate" and "equal" can not be used conjunctively in a situation of this kind; *there can be no separate equality.*

Marshall, Hall, and the others dismissed any syllogism that might be used by the state to infer that one could equally conclude that separation of the races suggested inferiority of the *white* group. After all, they maintained: *Negroes,* not whites, were aggrieved; *Negroes,* not whites, were discriminated against; *Negroes,* not whites, were being relegated to an inferior position because "the entire device of educational segregation has been used historically and is being used at the present to deny equality of educational opportunity to Negroes."

To prove that the "separate but equal" doctrine lacked any social justification, the NAACP lawyers cited eighteen "authoritative" sources throughout much of their argument, including government reports, articles in law journals, sociological publications, and other statistical information. Citing Gunnar Myrdal's *An American Dilemma* and Carey McWilliams's article "Race Discrimination and the Law," the Negro lawyers noted in the brief that "qualified educators, social scientists and others have expressed their realization of the fact that 'separate' is irreconcilable with 'equality' . . . since the very fact of segregation establishes a feeling of humiliation and deprivation to the group considered to be inferior." Moreover, they continued, both Negroes and whites suffer from segregation, in that discrimination lowers the economic, political, legal, and moral standards of whites and brings about an atmosphere of mutual distrust and hatred. Employing a study by Otto Klineberg, Marshall and his colleagues attempted to invalidate the rationale for separate education which maintains that "Negroes have an inferior mental capacity to whites," by arguing that it has "no rational, no factual justification." Finally, in support of integrated public schools, the advocates for the petitioner cited a study by Lloyd Warner of children in an integrated New Haven school district which evidenced no color consciousness among the students, who consequently experienced no racial discrimination.

Concluding their argument, the advocates pleaded with the Court that if it was unwilling to invalidate the doctrine of "separate but equal" facilities per se, at least not to allow it to stand in the present case.

On January 12, 1948, just four days after the case had been argued, the Supreme Court of the United States in a per curiam decision overruled the Oklahoma Supreme Court. Relying on its earlier decision in the *Gaines* case, the Court avoided most of the points touched upon by the Legal Defense and Educational Fund and held that Oklahoma "must provide such education for her in conformity with the Equal Protection Clause of the Fourteenth Amendment and provide it as soon as it does for applicants of any other group."

Five days following the Court's decision, the Oklahoma Law School was faced with the alternatives of either enrolling Sipuel—who was now Mrs. Fisher—or of refusing admission to all new applicants until a separate institution for Negroes was created. Consequently, the regents designated a roped-off area in the State Capitol as a makeshift law school, to which they assigned three teachers. Mrs. Fisher refused to enroll on the grounds that this ad hoc arrangement did not satisfy the "equality" required by the Fourteenth Amendment.

On January 26, NAACP lawyers Marshall, Hall, Hastie, Perry, and Dudley filed a brief in support of a petition for writ of mandamus with the Supreme Court of the United States, claiming that the action of the regents was inconsistent with the Court's decision in *Sipuel* to provide "such education as soon as it does for applicants of any other group." Citing studies compiled by sociologists and educators, the Director-Counsel and his associates argued that, besides tangible facilities, the free exchange of ideas and views of representatives from all groups is also necessary for an equal education in a democratic society. The motion noted:

> Equally essential to a proper legal education in a democratic society is the interchange of ideas and attitudes which can only be effected when the student body is representative of all groups and peoples. Exclusion of any one group on the basis of race, automatically imputes a badge of inferiority to the excluded group—an inferiority that has no basis in fact. The role of the lawyer, moreover, is often that of a law maker, a "social mechanic," and a "social inventor." A profession which produces future legislators and social inventor to whom will fall the social responsibilities of our society, can not do so on a segregated basis.

On February 16, 1948, in a 7–2 per curiam decision in *Fisher* v. *Hurst,* the Court was unwilling to yield on the established requirement of equal tangible facilities. It held that the creation of a separate law school for Negroes by Oklahoma complied with the Equal Protection Clause of the Fourteenth Amendment and thus denied the motion for a writ of mandamus. Mr. Justice Rutledge, who dissented along with Mr. Justice Murphy, wrote in his dissenting opinion:

> It is impossible . . . for the state's officials to dispose of petitioner's demand for a legal education equal to that afforded to white students by establishing overnight a separate law school for Negroes or to continue affording the present advantages to white students while denying them to petitioner.
> Oklahoma should end the discrimination . . . at once, not at a later date, near or remote.

Subsequently the Oklahoma legislature amended state law to allow the admission of Negroes to the university's Law School, but only on a segregated basis; however, since school officials felt that such a practice would be overturned by the Supreme Court of the United States, Mrs. Fisher was not kept segregated from her classmates after her admittance.

The Court's decision in the *Fisher* case was only a momentary setback for the Legal Defense and Educational Fund. In a case adjudicated in the lower courts just prior to the *Sipuel* decision, Marshall and his staff were preparing an even more powerful attack on the "separate but equal" doctrine.

The case centered on Herman Marion Sweatt, a Negro postal clerk, who in 1945 applied for admission to the University of Texas Law School at the opening of the 1946 term. He was refused on the basis of racial policy. Since Texas had no separate law school for Negroes, Sweatt filed suit in the District Court of Travis County to compel his admission. The state court postponed the trial of suit and granted the regents of the university a six-month period to create a "separate law school for Negroes substantially equal to the one at the University of Texas." In response, university officials adopted an order calling for the opening of a separate law school for Negroes in February 1947. Thereafter the District Court ruled against Sweatt, and upon appeal, the Texas appellate court upheld the earlier decision.

On March 3 the Texas Legislature created the School of Law of Texas Southern University in Austin, Texas. The proposed institution would have no independent faculty—four members of the university faculty were to teach the entire program—and very few of the 10,000 volumes ordered for its library had arrived. Moreover, the new school was not accredited; it consisted of three rooms in the basement of a building. Sweatt refused to apply and filed a petition for a writ of certiorari to the Supreme Court of the United States. The Court granted certiorari in the October term, 1949.

Arguing the cause for the petitioner were NAACP lawyers from New York, including Marshall, Carter, Ming, Nabrit, and Williams; and from Texas, W. J. Durham and U. Simpson Tate. In the brief Marshall and the others made essentially the same points that had been raised in *Sipuel* and *Fisher*. Studies proved that there are no essential differences in the ability to learn between Negroes and whites. Segregation is socially and morally destructive to both the majority and minority groups, and a feeling of mutual distrust inevitably develops. "Qualified educators, social scientists, and other experts have expressed their realization of the fact that 'separate' is irreconcilable with 'equality.' " Segregation imposes a "badge of inferiority" on the group separated from the rest of society. And the doctrine of "separate but equal" as expounded in the *Plessy* decision had no social or legal justification.

On the specifics of the case, the Negro lawyers assailed the measurable and immeasurable facets of the "equality" provided by Texas in creating the Negro law school. The University of Texas Law School, they contended, had a permanent faculty of sixteen professors, a library containing in excess of 65,000 volumes, and an enrollment of 850 students; it provided practice courts for its students, published an established law review, and maintained a chapter of the country's most renowned honorary legal fraternity; its graduates were recognized as the leading members of the bar in the state. On the other hand, the NAACP lawyers continued, Texas Southern University Law School had only a faculty of five permanent members, housed some 16,500 volumes in its library, provided one practice or moot court, maintained a legal-aid association, and had graduated only one alumnus who was at present a member of the state bar. Marshall and his colleagues stressed the fact that the intangible facilities are as unequal as the tangible ones. The University of Texas Law School was recognized as the best law school in the state and one of the leading institutions in the nation; how could such immeasurable qualities as "prestige" and "reputation" be accorded equally to the separate institution for Negroes? The requirements of the Fourteenth Amendment have not been met by Texas in this case, the advocates continued, since no "separate equality" exists. The respondents, they concluded, can only satisfy the "equality" required by admitting Sweatt and others similarly situated, to the *best* available law school in the state—that of the University of Texas:

> If an enlightened citizenry is a necessary factor in the equation of democracy, then it follows that education is an integral part of the democratic process. Assuming that education is merely a privilege, it is one of such a particular and precious nature that those entrusted with its administration have a compelling duty rather than mere discretionary power to see that no distinctions are made on the basis of race, creed or color. Unless Texas has some purpose other than these democratic objectives . . . it must permit all persons without regard to class or race to participate in these benefits on an equal basis.

On June 5, 1950, in a unanimous decision rendered by Chief Justice Vinson in *Sweatt* v. *Painter,* the Supreme Court of the United States held that the equal-protection clause of the Fourteenth Amendment did indeed require that the petitioner be admitted to the University of Texas Law School. The Court agreed with the contention of the NAACP lawyers that there was no equality in the tangible features of the two institutions. Vinson stated:

> Whether the University of Texas Law School is compared with the original or the new law school for Negroes, we cannot find substantial equality in the educational opportunities offered white and Negro law students by the State. In terms of numbers of faculty,

variety of courses and opportunity for specialization, size of the student body, scope of the library, availability of law review and similar activities, the University of Texas Law School is superior.

In light of the earlier decisions of the Court in *Gaines, Sipuel,* and *Fisher,* this reason alone was sufficient grounds for the decision; the Court went further, however:

What is more important, the University . . . Law School possesses to a far greater degree those qualities which are incapable of objective measurement but which make for greatness in a law school. Such qualities, to name but a few, include reputation of the faculty, experience of the administration, position and influence of the alumni, standing in the community, traditions and prestige. It is difficult to believe that one who had a free choice between these law schools would consider the question close.

As to the challenge posed by the Negro lawyers that the doctrine of "separate but equal" be overturned by the Court, the Chief Justice replied that the Court need not "reach petitioner's contention that *Plessy* v. *Ferguson* should be reexamined in the light of contemporary knowledge respecting the purposes of the Fourteenth Amendment and the effects of racial segregation."

Uniquely, then, while going far to render the doctrine meaningless by stating that intangible qualities are "more important" in achieving equality than tangible ones, the Supreme Court of the United States nevertheless remained unwilling at that time to overrule the *Plessy* decision altogether. Marshall considered the *Sweatt* decision to constitute the first substantive break in the wall of segregated public education.

In a companion case decided the same day—*McLaurin* v. *Oklahoma State Regents* (1950)—the Legal Defense and Educational Fund challenged a state statute requiring segregated facilities for Negroes and whites in the Oklahoma University Graduate School.

The Brief for the Appellant related that George W. McLaurin, a Negro teacher, applied for admission to the graduate school of the University of Oklahoma in order to pursue courses leading to a doctorate in education—a degree not offered by Langston University, Oklahoma's Negro college. His admission was denied on the basis of state laws which forbade school authorities to staff integrated state schools. McLaurin sued for injunctive relief, and a three-judge District Court ordered his admission to the University on the basis of the *Gaines* and

Sipuel decisions. In response, the state legislature quickly amended its laws to permit the admission of Negroes but also provided that instruction "shall be given at such colleges or institutions of higher education on a segregated basis." Upon entering the university, McLaurin was required to sit at the separate desk in an anteroom adjoining the classroom; he was assigned a desk on the mezzanine floor of the library but was prohibited from using those in the reading room; and he was granted the use of a specified table at designated times, different from those of the white students.

His lawyers, Robert Carter and Amos Hall, then filed a motion with the District Court to remove the conditions imposed by the state; however, the Court ruled that Oklahoma had provided the "equality" required by the Fourteenth Amendment when McLaurin was admitted and that the contested treatment afforded him was not prohibited. Although the university eventually modified some of its requirements for "colored students" it still imposed systematic separation from white students. Consequently, Carter and Hall won an appeal for McLaurin to the Supreme Court of the United States.

The brief—principally the work of Thurgood Marshall, Robert Carter, Frank Reeves, Marion Perry, and Franklin Williams—contained the same social theories expounded in the *Sipuel* and *Sweatt* cases. The thrust of the argument was that the enforced discrimination branded McLaurin an inferior, humiliated him, and brought mental strain which interfered with his ability to study. Consequently, the NAACP lawyers maintained, the equal-protection clause of the Fourteenth Amendment required the university to extend to him the *same* treatment that it did to other students.

Again, speaking for a unanimous Court, Chief Justice Vinson agreed. Holding that such discriminatory treatment is precluded by the Fourteenth Amendment, the Chief Justice noted:

> Our society grows increasingly complex, and our need for trained leaders increases correspondingly. Appellant's case represents, perhaps, the epitome of that need, for he is attempting to obtain an advanced degree in education, to become . . . a leader and trainer of others. Those who will come under his guidance and influence must be directly affected by the education he received. Their own education and development will necessarily suffer to the extent that his training is unequal to that of his classmates.

State-imposed restrictions which produce such inequalities cannot be sustained.

The decisions of the Court in *Sipuel, Sweatt,* and *McLaurin* were extremely important to the strategy of the Legal Defense and Educational Fund in seeking to eliminate state-enforced segregated education. In evaluating these decisions in "Law and the Quest for Equality," Marshall felt that the Court had "seriously undermined the rationale of the *Plessy* case, at least with respect to public education." After 1950 it became obvious that no *separate* graduate or professional school could satisfy the standards of equality laid down by the Court.

In 1951 the University of Tennessee refused several Negro applicants admission to the graduate school solely on the basis of race. After a federal district court ruled that they were to be admitted and the order was not carried out, the NAACP Legal Defense Fund won an appeal to the Supreme Court of the United States. While the arguments in *Gray* v. *University of Tennessee,* (1952), were being heard by the Court, the University revised its admissions policy and accepted the Negroes. Even after the School Segregation Cases in 1954, Marshall and his staff were forced to bring a number of cases before the Court involving states' attempts to prevent Negro enrollment in graduate and law schools, in which it came to recognize that admission was a "personal and present" civil right not subject to violation by the state. In one case Florida courts attempted to apply the "deliberate-speed" rule of *Brown* v. *Board of Education,* (1955), to the state's law school when a Negro attempted to gain admission; the Supreme Court, however, ruling in *Florida ex. rel. Hawkins* v. *Board of Control* (1956), held that the case did not "present the problems of elementary and secondary schools" and that "there is no reason for delay." For all practical purposes, most state-imposed segregation in institutions of higher learning was at an end by 1957.

One reason why the NAACP had taken on the graduate and law schools first—besides the fact that the total void in Negro professional and graduate education in the southern states made "inequality" easier to prove—was simply because the South was less sensitive to integration of higher educational facilities than to that of the elementary schools. As Marshall had informed Professor Alfred Kelly of Wayne State University,

Those racial supremacy boys somehow think that little kids of six or seven are going to get funny ideas about sex and marriage just from going to school together, but for some equally funny reason youngsters in law school aren't supposed to feel that way. We didn't get it but we decided if that was what the South believed, then the best thing for the movement was to go along.

In both *Sweatt* and *McLaurin,* the Supreme Court of the United States had paid some homage to the sociological arguments of the NAACP lawyers and, while it was not yet ready to repudiate the "separate but equal" doctrine, it seemed only logical that it would inevitably do so. After these decisions it apparently made little or no difference to the Legal Defense Fund what steps the South took to provide equal facilities; its strategy aimed at overruling the *Plessy* decision had been implemented and would not be altered now.

The Brown Case: NAACP Strategy Rewarded

In the summer of 1950 a national meeting of interested lawyers was called in New York by the NAACP Legal Defense Fund. Marshall and his colleagues agreed that it was totally unreasonable to expect Negro children "to wait for twenty, thirty or forty years before the Jim Crow school might wither away." Moreover, the higher education cases evidenced the fact that educators and students "adjust themselves relatively easily to long overdue changes when the laws compelling segregation are overthrown through judicial intervention. Immediately following the conference, Marshall and his staff began the prosecution of five suits in equity in federal district courts at strategic points around the country.

The NAACP suits were filed on the part of local Negro children to compel their admission to segregated white elementary and secondary schools in Clarendon County, South Carolina; in Topeka, Kansas; in Farmville, Prince Edward County, Virginia; in the Chancery Court of the State of Delaware; and in Washington, D.C. In the four state class-action suits, NAACP lawyers called for the repudiation of the doctrine of "separate but equal" in light of the "equal protection of the laws" clause of the Fourteenth Amendment. In the fifth action, in Washington, the Negro advocates pleaded that the doctrine violated "due process of law" of the Fifth Amendment, since the children were being denied rights, personal and present. The NAACP Legal Defense Fund placed its best legal minds into offensive action: Marshall argued the South Carolina case; his assistant, Jack Greenberg, and Louis L. Redding argued the case in Delaware; James Nabrit, Jr., and George E. C.

Hayes in the District of Columbia; Robert Carter in Topeka, Kansas; and Spottswood Robinson in Virginia. The attorneys in all five cases, complying with NAACP strategy, introduced extensive sociological and psychological materials and solicited testimony from leading social scientists to show the damaging effects of segregated schools on both Negro and white children. Probably the most telling testimony was given by psychologist Kenneth B. Clark of New York City College, whose experiment had shown that when Negro children were asked to pick one of two dolls—one white and the other black—they invariably chose the white doll, explaining that it was "pretty" and "nice," while the colored one looked "bad." Nevertheless, in all but the Delaware case, the three-judge district courts were not impressed by this line of argument and upheld the validity of the segregated school systems. The district court in Washington refused to appoint a collegial panel of judges to hear the case on its merits. Only in Delaware was there initial success. Chancellor Collins Seitz of the State Court of Chancery held in *Belton* v. *Gebhart,* (1952), that the Negro children of Newcastle County must be admitted to the white public school, since the separate Negro schools were inferior; he further mentioned that the segregation "itself results in Negro children, as a class, receiving educational opportunities substantially inferior to those available to white children." On appeal, in *Gebhart* v. *Belton* (1952), the Delaware Supreme Court upheld the decision of the lower court, upon the narrow ground that the Negro schools were of poorer quality than the white schools.

The Director-Counsel expected these initial set-backs and decided upon two procedures by which to bring these class-action cases to the Supreme Court of the United States: first, the suits in Kansas, Virginia and South Carolina were to be brought to the Court on Appeal; second, the litigants in the District of Columbia case were to file for writs of certiorari. The first of the five cases acted upon by the Court—*Briggs* v. *Elliott* (1952)—involved the suit from Clarendon County, South Carolina, in which the decision was vacated and remanded to the district court. (Justices Black and Douglas dissented in this per curiam decision on the ground that the case should be decided by the Court on its merits rather than remanding it to the lower court for an assessment of the equalization of educational facilities in progress.) On March 3, 1952, the district court repeated its judgment that the Negro schoolchildren of the county were entitled to equal facilities but still refused to declare South Carolina's compulsory segregation law unconstitutional. Again, Marshall appealed the case to the Supreme Court of the United

States, along with the Topeka suit, which was now coming before the Court for the first time. In explaining the justification for the Court's jurisdiction in the *Brown* case, Marshall, Carter, and Greenberg emphasized the adverse effects of segregation on schoolchildren during their most formative years. Their statement expounded upon the findings of the district court in Kansas that sympathized with the sociological argument against state-enforced segregation but nevertheless upheld the state law:

It is at the elementary or primary education level that children, along with their acquisition of facts and figures, integrate and formulate basic ideas and attitudes about the society in which they live. When these early attitudes are born and fashioned within a segregated educational framework, students of both the majority and minority groups are not only limited in a full and complete interchange of ideas and responses, but are confronted and influenced by value judgments, sanctioned by their society which establishes qualitative distinctions on the basis of race. *Education cannot be separated from the social environment in which the child lives. He cannot attend separate schools and learn the meaning of equality.* [Emphasis added]

The statement then centered on those problems peculiarly confronting the Negro children under a segregated school system:

Segregated education, particularly at the elementary level, where the emotional aspects of learning are inextricably tied up with the learning process itself, must and does have a definite and deleterious effect upon the Negro child. It is particularly true that when segregation exists at the elementary level it is hard to distinguish between fact and fiction—the fiction in this instance, being an arbitrary classification on the basis of race.

In conclusion, the lawyers for the appellants argued that the Negro children were being denied the "equal protection of the laws" and the equality in treatment required by the Fourteenth Amendment:

Since elementary education is absorbed during the formative years of a child's life, it assumes a peculiar and more important role than education at any other level. . . . Negro children cannot be afforded the opportunity to develop fully their intelligence and their mental capabilities if their training is circumscribed and their development stunted by state practices which, at the very outset of their search for education, places them at a disadvantage with children belonging to other racial groups.

On June 9, 1952, the lawyers for the appellants and repondents in the South Carolina and Kansas cases were officially notified by telegram that the Supreme Court of the United States would hear their causes. Oral argument was originally set for the week of October 13, 1952; however, the Court later postponed argument until December 9 to allow the lawyers in the three remaining cases to file their briefs. The four state suits were consolidated under the title *Brown* v. *Board of Education.* That from the District of Columbia, *Bolling* v. *Sharpe,* (1954), was handled separately because it involved federal jurisdiction.

Extralegal strategy on the part of the NAACP Legal Defense Fund seemed to jell during 1952. The acting Solicitor General Robert L. Stern, convinced Attorney General James P. McGranery that the Truman administration should file an amicus brief in the segregation cases. Having even the moderate support of the federal government was of vital importance to Marshall and his colleagues if the Legal Defense Fund was to be successful before the Court. In addition, a total of nineteen amicus briefs were filed on the side of the Negro school children by concerned organizations such as the American Civil Liberties Union, the American Council of Human Rights, and the Congress of Industrial Organizations. The NAACP legal staff took precautions to see that overlapping of argumentation on the part of the amici was kept to a minimum. Finally, although the charter of the Legal Defense and Educational Fund prohibited "propaganda," beginning in the late 1940s the Director-Counsel repeatedly informed local chapters of the organization that they were "to conduct research, collect, collate, acquire, compile and publish facts, information, and statistics concerning education facilities and educational opportunities and the inequality in the educational facilities and educational opportunities provided for Negroes out of public funds." While local chapters were forbidden to engage in propaganda, therefore, they were encouraged to disseminate information for the purpose of enlightening the public on the "facts." Nevertheless, there was no guarantee that even if NAACP strategy was fully implemented, the Justices on the Supreme Court of the United States would be willing to overturn the *Plessy* doctrine.

The Vinson Court, before which the segregation cases would first be argued, was not an unknown quantity to Marshall and his staff. It was essentially the same court that the NAACP Legal Defense Fund had bombarded with social theories denouncing forced segregation since 1948. (Justice Minton, who was elevated to his position in 1949, was the only member of the Court in 1952 who had not taken part in the *Sipuel, Fisher,* and *Shelley* decisions.) It was hoped that the justices on the Court would now accept this argument for repudiating the "separate but equal" doctrine. The probability of the Vinson Court's doing so was given a less than even chance: certainly Justices Black, Douglas, and Burton would support the Negro appellants at this time; it is equally certain that Justices Minton, Reed, and Chief Justice Vinson, who had gone as far as he was willing to go in the *Sweatt* decision, would not; the three swing votes rested in the hands of Justices Clark, Jackson, and Frankfurter, none of whom was noted for extremely libertarian decision-making. Unless events dictated otherwise, it seemed likely that if the Supreme Court of the United States was to overrule the *Plessy* doctrine, it would be in the form of a close controversial vote.

Oral argument for the litigants in the five cases began on Tuesday, December 9. The NAACP briefs, filed three months earlier, outlined the points of attack made by Marshall, Carter, Nabrit, and the others. The argumentation therein was essentially the same as that presented by the Legal Defense Fund in the higher education cases. In *Briggs* v. *Elliott,* Marshall was primarily responsible for both the oral argument and the brief on behalf of the Negro appellants from South Carolina. Relying on what were by now familiar sources by social scientists, and on legal precedent from forty-six cases, Marshall presented social and legal justification for the Supreme Court to repudiate the "separate but equal" doctrine. The Director-Counsel argued that legally enforced racial segregation in the public schools of South Carolina denied the Negro children of the state that equality of educational opportunity and benefit required by the "equal protection of the laws" clause of the Fourteenth Amendment. Moreover, he continued, the compulsory-segregation laws of the state inflict on its public schools that racism which the Supreme Court of the United States has repeatedly declared unconstitutional in other areas of governmental action. Citing *Nixon* v. *Herndon,* (1927), and *Skinner* v. *Oklahoma,* (1942), Marshall attacked South Carolina for requiring racial classification without a controlling justification:

> A state legislative classification violates the equal protection clause of the Fourteenth Amendment either if it is based upon nonexis-

tent differences or if the differences are not reasonably related to a proper legislative objective. Classifications based on race or color can never satisfy either requirement and consequently are the epitome of arbitrariness in legislation.

Seizing the opportunity now presented to him, the counsel for the appellants pointed to the inevitable results of such state-enforced segregation—results supported by such leading social scientists as Myrdal, Johnson, and Dollard:

Segregation of Negroes as practiced here is universally understood as imposing on them a badge of inferiority. It brands the Negro with the mark of inferiority and asserts that he is not fit to associate with white people.

In addition, he maintained, authoritative evidence shows that there are no inborn differences between Negroes and whites in intellectual capacity or in the ability to learn.

Finally, the Director-Counsel concluded his argument by stating that the Court's earlier decisions in *Plessy* v. *Ferguson,* (1896), and in *Gong Lum* v. *Rice,* (1927), upholding "separate but equal" facilities in elementary education, are no longer valid under the equal-protection clause of the Fourteenth Amendment and, therefore, should not be applicable in this case. Marshall further contended that the Court had already recognized this fact in the higher-education decisions:

The Court rejected its earlier decisions . . . that "the state had power to make racial distinctions in its public schools without violating the equal protection clause" in *McLaurin* and *Sweatt* "in relation to racial distinctions in state graduate and professional education"—*we ask that you now apply this to public education.* [Emphasis added]

Additional authoritative support for the Court's overturning of the *Plessy* doctrine was presented by the NAACP lawyers in the form of an appendix to the appellants' briefs in the *Brown, Briggs,* and *Davis* cases. Entitled "The Effects of Segregation and the Consequences of Desegregation: A Social Science Statement," it was claimed by Marshall, Carter, and Robinson to have been "drafted and signed by some of the foremost authorities in sociology, anthropology, psychology and psychiatry who have worked in the area of American race relations." A total of thirty-two social scientists—including Otto Klineberg, Noel P. Gist,

Robert K. Merton, Theodore M. Newcomb, Robert Redfield, Arnold M. Rose, Samuel A. Stouffer, and Robin M. Williams—attested to the psychological and social damage done to both whites and Negroes—but especially to the latter group—by forced segregation. They uniformly assured the Court that desegregation, for the benefit of all concerned, could be accomplished without violence.

The allotted time for both sides came to an end on December 11, 1952, having produced a total of ten hours of oral argument in three days. Marshall had met a worthy opponent in John W. Davis, the former Solicitor General and the presidential candidate for the Democratic party in 1924, who argued the cause for South Carolina. At least one justice felt that Davis was probably the most learned advocate to appear before the Court. Davis had disputed the argument that segregation inflicted psychological damage on Negro schoolchildren; even the "doll" experiment had proven that the children consistently picked the white dolls, whether they attended segregated schools or not. The lawyer for South Carolina had argued that the only question of sufficient magnitude for adjudication was whether the framers of the Fourteenth Amendment had actually intended to eliminate segregated schools. If this were the case, he concluded, then Congress could never have allowed the existence of such schools in the District of Columbia.

In June 1953 the Supreme Court of the United States, in a memorandum decision held that it was necessary to clarify certain points before a decision could be reached; it assigned the cases for reargument on Monday, October 12, 1953. In addition, the Court requested the advocates on both sides to provide answers to a number of significant questions: What evidence was there that the authors of the Fourteenth Amendment, as well as the state legislatures that ratified it, understood the Amendment to mean the end of segregated public schools? If no such assumption had been made, was there any evidence that the supporters of the Amendment perceived that Congress might imply such a prohibition or that the federal courts might legitimately construe the Amendment to mean the elimination of such segregation? If the original intent remained unclear in both questions, was it within the Court's power to efface segregated public schools nevertheless? Finally, if the Court did decide to do so, how should the order be implemented?

Although disappointed by the Court's delay in deciding the case, the NAACP lawyers were optimistic about the direction indicated by the questions. It became apparent to them that the Supreme Court of the

United States was more than willing to overrule the "separate but equal" doctrine if only an acceptable rationale could be found. However, as Marshall pointed out, what first appeared to be a "golden gate" might well "turn out to be a booby trap with a bomb in it." Marshall and his colleagues were certainly not historians, and close examination of relevant documents, such as the debates recorded in the *Congressional Globe* for 1866, might produce evidence supporting the Southern position.

Several weeks after the Court's memorandum decision, the Director-Counsel called for a national conference of some 125 leading social scientists including historians, political scientists, constitutional lawyers, and educators, to assist in meeting the problems inherent in the historical development of the Fourteenth Amendment. Alfred H. Kelly, the noted constitutional historian, relates that Marshall wrote him in early July inquiring whether he would be willing to prepare a research paper "on the intent of the framers of the 14th amendment with respect to the constitutionality of racially segregated schools" to be presented for discussion at the conference. Kelly accepted the invitation.

The conference was held at the Overseas Press Club on West Forty-third Street in New York, with headquarters at the Algonquin Hotel, from September 25 to 27, 1953. It was attended by some fifty academicians and about thirty-five legalists, who, for the most part, were NAACP lawyers involved in the School Segregation Cases. The more prominent academicians and lawyers in attendance included Robert K. Carr, John Frank, Horace Bond, Walter Gellhorn, Milton Konvitz, Howard K. Beale, John Hope Franklin, and C. Vann Woodward. Having engaged in weeks of extensive research, Kelly told a group of Negro lawyers at one of the conference seminars that the outlook was not comforting. The Civil Rights Act of 1866 had apparently been specifically amended by the Radical Republicans to protect segregated public education, and the first section of the Fourteenth Amendment had been passed simply to constitutionalize the Civil Rights Act; therefore the Legal Defense Fund would have difficulty arguing that the intent of Congress in submitting the Amendment for ratification by the states had been to abolish state-enforced segregated schools. Kelly found that the lawyers appreciated his views and, in his words, "they obviously wanted me to clarify as far as possible the difficulties they would confront were John W. Davis and his staff as well prepared as they might be expected to be." Thereafter, discussion focused on a central point of strategy: should the Fund's lawyers employ a "generalized" or a "particularistic" approach in their historical argument? Lawyer Robert Ming argued vigorously that since the historical evidence that could be utilized favorably by the Negro lawyers was either too "scanty" or too "unconvincing," they ought to abandon any attempt at the particularistic approach of the framers' intent. Instead, Ming advocated that the NAACP bypass the Court's request and emphasize "the overall spirit of humanitarianism, racial equalitarianism, and social idealism which had dominated the rise of the abolitionist movement and which by implication thereby had determined the objectives of the Radical Republicans who had written the 14th Amendment.

As powerful as this argument might have been, Kelly was opposed to it; he argued against it on three critical points: It would not present a solid defense against the attack of the respondents, who might well prove that the framers' intent supported their position. It was still possible that the NAACP could build a sufficient historical case "in immediate terms." And the lawyers would nevertheless be forced to do so or take the immediate chance of incurring the direct censure of the Court and possible loss of the case. By this time, Kelly noted, most of the lawyers present "appeared to be plunged into a state of vast uncertainty" with respect to the historical approach they faced in particular and the basic strategy they should adopt in general. In this state of confusion the conference came to an end.

The question of the tactical position to take with respect to the historical requirements of the Court's request was a source of anguish for Marshall and his colleagues, and time was of the essence. Seventeen days before the opening of the conference an event occurred that gave new impetus to the NAACP's cause: Chief Justice Vinson—whom Daniel M. Berman considered the leading opponent on the Court of nullifying school segregation—died of natural causes. On September 30 President Dwight D. Eisenhower, who had succeeded President Truman eight months earlier, made a recess appointment of a new Chief Justice, Governor Earl Warren of California. Not only did Vinson's death change the composition of the Court; it also deprived the justices who were predisposed to favor the respondent states of their leader. Reargument of the cases, originally set for October 12, was rescheduled for December 7, 1953, thus giving the NAACP lawyers the additional time they so desperately needed.

About ten days after the conference the Director-Counsel requested that Kelly again fly to New York to assist directly in drawing up the brief; the scholar accepted the invitation. Arriving at the National Office of the NAACP on West Fortieth Street on October 15, Kelly conferred for the next five days with the best minds of the legal staff, including Marshall, Carter, Constance Motley, Jack Greenberg, Louis Redding, Spottswood Robinson, and Robert Ming. Also present at a number of the conferences during this period were John Hope Franklin, the historian; John A. Davis, the political scientist; and Kenneth Clark, the psychologist who had conducted the "doll" experiment. The NAACP lawyers placed Kelly in the role of the Devil's advocate and, according to him,

> they picked my brains on American constitutional history beginning with Lord Mansfield's case and going to *Gong Lum* and *Gaines.* It soon became clear that they did not expect soft answers. They wanted hard questions and hard answers of the kind they might encounter from the justices and opposing counsel when the cases were argued before the Court in December.

On Thursday morning, the day after his arrival, Kelly was called into Marshall's office, where the Director-Counsel asked him to assist Ming in hammering out a draft of the brief to be used before the Court. For the next three days the lawyer and the academician paced up and down, argued, dictated to a stenographer, and finally came up with what they considered an acceptable draft. Shortly thereafter Kelly returned to Detroit, only to be once again asked by Marshall to give further assistance by revising the draft. The constitutional expert arrived at NAACP headquarters on November 2 and remained for the next three days. Marshall explained that the brief was too generalized and did not go far enough. He asked Kelly, along with John Frank of the Yale Law School, to reconstruct the draft in such a way as to get past Justices Douglas and Frankfurter. Speaking of the brief in its present form, Marshall said: "I gotta argue these cases and if I try this approach, those fellows will shoot me down in flames." The Director-Counsel also informed Frank and Kelly that as he evaluated the new Warren Court, the NAACP did not have to win the historical argument by overpowering strides; "old nothin' to nothin' score," as he put it, "means we win the ball game."

The methods used by the NAACP Legal Defense Fund in general and by its Director-Counsel in particular in the preparation of its historical argument for the Court, as related by Dr. Kelly, were later subjected to severe criticism from some quarters of the press and of the Congress. His critics have implied that Marshall in this instance was willing to use any means, valid or invalid, to secure from the Court a decision overturning segregated public schools. In defense of Marshall's tactics in the School Segregation Cases, Kelly recently repudiated the charge that he had been willing to use "any means to a just end":

> This statement misconstrues the entire problem. Basically, it fails to take account of the American system of advocacy, which requires counsel handling a case to do everything legitimate and ethical within the tenets of the legal profession to win a case at hand. This is exactly what Marshall did. Marshall's behavior in this respect was not one whit different from theirs. The point I made in my 1961 paper was simply that briefs are not history—they have an *ex parte* quality. That is the nature of the American advocacy system, which uses techniques radically different than those of history or the social sciences. *The real question is whether or not Marshall behaved ethically within the traditions, tenets, and ethical standards of the legal profession. The answer to that is an emphatic yes, as anyone who takes the trouble to read briefs, counterbriefs and the like in "Brown," and who understands the advocacy system will understand.*

The brief was filed with the Supreme Court of the United States on December 5, 1953. In it, the lawyers for the appellants put forth the Kelly-Frank-Graham argument that the states in this case have taken a mistaken approach to the history of the adoption of the Fourteenth Amendment; that the Amendment was not proposed simply to constitutionalize the Civil Rights Act of 1866.

> The significance of the legislative history of the Fourteenth Amendment is that there can be no doubt that the framers were seeking to secure and to protect the Negro as a full and equal citizen subject only to the same legal disabilities and penalties as the white man. The Court decisions in aid of this fundamental purpose, we submit, compel the conclusion that school segregation, pursuant to state law, is at war with the Amendment's intent.

Citing a monograph released by the Selective Service System, Marshall and his colleagues argued that "it is too late to say this is a question of local rather than national interest," since the federal government has stated that "In every phase of living the United States must demonstrate that the American way of life exemplifies true democracy by eliminating majority-minority division and distinctions, thus having the same citizenship privileges and obligations for all." The lawyers continued by making various points. First, the Supreme Court of the United States, in the light of recent decisions, has rejected the theory that the states have a de jure right to segregate persons because of race or color. Second, state laws requiring the segregation of children in the public schools are a form of governmental classification of citizens without a controlling justification and, as such, are patently unconstitutional. Third, the appellees are in error when they claim that the Fourteenth Amendment provides no constitutional remedy with respect to segregated schools, since such discrimination enforced by state law denies to Negro school children "the equal protection of the laws." In conclusion, the advocates for the appellants pointedly remarked that "the Southern way of life" or any other local customs, mores or prejudices cannot prevail against the Constitution of the United States:

> This entire contention is tantamount to saying that the vindication and enjoyment of Constitutional rights recognized by this Court as present and personal can be postponed whenever such postponement is claimed to be socially desirable.

As anticipated by the strategists at the New York Conferences, John W. Davis in oral argument before the Court stressed the fact that "the Congress which submitted, and the state legislatures which ratified, the Fourteenth Amendment did not contemplate and did not understand that it would abolish segregation in public schools." Therefore, Davis continued, the Negro's case was simply an exercise in sociological debate, with no substantive evidence to prove that Negro children would be happier or become better students in integrated schools. The appellees were convinced, he concluded, that the *Plessy* doctrine had been "so often announced, so confidently relied upon, [and] so long continued" that its validity was no longer a justiciable matter for the Court.

The United States government also participated in oral argument as an amicus curiae, at the invitation of the Court. Before the government took its stand, there had been considerable debate among officials of the Department of Justice as to the position to be taken by the Eisenhower administration. Assistant Attorney General J. Lee Rankin and others in the Department had advocated a strong stand against the segregation statutes; however, the Attorney General, Herbert R. Brownell, believing that President Eisenhower would not approve a direct attack on the constitutionality of segregated schools, had opted for a more moderate approach. After a long and detailed discussion of the historical development of the Fourteenth Amendment, the government lawyers gave their view that the evidence was inconclusive with respect to the framers' intent; of all the possible conclusions that might be drawn from relevant materials, however, the one least supported by history is that the framers advocated "separate but equal" public schools. Consequently, the lawyers concluded there was no reason why the Supreme Court of the United States in the exercise of its equity powers could not strike down the "separate but equal" scheme. It should instead adopt a moderate implementation plan, the supplemental brief suggested:

> it is within the judicial power to direct such relief as will be effective and just in eliminating existing segregated school systems; and . . . if the court holds that laws providing for separate public schools for white and colored children are unconstitutional, it should remand the instant cases to the lower courts with directions to carry out the Court's decisions as expeditiously as the particular circumstances permit.

At one point during oral argument, Associate Justice William O. Douglas asked Assistant Attorney General Rankin for a clarification of the government's stand on the merits of the constitutional controversy. Rankin replied: "It is the position of the Department of Justice that segregation in public schools cannot be maintained under the Fourteenth Amendment." The Associate Justice was apparently satisfied.

On Monday, May 17, 1954, some five months after the reargument of the cases, the Supreme Court of the United States announced its decision in the four state cases. In a unanimous opinion delivered by Chief Justice Earl Warren, the Court disposed of the historical argument on the ground that the evidence presented was inconclusive with respect to the framers' intent toward segregated schools:

> Reargument was largely devoted to the circumstances surrounding the adoption of the Fourteenth Amendment in 1868. . . . This discussion and our own investigation convinced us that, although these sources cast some light, it is not enough to resolve the problem with which we are faced. At best, they are inconclusive. The most avid proponents of the post-war Amendments undoubtedly intended them to remove all legal distinctions. . . . Their oppo-

nents, just as certainly, were antagonistic to both the letter and the spirit of the Amendments. . . . What others in Congress and the state legislatures had in mind cannot be determined with any degree of certainty.

One significant reason for the inconclusiveness of the historical data, as the Chief Justice noted, was that the South did not have advanced public educational systems during the Reconstruction Era. As a result, the framers of the Fourteenth Amendment were not deeply concerned with the topic. "Today," Warren continued, "education is perhaps the most important function of state and local governments," and as such, "it is a right which must be made available to all on equal terms." Relying solely on the sociological argument presented by Marshall and his staff in 1952, the Chief Justice contended that segregated public schools, regardless of tangible factors, deprive the Negro children of equal educational opportunities:

To separate them from others of similar age and qualifications solely because of their race generates a feeling of inferiority as to their status in the community that may affect their hearts and minds in a way unlikely ever to be undone. . . . Whatever may have been the extent of psychological knowledge at the time of Plessy v. Ferguson, this finding is amply supported by modern authority. Any language in Plessy . . . contrary to this finding is rejected.

In delivering the Court's conclusion, Chief Justice Warren did not overturn the *Plessy* doctrine as being unconstitutional; rather, he contended that its application to public education was invalid:

We conclude that in the field of public education the doctrine of "separate but equal" has no place. Separate educational facilities are inherently unequal. Therefore, we hold that the plaintiffs and others similarly situated . . . are, by reason of the segregation complained of, deprived of the equal protection of the laws guaranteed by the Fourteenth Amendment.

Because the cases were class actions, because of the extensive applicability of the decision, and because of the great variance of local conditions, the Court requested that further arguments be given by all parties on the nature of the implementation of the decrees; accordingly, it restored the cases to its docket for reargument that term. The

Court also requested the Attorney General of the United States to participate once again.

Following immediately on the heels of the *Brown* decision, the Chief Justice announced another unanimous decision in *Bolling* v. *Sharpe*—the District of Columbia case. Warren recognized that the Fifth Amendment contains no "equal protection" clause. "But as this Court has recognized, discrimination may be so unjustifiable as to be violative of due process." He therefore concluded:

> Liberty under law extends to the full range of conduct which the individual is free to pursue, and it cannot be restricted except for a proper governmental objective. Segregation in public education is not reasonably related to any proper governmental objective, and thus imposes on Negro children of the District of Columbia a burden that constitutes an arbitrary deprivation of their liberty in violation of the Due Process Clause.

In less than an hour after the decisions were read, the Voice of America announced the news by shortwave to the countries of Eastern Europe. The United States Information Agency also transmitted news of the decisions—as a "victory for democratic principles and practices"—to the peoples of the Far East in China, Korea, Japan and Vietnam. The effect of the school segregation decisions was felt to be beneficial to United States foreign policy as a propaganda tool in combating the notion that "the Negro is universally abused as an inferior creature in America"; the immediate reaction of the American people themselves, however, reflected anything but unanimous support.

Although no acts of direct violence were evidenced in the South following the Court's decision, a vast multitude of Southern newspapers and journals lashed out against it. In addition, sixty-nine congressmen from Southern and border states produced a statement attacking the *Brown* decision, which read in part:

> The decision of the Supreme Court . . . [is] clear abuse of judicial power. . . . The original Constitution does not mention education. Neither does the Fourteenth Amendment or any other Amendment.

A considerable number of Southern officials no doubt agreed with the views expressed by E. B. McCord, the Superintendent of Education for Clarendon County, South Carolina. McCord was one of the defendants in *Briggs* v. *Elliott*, (1951); (1952); (1953); (1954). He stated publicly that there would be no mixed schools in his county as long as the present leadership could prevent them; writing in the Charleston *News and Courier* of August 4, 1954, he denounced integration as contrary to the Scriptures and to good sense.

On the other hand, the Court was supported in its decision by an overwhelming majority of lawyers, public officials, and academicians in the states outside the South. Louis H. Pollak, former Dean of the Yale Law School, believed that "except for waging and winning the Civil War and World Wars I and II, the decision in the School Segregation Cases was probably the most important American governmental act of any kind since the Emancipation Proclamation." "Because of my participation," Marshall noted recently, "I perhaps could overestimate *Brown*'s importance; I doubt it though."

A more telling criticism with respect to the opinion of the Court in *Brown* has been one launched by a number of scholars who protested against the Court's reliance on sociological data rather than on the historical or legal argument. A central point of concern was footnote eleven in the opinion, wherein the Court cited the works of seven leading psychologists and other social scientists (most of them introduced by Marshall and his colleagues) to show the detrimental effects of segregation on Negro school children. Charles E. Silberman, author and lecturer in Economics at Columbia University, has written of the Court's opinion:

> whether segregation is harmful or not is quite beside the point: the Constitution guarantees every citizen equal treatment under the law, whether equality is good for him or bad. In this sense, the Court's citation in footnote eleven . . . was an unfortunate irrelevance that directed attention away from the main thrust of its opinion—an opinion that had been clearly anticipated several years before.

Historian Alfred Kelly agrees that the historical argument was more constitutionally salient than that of the psychologists and sociologists. In a personal letter to the author on June 18, 1968, he noted: "I would have preferred to see the Court use a historical argument . . . and to have overruled Plessy on that ground. I think it might have done so."

Nevertheless, the *Brown* decision stands as the greatest legal victory for the NAACP Legal Defense and Educational Fund during Marshall's tenure as Director-Counsel. Since 1948 the NAACP, as an organized interest group, had applied increasing pressure on the Court to effectuate a dramatic change in judicial policy for the benefit of American Negroes. Its legal arm had financed and argued case after case before the Court in order to achieve this objective. In doing so, it had relied chiefly on sociological argumentation and had provided the members of the Court with an "escape clause" if and when the historical evidence proved to be an insufficient tool in overturning the "separate but equal" concept. This is exactly what happened in the *Brown* case. The historical data, while proving to be inconclusive on the framers' intent, was valuable because it meant that the Court was free to prohibit segregated public schools based on other considerations. In essence the Court made a political decision and, aware of the social and legal consequences involved, deliberately restructured constitutional law to that end.

On November 15, 1954, the NAACP lawyers filed their brief on further reargument of the means of implementation—Brief for Appellants in Nos. 1, 2 and 3, and for Respondents in No. 5 on Further Reargument, 349 U.S. 294.

It was the position of Marshall and his fellow lawyers that "only a decree requiring desegregation as quickly as possible as prerequisite administrative and mechanical procedure can be completed will discharge judicial responsibility for the vindication of the constitutional rights of which appellants are being deprived." In assessing developments since the Court's decision of May 17, the lawyers for the plaintiffs pointed out that the Topeka School Board did adopt a resolution terminating segregated public schools "as rapidly as is practicable." However, they continued, statistics show that only 123 out of 700 Negro school children in Topeka now attend integrated schools, while the other 85 percent "are still being denied the constitutional rights for which appellants sought redress in their original action." (The NAACP was here attending a de facto rather than a de jure situation, since the resolution was pursuant to the *Brown* decision.) The lawyers demanded the immediate admission of the complaining children, and the admission of others similarly situated by the beginning of the next academic term in September, 1955.

Citing a study by Kenneth B. Clark, the lawyers lashed out at the assumption that "gradual as opposed to immediate desegregation is the better, smoother or more effective mode of transition":

On the contrary . . . gradualism, far from facilitating the process, may actually make it more difficult; that in fact, the problems of transition will be a good deal less complicated than might be fore-cast by appellees. Our submission is that this, like many wrongs, can be easiest and best undone, not by "tapering off" but by forth-right action. . . .

Moreover, "piecemeal" schemes have been shown to increase resistance of people, to change. . . . "They feel arbitrarily se-lected as experimental animals." Other members of the commu-nity observe this and their anxieties are sharpened.

Several months later the Legal Defense Fund lawyers in their reply brief pointed out that the arguments now used by the respondent states for gradualism, were essentially the same arguments advanced by the opposition in support of the "separate but equal" concept. Considering the similarity of the appellees' briefs of 1952 and 1954, Marshall and his associates concluded:

The impossibility of procuring community acceptance of desegre-gation, urged earlier as a ground for decision on the merits, now turns up as an argument for indefinite postponement with no con-vincing reasons given for supposing that community attitudes will change within the segregated pattern.

In both the brief and in oral argument before the Court, Attorney General of the United States Herbert Brownell, Jr., argued for an ef-fective gradual adjustment to desegregated public school systems and urged that the Court remand the cases to the lower courts with instruc-tions to enforce the Court's decision "as rapidly as the particular cir-cumstances permit." Concerning deliberate attempts to delay on the part of the states, Brownell contended:

In the absence of compelling reasons to the contrary . . . there should be no unnecessary delay in the full vindication of the con-stitutional rights involved in these cases, and if any delay is re-quired, it should be kept to a minimum.

In arguing for delay at best, or gradual implementation at worst, the respondent states were assisted by the filing of amici curiae briefs on the part of the attorneys general of Arkansas, Florida, Maryland, North Carolina, Oklahoma, and Texas.

On May 31, 1955, Chief Justice Warren, again speaking for a unani-mous Court in Brown v. Board of Education of Topeka, remanded the cases to the lower courts with directions to take steps necessary and proper "to admit to public schools on a racially nondiscriminatory basis with all deliberate speed the parties to these cases." Warren took notice of the fact that a good number of states, including some not immediately involved in the cases, had already taken "substantial steps" to comply with the Court's earlier decision. The Chief Justice ruled that in formulating decrees, the district courts could consider such administrative problems as the physical condition of particular schools, the related transportation systems, revision of school districts, and other factors; however, "the burden rests upon the defendants to establish that such time is necessary to the public interest and is consistent with good faith compliance at the earliest practicable date."

In exercising its equity powers, the Court embraced the deliberate-speed rule on the basis that it could secure the rights of the Negro litigants but, at the same time, allow the federal district courts to facilitate a reasonable, yet prompt, start toward compliance. It also presumed that the federal courts would act firmly and with good faith. Accordingly, the Court's mandate did not become effective until June 25. Immediately following the decision, the NAACP instructed its branches to file petitions with school boards during the summer and to file desegregation suits in the courts if no action had been taken by the fall. Even though the Court's solution was at variance with that offered by the counsel for the appellants at the time, Marshall was optimistic over the outcome:

> The decision was a good one. The Court has reaffirmed its pronouncement that segregation is unconstitutional and throughout the opinion stress is placed upon the necessity for full compliance at the earliest practicable date. Delays may be occasioned by various devices. This would result in any case. We can be sure that desegregation will take place throughout the United States—tomorrow in some places, the day after in others and many, many moons hence in some, but it will come eventually to all. We look upon the . . . decision as a ticket which is now available to every parent and child who needs it and wants to use it.

The Director-Counsel and his assistant, Robert L. Carter, felt that the net result of the Court's mandate might be the unification of the country behind "a nationwide desegregation program" and that, if this should indeed come to pass, "the Court must be credited with having performed its job brilliantly." But human nature and Southern resistance to the concept of integration proved this view to be overly optimistic. Eleven years after the Court's solution, Loren Miller was forced to conclude:

> The harsh truth is that the first Brown decision was a great decision; the second . . . was a mistake. . . . In the 1955 case, the Court held that a *personal* and *present* constitutional right could be deferred and extended gradually to those who were entitled to exercise it by virtue of a constitutional amendment. There was no constitutional warrant for such a ruling.

The Court's decree seemed to encourage the Southern states to devise an almost endless series of plans designed to thwart desegregation. In the decade following the School Segregation Cases, the most difficult job for the Legal Defense Fund was to make the abstract doctrine of desegregated public schools a reality.

Nevertheless, the monumental decision of the Supreme Court of the United States to strike down the long-standing principle that government, whether state or national, could legitimately classify children according to race or color in the admission to elementary and secondary public schools, seemed to reaffirm Marshall's belief in the force of law. In his address "Law and the Quest for Equality" he noted:

> The Negro who was once enslaved by law became emancipated by it, and is achieving equality through it. To be sure law is often a response to social change; but as I think *Brown* v. *Board of Education* demonstrates, it can also change social patterns. Provided it is adequately enforced, law can change things for the better, moreover, it can change the hearts of men, for law has an educational function also.

Racial Injustice in Korea

During the period in which the NAACP was launching its legal attack against segregated public schools, it was also deeply concerned with the treatment of Negro servicemen in Korea.

Since the Civil War, military staffs in the American Armed Services have always felt themselves confronted by two questions with respect to Negro personnel: Do they have the mental and educational qualifications to be used in the full range of military vocations? Shall they be utilized only in exclusively Negro units? Consistently the answer to the first question has been negative and the answer to the second affirmative. The United States Army was particularly rigid in this assessment.

The Army had maintained Negro units since the creation of two cavalry and two infantry regiments in 1866. During World War I the Army placed Negroes in supply and support units and in two combat units, and despite the fact that the War College made an interbellum recommendation that Negro units of division size be discontinued, the Army reactivated two black divisions during World War II. As late as the fall of 1945 the Army's Gillem Board, composed of general officers, concluded that the maintainance of segregated units was a necessity and suggested the retention of a quota system directly proportional to the civilian population.

On July 26, 1948, President Truman issued Executive Order 9981, calling for the integration of the armed forces and established an advisory committee to assist in its implementation. The President's Committee on Equality of Treatment and Opportunity in the Armed Services investigated those formal service regulations charged with being discriminatory and made recommendations for policy changes in the Army, Navy, and Air Force. As a result, the Air Force instituted new policies to effectuate an integrated service in July 1948; the Army ultimately adopted the recommendations of the President's Committee between September 1949 and March 1950.

Frequent reports of Negroes' indolence and pusillanimity, requiring a disproportionate number of courts-martial, persisted both in World War I and in World War II. In the latter conflict the NAACP was involved in literally hundreds of cases involving official discrimination in the trials of Negro servicemen. One such case involved the convictions of fifty Negro sailors at Port Chicago, California, by a court-martial board of the Twelfth Naval District for alleged refusal to load ammunition. The men received prison sentences ranging from five to fifteen years. On appeal the Navy allowed the Legal Defense Fund to file briefs and to appear on behalf of the defendants when the case was reviewed in Washington. The NAACP lawyers were able to have all the sentences substantially reduced.

With the outbreak of the Korean War, the NAACP was again flooded with requests for assistance on the part of Negro soldiers who were allegedly being victimized by racially abusive courts-martial. In one sensational case thirty-nine Negro soldiers were convicted and sentenced for violation of the seventy-fifth Article of War—"misbehavior in the presence of the enemy," or cowardice. One of the soldiers, Lieutenant Leon A. Gilbert, was sentenced to death by a court-martial board just 200 yards behind the battle lines on September 6, 1950. All thirty-nine had pleaded not guilty and asked the NAACP to intervene. After examining the trial records, the Director-Counsel of the Legal Defense and Educational Fund believed something to be seriously wrong. The convicted personnel were members of the Twenty-Fourth Infantry Regiment, which had won the first significant United Nations victory in retaking Yechon on July 28, after a sixteen-hour battle. The Third Battalion of this all-Negro regiment had fought its way up and down Bloody Peak Mountain, suffering extremely heavy losses until the men had taken and held it. "It seemed hard to believe," wrote Marshall, "that these men could change over from heroes to cowards, all within a few days, even under the violent pressures of warfare."

The Director-Counsel needed the facts of each individual case, if any appeals were to be submitted; accordingly, Walter White, the Executive Secretary of the NAACP, cabled General Douglas MacArthur for permission to allow Marshall to travel to Tokyo, where the prisoners were being held. In a reply cable, the General refused. Marshall recalls, in the same article, that it claimed:

> Not the slightest evidence exists here of discrimination as alleged. As I think you know in this Command there is no [sic] slightest bias of its various members because of race, color or other distinguishing characteristics. Every soldier in this Command is measured on a completely uniform basis with the sole criteria his efficiency and his character.

After further pressure was applied, General MacArthur finally yielded and withdrew his objection to Marshall's visit. Marshall left New York for the Pacific on January 11, and he spent five weeks in both Japan and Korea with the full cooperation of the Far East Command. After interviewing hundreds of enlisted men and officers, including those at the Twenty-fifth Division Headquarters in Korea, as well as those at Eighth Army Headquarters, Marshall came to a number of disturbing conclusions concerning the treatment of Negro soldiers.

The Negro lawyer discovered that between the time of Lieutenant Gilbert's conviction and the time of his visit to Korea in late February, there had been a total of eighty-two cases which resulted in general court-martial trials; in these cases, fifty-four of the defendants were Negroes, twenty-seven were white, and one was Japanese. The charges filed against the Negro defendants were for violation of the Seventy-fifth Article of War. Further investigation disclosed the following summary of the actual results of the trials for alleged violation of the Seventy-fifth Article during this six-month period:

	Negro	White
Charges withdrawn	23	2
Charges reduced to AWOL	1	0
Aquittals	4	4
Sentenced	32	2
Charges Filed:	60	8

The sentences eventually given to the defendants by the general courts-martial:

	Negro	White
Death	1	0
Natural Life	15	0
50 Years	1	0
25 Years	2	0
20 Years	3	0
15 Years	1	0
10 Years	7	0
5 Years	2	1
3 Years	0	1
	32	2

Upon comparing the investigation reports at the Judge Advocate's office with the statements of the men charged with this crime, Marshall concluded that not only did the investigating officers completely ignore the explanations given by the accused, but also that "scant effort was made to find out what was true and what was not." In many instances he found that some of the accused were completely innocent but had made no attempt to defend themselves because they were convinced they had no chance of obtaining an acquittal. In others, the court-appointed counsel made little or no attempt to verify the statements of the accused. In nearly every case Marshall discovered that the morale of the men had been at a "disastrously low ebb" because casualties had been high and their "white officers were in many instances Southerners who had brought their prejudices with them" when assigned to duty with the Twenty-fourth Infantry.

Finally, the Director-Counsel found that four of the trials in which Negroes had been sentenced to life imprisonment were conducted in a time span ranging from forty-two to fifty minutes. "I have seen many miscarriages of justice," he noted later, "but even in Mississippi a Negro will get a trial longer than 42 minutes, if he is fortunate enough to be brought to trial."

In his report to the Army's Far East Command in the Dai Ichi Building, Tokyo, Marshall placed ultimate responsibility for these courts-martial upon General Douglas MacArthur himself. True, Marshall admitted, the Major General in command, not MacArthur, had the direct responsibility for the disposition of the individual cases; MacArthur, however, had both the authority and the responsibility for the maintenance of racial segregation in the Far East Command. He pointed out that at Command Headquarters not one Negro belonged to the elite honor guard, the football team, or even the band. When MacArthur's Chief-of-Staff, Major General Doyle O. Hickey, replied that the General had ordered a study of this problem, Marshall pointedly replied that it had taken the United States Air Force exactly one day to completely end segregation in that branch of the armed forces.

Throughout the period 1951–1952 the Legal Defense Fund represented thirty-nine convicted men of the Twenty-fourth Infantry before the Office of the Judge Advocate General in the Pentagon in Washington. The NAACP lawyers obtained substantial reductions of sentence for thirty of the Negro soldiers. In addition, President Truman commuted the death sentence of Lieutenant Leon Gilbert to life imprisonment. Subsequently the Legal Defense Fund prevailed upon the Judge Advocate General's Office to reduce the sentence to twenty years.

In another court-martial case involving the rights of accused Negroes, Marshall and his staff availed themselves of the legal process up to and including the Supreme Court of the United States. Robert W. Burns, Calvin Dennis, and Herman P. Dennis, Jr., all Negro servicemen in the United States Air Force in the Far East Command, were tried separately by a general court-martial convened on the Island of Guam for the rape-murder of Ruth Farnsworth, a white civilian. On May 9 and May 29, 1949, the defendants were sentenced to death. These judgments were upheld and found legally sufficient by the Judge Advocate General's Board of Review and the Judicial Council, and the sentences of death were ordered executed by the President. Petitions for new trials were made on behalf of the defendants by the Legal Defense Fund. The NAACP lawyers claimed that each of the accused had been held for weeks incommunicado and without due process by civilian authorities on Guam. Each had been subjected to continuous questioning and beatings and had been denied edible food before coming to trial. In no instance were the defendants allowed counsel during questioning, nor were they informed of their protection against compulsory self-incrimination as required under Sections 686 and 780 of the Penal Code of Guam and the Fifth Amendment. These efforts had resulted in Calvin Dennis' being a witness for the prosecution at the court-martial and giving testimony which he later repudiated as false, perjured, and suborned by the prosecution. In the case of Herman Dennis, the police took pubic hairs from his person which were subsequently used against him as evidence. Subsequently he made four confessions to the civilian authorities between January 11 and 14, 1949, which Marshall and his colleagues claimed were obtained through physical and mental duress, protracted interrogation, threats, promises, and the use of a lie detector. The petitions for new trials were denied on January 28, 1952.

Having exhausted all available remedies provided within the military establishment, the lawyers for the accused filed petitions for a writ of habeas corpus with the Federal District Court in Washington, D.C. On April 10, 1952, the court dismissed the petitions on the grounds that the litigants had raised no questions reviewable by civil courts. On appeal the United States Court of Appeals for the District of Columbia, with one judge dissenting, affirmed the decision of the lower court and held that only "exceptional cases" from the military courts would be considered by the federal courts. Subsequently, the Supreme Court of the United States granted the petitioners certiorari.

Marshall was largely responsible for the brief, while Robert L. Carter argued the case before the Court. In Brief for Petitioners, filed January 29, 1953, the Director-Counsel and his associates argued that the Court of Appeals had erred in not remanding the case to the lower federal court for a hearing because "on habeas corpus a district court must make its own independent determination and evaluation of the evidence relating to the claimed invalidity of the judgment of the military tribunal." The lawyers cited recent decisions by the Court in which, at least by inference, it had held that on a writ of habeas corpus a civil court may inquire into whether guarantees of due process have been observed by the military tribunal. These were *Wade* v. *Hunter,* (1949); *Humphrey* v. *Smith,* (1949); and *Whelchel* v. *McDonald,* (1950). They continued:

All persons tried in our civil courts are protected by the Constitution and may attack their convictions by habeas corpus on the grounds that their trials failed to conform to requisite constitutional standards. It would be strange indeed if American citizen soldiers, whose primary duty is to defend our country and to preserve our democracy, are deprived of rights which our Courts will scrupulously guard when asserted by those whose purpose is the destruction of our institutions.

Marshall and his colleagues conceded that if the military services were composed entirely of professional soldiers, there might be some logic in allowing the court-martial system to determine conclusively the meaning and application of constitutional provisions; however, in the present day they are mostly composed of conscripted American citizens, whose rights must be safeguarded by the civil courts. The advocates for the petitioners contended that theirs was a prima facie case of denial of fair pre-trial procedures by the civilian authorities and trial procedures by the military tribunal, inasmuch as violation of the "due process" clause of the Fifth Amendment was prohibited by a number of decisions by the Court. In support they cited *Betts* v. *Brady,* (1942); *Watts* v. *Indiana,* (1949); *McNabb* v. *United States,* (1943); *Rochin* v. *California,* (1952); and *Lisenba* v. *California,* (1941).

On June 15, 1953, with only Justices Black and Douglas dissenting, the Court handed down its decision in *Burns* v. *Wilson,* to affirm the judgments of the lower courts. Chief Justice Vinson announced the decision in an opinion in which Justices Reed, Burton, and Clark joined:

The military reviewing courts scrutinized the trial records before rejecting petitioners' contentions. In lengthy opinions, they concluded that petitioners had been accorded a complete opportunity to establish the authenticity of their allegations, and had failed . . . that each petitioner had declared, at the beginning of his trial, that he was ready to proceed; that each was ably represented; that the trials proceeded in an orderly fashion—with that calm degree of dispassion essential to a fair hearing on the question of guilt.

Thus concluded a decade in which the NAACP and its Legal Defense Fund had assisted in embodying more substantive and procedural rights in American constitutional law for the benefit of the Negro than had been witnessed in any similar period. A panorama of rights had been involved in seventeen cases argued before the Supreme Court of the United States, ranging from interstate transportation, state primaries, and procedural rights of the accused to restrictive covenants and education at all levels. Fund lawyers were successful in all but four. However, the actual enforcement of these decisions presented a most difficult task for Marshall and his staff in the decade to follow.

4

Signs in the Wind: 1956–1961

AFTER THE ISSUANCE OF THE COURT'S MANDATE CONCERNING SCHOOL IN-
tegration in 1955, a number of Southern states reacted by adopting
policies of "massive resistance" and "interposition." The implementation of massive resistance included the passage of school laws intended
to thwart the force of the Court's desegregation decision. These included statutes allowing local school boards to rearrange students
among various districts in order to maintain segregated facilities; repealing laws requiring compulsory attendance, thus inviting parents to
withdraw their children from integrated schools; laws providing for
state-supported segregated private schools; acts permitting the withdrawal of state funds from any school system that complied with the
desegregation decree; and state laws threatening the direct closing of
public schools if integration became inevitable.

Defenders argued that the doctrine of "interposition" had a more
compelling legal-historical basis than did the policy of "massive resistance." The concept that the state could interpose itself, *parens patriae,*
between its citizens and the national government if it acted in an unconstitutional manner had as its antecedents the Virginia and Kentucky
Resolutions of 1798, the Hartford Convention of 1814, and the South
Carolina Nullification Ordinance of 1832. Alabama, Georgia, Louisiana, Mississippi, South Carolina, and Virginia adopted such resolutions
within two years following the *Brown* decision.

Between 1956 and 1961 the NAACP Legal Defense Fund countered
Southern resistance with a no less massive program of litigation in
order to force an end to segregated public schools. As Marshall pointed
out, the *Brown* decision "probably did more than anything else to
awaken the Negro from his apathy to demanding his right to equality."
As late as 1958, however, the *Southern School News* reported that four
years after the School Segregation Cases in the seventeen Southern
and border states, elimination of de jure segregation had begun or

been completed in only 764 of 2,889 school districts; none of the school districts in Alabama, Florida, Georgia, Louisiana, Mississippi, South Carolina and Virginia had, as yet, complied with the law. The litigation that ensued often brought with it racial turmoil, rioting, and open hostility that necessitated the intervention of local and state forces and on occasion even the federal government.

The Aftermath of the School Segregation Cases

Following the "all deliberate speed" rule, a resultant tide of litigation swamped the federal courts. The Legal Defense Fund brought suits in a variety of areas, including education, local and interstate transportation, freedom of association, criminal procedure, recreational facilities, professional sports, and sit-down demonstrations.

In the first five years following the second *Brown* decision, Marshall and his colleagues brought seven major education cases before the Supreme Court of the United States; they were *Lucy* v. *Adams,* (1955); *Florida ex rel. Hawkins* v. *Board of Control,* (1956); *Frasier* v. *University of North Carolina,* (1956); *Florida ex. rel. Hawkins* v. *Board of Control,* (1957); *Cooper* v. *Aaron,* (1958); *Faubus* v. *Aaron,* (1959); and *Bush* v. *Orleans Parish School Board,* (1960). Only four of them bear considerable discussion. Autherine J. Lucy and Polly Anne Myers, two Negro citizens of Alabama, had been seeking admission to the University of Alabama since September 1952 but had been denied admission solely on account of their race and color. Consequently they brought suit against William F. Adams, the Dean of Admissions at the University, in the Federal District Court of the Northern District of Alabama. Speaking for the Court, Judge Grooms held that the Negroes had been denied the "equal protection of the laws" of the Fourteenth Amendment and permanently enjoined the Dean, "from denying the plaintiffs and others similarly situated the right to enroll in the University of Alabama and pursue courses of study thereat"; the United States Court of Appeals, Fifth Circuit, however, suspended the injunction. Counsel for the petitioners—including Marshall, Constance Baker Motley, Arthur D. Shores, and Robert L. Carter, applied to the Supreme Court of the United States on September 13, 1955, for injunctive relief. In a per curiam decision, the Court reinstated the injunction in accordance with its earlier decisions in *Sipuel, Sweatt,* and *McLaurin.* Threats of physical harm followed, and while attending classes on February 6, 1956, Miss Lucy was pelted by rocks and eggs thrown by university students and citizens of Tuscaloosa. The following day the University trustees suspended the young woman indefinitely, for her own safety and "for the safety of the students and faculty members." Thurgood Marshall, who had been with her during the violence, again appeared before the district court in Birmingham. He argued that the University had punished his client for complying with the law but had done nothing about those who had engaged in the disruption. On February 29 Judge Grooms held that the University had to reinstate the Negro student by March 5. Immediately following the court's decision, the trustees permanently expelled Lucy for the accusations she and her counsel had made in the contempt actions before the court. At this point the case suddenly died a natural death—Lucy flew to New York for rest and medical attention, did not attempt to reenter the University, and was married in Dallas, Texas, on April 22.

A more violent disturbance took place two years later when Arkansas attempted interposition with respect to the desegregation of Little Rock's Central High School. Six days after the first *Brown* decision the Little Rock District School Board made public its intention to comply with the constitutional requirements outlined by the Court. On May 24, 1955, seven days prior to the second *Brown* opinion, the Board approved a plan prepared by the Superintendent of Schools which provided for desegregation to begin at the senior high-school level in the fall of 1957, to follow with gradual desegregation at the junior-high and elementary levels, and to achieve complete desegregation by 1963. Other state officials were utterly opposed to compliance with the Court's decision, however. In November 1956, at the urging of Governor Orval Faubus, an amendment was attached to the Arkansas Constitution which commanded the State General Assembly to oppose "in every constitutional manner the un-constitutional desegregation decisions of . . . the United States Supreme Court." Consequently in 1957 the General Assembly enacted a statute which suspended compulsory-attendance regulations for students attending desegregated schools.

The School Board and related officials nevertheless continued preparations to initiate the program and scheduled John Aaron and eight other Negro children for admission to Central High School in September, 1957. On September 2, the day before the plan was to be implemented, Governor Faubus precipitated a confrontation which reached near-riot proportions when he dispatched units of the National Guard to the school grounds in order to place the school "off-limits" to the black children. The following day the Board requested the Negro students not to attend the school "until the legal dilemma was solved" and petitioned the United States District Court for the Eastern District of Arkansas for instructions. Speaking for the court, Judge Harry J. Lemley ordered the Board and the Superintendent of Schools to carry out the plan without further delay. For the next three weeks the Negroes attempted to enter the high school but were physically prevented from doing so by the Arkansas National Guard, pursuant to the orders of the Governor. On September 20, at the urging of the children's counsel—headed by Thurgood Marshall; Wiley A. Branton of Pine Bluff, Arkansas; and Attorney General Brownell, who filed an amicus curiae petition—the district court granted a preliminary injunction enjoining the Governor and the officers of the National Guard from further interference with the Board's desegregation plan.

On Monday, the following day, the Negro children entered the school under the protection of members of the State Police and the Little Rock Police Department; however, in view of the presence of an unruly mob of protesting whites, the children were again withdrawn. Finally, on September 25, President Eisenhower felt compelled to dispatch federal troops to the high school to ensure the safe admission of the Negro students. (The President acted on the advice of Attorney General Brownell, who argued that Section 333, Title 10, of the United States Code authorized the Chief Executive to suppress riots and insurrections which interfered with the execution of either federal or state law.) One month later these troops were replaced by federalized National Guardsmen, who remained on duty until the end of the school year.

On February 20, 1958, because of the racially tense environment of Little Rock, the School Board and the Superintendent of Schools filed a petition in the district court asking for a postponement of two and a half years of the desegregation program. On June 20 the district court granted the relief requested by the school agencies on the ground that there was "tension and unrest among the school administrators, the classroom teachers, the pupils, and the latter's parents, which inevitably had an adverse effect upon the educational program" and that the situation, as a whole, was "untolerable." Thereafter, Marshall and his fellow lawyers appealed to the United States Court of Appeals for the Eighth Circuit and asked for a stay of the lower court's judgment.

On August 18 the court of appeals, not acting on the petition for a stay, reversed the decision of the district court, but three days later it stayed its own mandate to allow the School Board to petition the Supreme Court of the United States for certiorari. Thereupon the Court, convened in a special term in August, began hearing arguments in *Cooper* v. *Aaron* on September 11, 1958.

Marshall and Branton, who argued the cause for the respondent school children before the Court, also contributed heavily to the brief. They were aided by NAACP and other lawyers from New York and Arkansas, including Elwood H. Chisolm, William Coleman, Jr., Irma Robbins Feder, Jack Greenberg, Louis H. Pollak, and William Taylor. In the short eleven-page Brief for Respondents in William G. Cooper, et al., Members of the Board of Directors of the Little Rock, Arkansas, Independent School District & Virgil T. Blossom, Superintendent v. John Aaron, et al., filed September 10, 1958, the lawyers argued that the rights of the Negro children must be enforced regardless of local public hostility:

> Neither overt public resistance, nor the possibility of it, constitutes sufficient cause to nullify the orders of the federal court directing petitioners to proceed with their desegregation plan. This Court and other courts have consistently held that the preservation of the public peace may not be accomplished by interference with rights created by the federal constitution.
>
> . . . Here one state agency, the School Board, seeks to be relieved of its constitutional obligation by pleading the *force majeure* brought to bear by another facet of state power. To solve this problem by further delaying the constitutional rights of the respondents is unthinkable.

There is no basis, the brief continued, for presuming that the state authorities charged with the responsibility of enforcing the law will not be able to do so. Moreover, Marshall and his colleagues warned:

> Even if it be claimed that tension will result which will disturb the educational process, this is preferable to the complete breakdown of education which will result from teaching that courts of law will bow to violence.

The lawyers for the respondents maintained that mob violence and riots did not provide a sufficient justification for the School Board and the Superintendent to avoid their clear-cut constitutional duty to comply with federal court orders requiring the gradual desegregation of the public schools. Such expediency at the expense of the rights of school children on the part of state officials, they continued, constitutes a denial of "equal protection of the laws" guaranteed by the Fourteenth Amendment. In addition, Marshall and the others contended, significant ramifications in the adjudication of this case must be considered:

> This case involves not only vindication of the constitutional rights declared in *Brown,* but indeed the very survival of the Rule of Law. This case affords this Court the opportunity to restate in unmistakable terms both the urgency of proceeding with desegregation and the supremacy of all constitutional rights over bigots—big and small.

On August 28, 1958, J. Lee Rankin, the Solicitor General, filed the Brief for the United States as Amicus Curiae. The government's position was that the decision of the Court of Appeals was "correct" and should be upheld; that the proper state authorities were indeed capable of maintaining domestic tranquility and of protecting the rights of the Negro respondents.

An interesting side point was the fact that Senator J. William Fulbright of Arkansas also filed a friend-of-the-court brief, but one which supported the position of the petitioners. Fulbright defended the decision of the district court, as announced by Judge Lemley, to suspend the desegregation program. The record plainly shows, the Senator contended, that the district court had attempted to carry out the plan but the "disruptive conditions" to the educational system which resulted, prohibited further implementation.

In a unanimous decision the Court upheld the order of the court of appeals on September 12, as it clarified in an opinion printed later that month. (The *Cooper* decision, incidentally, is unique in that it was signed by all nine judges.) It lashed out at the state's attempt to thwart its ruling in the *Brown* decision:

> The constitutional rights of respondents are not to be sacrificed or yielded to the violence and disorder which have followed upon the actions of the Governor and Legislature . . . law and order are not to be preserved by depriving the Negro children of their constitutional rights. The record before us clearly establishes that the growth of the Board's difficulties to a magnitude beyond its unaided power to control is the product of state action. . . . The controlling legal principles are plain. The command of the Fourteenth Amendment is that no "state" shall deny to any person

within its jurisdiction the equal protection of the laws . . . the Brown case can neither be nullified openly and directly by state legislators or state executive or judicial officers nor nullified indirectly by them through evasive schemes for segregation whether attempted "ingeniously or ingenuously."

The Court pointed out that because of Article VI of the Constitution and judicial interpretation as expounded in *Marbury* v. *Madison,* (1803), the decisions of the Supreme Court of the United States on constitutional issues are the "supreme law of the land." As such, the Court concluded, the principles announced in the *Brown* decision,

and the obedience of the States to them . . . are indispensable for the protection of the freedoms guaranteed by our fundamental charter for all of us. Our constitutional ideal justice under law is thus made a living truth.

Even after the Court's decision, the contest between federal and state authority did not end in Arkansas. Immediately following the *Cooper* opinion, Governor Faubus, through legislative authorization, ordered the withholding of state funds from racially mixed public schools and proclaimed them closed for the ensuing school year. In June 1959 the district court, ruling in *Aaron et al.* v. *Faubus, Governor of Arkansas,* found these actions violative of "due process of law" and "equal protection of the laws" as provided by the Fourteenth Amendment. On appeal to the Supreme Court of the United States, Thurgood Marshall and Wiley A. Branton again argued the cause of the Negro appellees. In a per curiam decision in *Faubus* v. *Aaron,* the Court affirmed the decision of the lower federal court; in September desegregation was accomplished in Little Rock high schools without incident.

In 1960 similar litigation was brought to the Supreme Court of the United States by Marshall, Constance Baker Motley, and A. P. Tureaud of New Orleans, all affiliated with the NAACP, in *Bush* v. *Orleans Parish School Board,* with respect to Louisiana's attempt at interposition. At the urging of Governor Jimmie Davis, the Louisiana legislature had enacted a number of statutes designed to prevent the New Orleans Parish School Board from carrying out partial desegregation of the public schools in that city. It reasoned, inter alia, that the State "had interposed itself in the field of public education over which it has exclusive control." After a three-judge federal district court temporarily enjoined enforcement of the statutes as being unconstitutional, Louisiana officials asked the Supreme Court of the United States to grant a motion for stay. The Court upheld the decision of the lower court and the motions for stay were denied.

The nub of the decision of the three-judge court is this: "The conclusion is clear that interposition is not a *constitutional* doctrine. If taken seriously it is illegal defiance of constitutional authority."

In the late 1950s a number of Southern states, recognizing the effectiveness of the NAACP and the Legal Defense and Educational Fund in the civil-rights litigation, either evoked old laws or enacted new ones to exclude such organizations from the state altogether. A long series of litigation seemed inevitable.

Principal points of concern for the NAACP and its legal arm were the states of Alabama and Virginia, though during the same period the two organizations were involved in similar suits against the states of South Carolina and Texas. The Attorney General of Alabama, John Patterson, filed a bill of complaint against the NAACP on June 1, 1956, alleging that the Association had failed to comply with Article 12, Section 232, Constitution of Alabama, 1901; Title 10, Sections 192, 193, 194 Code of Alabama, 1940, the state law requiring the registration of foreign or out-of-state corporations. Patterson argued that the NAACP, which was established in Alabama in 1918, was "causing irreparable injury to the property and civil rights of the residents and citizens of the State" and should therefore be banned from the state. In litigation before the state court the trial judge issued an order requiring the NAACP to produce its records and papers, including its membership lists. The Association agreed to produce all its papers except a list of its members, on the ground that such a disclosure would result in both official and nonofficial harassment of individual members. The judge responded by finding the Association in contempt of court, by imposing a preliminary fine of $10,000, and by threatening an additional $90,000 fine unless the list was produced within five days. Refusing to comply with the order of the court, the NAACP appealed to the Alabama Supreme Court. The court upheld the earlier decision, and the $100,000 fine was imposed. The case was then brought before the Supreme Court of the United States for review as *NAACP* v. *Alabama ex rel. Patterson.*

Robert L. Carter and Arthur D. Shores argued the case for the Association while Marshall and others drew up the Brief for Petitioner, No.

91, filed on September 21, 1957. The lawyers reasoned that the NAACP, in addition to a number of other organizations, has the constitutional right to exist and to advance beliefs in an open democratic society regardless of popular opposition to these views. The brief contended:

> Solution of the American race problem—one of the great social issues of this era—is the cause to which petitioner and its members are devoting their efforts and energy. The right to free discussion of the problems of our society and to engage in lawful activities aimed at their alleviation is one of the unique and indispensable requisites of our system. . . . The fact that some may view the ideas . . . its members espouse as ill-advised or even infamous is of no moment.

In this case, Marshall and the others contended, Alabama has deprived the Association and its members of the right to freely associate and to express ideas without providing "due process of law" as guaranteed by the Fourteenth Amendment:

> The right of freedom of association and free speech is accorded to dissident and unpopular minorities as well as those advocating ideas or engaging in activities of which those in power approve.
>
> The unimpaired maintenance of freedom of association and free speech is considered essential to our political integrity . . . and their safeguard in our basic law postulates a belief in the fundamental good sense of the American people.

An amici curiae brief was filed jointly by twelve other interested organizations having branches in Alabama including the American Baptist Convention on Christian Social Progress, the Anti-Defamation League of the B'nai B'rith, and the Japanese American Citizens League. In support of the NAACP, counsel for the amici argued that Alabama's action violates the First, Fifth, and Fourteenth Amendments. He warned, moreover, that state's "persecution" of the NAACP was only the first step in eliminating all opposition to racial segregation:

> It has become perfectly obvious that Alabama not only is attempting to maintain its statewide pattern of segregation but is also working for the destruction of all organized opposition to this policy. . . . Today, it is the NAACP that is subjected to attack. To-

morrow, the same measures may be taken against any group that supports a cause opposed by state officials.

On June 30, 1958, Associate Justice Harlan, speaking for a unanimous Court, reversed the decision of the Alabama Supreme Court. Harlan noted:

> It is not sufficient to answer, as the State does here, that whatever repressive effects compulsory disclosure . . . may have upon participation by Alabama citizens in petitioner's activities follows not from *state* action but from *private* community pressures. The crucial factor is the interplay of governmental and private action, for it is only after the initial exertion of state power represented by the production order that private action takes hold.

Since the state had no controlling justification in requiring the disclosure of membership lists, Harlan reasoned, "the deterrent effect on the free enjoyment of the right to associate" violated "due process of law" as protected by the Fourteenth Amendment. Accordingly, the Court dismissed the charge of civil contempt and the $100,000 fine and remanded the case to the state supreme court for "proceedings not inconsistent with this opinion." The litigation, however, did not end here.

The state supreme court, on remand, affirmed the contempt citation, as well as the fine imposed on the Association, on the grounds that the organization had not in fact done everything ordered except produce the membership lists. Again the Legal Defense Fund brought the case before the Supreme Court of the United States for review, with the Director-Counsel arguing the cause for the Association. On June 8, 1959, the Court, in a per curiam decision on *NAACP* v. *Alabama ex rel. Patterson,* reversed the decision of the lower court and remanded the case: "It is now too late for the State to claim that petitioner had failed to comply with the production order in other respects, that issue being foreclosed by this Court's prior disposition of the case." Because of the adamant refusal of the Alabama Supreme Court to decide the case on its merits, it took another five years and an additional two decisions by the Supreme Court of the United States to settle the matter permanently in the NAACP's favor.

Legislation brought about by state officials in Virginia also posed a serious threat to the activities of the NAACP Legal Defense Fund. In 1956 the General Assembly of Virginia enacted five statutes requiring the registration of persons or corporations who rendered financial assistance in litigation and who engaged in the public solicitation of funds for that purpose; it also established procedure for the suspension and revocation of state attorneys' licenses in violation of the law. The Legal Defense Fund brought separate actions for declaratory and injunctive relief on its own behalf and on behalf of the NAACP against the state's Attorney General, Albertis S. Harrison, and five other Commonwealth attorneys. A three-judge federal district court declared three of the statutes void but held that the remaining two must first be authoritatively construed by the state's courts. The case was then appealed to the Supreme Court of the United States as *Harrison* v. *NAACP et al.,* (1959).

Marshall argued for the appellees; with him on the Brief, No. 167, filed May 16, 1959, were Robert Carter, Oliver Hill, Spottswood Robinson III, William T. Coleman, Jr., Jack Greenberg, Constance Baker Motley, Louis Pollak, Charles L. Black, Jr., Irma Feder, and Elwood H. Chisolm. The lawyers maintained that the Virginia statutes not only curtailed the lawful activities of the two organizations and their members, but also struck at the basic civil rights and liberties guaranteed by the Constitution. At no point did Marshall and his associates deny that their membership corporations engaged in the solicitation of funds or the subsidization of litigation. Instead they argued, as in the *Alabama* cases, that "compulsory disclosure of organizational affiliates where economic reprisals and other manifestations of public hostility will ensue" violated the "due process" clause of the Fourteenth Amendment, that here, as in Alabama, the record fell short of demonstrating a controlling justification for Virginia's curtailment of the right of association or for its use of statutory barratry. The Director-Counsel and his colleagues concluded:

> Group sponsorship of litigation is as indigenous to twentieth century America as group sponsorship of welfare charities. . . . It appears that no court in the United States has ever denied the right of individual or group sponsorship of litigation as involved here where the members of the group have a common or general or patriotic interest in the principle of law to be established. Indeed the courts have expressly upheld it.

In a 6–3 decision—with Chief Justice Warren and Justices Douglas and Brennan vehemently dissenting—the Court handed the organizations a temporary setback by vacating the judgment of the district court and remanding the case for further consideration. Speaking for the majority, Justice Harlan held that the district court should not have declared any of the statutes unconstitutional "until the state courts had been afforded a reasonable opportunity to pass upon them." He concluded that the statutes involved

> leave reasonable room for a construction by the Virginia Courts which might avoid in whole or in part the necessity for federal constitutional adjudication or at least materially change the nature of the problem.

Within three years the state courts declared most of the laws unconstitutional except Chapter 33, which was directed against persons who solicit business for lawyers. In *NAACP* v. *Button,* (1963), brought about by the NAACP, the Supreme Court of the United States declared this statute to be invalid as well.

Marshall and his staff also showed justifiable concern in the early 1960s for the rights of accused Negroes. In 1959 Charles Clarence Hamilton, a Negro citizen of Alabama, was convicted and sentenced to death for "burglary with intent to ravish" and the rape of a white woman. In violation of Alabama law, Hamilton was not provided with counsel during arraignment, a critical stage in the state's criminal procedure. Only during arraignment may the defense of insanity be pleaded, or pleas in abatement or motions challenging the composition of the grand jury be made—all of which was unknown to Hamilton, who had pleaded not guilty. Moreover, after counsel was provided, the defendant became dissatisfied with his lawyer and "ignorantly" attempted to defend himself. The Legal Defense Fund was then requested to join the case.

On August 15, 1960, the Director-Counsel and his associates petitioned the Supreme Court of Alabama to grant leave to file a writ of error coram nobis, but the motion was denied in *Hamilton* v. *Alabama.* However, on November 15 Associate Justice Black ordered a stay of execution pending litigation to the Supreme Court of the United States. Constance Baker Motley argued the case before the Court, with the assistance of Marshall, Greenberg, Nabrit, and two Association lawyers from Birmingham, Orzell Billingsley, Jr., and Peter A. Hall.

In both the Brief for the Petitioner, filed August 25, 1961, and in oral argument, the Counsel for the plaintiff reasoned that the right to an attorney is so essential in cases in which the death penalty may be imposed that it cannot be arbitrarily limited "by a rule requiring demonstration of the amount of prejudice resulting from a denial of representation at a particular stage." Certainly, the brief argued, the defendant was "disadvantaged" by the actions of the state in this instance:

> Absence of counsel at arraignment must have been by any reasonable appraisal of . . . the issues posed by this case, prejudicial in and of itself. . . . Indeed, arraignment is so crucial a stage of criminal litigation that state law concerning appointment of counsel generally provides that the right attaches at or before arraignment. . . . Petitioner alone could hardly have been expected to know that he might have, for example, negotiated, in exchange for a plea of guilty to a lesser offense, a lighter sentence.

To compound the injustice afforded the defendant, Marshall and his fellow lawyers continued, the trial itself was "riddled with explosions" caused by Hamilton's conflict with the court, his "awkward efforts" to conduct his own defense, arguments with his counsel, his lawyer's efforts to withdraw, and his ultimate censure by the court. They concluded that their client had been denied "due process of law" provided by the Fourteenth Amendment and pleaded that the judgment of the lower court be reversed.

On November 13, 1961, the Court reversed the decision of the state supreme court. Speaking for a unanimous panel, Justice Douglas found that, regardless of the importance of arraignment in other states, in Alabama it plays such a crucial role that it may affect the whole trial:

> When one pleads to a capital charge without benefit of counsel, we do not stop to determine whether prejudice resulted. . . . Only the presence of counsel could have enabled this accused to know all defenses available to him and to plead intelligently.

In another criminal action—*Anderson* v. *Alabama*, (1961)—Jack Greenberg, Thurgood Marshall, and Alabama lawyers Billingsley and Hall persuaded the Supreme Court of the United States to reverse the conviction of a Negro defendant who had been found guilty of murder by an all-white Alabama jury in violation of the "equal protection" clause of the Fourteenth Amendment.

Inspired by the Court's decision in the *Brown* case, the NAACP Legal Defense Fund also took up the cause of Negro litigants in areas involving the use of public recreational facilities, interstate and local transportation, and participation in professional sports.

In 1955 Thurgood Marshall argued two cases before the Supreme Court of the United States with respect to state segregation of public recreational facilities. They were *Mayor and City Council of Baltimore* v. *Dawson;* and *Holmes* v. *Atlanta.* Dawson and other Negro citizens brought actions for declaratory judgments and injunctive relief against the enforcement of racial segregation in the use of public beaches and bathhouses maintained by the officials of Maryland and the city of Baltimore. The lawyers for the Negro plaintiffs—including Marshall, Carter, and Greenberg—brought the case to the United States Court of Appeals, Fourth Circuit. In a decision by Chief Judge Parker, joined by Judges Soper and Dobie, in *Dawson* v. *Mayor and City Council of Baltimore,* (1955), the court of appeals held that the segregation of such facilities was an invalid use of Maryland's police power and violated the "equal protection" clause of the Fourteenth Amendment.

Baltimore officials appealed the case to the Supreme Court of the United States. The Court, in a per curiam decision, affirmed the decision of the lower federal court. In the related case of *Holmes* v. *Atlanta,* decided immediately afterwards and also argued by Marshall, with the assistance of Carter and Atlanta attorney E. E. Moore, the Court remanded litigation involving the Negro use of a municipal golf course to the lower court with directions to enter a decree conforming with the *Baltimore* decision. Significantly, what Marshall and his colleagues had argued and the Court had eventually accepted was that the meaning of the *Brown* decision had to be construed and applied to other areas of state activity besides education; that the "separate but equal" doctrine had no place in the arena of legitimate state responsibility, including the use of public facilities.

Beginning in the mid-1950s, Negroes began to openly challenge the indignities they believed to be inflicted upon them by "Jim Crow" laws in the South requiring racial segregation in transportation. In 1956 Mrs. Flemming, a Negro resident of Charleston, South Carolina, assisted by lawyers Marshall, Carter, and Philip Wittenberg, brought suit against a public bus company because the bus driver required her to move to the back of the vehicle in accordance with South Carolina law. The United States Court of Appeals, Fourth Circuit, held in *Flemming* v. *South Carolina Electric & Gas Company,* (1956), that the driver acted "under color of state law" and that the segregation statute was in violation of "equal protection of the laws" provided by the Fourteenth Amendment. On April 26, 1956, the Supreme Court of the United States affirmed the judgment of the lower court without opinion. In the same year Marshall and his staff handled litigation arising over a Negro boycott of segregated buses in Montgomery, Alabama, which involved more violent overtones.

On December 1, 1955, Mrs. Rosa Parks, a Negro citizen and resident of Montgomery, refused to heed the request of a bus driver that she move to the rear of the bus into the area reserved for Negroes. Her subsequent arrest signaled the beginning of nonviolent protest in the American civil-rights movement. A relatively unknown Baptist minister, Martin Luther King, Jr., was named President of the Montgomery Improvement Association. The organization boycotted the use of city buses by Negroes, created voluntary car pools, and instructed Negro citizens on the philosophy of nonviolent resistance to evil as expounded by Thoreau and Mahatma Gandhi. So successfully was economic pressure brought to bear on the city that Dr. King was arrested and his life was threatened. In February 1956 Dr. King left Montgomery to meet with friends in Atlanta to decide whether he should return to the city and continue the boycott. After King decided to return, A. T. Walden, a Negro attorney, contacted Arthur Shores, NAACP counsel in Alabama, and Thurgood Marshall in New York. Both men assured King's friend that the minister would have the best legal protection. The boycott continued, and when city officials refused to change their segregation policies, it was decided to take the matter to the courts.

In an opinion by Circuit Court Judge Richard Rives, the federal court noted in *Browder* v. *Gayle*, (1956), that since "the Court has first weakened the vitality of, and has then destroyed, the separate but equal concept," the statutes are unconstitutional as violations of the Fourteenth Amendment. The decision, along with a companion case argued by Marshall and Carter, was appealed to the Supreme Court of the United States as *Owen* v. *Members of the Alabama Public Service Commission.* On November 13, 1956, the Court bypassed an opportunity to declare the *Plessy* doctrine "null and void," and affirmed the judgment of the lower court in a per curiam decision in *Gayle* v. *Browder.* Nevertheless, the victory brought the bus boycott and its leader, Dr. King, to national attention and won the respect of many of America's Negroes. Subsequently, King and a number of other Negro clergymen—including his father, Martin Luther King, Sr., Reverend Wyatt T. Walker, and Reverend Ralph Abernathy—founded the Southern Christian Leadership Conference (SCLC). Since 1956 the organization has played a prominent role in the civil rights movement by its usage of nonviolent resistance to challenge what it considers "evil" laws.

The decisions by the Court did not end state efforts to require segregation in local or even interstate transportation facilities by the use of "trespassing" laws. In 1960 a Negro law student named Bruce Boynton was arrested and convicted in Virginia courts for refusing to leave the white section of a Richmond bus-terminal restaurant. He was convicted of violating state law which made it a misdemeanor for any person "without authority of law" to remain upon the premises of another after having been forbidden to do so. Boynton's counsel—including Marshall, Greenberg, Pollak, Motley, and two Virginia lawyers, Martin A. Martin and Clarence W. Newsome—brought the case before the Supreme Court of the United States by filing their brief on November 7, 1960. Marshall and his associates argued in the Brief for Petitioner in *Boynton* v. *Virginia* that in the case an interstate traveler merely sought refreshment and, after observing that the Negro section was filled to capacity, was barred solely because of his race. Obviously, the brief continued, this was a case of a private person—the proprietor of the restaurant—who employed the force of state law to disrupt the flow of interstate commerce in violation of Article I, Section 8, Clause 3. In addition, Marshall and the others reasoned, the conviction resulted in a denial of the plaintiff's constitutional rights as protected by the "due process" and "equal protection" clauses of the Fourteenth Amendment.

In a 7–2 decision, overriding the dissents of Justices Whittaker and Clark, the Court held the Virginia statute unconstitutional and reversed the conviction. Speaking for the majority, Justice Hugo Black noted that the law violated Section 216 (d) of the Interstate Commerce Act forbidding any interstate carrier to subject any person to unjust discrimination:

> [When a] bus carrier has volunteered to make terminal and restaurant facilities available to its interstate passengers as a regular part of their transportation . . . [they] must perform these services without discriminations prohibited by the Act.

In their final area of legal activity during this period, the lawyers of the Legal Defense Fund asked that the principles of the *Brown* decision be applied to those professional sports falling under state jurisdiction. In 1959 Joseph Dorsey, Jr., a Negro prizefighter, brought a class-action suit and sought an injunction to restrain the Louisiana State Athletic Commission from enforcing rules prohibiting athletic contests between

Negroes and whites. Rule 26 of the Rules and Regulations adopted by the Commission provided that

> There shall be no fistic combat match, boxing, sparring or wrestling contest or exhibition between any person of the Caucasian or "white" race and one of the African or "Negro" race; and, further, it will not be allowed for them to appear on the same card.

Marshall argued the case for the Negro athlete and was assisted by Jack Greenberg, James Nabrit, Jr., and Louisiana NAACP counsel Prudhomme F. Dejoie. The United States District Court for the Eastern District of Louisiana held in (1959) that the statute was unconstitutional on its face as a violation of the Equal Protection Clause of the Fourteenth Amendment. On appeal, the Supreme Court of the United States affirmed in *State Athletic Commission* v. *Dorsey,* (1959), the district court's decision without opinion.

Racial Turmoil: From the Streets to the Courts

During the height of the Montgomery bus boycott the Reverend Martin Luther King, Jr., after being arrested himself, was reported to have said:

> We must continue our struggle in the courts. Above all, we must continue to support the NAACP. Our major victories have come through the work of this organization. One thing the gradualists don't seem to understand: We are not trying to make people love us when we go to court; we are trying to keep them from killing us.

Nevertheless, the creation of the Southern Christian Leadership Conference late in 1956 heralded a new age, in which American Negroes became increasingly impatient with the judicial process and began to protest actively against discrimination in businesses, at lunch counters, in theaters, in restaurants, and in the streets. The movement, essentially nonviolent in nature, was directed at the racially discriminatory policies of both local and state governments and of private parties as well.

The use of the "sit-in" demonstration had its beginnings on February 1, 1960, when four Negro students from North Carolina Agricultural and Technical College at Greensboro refused to leave a segregated lunch counter in a Woolworth store after being denied service. They were arrested for disturbing the peace. The technique attracted national attention, and its use quickly spread throughout the cities of the South. Efforts to coordinate the movement led to the creation in 1960 of the Student Nonviolent Coordinating Committee (SNCC) with headquarters in Atlanta, Georgia.

In March lawyers of the NAACP Legal Defense Fund drafted a master plan for defending the Negro demonstrators. At a conference of sixty-two lawyers in New York, representing more than a thousand Negro defendants in the South, the Director-Counsel announced, according to *The New York Times* of March 20, 1960, that state use of "disturbing the peace" statutes to convict the sit-in demonstrators would be challenged as violations of the Fourteenth Amendment. Subsequently, as reported in the Nashville *Banner* on April 7, 1960, Marshall committed "the whole force of the NAACP" behind the students in the sit-in demonstrations. Finally, in 1961, Marshall and his staff were able to present the question to the Supreme Court of the United States in *Garner* v. *Louisiana.*

Garner and fifteen other students were arrested in Baton Rouge, Louisiana, for disturbing the peace after they refused the proprietors' requests to leave lunch counters in a Kress Department store, in a drug store, and in a bus terminal. In each instance the Negroes were refused service and remained silently in their seats until they were arrested for violating state law which proscribed any act that "would foreseeably disturb or alarm the public." In three cases that were later combined, the trial cuurt found the defendants guilty and sentenced each of them to a thirty-day jail term and a fine of $100, which was later upheld by the Supreme Court of Louisiana.

Jack Greenberg, Thurgood Marshall, and two Louisiana lawyers, A. P. Tureaud and Johnnie A. Jones, who served as counsel for the defendants, on December 31, 1962, submitted to the Supreme Court of the United States a Petition for Writ of Certiorari. Greenberg, who eventually argued the case, and Marshall, who headed up the team responsible for the brief, argued that the State Supreme Court's decision affirmed a criminal conviction based upon no evidence of guilt and was therefore in conflict with recent decisions of the Court. Indeed, they continued, the demonstrators were neatly dressed and remained quiet; there was no disturbance; no one was alarmed; and no disorder resulted. Greenberg, Marshall, and the others reasoned that the young Negro defendants were convicted under a statute that was so vague, indefinite, and uncertain as to offend the concept of "due process of law" protected by the Fourteenth Amendment.

In conclusion, Marshall and his associates attacked the use of state "disturbing the peace" statutes to enforce racial segregation in public facilities:

[The lower court's decision if] allowed to stand, would be completely subversive of the numerous decisions throughout the federal judiciary outlawing state-enforced racial distinctions. Indeed, the segregation here is perhaps more insidious than that accomplished by other means for it is not only based upon a vague statute which is enforced by the police according to their personal notions of what constitutes a violation and then sanctioned by state courts, but it suppresses freedom of expression, as well.

On December 11, 1961, the Court unanimously reversed the convictions of all of the Negro defendants. There were four separate concurring opinions—one each by Justices Douglas, Frankfurter, and Harlan, and a majority opinion written by Chief Justice Earl Warren. He spoke for the majority by noting:

[as] these records contain no evidence to support a finding that petitioners disturbed the peace, either by outwardly boisterous conduct or by passive conduct likely to cause a public disturbance, we hold that these convictions violated petitioners' rights to due process of law guaranteed them by the Fourteenth Amendment. . . . The undisputed evidence shows that the police . . . were left with nothing to support their actions except their own opinions that it was a breach of the peace for the petitioners to sit peacefully in a place where custom decreed they should not sit. Such activity . . . is not evidence of any crime and cannot be so considered either by the police or the courts.

The Garner litigation was the last case in which Thurgood Marshall actively participated for the NAACP Legal Defense and Educational Fund. His record as an advocate for civil rights before the Supreme Court of the United States had won him acclaim from the protagonists of the civil-rights movement as well as grudging respect from its antagonists. Senator Richard B. Russell, Democrat from Georgia, remarked that Marshall apparently exercised "an almost occult power" over the members of the Supreme Court of the United States. Many constitutional scholars would probably agree with the assessment of Marshall's efforts for the NAACP and its legal arm, confided by Henry J. Abraham in a letter to the author on April 10, 1969:

Thurgood Marshall's contributions to the amelioration of the Negroes' lot, and, through them, to the causes of civil rights, in general, have been unquestionably significant. Both as a symbol and as a legal tactician, his work was crucial, particularly in the 1940's and 1950's. Especially his strategy in the *Brown* case, and its antecedent events, looms giant.

In January and February 1960 Marshall served as a consultant at the Constitutional Conference on Kenya held in London. After observing him on two occasions during the Conference, news correspondent Eric Sevareid remarked:

What stayed with me, what was to me impressive and humbling, was that in everything the man said, on both occasions, in his every expression and gesture, one was made conscious of the presence . . . of an American, period.

Journalist Juan Williams wrote this essay for the Washington Post Magazine *(January 7, 1990). In it he focuses on Marshall's work during his tenure with the NAACP.*

Marshall's Law

IN THE SEGREGATED SOUTH, WHEN HOPE DIMMED, OPPRESSED BLACKS USED to whisper his name. His legal strategy fueled the triumphs of the civil rights movement. Now Thurgood Marshall—the first black Supreme Court justice and still the most powerful black person in America—looks back on his historic career.

A tall, thick, aging black man steps out of a limousine and slowly makes his way into the Sheraton-Washington Hotel. As he trudges toward the ballroom where he is scheduled to give one of his rare speeches, black bellhops and maids and doormen freeze in place, pointing. Black waiters and waitresses begin streaming out of the kitchen for a glimpse of the man. Elderly black people, some with tears in their eyes, stand on tiptoes to see better and wave.

A white man, obviously awed by the emotional reaction of those around him, taps a black man on the arm: "What's goin' on? Who *is* that guy?"

"That's *Thurgood Marshall.*"

The white man seems almost confused: "He's one of those Supreme Court judges, right?"

To many, if not most, white Americans, Thurgood Marshall is not a lot more than "one of those Supreme Court judges." They don't doubt that he is an important and honored man in American life, but he is only one of hundreds of equally important and powerful people in the country. Many saw his appointment to the court by Lyndon Johnson as a political response, even a gesture of appeasement, to the power of the civil rights movement.

In American universities and law schools, the opinions of Thurgood

Marshall aren't ranked with those of John Marshall or Louis Brandeis. Within the realm of the high court and its place in history, white America may never afford Marshall its highest honors.

Yet if whites could see Thurgood Marshall more clearly, they might see the most important black man of this century—a man who rose higher than any black person before him and who has had more effect on black lives than any other person, black or white. Perhaps even more important to many blacks, Marshall got where he is the hard way —by risking his life and reputation to help them.

Twenty-two years ago, even before Marshall broke the 178-year color barrier on the Supreme Court, *Newsweek* magazine wrote: "In three decades he has probably done as much to transform the life of his people as any Negro alive today, including Nobel laureate Martin Luther King." The accolade was deserved. Marshall built his reputation slowly, in backwater southern towns, overwhelmed but not overmatched by a twisted white justice wrought by judges and sheriffs who had few second thoughts about beating in black heads. Often the only hope among blacks in these small communities was expressed in a quiet, angry threat, whispered like code: *Thurgood is coming.*

"When I think of great American lawyers, I think of Thurgood Marshall, Abe Lincoln and Daniel Webster," says Thomas G. Krattenmaker, a professor of constitutional law at Georgetown University Law Center. "In this century only Earl Warren approaches Marshall. He is certainly the most important lawyer of the 20th century."

Marshall is the only black leader in American history who can argue that he defeated segregation where it really counts—in court. Devising a legal strategy based on the Constitution, he forced rights to be extended equally to even the poorest and most disadvantaged citizens. Martin Luther King Jr. would not have won his first victory, the Montgomery, Ala., bus boycott, if Marshall's legal team at the NAACP had not first won a Supreme Court ruling outlawing segregation on buses. And it was Marshall who argued *Brown* v. *Board of Education* before the Supreme Court, ending segregation in public schools.

"For black people he holds special significance because it was Thurgood, Charles Houston [Marshall's law professor] and a few others who told us we could get justice through interpretation of the law," says Duke law professor John Hope Franklin, author of *From Slavery to Freedom: A History of Negro Americans.* "Marshall was at the head of these lawyers who told us to hold fast because they were going to get the law on our side. And they did."

Once on the court, Marshall continued the battle, fighting against the death penalty and for individual rights—freedom of the press, privacy and due process. His efforts have not gone unnoticed. "He is almost an exact contemporary of mine," says Erwin Griswold, a former dean of the Harvard Law School and former solicitor general who is regarded as an expert on the Supreme Court. "I have watched him for all these years. First, he was an extremely resourceful and energetic advocate in the late 1930s and 1940s, trying difficult cases all over the South with great skill and often much courage. He changed America. And then as a judge on the court of appeals and as solicitor general he upheld the best standards of the legal profession. And now he has been on the Supreme Court for 22 years and has had a distinguished record not only through votes on civil rights but on technical legal questions of varying issues. He has been a strong constitutional influence for the proper, sound development of the law and ranks among the strongest members of the Supreme Court in this century."

"Thurgood Marshall is the living embodiment of how far we Americans have come on the major concern in our history—race—and how far we've got to go," says Drew Days, professor of law at Yale and former assistant attorney general for civil rights. "He has been a conscience. In the law he remains our supreme conscience."

Marshall has argued more cases before the court—32—than any justice now sitting. He won 29 of them. Marshall alone among the justices can say he has defended a man charged with murder. And only Marshall can say what it feels like to be black in America.

He has been much more than a minority spokesman. Says John Hope Franklin: "If you study the history of Marshall's career, the history of his rulings on the Supreme Court, even his dissents, you will understand that when he speaks, he is not speaking just for black Americans but for Americans of all times. He reminds us constantly of the great promise this country has made of equality, and he reminds us that it has not been fulfilled. Through his life he has been a great watchdog, insisting that this nation live up to the Constitution."

But in black America, Thurgood Marshall has become a doubly potent symbol: the protector fighting for the rights of individuals in a white-majority society still stained with racism, and the personification of black achievement. No black American has ever held a higher government office, and none will until a black person is elected president.

* * *

Thurgood Marshall's thinning silver hair is combed straight back. At 81, his wife and friends complain, he is heavier than ever because he refuses to exercise. He wears two hearing aids, and sometimes his still smooth face is suddenly etched with tears caused by glaucoma that keeps him from driving and forces him to hold papers close to his eyes as he reads. But he reads constantly. His massive desk at the court is covered with papers, letters, law books and pictures.

There is a picture of his grandson, Thurgood William Marshall (whose middle name honors Marshall's friend Justice William Brennan). Also on the desk is a small bust of Frederick Douglass, the black anti-slavery writer who is Marshall's hero. And there is a picture of Marshall with his wife. It was taken recently after Marshall finally agreed to have painted the portrait of him that will hang in the Supreme Court after his death.

Save for a 1988 documentary he did with Carl Rowan, Marshall hasn't given any interviews while on the court. As he talks about his extraordinary career, his voice is gruff; he often mumbles or gives brusque answers to questions.

Marshall's life is a reflection of the changing 20th century. It began in a sharply segregated town of ordinary people—Baltimore—in 1908. Baltimore was a town where blacks attended "colored schools" run by a white superintendent who said he wouldn't build a swimming pool for students because "Negroes don't deserve swimming pools." It was a town where the parochial schools let students out 10 minutes earlier than the black public schools to minimize fights between the two groups. Not a single department store in Baltimore was open to blacks, not a single restroom that blacks could use was to be found downtown.

"The only thing different between the South and Baltimore was trolley cars," recalls Marshall. "They weren't segregated. Everything else was segregated."

As a boy, Marshall did not have a burning desire to fight segregation. He says he rarely felt uncomfortable about race. He lived in a nice house on Druid Hill Avenue, and both of his parents worked. His mother taught kindergarten, and his father held a variety of jobs, including working as the steward at the prestigious Gibson Island Club on Chesapeake Bay. Marshall was the great-grandson of a slave named Thoroughgood—Marshall shortened it to Thurgood—but both his grandfathers owned large grocery stores in Baltimore.

As young Thurgood grew, his parents and grandparents encouraged him to adjust to segregation, not to fight it. There was even teasing about it, family jokes. Marshall's father, William Canfield Marshall, a pale-skinned, blue-eyed man who could have passed for white, used to say, "There's a white man in the woodpile," or "That's mighty black of you."

"Well, the truth is you learn to take it," Marshall says. "I was taught to go along with it, not to fight it unless you could win it. The only thing was if somebody calls you a nigger." His father ordered Marshall to fight if anyone called him that.

Marshall's high school life was full of circumstances that would later prove to be significant. As a mediocre student and a cutup, he was frequently punished, made to read the U.S. Constitution aloud. By the time he graduated from high school, he knew it by heart. The school he attended was located next to a police station. Marshall remembers spending afternoons listening to the police beat up black prisoners and tell some to shut up before they talked themselves into a death sentence. For amusement, Marshall's father would occasionally take his son down to the local courthouse to watch trials.

In September 1925, Marshall went off to Lincoln University in Oxford, Pa., a premed student hoping eventually to graduate from dental school. But he had problems at Lincoln. He and the biology teacher argued constantly, and Marshall failed the course. He was thrown out of the college twice for fraternity pranks.

Then, in his junior year he married Vivian "Buster" Burney, a beautiful, energetic student at the University of Pennsylvania he had met on a weekend trip. In some ways he began to settle down. In other ways he was just beginning to become unsettled.

At Lincoln, a school for bright, black males founded by a Presbyterian minister and staffed by an all-white faculty, Marshall at first showed little interest in civil rights issues. Some of his fellow students began to argue with him about his indifference. They would ask him why he hadn't challenged segregation in Baltimore, why he hadn't used white bathrooms or sat in the white sections of movie theaters. Then came a school-wide vote: Should the Lincoln faculty be integrated? Marshall voted with the majority—two-thirds of Lincoln's upperclassmen—to keep the faculty all-white.

Classmates wanted Marshall on their side—for integration—when the issue came up again. Among them were Cab Calloway, who went on to fame as a cabaret dancer; Langston Hughes, the writer, who later described Marshall at college as "the loudest individual in the dormitory, good-natured, rough, ready and uncouth"; U. Simpson Tate, who later worked with Marshall on civil rights cases; and Nnamdi Azikiwe, who became president of Nigeria. (Kwame Nkrumah, who became president of Ghana, also went to Lincoln and became a friend of Marshall's, although he graduated much later.)

Hughes in particular pressed Marshall on the faculty integration question, arguing that lack of support for black teachers was evidence of the students' "belief in their own inferiority." The debate started a radical shift in Marshall's thinking. His mother had taught him to go along so he could get along in a segregated world, but his father's more subtle message, he began to realize, was to fight. Confused, Marshall went to his favorite professor, sociologist Robert M. Labaree. Labaree told Marshall he should be fighting segregation and the faculty should be integrated.

When the issue came up again, Marshall voted for integration. The faculty was integrated two years after that vote.

After graduating from Lincoln in 1930 with a degree in humanities, Marshall enrolled at Howard University's all-black law school in Washington, making daily train trips there from his parents' home in Baltimore, where he lived with his wife.

In law school, the same message Marshall had heard from his father, from Labaree and from his college classmates—don't accept segregation—started to come at him again. Charles H. Houston had transformed Howard's law school from a "dummy's retreat" night school to a rigorous day school for students committed to using legal knowledge to change segregated society. Marshall would later say that everything he knew about the law Houston had pounded into his head. "He taught us with an emphasis on the Constitution," Marshall recalls. "And basically, he said you had to be not as good as the average white lawyer, you had to be better, because you wouldn't get a break on an even basis. He would tell us that the secret was hard work and digging out the facts and the law.

"When I was in law school in my first year, I lost 30 pounds solely from work, intellectual work, studying. And that's how you get ahead of people." Marshall says Houston's message to him was that "lawyers were to bear the brunt of getting rid of segregation, and he made public statements that we would become social engineers rather than lawyers." Although his class began as a group of more than 30 students, only six graduated. The No. 1 student was Thurgood Marshall.

Among the lecturers for the school, then located at Fifth and D streets NW, Houston brought in stars like Felix Frankfurter and Clarence Darrow. Marshall remembers Darrow telling him that a good lawyer studied sociology as much as he studied the law. Years later, when Darrow died, his widow gave all his cases dealing with civil rights to Marshall.

In his last year of law school, Marshall and some of his classmates began reviewing the D.C. Code "just for fun," only to discover it prohibited blacks from voting. The discovery became a cause, and eventually Congress put a civil rights clause into the code. For the first time, Marshall focused on what would become his life's work—fighting segregation.

After graduation, in an effort to impress on his star pupil the devastation of segregation, Houston took Marshall with him on a trip through the South. Traveling anonymously in Houston's old automobile, and prohibited from patronizing most motels and restaurants, they stayed overnight with local black lawyers and ate from bags of fruit they carried with them.

Shortly after their return, Houston had Marshall assist him in the case of George Crawford, a black man charged with murdering a white man in Loudoun County, Va. After a strong defense, Crawford was convicted and given life.

"We won it," Marshall says. "If you got a Negro charged with killing a white person in Virginia and you got life imprisonment, then you've won. Normally they were hanging them in those days."

Houston went on to New York to run the NAACP's Legal Defense and Educational Fund while Marshall returned to Baltimore to open a one-man law firm. His mother took the rug off her living room floor and put it in his otherwise bare office. He took what cases he could get, developing a reputation as a lawyer who would help poor blacks.

"A woman walked into my office one day, a colored woman from South Carolina, and she had a case and she didn't have any money," Marshall remembers. "So I said, 'Well, madam, please tell me: How did you happen to get to me?' And she said, 'In my home town in South Carolina, when we has trouble we goes to the judge, and the judge tells us what to do. So I went over to the courthouse, and when I saw the sign "Judge," I went in and told him of my problem and he said, "We don't operate that way up here. You need a lawyer." ' And she said she didn't have any money. And he said, 'You go down to this lawyer Marshall. He's a freebie.'

"So I said, 'I've got to stop that nonsense right now.' "

Though he couldn't afford it, Marshall still made time for the fight against segregation. Representing the local NAACP, he negotiated with white store owners who sold to blacks but would not hire them. He joined John L. Lewis's effort to unionize black and white steelworkers. And he convinced a college graduate who wanted to go to law school to apply to the University of Maryland, which did not accept blacks into its law school program. Marshall had considered applying to Maryland himself after he graduated from college but decided it would be hopeless. Now he was taking the law school to court.

Houston came to Baltimore and helped argue the case. During the proceedings, Marshall told the court: "What is at stake here is more than the rights of my client; it is the moral commitment stated in our country's creed." No one expected Marshall and Houston to win; they were simply trying to set up a case that could be appealed. "We were hoping to get to the Supreme Court any way we could," Marshall says. "But Judge Eugene O'Dunne said no. He said we won right there."

"The colored people in Baltimore were on fire when Thurgood did that," recalls Juanita Jackson Mitchell, an NAACP activist in Baltimore. "They were euphoric with victory . . . We didn't know about the Constitution. He brought us the Constitution as a document like Moses brought his people the Ten Commandments."

It was during these heady, early days of practice that many of Marshall's ideas about the fallibility of the law would be developed. For example, his repeated contact with black defendants accused of capital crimes helped convince him that his fellow man should not be given the power to condemn others to death. He remembers many stories about lives that could easily have been snuffed out by the capriciousness of the white man's law.

One night, he says, he got a call from Frederick, Md., warning that a lynching was about to take place. A black man had been charged with attempting to rape the white daughter of a bank president. Marshall got into his '29 Ford and raced to Frederick. A local judge had stopped the lynching, but he told Marshall it had been close. A mob had captured a suspect and brought him to the young woman to be identified.

"She was laying on the sofa in her home in pain because he broke her jaw," Marshall says, "and she said, 'Yeah, that's him.' And the mob was ready, and they barely got him to the front door when she said, 'Wait a minute. Bring him back.' And they brought him back in, and she said, 'That's not the man.' So the chief of police said, 'Now why did you change your mind like that?' She said, 'The guy that attempted to rape me had his belt buckle on the side, and that one's got it right there.' So they went out, and they found a guy that looked like this guy's twin brother. And they weren't even related. Now you see how easy that would have been? That innocent man would have been lynched."

In 1936, after three years of private practice, Marshall was invited by Houston to join the NAACP's national office in New York as assistant special counsel. Two years later, Houston returned to his family practice in Washington. Marshall was appointed to fill Houston's position, and for the next 20 years he traveled the country using the Constitution to force state and federal courts to protect the rights of black Americans. The work was dangerous, and Marshall frequently wondered if he might not end up dead or in the same jail holding those he was trying to defend.

In the early 1940s, for example, he was changing trains in a small town in Mississippi when "I got hungry and I saw a restaurant, so I decided that I'd go over there and put my civil rights in my back pocket and go to the back door of the kitchen and see if I could buy a sandwich. And while I was kibitzing myself to do that, this white man came up beside me in plain clothes with a great big pistol on his hip. And he said, 'Nigger boy, what are you doing here?' And ·I said, 'Well, I'm waiting for the train to Shreveport.' And he said, 'There's only one more train comes through here, and that's the 4 o'clock, and you'd better be on it because the sun is never going down on a live nigger in this town.' I wasn't hungry anymore."

A few years later, Marshall was defending two black men accused of shooting a policeman. The shooting occurred after a black youngster and a storekeeper got into a fight over the cost of repairing a broken radio. The youngster beat up the man and ran away. A mob, including the police, pursued him into the black section of town and shot randomly into homes. Shots were fired back from neighborhood houses, and a policeman was hit. At the end of the trials—one man was found guilty, the other innocent—Marshall went in search of a bottle of liquor to unwind with.

"The bootlegger said, 'I'm sorry, I had just vodka and whiskey, and I just sold the last two bottles to the judge," Marshall remembers. So he and the other lawyers left town, only to be stopped by police, who searched the car for liquor, without success. When the car had been driven on a few hundred yards, it was stopped again. After much finger pointing, the police agreed that the tall man in the back seat was "the one we want." Marshall was arrested for drunken driving.

"The justice of the peace was a little, short man—5-4, elderly and about 60. He said, 'What's up?' And they said, 'We got this nigger here for drunk driving.' And he says, 'Boy, you want to take my test? I never had a drink in my life, and I can smell a drink a mile off. You want to take a chance?' I said, 'Well, sure, I'll take a chance.' He said, 'Blow your breath on me.' I blew so hard he rocked. When he got himself together, he said, 'This man hasn't had a drink in 24 hours. What the hell are you talking about?' I turned around, and the police were gone."

Another time, when Marshall went to Dallas to challenge the city's refusal to seat blacks on juries, the police chief "called the top personnel, the captains and lieutenants, and made a speech to them one morning that said a newspaper reported that a nigger lawyer named Marshall was coming down from New York to disrupt our procedures. And he wanted them to know that he was instructing them not to do anything about it, not to touch Thurgood Marshall, because he personally would take him and kick the shit out of him. I sort of considered the idea of having a bad cold or something and not going down there."

Instead, Marshall called the governor and requested protection from a state trooper. But one day as he left the courthouse, Marshall came face to face with the chief. "And when he saw me, he said, 'Hi, you black son of a bitch, I've got you.' And I ran. And the state trooper pulled out his gun and said to the chief, 'You stay right there.' "

Living out of suitcases, hopping trains into and out of small towns dedicated to white supremacy, Marshall lived the segregated life he was challenging, often finding the irony ridiculous. Once, in North Carolina, he told a judge that he had eaten the same exquisite meal, drunk the same expensive wine and been served at the very same segregated restaurant the judge had dined in the night before. The only difference, Marshall said, was that "you had yours in the dining room, and I had mine in the kitchen."

Though many of his clients were ushered off to years in prison despite their innocence, the risks Marshall took paid off in a mass of legal precedents. Among the successes: He ended the use of racially restrictive covenants to keep blacks from buying houses; he argued the case that ended the all-white primary system in Texas (Marshall had already garnered such a reputation among blacks that during the Texas case Duke Ellington stopped his tour for a week to sit in the courtroom and watch Marshall in action); and he won cases calling for black teachers to be paid salaries equal to those of whites.

Between cases, Marshall was constantly involved with other events and personalities in the struggle between American blacks and whites. He was denounced by Muslims as a "half-white son of a bitch." He met Malcolm X once and "we spent the whole time calling each other a bunch of sons of bitches." Once, after he had been threatened by some Muslims on the street, the New York police commissioner came to his house with a beautifully wrapped gift—a gun. Marshall refused.

At the invitation of various federal and state officials, he investigated almost every race riot between 1940 and 1960. He recalls in particular a Detroit riot that began after a rumor was spread among blacks that a white Marine had raped a 7-year-old black girl. In white Detroit, a rumor was spread that a black man had raped a 7-year-old white girl. "The one thing you get out of race riots," he says, "is that no guilty person ever gets hurt. The innocent people get hurt."

In the late 1940s, Branch Rickey, the general manager of the Brooklyn Dodgers, called him to ask if he would help a young ballplayer named Jackie Robinson straighten out his financial affairs.

At the request of President Truman, Marshall traveled to the Far East in 1951 to review treatment of black soldiers under Gen. Douglas MacArthur. Marshall remembers asking MacArthur why there were no blacks in the elite group guarding the general. He was told none were qualified by their performance on the field of battle.

"I said, 'Well, I just talked to a Negro yesterday, a sergeant who has killed more people with a rifle than anybody in history. And he's not qualified?' And he [MacArthur] said, 'No.' I said, 'Well now, general, remember yesterday you had that big band playing at the ceremony over there?' He said, 'Yes, wasn't that wonderful?' I said, 'Yes, it's beautiful.' I said, 'Now, general, just between you and me: Goddammit, don't you tell me that there's no Negro that can play a horn.' That's when he said for me to go."

Today Marshall says the general was a racist: "What else can you say? Every other branch of the armed forces was desegregated, but he wouldn't budge. And when he left, the Army desegregated too. Right away."

Marshall's greatest victory came in 1954, when he led the legal team that challenged school segregation before the Warren court. As the case progressed, three secret dramas unfolded.

First, Marshall heard that President Eisenhower had pressured Chief Justice Earl Warren to retain school segregation. Marshall says that Ralph Bunche, former U.S. undersecretary to the United Nations, told him that at a White House dinner he heard Warren tell Eisenhower off in no uncertain terms: "I thought I would never have to say this to you, but I now find it necessary to say to you specifically: You mind your business, and I'll mind mine." Later, Marshall said Eisenhower's attempt to pressure Warren was the "most despicable job any president has done in my life."

Second was Marshall's mental combat with Justice Felix Frankfurter. Throughout the case, the justice had peppered him with questions. At one point, just before recessing for the day, Frankfurter asked him if the case would be affected if the 14th Amendment to the Constitution had not been intended to end segregation. "My God, the light went on, which meant you had to come back in the morning," recalls William T. Coleman, who worked with Marshall on the case. "Well, from 5 o'clock until 7 o'clock in the morning—the work that went into how do you answer that question!"

Later, Marshall discovered that it was Frankfurter who had put the phrase "all deliberate speed" into the decision, creating a loophole that allowed segregationists to delay the integration of schools instead of immediately obeying the court order.

"If he'd pushed me one more time in the school case," Marshall says, recalling the argument 35 years ago, "I was going to say, 'And may it please the court, I wish to mention the fact that we have not come as far as some people think and as far as other people think. For example, if this case involved a Jewish kid, I don't think we'd have this problem.' And I was going to say it. I was going to say it."

The third drama involved Justice Stanley Reed, a Kentuckian. Marshall had been told that Reed had independently hired a clerk to write a dissent to the opinion. In Marshall's mind, the question was: How many justices will join in Reed's dissent?

As the decision came down, Marshall was watching Reed's eyes. "When Warren read the opinion," he says, Reed "looked me right straight in the face the whole time because he wanted to see what happened when I realized that he didn't write that dissent. I was looking right straight at him, and I did like that [a nod of the head], and he did like that [a nod in response]." The decision was unanimous.

Marshall would later comment that the Brown decision "probably did more than anything else to awaken the Negro from his apathy to demanding his right to equality."

In February 1955, Marshall's wife, Buster, began to fail from cancer. He stayed at home with her for the last weeks of her life, not answering phone calls, not going out except to get food. "She would have done the same thing for me," he says.

He remained single for a year, dating Cecilia Suyat, a secretary who worked at the NAACP. Finally, he asked her to marry him. She said no.

Suyat, who is of Philippine ancestry, thought Marshall would come in for too much criticism if he married her. "They called me a foreigner," she says. "No, with his stature I just didn't want to bring any controversy into it." Eventually, however, she agreed.

Although Marshall's associates and friends at the NAACP didn't object to the marriage, a newspaper in Mississippi did. "They had a front-page editorial that said that Thurgood Marshall, just like his predecessor Walter White, has broken down and admitted his racial prejudice by marrying a white woman," Marshall says. "And I wrote a letter back to them, and I said, not that I object to it, but I just think you ought to be accurate. And I don't know which wife you're talking about, but I have had two wives, and both of 'em were colored." The editor of the newspaper wrote his response on Marshall's letter and sent it back: "So what?"

Between 1955 and 1960, Marshall's legal team at the NAACP filed seven major cases dealing with the right of black children to an education. In 1957 he represented the nine black Little Rock, Ark., students who tried to integrate Central High School, challenging segregationist Gov. Orval Faubus and Arkansas moderate Sen. J. William Fulbright (who filed a brief with the court opposing desegregation because it might create "disruptive conditions"). Marshall, in his arguments to the court, countered: "Even if it be claimed that tension will result which will disturb the educational process, this is preferable to the complete breakdown of education which will result from teaching that courts of law will bow to violence."

Nevertheless, the threat of violence hanging over the Little Rock case was real. Wiley Branton, Marshall's co-counsel, once recalled that fear of firebombs in Little Rock's black community prompted whole neighborhoods to keep their lights out after dark. Marshall and Branton slept in the same room in the home of Daisy Bates, the head of the local NAACP. Branton joked that he would put Marshall's luggage on the bed nearest the window, but that Marshall would sneak into the room and move his gear to the bed farthest away.

By 1959, Marshall was known internationally as "Mr. Civil Rights," and in polls among black Americans he either beat or tied Martin Luther King Jr. for the title of most important black leader. Presidential candidate John F. Kennedy called to ask for campaign advice.

In 1960 Marshall traveled to Kenya and England, where he worked for three months to draft a constitution for the soon-to-be independent republic of Kenya—a constitution, ironically, that included safeguards for the rights of the white minority.

About this time Marshall began talking about joining a private law firm and "making money." But he was also intrigued by the idea of becoming a judge. As a young Baltimore lawyer, he had dreamed of becoming a local magistrate. Now the prospect of a federal judgeship on the appeals court level intrigued him.

After Kennedy won the election—a close victory that would have been impossible without overwhelming black support—pressure began to build to appoint blacks to important jobs. Marshall saw a vacancy on the U.S. Court of Appeals and let it be known that he wanted it. Attorney General Robert Kennedy fought the idea. He told his brother the political cost of getting Marshall, a man despised by southern segregationists, confirmed by the Senate would be too high.

Marshall recalls arguing face to face with Robert Kennedy, who was trying to get him to take a district court job instead: "He said, 'Well, you can't go on the Court of Appeals.' I said, 'There is an opening.' He said, 'But that's already filled.' I said, 'So?' He said, 'You don't seem to understand. It's this [the district court job] or nothing.' I said, 'I do understand. The trouble is that you are different from me. You don't know what it means, but all I've had in my life is nothing. It's not new to me. So goodbye.' And I walked out."

With pressure from black voters building, Louis Martin, the president's principal black adviser, convinced John Kennedy to ignore his brother's caution and nominate him for an appellate seat. But when Kennedy did send Marshall's name to the Senate Judiciary Committee, Marshall wasn't scheduled for confirmation hearings for eight months. In the book *Kennedy Justice,* Committee Chairman James Eastland of Mississippi is quoted as instructing Robert Kennedy to tell the president that Eastland would "give him the nigger" if Kennedy would nominate conservative judge Harold Cox of Mississippi to a district court. After Kennedy nominated Cox, Marshall was confirmed by the Senate.

In 1965, Lyndon Johnson named Marshall as his solicitor general. Representing the government before the Supreme Court, he twice volunteered information about illegal wiretaps that caused the court to throw out the government's case. He also argued one of the cases that resulted in the court voting to adopt the Miranda rule, which requires police to inform suspects of their rights.

Marshall's nomination to the Supreme Court in 1967, like his nomination to the Court of Appeals, was a difficult affair. Four senators on the Judiciary Committee, all southerners, opposed him—Strom Thurmond of South Carolina, James Eastland of Mississippi, John McClellan of Arkansas and Sam Ervin of North Carolina. An openly segregationist Thurmond asked Marshall 60 questions on constitutional history and the meaning of the 13th, 14th and 15th amendments. Nevertheless, Marshall was confirmed by a vote of 69 to 11.

Over the years, Johnson had discovered that he and Marshall shared an appreciation for fine bourbon and political talk. In January 1973, a week before he died, the former president telephoned Marshall and spoke about how dearly Marshall's appointment had cost him.

Marshall remembers that Johnson was "heartbroken" about his decision not to seek reelection in 1968. And while his withdrawal from the race is usually associated with the country's bitter division over the Vietnam War, Johnson told Marshall during that phone conversation that it was his appointment of blacks to high offices that destroyed his chances.

In a sealed 1977 interview, which was given to Columbia University on the condition that it be opened only with his permission and which was unsealed for the first time for this article, Marshall said that Johnson felt he couldn't win reelection because he had appointed a black to the Supreme Court. "He thought that moving me here was what killed him off," Marshall said in the interview.

"You mean that was more critical than the Vietnam War?" asked the Columbia University interviewer.

"He felt that they [Johnson's enemies] used the Vietnam War as the excuse," Marshall said. "He told me that as late as about a week before he died."

Marshall said he talked with Johnson the day he was confirmed to sit on the high court. Johnson said: "Well, congratulations, but the hell you caused me. Goddammit, I never went through so much hell . . ."

In their last phone conversation, Johnson told Marshall: "More and more I'm sure I'm right, and I'm going to write about it." Today the justice speaks of Johnson with passion. "I loved that man," he says.

When Marshall came to the Supreme Court in 1967, his first order of business was to ask Earl Warren what had happened 13 years earlier to the dissent Stanley Reed never wrote in the Brown case. Warren told him it would be best if he forgot about the subject and quit asking questions.

"Since I've been on this court," Marshall says, "I've been able to find out everything about the past but the Brown case. Nobody will talk."

Throughout his time on the court, Marshall has remained a strong advocate of individual rights. His position has not changed, but as his fellow justices came and went, Marshall began to find himself on the ideological left. When he joined the Warren court in 1967 he was in the middle, part of a liberal, activist majority. By the early 1970s, on Warren Burger's court, he was part of a four-man minority. On the conservative Rehnquist court, he is at the far left with only one compatriot, William Brennan.

He has remained a conscience on the bench, never wavering in his devotion to ending discrimination. In the midst of the benign 1987 celebration of the bicentennial of the Constitution, Marshall declared the document "defective" for failing to deal with slavery or the rights of women. When the nine members of the Supreme Court were invited to attend a reenactment of the Founding Fathers' deliberations, Marshall refused to go. Later he told an interviewer: "If you are going to do what you did 200 years ago, somebody is going to give me short pants and a tray so I can serve coffee."

And it was Marshall who earlier this year described the court's recent rulings limiting minority set-asides and the rights of employees to sue for discrimination as "a retrenching of the civil rights agenda" that has the nation running "full circle" back to the days before 1954.

In court conferences Marshall tells stories from his years in the segregated South. Though the stories are usually funny, several justices say they leave "an aftertaste," a reminder of the nation's dismally racist history. Even on the bench, Marshall works on his colleagues. Chief Justice William Rehnquist once asked why the government had to offer psychiatric care for suspects. Replied Marshall sarcastically: Why not skip everything, including the trial, and just "shoot them when you arrest them?"

"The only time Thurgood may make people uncomfortable," says Justice Brennan, "and perhaps it's when they should be made uncomfortable, is when he'll take off in a given case that he thinks . . . is another expression of racism." In conference, Brennan says, "there's no question about where Thurgood stands, no matter how uneasy it may make any of us." Marshall, Brennan continues, thinks that the court's recent record on civil rights "shows innocently or otherwise that there's still racism. I agree that there is. There is no question. But I will not accept the suggestion that it may also be true of our colleagues [on the court]."

Marshall does not call his colleagues racist, but he is frustrated by what he sees as their lack of awareness of the effects of racism on American society. "They need to stop looking for excuses not to enforce the 14th Amendment as it was intended to be enforced," he says.

He worries about the court sticking its nose into racial issues that seem already worked out: agreements on busing, school admissions, hiring and contract set-asides. "The only problem we've got now is everybody agrees to do it and the court moves in and says no. Now, that's what I object to . . . I don't see why it's the business of the court to come in over the top of all of that and say because of our majesty we say, 'No!' "

At times he becomes terribly frustrated about failing to change his colleagues' minds. "I mean, I didn't persuade them on affirmative action, did I? I didn't persuade them in the Bakke case [the decision outlawing a quota system for admission of blacks to a medical school]." And he is constantly aware of their innocence. "What do they know about Negroes?" he says. "You can't name one member of this court who knows anything about Negroes before he came to this court. Name me one. Sure, they went to school with one Negro in the class. Name me one who lives in a neighborhood with Negroes. They've got to get over that problem, and the only way they can do it is the person himself. What you have to do—white or black—you have to recognize that you have certain feelings about the other race, good or bad. And then get rid of them. But you can't get rid of them until you recognize them.

"There's not a white man in this country who can say, 'I never benefited by being white,' " said Marshall. "There's not a white man in the country who can say it. Maybe he doesn't know it. For example, all these graduates from Harvard [four of the current Supreme Court justices graduated from Harvard's law school]. They were one of 300 students, and there were two Negroes."

A principal benefit of having him on the court, Marshall believes, is that his fellow justices "know that whatever they do is going to be exposed."

Marshall blames former president Reagan for some of the backsliding on civil rights and has called him the worst president on civil rights in his lifetime. Asked recently if he had ever wanted to be chief justice, Marshall showed a spark of interest, but when it was suggested that Reagan could have appointed him, he said, "I wouldn't do the job of dog-catcher for Ronald Reagan."

Occasionally, Marshall's frustration with his colleagues over racial issues is on view in his dissents. After the court ruled against a contract set-aside plan for minorities in Richmond last year, Marshall wrote: "Racial classifications drawn for the purpose of remedying the effects of discrimination that itself was race-based have a highly pertinent basis: the tragic and indelible fact that discrimination against blacks and other racial minorities in this nation has pervaded our nation's history and continues to scar society."

The Bakke decision, which came down in 1978, particularly incensed Marshall. "I did a lot more research on it because I wanted to win it, and there were times when I almost won it," he says. "I still stand by every word I've said in my opinion."

Marshall wrote in dissent: "It must be remembered that during most of the past 200 years the Constitution as interpreted by this court did not prohibit the most ingenious and pervasive forms of discrimination against the Negro. Now, when a state acts to remedy the effects of that legacy of discrimination, I cannot believe that this same Constitution stands as a barrier. At every point from birth to death the impact of the past is reflected in the still disfavored position of the Negro. In light of the sorry history of discrimination and its devastating impact on the lives of Negroes, bringing the Negro into the mainstream of American life should be a state interest of the highest order."

Despite his strong support for affirmative action, Marshall does not believe there must be a permanent black slot on the Supreme Court. "I don't think there should be another 'Negro' justice," he says, when asked if he should be replaced by another black person. "I think the next justice should be a qualified person."

No Jewish justice, he notes, was named to replace Arthur Goldberg. "I would propose that they get a good person," he says. "The best person they can find, and I would hope that it would be a Negro. But a good one. Not a [William] Lucas," he adds, referring to the former

Michigan gubernatorial candidate whose nomination as the Bush administration's assistant attorney general for civil rights was rejected by the Senate.

Last year, at a congressional black caucus dinner in his honor, Marshall was saluted for a lifetime of service. When he stood to speak, he looked over the large crowd, then stared at a large, mounted photograph of himself that had been given to him. He pointed at the picture and said, "You know, what worries me about this thing, and I ask you to look at it—doesn't it look like a memorial? Well, I've got news for you that I will try to put in the best English available: I ain't dead yet!"

One of the more morbid aspects of the history of the Supreme Court is the constant discussion of the justices' ages and how much longer they will be able to serve. Presidents are forever eager to influence the balance of the court by making as many appointments during their terms as possible. Marshall has never been pleased by the death watch, but he's used to it; for two decades, he has been dealing with those who are anxious to see him replaced.

In 1970, when he was in Bethesda Naval Hospital with pneumonia, a doctor walked into his room one afternoon and informed him that President Nixon had asked for his medical reports. The president apparently wanted to see how close Marshall was to death and thus how close the Republicans were to being able to name a conservative successor. Marshall told the doctor he could send the medical records to Nixon but only with two words written on the outside of the folder. The doctor agreed. Then Marshall wrote on the folder in large black script: "NOT YET!"

He has even heard the same morbid questions from Democrats. In 1979, he says, two White House aides called him and suggested that he quickly quit the court so President Jimmy Carter could name a new justice. The aides reminded Marshall of his heart attack, his difficulties with blood clots and his bouts of pneumonia. They painted a sad picture of the possible replacements that a Republican like Ronald Reagan might select for the court. The justice slammed the phone down. But that didn't stop it.

Reporters started calling day and night about his imminent resignation. One said he had confirmed that the justice had had a pacemaker installed and that was why he was stepping down. No, said an exasperated Cecilia Marshall, the judge does not have a pacemaker. When another reporter called to say she *knew* Marshall had resigned, his wife said, "You reporters know more about my husband than I do—I only sleep with him." Then there was a false radio report that Marshall had died, prompting Warren Burger to have his secretary call Cecilia and urge her to remain calm. "I said, 'Well, I'm very calm because he's there in the living room having his dinner.' "

These days Thurgood Marshall is straightforward about how soon he will retire. "I have a lifetime appointment and I intend to serve it," he says. "I expect to die at 110, shot by a jealous husband."

Constance Baker Motley is a federal judge for the United States Southern District of New York. She worked closely with Thurgood Marshall from 1945–1961 in the NAACP Legal Defense and Education Fund, Inc. In this essay, My Personal Debt to Thurgood Marshall, *written for the* Yale Law Journal *(November 1991), Judge Motley describes working with Marshall and his impact on her career.*

MY PERSONAL DEBT TO THURGOOD MARSHALL

Constance Baker Motley

NOW THAT THURGOOD MARSHALL HAS ANNOUNCED HIS DECISION TO RETIRE as a Justice of the Supreme Court, assessments of his life and contributions to the development of American constitutional law are beginning to pour in and, even in this conservative climate, they are all favorable. When viewed against the background of American history over the past half century, the totality of his contributions to the restructuring of American society has rendered him larger than life. However, I fear that his personal, unique contributions to the advancement of women in the law—a profession once totally dominated by men—may be lost in the review of the multitude of events and judicial opinions which now compose his life. My tribute acknowledges my personal debt to Thurgood Marshall for aiding my career at a time when nobody was hiring women lawyers.

My first job interview was an accurate sign of the times. It was October 1945. World War II had abruptly ended a few months earlier, and I was in my final year at Columbia Law School. The women in my class had high hopes but few offers. I learned from my classmates that a small midtown firm was looking to hire a recent graduate. When I appeared for my interview, a balding, middle-aged white male appeared at a door leading to the reception room where I was standing.

The receptionist had not even asked me to have a seat. Even after the door to the reception room quickly closed, she still did not invite me to sit down. She knew as well as I that the interview was over.

When I returned to school, another classmate, an African-American male from North Carolina, Herman Taylor, told me about a law clerk vacancy at the NAACP Legal Defense and Educational Fund, Inc. (the Inc. Fund). I hurried down to the Inc. Fund offices on lower Fifth Avenue for an interview, and Thurgood Marshall hired me on the spot. Marshall told me about his admiration for African-American women who had the courage to enter the legal profession. He also told me about Florence Lucas, an African-American woman who was practicing in Queens and who had put herself through law school by working in a laundry at night. When I finished Columbia Law School in June 1946, Marshall received Board approval to hire a woman lawyer. I was a member of the Inc. Fund staff until 1965.

Thurgood Marshall had no qualms about women being given equal employment opportunities. His mother was a school teacher and his father was a dining car steward. Over the years, he told me about every successful African-American woman he encountered. Marshall was born and grew up in America at a time when nobody had to tell him that African-American males were on the bottom rung of the ladder in every conceivable professional endeavor and that African-American women were not even on the ladder.

When I joined the staff of the Inc. Fund as a clerk in 1945 it was a fledgling public interest law firm with two full-time lawyers in addition to Marshall, one part-time lawyer, and three secretaries. The annual budget was about $30,000. The law library consisted of a single set of Supreme Court Reports. Since my main responsibilities included research and writing, and we had no library facilities, Marshall suggested that I join the New York City Bar Association (the Association) so that I could use its law library. After securing membership, I presented myself at the front door of the Association on 44th Street in Manhattan. When I got there I saw the "gate keeper" standing at his desk immediately inside the door. He was an elderly white man with snow-white hair who appeared to be one year older than God. He was talking with an Association lawyer. When I approached the desk, the "gate keeper" continued his conversation and never even looked at me. The "gate keeper" obviously assumed that I was a mere messenger. The one or two other women members of the Association at that time had joined so recently that a women's rest room had not yet been provided.

When the "gate keeper" finally addressed me an embarrassing two minutes or so later, he said politely, "May I help you," with a quick motion of his head in my direction. When I replied that I wanted to use the library, the "gate keeper," again without looking in my direction, said, "You must be a member." When I assured him that I was a member, he finally ceased his conversation and turned his head fully in my direction for the first time. As if he had seen a ghost, he shouted in disbelief, "*You a member* of this Association." "Yes," I replied. "What is your name," was his retort. "Mrs. Motley," I said, guarding against what all African-American women guarded against in those days. When he found my name on the membership list, he exclaimed, "Oh, right this way, *Constance.*" This story is one of the many stories in Marshall's "Stories Repertoire." The Association, forty years later, now has its first African-American president.

Around 1948, Marshall sent me to Baltimore to sit in on a case that was being tried by the founder of the Inc. Fund and Thurgood Marshall's mentor, the great Charles Hamilton Houston. Houston was the Dean of Howard Law School when Thurgood Marshall studied there. In the case I was watching, Houston was representing a black woman against the University of Maryland's School of Nursing. Marshall wanted me to learn from the master. To this day I have never seen a better prepared trial lawyer. Houston had a notebook in which every question he was going to ask was written out. His advice to me was: "Never ask a question which you have not previously considered." Every exhibit he was going to introduce was carefully laid out on a table. He allowed me to sit next to him at the counsel's table so that I could see and hear every move he made.

As part of my early training, Thurgood Marshall accompanied me to two trials. One of these trials, which was before the Commissioner of Education for the State of New York, involved segregated schools in Hempstead in 1949. (Hempstead now has an African-American mayor.) The other trial was a contempt hearing against the Board of Trustees of the University of Alabama. During the course of that hearing, we stayed in the Birmingham home of local attorney Arthur Shores. His home had been bombed on at least fifteen occasions. (Birmingham now has an African-American mayor.) At night we were guarded by African-American men with machine guns, and during the day others carrying handguns escorted us to and from court.

Among the better known cases that I personally tried were those against the Universities of Mississippi, Georgia, and Alabama, and

Clemson College in South Carolina. As a result, James Meredith, the plaintiff in the University of Mississippi case, became a national hero in 1962. Charlene Hunter Gault and Hamilton Holmes, the plaintiffs in the University of Georgia case, brought Georgia kicking and screaming into the twentieth century in 1961. George Wallace and Alabama finally gave up massive resistance to desegregation in 1963. And now South Carolina brags about Harvey Gantt, the plaintiff in the Clemson College case in 1962, who became mayor of Charlotte and recently ran unsuccessfully against Jesse Helms for the United States Senate. During my career with the Inc. Fund, I participated in civil rights cases in federal courts in eleven states and the District of Columbia. Out of the ten cases I argued before the United States Supreme Court, I won nine. One particularly busy day in 1962, I argued four cases on appeal in the Fifth Circuit.

By the time I left the Inc. Fund in February 1965 to become the first woman President of the Borough of Manhattan, I was one of the best known civil rights lawyers in the country. A year earlier I became the first African-American woman and the second woman ever elected to the New York State Senate. In 1965, there were still not very many women who had actually tried cases as the chief counsel. You could count on one hand the number of women who had argued a case before the United States Supreme Court. When I first joined the Marshall team in 1945, women lawyers were a rarity in most courthouses and virtually unheard of outside New York City. I remember that when Thurgood Marshall sent me to Jackson, Mississippi, in 1949 to assist Robert Carter with a case involving the equalization of "Negro" teachers' salaries, the whole town turned out to see the "Nigra" lawyers from New York—one of whom was a woman.

Beginning in 1946, when Thurgood Marshall argued the case striking down segregation on interstate buses, *Morgan* v. *Virginia*, he allowed me to accompany him to virtually every case he argued, including *Brown* v. *Board of Education*, the *School Desegregation Cases*. Since the Nation's Capital was a racially segregated town, I usually ended up staying at a so-called "Negro" hotel, which was no more than a private rooming house in a "Negro" residential area. We stayed in such hotels until 1964 when the Congress reenacted the Civil Rights Act of 1875, making it possible for us to stay in white hotels and eat in white restaurants. The *Restrictive Covenant Cases* were argued in 1947. The following year, *Spiuel* v. *University of Oklahoma* which involved the admission of a "Negro" woman to the law school of the University of Oklahoma, was argued. In 1949, *Sweatt* v. *Painter* resulted in the admission of Heman Sweatt to the University of Texas Law School. Finally, in 1952, when the *School Desegregation Cases* were argued in the Supreme Court for the first time, Marshall moved for my admission to the Supreme Court Bar.

My son was born in May 1952. Although the policy at the NAACP—of which the Inc. Fund was part in those days—was to have women take a leave of absence after six months of pregnancy, Marshall simply ignored the pressure brought on him to have me go on leave after six months. I worked until one week before my son arrived. I was the only professional woman employed by the NAACP or the Inc. Fund at that time. All the other women were clerical or semi-professionals and, if pregnant, had left long before the ninth month. I set a new standard for women with Marshall's tacit approval. Thus, there was a big smile on my face when I read Marshall's opinion for the court on pregnancy leaves and Title VII in *California Federal Savings and Loan* v. *Guerra.*

During his career with the Inc. Fund, Thurgood Marshall argued or participated in about thirty-two cases before the Supreme Court. He was involved in a much greater number of lower court cases. Marshall also had an invaluable training program for lawyers who worked for him. Prior to each Supreme Court argument, he invariably practiced before a panel of Howard Law School faculty members. Not only did Marshall's staff members attend these moot court sessions, but on occasion we participated as well. In addition, we were included in the preparation of cases. All of Marshall's major cases before the Supreme Court benefitted from weeks of discussions with experts and academics in constitutional law. For the *School Desegregation Cases*, these conferences took place over a two-year period and included historians, sociologists, and psychologists.

In January 1966, President Johnson submitted my name to the United States Senate for its "Advice and Consent" to my nomination as a United States District Judge. At the time, only two other women were federal district judges: Sarah Hughes in Texas, who swore in Johnson after Kennedy was assassinated in 1963, and Bonita Matthews in the District of Columbia. Florence Allen, the first woman federal judge, was then on the Court of Appeals for the Sixth Circuit. President Johnson had initially submitted my name for a seat on the Court of Appeals for the Second Circuit, but the opposition to my appointment was so great, apparently because I was a woman, that Johnson had to withdraw my name. I remember how stunned both Johnson and Marshall were by the strength and intensity of the opposition. When I went to Washington for the announcement of my appointment, Johnson told me that the first opening in the Supreme Court would go to Thurgood Marshall. At the time, Marshall was the Solicitor General of the United States. Johnson stepped down in 1968, but not before appointing Thurgood Marshall to the Supreme Court.

President Johnson also told me that Ramsey Clark, who was then the Attorney General of the United States, was the first person to bring me to his attention. He said that Clark was in the Supreme Court one day when I argued a case. After the argument Clark went directly to the White House and urged Johnson to appoint me to the bench. Thurgood Marshall held my hand during the entire process. When my name finally reached the Senate floor in August 1966, Senator Eastland of Mississippi, who headed the Judiciary Committee, led the opposition. He had held up my nomination as well as the nomination of every other African-American appointed to the federal bench during the sixties, including Marshall's nomination to the Second Circuit in 1962 and his nomination to the Supreme Court in 1968. I was finally confirmed by the Senate in August 1966 and became the first African-American woman appointed to the federal bench. Marshall came to my swearing in as a district court judge.

When Marshall was appointed to the Second Circuit, there was not a single African-American employee in the United States Courthouse in Manhattan except for the elevator operators. Thurgood Marshall served as the only African-American judge in that courthouse from 1961 to 1965. Before his appointment to the bench, Thurgood Marshall had spent his entire life in the African-American Community, so to speak, so he knew how lonely I would be, with the double handicap of being a woman and black. At the time of my appointment, there were only about seven other African-Americans who had been appointed to the federal bench. It was not until 1970 that the United States Attorney's Office for the Southern District of New York decided that women were as capable as men at handling federal criminal prosecutions. Shira Neiman, who was hired in 1970, was the first woman in the Criminal Division. Before that, Patricia Hynes, who worked in the Civil Division, was the only woman in the United States Attorney's Office in the Southern District.

When I was introduced as a new judge at a Second Circuit Judicial Conference, the master of ceremonies said, "And now I want to introduce Connie Motley who is doing such a good job on the District

Court." In contrast, everyone else was introduced with a full blown curriculum vitae. Simiarly, in 1968 when I was introduced by the chairman of the Seminar for New Federal Judges, my introduction went as follows: "Judge Motley has served on the Board of United Church Women and the Board of Trustees of the Y.W.C.A." Former Supreme Court Justice Tom Clark, who was helping to chair the meeting, was so astounded by this introduction that he asked the master of ceremonies to let him have the microphone. Clark then told the assembled new judges about the ten cases I had argued before him when he was still on the bench. Later Justice Clark told me about the disparagement of Shirley Hofstedler, who had just been named by President Carter to the Ninth Circuit, by a group of men at the golf course. The thing which amazed him was that none of the judges had ever met Shirley Hofstedler. One of the most critical lessons I learned from my mentor, Thurgood Marshall, was to laugh off these ludicrous, antifeminist affronts which were regularly hurled in my direction. Eventually, they all ended up in Marshall's "Stories Repertoire."

After his appointment to the Supreme Court, I saw Thurgood Marshall at least once a year at the Second Circuit Judicial Conference, since he was our Circuit Justice. He pushed unsuccessfully for my appointment to Second Circuit Court Committees. He had a great big smile on his face when I became the Chief Judge of our court and thus appointed the members of all of our twenty-four court committees at the district court level.

Now I am a Senior United States District Judge, having taken senior status on October 1, 1986. I was the Chief Judge of our court, the largest federal trial court in the country, from June 1, 1982 until October 1, 1986. Our full complement was twenty-seven judges. Only one other woman had ever served as a chief judge of a federal district court prior to myself. I was the only woman on our court until June 1978, when Mary Johnson Lowe, another African-American woman, was appointed by President Carter. Carter appointed about forty women to the federal bench during his term. One of Thurgood Marshall's biggest disappointments is that I never was elevated to the Court of Appeals. The opposition to me as a woman and a "liberal" has remained. As Gabe Pressman said when I was sworn in to the District Court: "She just made it, because now the tide has turned."

If it had not been for Thurgood Marshall, no one would ever have heard of Constance Baker Motley.

Paul Gewirtz, now a professor of law at Yale University, clerked for Thurgood Marshall during the 1971 term. In this essay, which originally appeared in The Yale Law Journal *(November 1991), Professor Gewirtz pays tribute to Marshall's accomplishments as a lawyer and judge and provides insight into his wonderfully human character.*

THURGOOD MARSHALL
Paul Gewirtz

THURGOOD MARSHALL'S LIFE AS A CIVIL RIGHTS LAWYER INSPIRED MY decision to go to law school, so it was the greatest of dreams fulfilled when I came to work as his law clerk at the Supreme Court. Now, as he leaves the Court, it is an honor to mark his retirement in these pages.

Marshall is an extraordinary figure in American legal history. He has lived many lives—indeed, while others marvel over his professional durability at the age of eighty-three, I actually think of him as having compressed more than a hundred years of living into that time span. He was the country's greatest civil rights lawyer during the greatest period for civil rights advances in our history, and in that role he lived a life of relentless intensity and danger, and one of transforming achievement. He was a United States Court of Appeals Judge. He was Solicitor General of the United States (his favorite job, he has often said with complete seriousness—an advocate's job in which he spoke for "the United States," not simply a faction or insurgent part of the whole). Finally, he became a Justice on the Supreme Court of the United States during one of its most dramatic periods of change. While he was a top government official for much of this time—an insider and a colleague of the advantaged—he spent his entire career trying to protect the disadvantaged and identifying with them.

The centerpiece of his public life is and always will be *Brown* v. *Board of Education*. Marshall did not win *Brown* alone, and never claimed to have done so, but he was the guiding force and justly became the symbol of the triumph. Much has been written about the long litigation campaign leading to the Supreme Court's unanimous decision in *Brown*. But one aspect of Marshall's achievement is rarely emphasized: to do what he did required an heroic imagination. He grew up in a ruthlessly discriminatory world—a world in which segregation of the races was pervasive and taken for granted, where lynching was common, where the black man's inherent inferiority was proclaimed widely and wantonly. Thurgood Marshall had the capacity to imagine a radically different world, the imaginative capacity to believe that such a world was possible, the strength to sustain that image in the mind's eye and the heart's longing, and the courage and ability to make that imagined world real. The predicate for the great achievement of *Brown* was to imagine something better than the present—to resist the acquiescence, passivity, fear, and accommodation that overcome so many, to defy an insistent reality with imagination and then to fight for what was imagined.

Brown changed the world. And because of that, Thurgood Marshall's life stands for the idea that law can change the world and that the Supreme Court can be a powerful force in fulfilling our best public values. That was what drew me to the law, and what has drawn so many others. *Brown*, then, is not just a case; its importance cannot be assessed just by totalling up what ending enforced school segregation may have accomplished. Its importance cannot be assessed even by recognizing that it gave broad legitimacy to the modern political struggle for racial equality. Its broadest importance is its embodiment of a conception of law and of the courts.

The naming of Thurgood Marshall to the Supreme Court, therefore, was an act of the greatest importance. His becoming a part of the Court showed how much he had changed the world—in many ways it was the most striking indication of the transformation he had wrought. For all of his imaginative heroism, it is hard to believe that in the 1930's, '40's and '50's Marshall ever imagined that he might someday sit on the Court, be more than an insurgent advocate waiting for others—the Justices—to vindicate him. He created the world that made his own ultimate personal triumph possible. He would now share the power to decide. His becoming a Justice became part of what *Brown* meant.

The perspective he brought to the Court was unique. The other Justices had diverse life experiences, and many were major public figures in their own right. But Marshall brought something distinctive to the Court. The distinctiveness was not simply that he was the first black to sit on the Court, but that he had spent much of his professional life working among the oppressed and the insurgent. To be sure, by the time Marshall came to the Supreme Court he knew more Presidents and Congressmen than most Justices, and he knew their needs and their weaknesses; indeed, they were the subject of many of his best stories. But Marshall also knew the other side of the tracks, not simply as an observer but as one who had called it home; and he always thought of himself as an activist on its behalf. He brought to the Court a sense of how the world worked, and how it worked against those at the bottom. He knew what police stations were like, what rural Southern life was like, what the New York streets were like, what trial courts were like, what hard-nosed local political campaigns were like, what death sentences were like, and what being black in America was like—and he knew what it felt like to be at risk as a human being. Most importantly, perhaps, he knew the difference that law could make in all those places. None of his experiences with the harshness of life made him bitter or cynical about law's possibilities. He knew well how law could trample individuals, but he remained faithful to an ideal of what it could do to protect individuals.

Marshall is, as Louis Pollak once called him, "larger-than-life." In his presence one thinks: This man has genuinely lived. That is partly because of what one knows of him, partly from the vast and shifting fields of reference in his fecund supply of stories, and partly from the earned aura given off by someone who has experienced life especially intensely. For all of that, he is utterly human. He is earthy, compassionate, determined, funny, and proud. He does not act like someone taken with his own legend—indeed, at times he seems to defy people's expectations of who he is. He is outwardly unsentimental. He never coddled his law clerks, and almost never praised them. Yet he is in fact a man of strong sentiment and loyalty. The day after I argued my first Supreme Court case I was back at home in my study reading when the phone rang. "Paul, it's Thurgood Marshall. I just wanted to tell you that you were really great yesterday and that I was so proud of you." My fantasies about arguing before the Court—and there were many—had not included such a moment. "Now, remember, that doesn't mean you're going to win," he quickly added, "but I just wanted you to know you did a great job."

He came to the Court during what seemed the heyday of the Warren

Court, but the Court's membership rapidly changed. He wrote many important majority opinions, but soon found himself a frequent dissenter from a considerable portion of the Court's work. He found that discouraging, but in some sense it was his more accustomed position. While he would have devoutly wished to have ended his career as a comfortable member of the Court's majority, his role as dissenter was perhaps more authentic for him, or at least more continuous with what had come before.

For me at least, it is his dissents that sound with the greatest power and resonance, whether or not one agrees with their ultimate conclusions. I particularly have in mind his dissent in *San Antonio Independent School* v. *Rodriguez*, the case that marked the true end of the Warren Court, and perhaps most especially his dissent in *Milliken* v. *Bradley*, in which the Court rejected the appropriateness of most interdistrict relief in school desegregation cases. The *Milliken* dissent emerged from the core of Marshall's pre-Court experience and ended with a sad and angry prophecy:

> Desegregation is not and was never expected to be an easy task. Racial attitudes ingrained in our Nation's childhood and adolescence are not quickly thrown aside in its middle years. But just as the inconvenience of some cannot be allowed to stand in the way of the rights of others, so public opposition, no matter how strident, cannot be permitted to divert this Court from the enforcement of the constitutional principles at issue in this case. Today's holding, I fear, is more a reflection of a perceived public mood that we have gone far enough in enforcing the Constitution's guarantee of equal justice than it is the product of neutral principles of law. In the short run, it may seem to be the easier course to allow our great metropolitan areas to be divided up each into two cities —one white, the other black—but it is a course, I predict, our people will ultimately regret. I dissent.

Justice Marshall's views evolved while he was on the Court. Always a patriot, he nevertheless became more skeptical of the government's professed need to promote national interests by restricting individual liberty. He had a strong distaste for flag burners and others who attacked our country, but he disciplined that distaste and supported their First Amendment claims, as he concluded the Constitution required him to do.

Always an egalitarian on racial matters, he broadened his own understanding of the meaning of equality to other social groups. Interestingly, when affirmative action issues first started to emerge in bold relief, I can recall, he was very uneasy with race-conscious hiring, admissions, and set-asides as a corrective for past discrimination. In time, he became their most passionate defender on the Court. He came to that position, I think, in much the same way many others did: reluctantly, through a gradually developed judgment that, against the backdrop of centuries of oppression, colorblind measures would not work, or at least not work fast enough, to achieve a significantly greater inclusion of minorities in mainstream American life. Those who have tried to quote back at the Justice his endorsement of colorblind remedies at the time of *Brown* ignore the fact that judges continue to change while in office, and that the life revealed in cases continues a judge's education.

The departure of Justice Marshall, of course, is not just the end of a great man's career on the Court, but also the end of a large chapter in the Court's history, the breaking of the final link to the Warren Court. At the end, Justice Marshall was an isolated figure on the Court, not only deprived of majorities in the cases that mattered most to him, but deprived even of the shared memories and dissenting faith provided by Justice Brennan. For that reason, his departure produced in many an elegiac mood that Justice Brennan's departure had not. Linda Greenhouse of *The New York Times*, writing on a daily deadline, captured that sense exactly:

> Thurgood Marshall . . . knows the Court's potential as an instrument for social change better than almost anyone who has ever served there. Even in advanced age, in evident anger and sorrow, his continued presence on the bench made him a powerful symbol of the era when the Court demonstrated that potential to a remarkable degree. His departure crystallizes a moment when a historic tide, long in the ebbing, has finally run out and a new history of uncertain dimension has begun to unfold.

In law, of course, the link to the past is never fully cut because those who come before always provide some authority for those who come after. History itself is authority, and history can never be permanently erased. The central legal strategy leading up to *Brown*, like the central political strategy of figures such as Martin Luther King, Jr., was to invoke Americans' historic ideals as the basis for insisting that America's racial practices had to change. We, after all, were a country conceived with the proclamation that all men are created equal, and we have often reproclaimed that faith. *Brown* did not embody some radical new principle, but rather was seen as the fulfillment of promises made a century or two earlier in the Declaration of Independence, in the Fourteenth Amendment, and in cases like *Strauder* v. *West Virginia*, whose sweeping rationale had been ignored in subsequent decisions. The appeal in *Brown* was not to ideas outside the central American tradition, but to the core of that intellectual tradition itself. That is why Thurgood Marshall's intuitively patriotic response to flag burning or Communists should never have surprised me: the premise of the great litigation campaign leading up to *Brown* was that what blacks had to work with, their best hope, was America's own ideals, the symbols of its democratic faith.

The Justice's dissents of the past two decades, progressively harsher and more numerous, also appealed to the country's historic ideals. But they were also appeals to the future—at least implicitly a beacon to some later day when the Court might change and perhaps follow the alternative path laid out by today's dissent.

As the new Court consolidates its membership and direction, the great historic question is this: A hundred years from now, will the Warren Court be seen as a parenthesis in the history of the Court—an essentially aberrant deflection from the true path of the Court's development? Or will the newly emergent late twentieth century Court itself be seen as the parenthesis, the aberrant deflection? There is, of course, no way to know; "[t]here is no pulling open the buds to see what the blossom will be." There may, in fact, be no ultimate answer. But if the Warren Court is the parenthesis, Marshall's dissents will be ignored; if the Rehnquist Court proves to be the aberration, then Marshall's dissents will be rediscovered and will provide authority and guidance for the future. Dissenters (whether the Marshalls or the Scalias) hope to become like Holmes and Brandeis—prophets vindicated by the future, dissenters who became great prophets because (indeed, only because) they were vindicated by history.

If we can predict anything about our constitutional future, though, we know that Thurgood Marshall is indelibly impressed upon it. Perhaps more clearly than any other recent member of the Court, he is an historic figure. He fundamentally changed our world for the better, which can be said of very very few lawyers. And he deservedly has become a symbol of America's possibilities—the possibility that we can redeem our terrible racial past, that our constitutional ideals are part of our strength as a nation, and that a life in the law can be a life of the largest purpose and achievement.

In this essay written for the American Bar Association Journal *(September 1991 issue), attorney Glen Darbyshire recalls his clerkship under Associate Justice Marshall and offers his insights into the man as well as the attorney.*

Clerking for Justice Marshall

PURELY BY COINCIDENCE, I TELEPHONED JUSTICE MARSHALL'S CHAMBERS at midday on June 27 to convey my decision to leave big-firm practice in Atlanta and move farther south to Savannah. His longtime secretary, Mrs. McHale, had just returned from the White House to deliver a letter announcing the justice's retirement from the Court.

I was completely unprepared for this development, and, when Mrs. McHale put me through to him, I could only stammer on about what a great contribution he had made to this country as a lawyer and judge, and how grateful I was to have had the opportunity to serve as one of his law clerks for a year.

"The Judge" (as he insists that his law clerks call him in lieu of "Mr. Justice") would listen to none of this, and instead fondly recalled his experiences in the '30s and '40s trying criminal and civil rights cases in the low country regions of Georgia and South Carolina.

Savannah would be a "beautiful city" in which to practice law and raise a family, he said, noting that he had begun private practice in his hometown, Baltimore, after completing law school in the midst of the Depression. Justice Marshall needled me for being "tired of the money," reminded me to volunteer for pro bono cases, and ended our conversation, as he always has, with the reminder that I had come to clerk in Washington from the rural South: "Come see me, *boy.*"

This was vintage Marshall. Lacking the slightest pretension and being uncomfortable with any display of adulation, he invariably will find a humorous way to deflect praise and change the subject to one he finds more important. In fact, of all the awards and honors Marshall has received through the years, only one item can be found in his office that suggests pride in his accomplishments. On his desk rests a small block of plastic like those collected by corporate lawyers to commemorate their major deals.

But this memento does not contain a miniature shareholder prospectus. Inside is a reproduction of the front page of *The New York Times* announcing the Supreme Court's 1954 decision in *Brown* v. *Board of Education*. Marshall is pictured, with other lawyers who assisted him in that case, standing on the marble steps in front of the Court.

Marshall's limited interest in gratuitous praise does not discriminate: He doles it out as rarely as he allows himself to receive it. The closest my three co-clerks and I ever came to receiving an outright compliment followed publication of his 1987 speech on the bicentennial of the Constitution. He initially had decided against participating in the celebration, bristling in particular at a suggestion that the Supreme Court convene at Independence Hall in Philadelphia where, he said, he only would attend "wearing breeches and serving tea."

Marshall eventually decided, however, to give a short speech calling attention to the failure of the original document to abolish slavery and enfranchise women and Afro-Americans. The collaborative efforts of his law clerks produced a draft that pleased him, and the speech received wide media attention. On the morning after newspaper coverage of the speech, he lumbered in through our office and said, "Hey, hey, front page." Our eyes lit up with pride, as he continued down a hall and through his secretary's office and the library. Well into his office, he added, in a voice just loud enough for us to hear, "No picture."

Without such moments, the job of clerking would have produced mostly memories of a relentless flow of paper and long days of reading briefs and typing memoranda. Marshall was the only justice who had his law clerks prepare a memorandum analyzing every petition for certiorari and response filed in the Court—on average more than 100 petitions were filed each week. In addition, a bench memorandum would be prepared for each of the approximately 150 cases granted review, and after oral argument there would be majority, concurring and dissenting opinions to draft.

Given Marshall's view that the death penalty is unconstitutional in every case, emergency applications for stays of execution received careful attention. Copies of the briefs filed in the lower courts would come in by telefax while those courts considered the applications, but it was often well into the night when a formal application would be filed in the Supreme Court.

Other justices might circulate a memorandum before leaving for the day, indicating how they would vote unless new arguments were raised, but Marshall insisted that a law clerk call him at home after the application had been filed so that he could consider the merits and dictate a memorandum conveying his vote. On more than one occasion he was rousted from bed well past midnight by a law clerk's call. He would allow an explanation of the arguments, to be followed each time by his ringing pronouncement: "I *always* vote to grant the stay (click)."

Marshall judged from an instinct honed by his experiences as a lawyer and not from an encyclopedic knowledge of legal technicalities. In our afternoon conferences, he would relate events he had encountered in practice that gave insight to his views on each of the cases to be decided. He never allowed academic theories to restrict his consideration of bare facts, and his questions from the bench were often brutally blunt.

He told us once in chambers how he appreciated most the lawyers whose arguments would lead to a point just short of the desired conclusion, leaving the judges to make the final connection, instead of lawyers who simply reiterated the conclusion again and again. He also joked about how in practice he would place important arguments in footnotes of his briefs, because he knew the law clerks would point them out in an attempt to impress their judge. Anecdotes like these kept us humble.

Perhaps more than any other justice, he gave his law clerks creative freedom in drafting opinions. He would define the central focus and rationale and then allow the clerks to organize the arguments consistent with his prior opinions.

Nonetheless, his review of draft opinions could be exacting. He edited with a thick blue pencil that could, with a single stroke, obliterate pretentious or ineffective wording. He would not tolerate a long opinion if it could be avoided. His law clerks, before submitting drafts to him, followed a detailed procedure for reviewing and editing them for substantive or grammatical errors—all in a determined effort to avoid the blue pencil.

Marshall is a big man. More than six-feet tall, with well over 200 pounds on a barrel-chested frame, he gives a commanding presence, even when attired in the unassuming, off-the-rack style suits he has collected over the last few decades. He once grumbled mightily about having to put on a tuxedo for a formal dinner at the Court during our clerkship, but the effect was stunning. His arms are long and his hands are big and thick. A handshake with his arm on your shoulder has a crushing effect.

Had he not become a lawyer, he may have dreamed wistfully of becoming a prize fighter; he thoroughly enjoys recounting the late-night parties he attended in Harlem with Joe Louis and entourage. His combative spirit is evident in the tone and strength of his dissents, of which he once declared: "I enjoy the fight. I agree with the old saying, 'I love peace, but I adore a riot.' You've got to be angry to write a dissent."

Marshall's heart is as big as his frame. He has a profound sense of humanity that is rooted in his years of living with and litigating on behalf of the disposed and downtrodden. Wherever he went, he imbibed the local culture—its entertainment, food and drink. He told us of shark meat sun-dried on clotheslines in South Carolina, moonshine in Appalachia, and steak tartar in Manhattan. He can dictate from memory the precise steps for making Maryland she-crab soup. He has been known to place small wagers at the roulette and blackjack tables in Atlantic City, and, if he makes any money, he never tells.

Marshall is, moreover, a consummate storyteller, as we first learned at an informal cocktail party of justices and law clerks when the term began. Twenty minutes into the affair, nearly half of the clerks were gathered around him listening to raucous tales while the rest of us discussed our law schools and geographic origins with other justices.

Marshall often reminisced about his early days as a sole practitioner in Baltimore, explaining how, when relief was needed from the pressures of work, he would break for lunch and visit the local aquarium. There he would watch the fish swim in lazy circles without a care in the world. In 1965, he was quoted as describing his philosophy on living this way: "I intend to wear life like a very loose garment and never worry about nothin'." This exuberance has survived his tenure on the Court.

Not that he lacks an irascible streak. His sharp criticisms of politicians have been particularly well-publicized, and his targets have included civil rights opponents and certain proponents alike. Concerns about his health may have contributed to an occasional cantankerous episode, but more often as not they became a source of humor. For example, while hospitalized in the early 1970s, he responded to President Nixon's request for copies of his medical records by authorizing their release, but only after first writing in bold letters on the cover of the file: "Not yet!"

During our clerkship, on doctors' orders, he and Justice Powell would take daily walks around the exterior hallway of the Court, which essentially amounted to indoor walks around the block. Justice Powell would walk in one direction and Marshall in the other. Occasionally, their walks would overlap and they would pass in front of our office. Marshall's mood could always be gauged from his responses to Powell's predictable "Good morning, Thurgood." These ranged from a curt "What's so good about it?" to a jovial "I'm gaining on you."

Marshall would become especially cantankerous when he perceived an approach that singled him out as an Afro-American. Though it is historical fact that many of his accomplishments were "firsts" for black America, he insists that such distinctions are irrelevant.

After all, when he was appointed to the Supreme Court in 1967, there were few if any lawyers who, regardless of race, could match his 29 winning arguments before the Court, much less his other contributions as a lawyer for the NAACP, a circuit judge, and then solicitor general. Still, he resented being singled out for his views as a spokesman for black America. When a reporter called to ask what he planned to do on the newly designated national holiday honoring Martin Luther King Jr., he bellowed, "The same damn thing I do on every holiday—stay home." And he slammed the phone down on its hook in disgust.

Marshall often has repeated the words of an old Pullman porter who, like himself, had travelled all over the United States, but had never been any place "where he had to hold his hand up in front of his eyes" to remember that he was a man of color.

But Marshall did discover such a place when he travelled to Kenya as an American representative for the celebration of that country's independence in 1963 and in 1978 at the death of its first president, Jomo Kenyatta. Marshall had participated in an international conference in 1960 that drafted a constitution for the new republic, and he had come to know Kenyatta as a friend. Marshall is an honorary Kikuyu tribal chief. In his office a ceremonial animal-skin cape drapes a chair, and a large, colorful replica of the official seal of Kenya hangs prominently over the mantel.

He loves to tell how he patiently explained the due process and taking clauses of the new Kenyan constitution to Masai tribesmen, who to this day have resisted modern trends and continue to live and herd their livestock among the wild animals of Kenya's southern plains. After his detailed assurances that access to their grazing lands could not be taken by the new government without compensation, the Masai declared: "If they come, we will kill them." Marshall exclaimed: "Now, you've got it!"

His African political ties are extensive, and for years he was included among the dignitaries invited to meet with African heads of state when they visited the United States. However, this practice was curtailed without explanation during the Reagan administration at a time when, ironically, African leaders were coming to America seeking foreign aid under gathering clouds of alleged human rights violations. Marshall never complained about being excluded, but the absence of his credible voice on such issues was apparent.

The contributions of Marshall to the legal profession and to this country have made him a living legend. The clerkship experience offered to those fortunate enough to work for him the opportunity to see that he is indeed very human—complex, temperamental and full of life.

He instilled in his clerks an abiding respect for the Constitution and its amendments protecting individual freedoms and human rights, and for the Court as an institution capable of ensuring that the poor and powerless are not neglected or treated unfairly. Having taken on unpopular causes long before they became fashionable, he has never wavered in his view of the lawyer's role: "You either work to improve society, or you become a parasite on it."

It has been nearly 60 years since he obtained his law degree, 24 of which he has devoted to service on the Court. As for his retirement, this former law clerk can say, without reservation, "You've earned it, *boss.*"

Martha Minow, a Harvard Law School professor, clerked for Associate Justice Marshall in 1980–81. In this tribute to Marshall, which appeared in the Harvard Law Review *(November 1991), Professor Minow shares her memories of her clerkship with Marshall and evaluates his professional contributions.*

A Tribute to Justice Thurgood Marshall

JUSTICE THURGOOD MARSHALL TAUGHT HIS LAW CLERKS TO PICK their battles carefully. A clerk might be tempted to pursue every plausible argument presented to the Supreme Court. Known as the champion of the rights of the excluded and oppressed, Justice Marshall nonetheless taught his clerks that we—and he—would be worn out by trying to fight for every conceivable claim. Exhaustion would not help anyone. Fighting every battle would not leave time to fight any of them successfully, to work effectively with colleagues on the Court, or to sustain the moral authority that accompanies considered, deliberate judgments.

In light of this lesson, the occasions when Justice Marshall chose to dissent are especially revealing. Indeed, a review of his dissents over his twenty-four years on the Court demonstrates how a Justice of the Highest Court can through his attention to injustice bear witness to the ideal of justice. Justice Marshall showed how a member of the Supreme Court can insist on telling the truth about the world and about the effects of the Court's actions on living, breathing people. For the Court and for the world, he bore witness to neglected or suppressed perspectives, to historical promises unfulfilled or betrayed, and to the ideal of a legal process more enduring than human mistakes. And he did it all with zest, humor, and enormous capacity to imagine and appreciate the details of other human beings' lives.

The Supreme Court of the United States has not for the most part attended to lives unlike those of its members. In his dissents, however,

Justice Marshall paid acute attention to people neglected, the misunderstood, and the politically underrepresented. He showed special concern for poor people, prisoners, minors, older people, minority political parties, persons with disabilities, Native Americans, members of religious minorities, immigrants and noncitizens, fathers, women, anyone who might need an abortion, rock music fans, students, people with long hair, residents of Puerto Rico, protesters, and members of racial minorities. This list may seem long, although it reflects only a small portion of the Court's docket. But long is the list of people who have been misunderstood or disregarded by the Court. In his dissents on behalf of members of these groups, Justice Marshall acted upon his belief that *all* Americans are worse off when a minority is worse off. At the same time, his dissents vivified the points of view and the needs of people apparently unknown or dismissed by the majority.

Thus, when the majority characterized as innocuous the closing of a street in Memphis that had connected a white residential neighborhood and an African American neighborhood, Justice Marshall explored the economic and symbolic injuries to the African Americans. "Now the Negro drivers are being told in essence: 'You must take the long way around because you don't live in this "protected" white neighborhood.' " When the Court's majority found no constitutional defect in a state law allowing school districts to charge a fee for bus transportation, Justice Marshall condemned the Court's " 'callous indifference to the realities of life for the poor.' " He continued:

> These realities may not always be obvious from the Court's vantage point, but the Court fails in its constitutional duties when it refuses, as it does today, to make even the effort to see. For the poor, education is often the only route by which to become full participants in our society. In allowing a State to burden the access of poor persons to an education, the Court denies equal opportunity and discourages hope.

People live in concrete, particular contexts. By devoting portions of his dissents to detailed descriptions of litigants' lives, Justice Marshall paid tribute to the dignity of people who lost their claims. He examined how a seemingly modest fee for bankruptcy filings could put the protection of bankruptcy beyond the reach of poor people: "A sudden illness, for example, may destroy whatever savings they may have accumulated, and by eliminating a sense of security may destroy the incentive to save in the future." A statute requiring parental notification before a minor may obtain an abortion "forces a young woman in an already dire situation to choose between two fundamentally unacceptable alternatives: notifying a possibly dictatorial or even abusive parent and justifying her profoundly personal decision in an intimidating judicial proceeding to a black-robed stranger."

Justice Marshall's attention to people's particular circumstances contributed to his original but as yet unprevailing conception of equal protection scrutiny. He rejected the current categorical approach that sorts cases into those requiring strict scrutiny and those deserving only a rationality inquiry. He called for an examination of the nature of the category and its burden with the intensity of scrutiny adjusted accordingly in each instance. His view, I believe, reflected a devotion to contextual approaches and his suspicion of formalistic reasoning. It also expressed real interest in the particularities of people's lives.

Justice Marshall's dissents frequently examined the social, emotional, and political constraints that interfere with individuals' free choices or limit the scope of their knowing consent. His inquiries contrast sharply with those of a Court majority increasingly willing to infer waivers of constitutional rights. Look at the facts, urged Justice Marshall; imagine what a person would feel under those circumstances and then see the external conditions precluding free choice. In evaluating a person's willingness to be interrogated and thereby to relinquish the right against self-incrimination, it matters, wrote Justice Marshall, whether you know which charges have been brought against you. "Additional questioning about entirely separate and more serious suspicions of criminal activity can take unfair advantage of the suspect's psychological state, as the unexpected questions cause the compulsive pressures suddenly to reappear."

Similarly, when an individual taken from the police station and placed in a squad car asks, "Well, what is going to happen to me now," he has not indicated a desire to continue an interrogation. Look at the context, Justice Marshall demanded. If this question "had been posed by Jean-Paul Sartre before a class of philosophy students, it might well have evinced a desire for a 'generalized' discussion. But under the circumstances of this case, it is plain that respondent's only 'desire' was to find out where the police were going to take him."

Judges should acknowledge the limits of voluntary and knowing choice and greet with skepticism justifications offered by government officials charged with harming or overbearing private individuals. Justice Marshall emphasized what every welfare recipient knows, but what the Supreme Court majority seemed not to: a visit by the state social worker is not purely benevolent. He refused to condone governmental officials who fail to tell prisoners of alternate remedies for their grievances and who then point to those alternatives to avoid liability for their own deficiencies. And he held out the vision of a society in which individuals do not owe a greater loyalty to the government than they do to themselves or their friends.

For Justice Marshall, then, it was worth fighting with his colleagues when they ignored the temptations government officials often have to deceive in order to achieve their goals. He fought to fulfill the Court's duty to guard against those failings. This mission meant telling and facing up to the often dark truth about government. It meant not forgetting that government employees are human, too; they will sometimes lie and use tricks contrary to the directives of the Constitution and to the demands of fairness. Officials may shade their testimony to secure convictions. Given the chance, they may try to bypass constitutional restrictions and take advantage of the psychological vulnerabilities of people they suspect of committing crimes. From Justice Marshall's vantage point, the Court's refusal to guard against these inevitable dangers not only undermines the values that the Constitution is supposed to protect, but also "erode[s] respect for law among those charged with its administration."

The most serious erosion of respect for law occurs if the Court itself dissembles about the effects of its actions. The Court teaches by its example, and its worst mistakes arise when it betrays in its very methods the values it is supposed to uphold. Therefore, the Court's lack of candor about its own actions provoked some of Justice Marshall's most impassioned dissents. For example, in *McCleskey* v. *Zant,* the majority announced and retroactively applied a new rule limiting habeas corpus by shifting to every petitioner who brings more than one petition the burden of excusing the failure to raise that claim earlier and showing how the error actually caused an injustice. Justice Marshall hammered at the Justices in the majority for approving that rule because they failed to face how the rule "encourages state officials to *conceal* evidence that would likely prompt a petitioner to raise a particular claim on habeas." He concluded: "Whatever 'abuse of the writ' today's decision is designed to avert pales in comparison with the majority's own abuse of the norms that inform the proper judicial function."

With the Court's lack of candor may come amnesia about its past and about the histories of its litigants; this warning is another persistent and powerful theme in Justice Marshall's dissents. He insisted that shameful episodes in judicial decisionmaking are not to be hidden from view, but remembered and recalled precisely when they are in danger of repetition:

> History teaches that grave threats to liberty often come in times of urgency, when constitutional rights seem too extravagant to endure. The World War II relocation-camp cases, and the Red scare and McCarthy-era internal subversion cases, are only the most extreme reminders that when we allow fundamental freedoms to be sacrificed in the name of real or perceived exigency, we invariably come to regret it.
>
> In permitting the Government to force entire railroad crews to submit to invasive blood and urine tests, even when it lacks any evidence of drug or alcohol use or other wrongdoing, the majority today joins those shortsighted courts which have allowed basic constitutional rights to fall prey to momentary emergencies.

Forgetting the Court's history could mean repeating it; forgetting American history could also mean disguising the severity of a problem or diminishing the power of past struggles. When the Court's majority rejected the affirmative action plan adopted by the city of Richmond, Virginia, Justice Marshall reminded the Court of that city's history as the capital of the Confederacy and of the history of discrimination that prompted the adoption of the plan. Only indifference to such history could support the majority's decision to subject race-conscious measures to remedy past oppression to the same strict scrutiny review applied to race-conscious oppression of minority groups. Justice Marshall's insistence on historical memory became an integral part of his jurisprudence of candor. Without attention to history, a majority of the Court could reason that because Congress has adopted legislation to advance the interests of people with mental retardation, such people are not a politically powerless group and have no need for greater judicial protection than any group "that wins some political battles and loses others."

History helped Justice Marshall compare the isolation of persons who have mental retardation with the stigma of racial discrimination and analogized the oppressive use of stereotypes in rules governing Negroes, women, and persons with disabilities. He also analogized a demonstration against homelessness through sleeping in a park to demonstrations against racial segregation through sit-ins and stand-ins.

Steeped in the nation's past, Justice Marshall pointed to legal and political promises unfulfilled and purposes unredeemed. The ideas underlying the founding of the nation, the framing of the Constitution, the adoption of the Reconstruction Amendments, and the civil rights movement were worth the fight. Those ideas also serve as a basis for allegiance to the legal system and to the rule of law.

Thus, he also used dissents to emphasize that legal institutions should follow proper procedures, perform with at least minimum competence and impartiality, and be held accountable for their actions. He believed that "the crucial task is not so much to define our rights and liberties, but to establish institutions which can make the principles embodied in our Constitution meaningful in the lives of ordinary citizens." Besides the critical need for competent courts, juries, agencies, and legislatures, Justice Marshall looked to private attorneys to vindicate rights.

Justice Marshall's repeated dissents against restricted access to the court system embodied both his faith in the system and his demand that its promises be fulfilled. In particular, the Court's recent curbs on in forma pauperis petitions prompted Justice Marshall's strenuous objections. Denying permission to proceed without fee payment for petitions deemed by the Court to be frivolous or malicious produces an invidious distinction between paying and poor litigants because paying litigants have no comparable constraint.

Monetary restraints on access to the electoral system also warranted sharp and insistent dissent. Committed to full access to legal institutions, Justice Marshall objected to rules of electoral politics that barred minority parties from participation in general elections, not only primary elections. Justice Marshall maintained that participation in politics may have purposes beyond victory; access for a minority can broaden the majority's access to ideas. "The minor party's often unconventional positions broaden political debate, expand the range of issues with which the electorate is concerned, and influence the positions of the majority, in some instances ultimately becoming majority positions." In an especially telling phrase, Justice Marshall continued to defend access for the minority party that may have no chance of winning: "[I]ts very existence provides an outlet for voters to express dissatisfaction with the candidates or platforms of the major parties."

Could it be that the dissenting Justice knew how he voiced the dissatisfactions of many citizens with the positions of the judicial majority? Certainly, he emphatically defended dissent and protest. Perhaps his dissents also voiced his commitment to the rule of law: the rules of the powerful would be worthy of respect if they enabled critique and challenge by those excluded, out-voted, or despised. Justice Marshall stressed that protesters should have as much opportunity to express themselves on Supreme Court grounds as they do at schools, libraries, private lunch counters, bus terminals, airports, and welfare centers.

Justice Marshall's commitment to dissent extended to his practice of dissenting religiously in a few selected areas long after his views had been rejected by the Court. In every death penalty case, Justice Marshall and his friend and colleague Justice Brennan included a restatement of their view that the death sentence violates the Eighth Amendment. Similarly, in denials of in forma pauperis petitions, summary treatment on the merits of petitions submitted for certiorari, and equal protection cases, Justice Marshall methodically registered his continuing protest.

It is common practice for Justices whose views have not prevailed with the majority to agree eventually to abide by the majority's decisions. But Justice Marshall was an uncommon Justice. He believed in a rule of law that permitted and respected dissent. He imagined and evoked the lived experiences of a range of human beings. He brought critical historical perspectives to the tasks of analyzing the facts and interpreting the Constitution in a process designed to enlarge legal guarantees of human dignity. He worked to redeem the promise of this nation whose greatness he celebrated by devotion to law and by dissent.

To imagine the Court without Justice Thurgood Marshall, we must listen for the moment when he would have cracked a joke we would relish and repeat. We must listen harder for the silence when he would have made vivid the experiences of the litigants or the historical context for the lawsuit. It is not easy to hear such silences, but because of his work on the Court, they will be heard. Justice Marshall has ensured that the law belongs not only to its drafters or to its official interpreters, but also to those who "refuse . . . to acquiesce in outdated notions of 'liberty,' 'justice,' and 'equality.' " May they—may we—pick our battles carefully, and draw strength from the struggles of the man from Maryland who "did what he could with what he had."

Now a District Court Judge for the southern district of the state of New York, Robert Carter was hired by Marshall in 1944 to serve as his assistant in the NAACP. The two worked together closely for fifteen years and together strove to outlaw racial segregation in public transportation, housing, and education. Carter recalls those days in this piece written for the Harvard Law Review *(November 1991).*

A Tribute to Justice Thurgood Marshall

IN THE LATE 1940s, WHEN THURGOOD MARSHALL AND I TRAVELLED TO the nation's capital for oral argument at the U.S. Supreme Court, we were required to stay at segregated hotels. Just prior to this particular trip, I had read a newspaper article reporting that the Sheraton Hotels had purchased the Wardman Park Hotel in the Northwest section of Washington, D.C. and had adopted a policy of nondiscrimination throughout its hotel chain. I suggested to Thurgood that we make reservations at that hotel, and he agreed.

As our taxi moved from the train station to the hotel, the driver—who was black—kept asking, "Are you sure you know where you're going?" or "You sure you haven't made a mistake?" Each time, Marshall assured the driver that he should continue on. For me, however, the pressure was mounting. I began to worry that I might have misread the newspaper article, and I felt responsible for getting my boss into what might turn out to be an embarrassing situation. When we finally arrived at the hotel after what seemed an interminable ride, the driver asked whether he should wait for us. Marshall said "No thanks."

When Thurgood and I walked up to the registration desk, the clerk blanched before our very eyes. The sight of us clearly distressed the clerk, and I was certain that he would not honor our reservations. Despite his patent disapproval, the clerk reluctantly assigned us our rooms. By this time, I had been reduced to such a state of anxiety that I could hardly sign my name on the registration form. Marshall, however, remained unruffled throughout. His demeanor, both in public and in private, gave no indication that he thought our presence was anything out of the ordinary.

On March 3, 1991, the nation watched in horror as a witness's videotape captured the brutality with which several white Los Angeles police officers had attacked Rodney King, a black man whom they had pulled over for speeding. Shortly afterwards, amidst public outcry across the country, the Federal Bureau of Investigation launched a nationwide review of all police brutality complaints in the past six years. Within a few months, the Community Relations Service of the United States Department of Justice initiated civil rights mediation efforts in the Los Angeles area to facilitate discussions between the police and minority groups. A California grand jury indicted a sergeant and three patrolmen in the beating, but it later cleared all of the other twenty-one policemen who had done nothing to stop their fellow officers. The prosecutor explained that "[h]owever morally wrong their failure to intercede, in California law there is no criminal statute under which these officers can be indicted." The prosecutor indicated that these officers might still be charged under federal civil rights statutes and that he was coordinating his efforts with the United States Attorney's Office in this regard.

That the public outrage at the Los Angeles police officers was as vociferous and widespread as it was, that several different governmental arms responded as quickly as they did, and that state prosecutors turned to the federal civil rights statutes of the post-Civil War Reconstruction era that had been resurrected after nearly a century of complete neglect are all part of the legacy left by Thurgood Marshall's leadership in the civil rights struggles of the 1940s, '50s, and '60s. In this sense, Marshall's direct participation in the Sheraton Park Hotel incident—his courageous and resolute determination to force at least one institution to live up to its promise of nondiscrimination—is dwarfed by comparison to his more indirect participation in shaping a world in which, thirty years later, incidents such as Rodney King's are simply not tolerated. Some of this indirect participation occurred during his long tenure as an Associate Justice of the Supreme Court, but it started long before that, during his time as the leading civil rights lawyer in the history of this country.

The incident at the Sheraton Park Hotel occurred at a time when public pressure had been building up to desegregate all public accommodations in the nation's capital, and Marshall had just begun to heat up the assault on the "separate but equal" doctrine. Marshall believed, as did many of us at the time, that once the issue of discrimination against blacks was resolved, the whole gamut of racial, religious, and ethnic discrimination would also soon be resolved. We also felt that the invalidation of state-sponsored segregation was the key to eliminating discrimination and that, if and when such segregation was outlawed, societal discrimination against blacks would ease and eventually disappear. Thus, a great deal was riding on each step we took in the effort to overturn the "separate but equal" doctrine—both in the courtroom and in our first-hand personal encounters with segregation.

The hotel incident illustrated that, whatever the strength of the general resistance to social change, when higher-ups announce a firm new policy, it will ultimately be followed. Such was the underlying theory of civil rights law enforcement so ably advanced by Thurgood Marshall; it was also the basis for his unwavering confidence in the potential for social progress through the rule of law.

However, that a black motorist in 1991—126 years after the Civil War and 27 years after the passage of the watershed Civil Rights Act of 1964—could be the victim of such violence at the hands of those entrusted to enforce the law, despite the public outcry afterwards, serves as a vivid reminder of how much American society has yet to change.

I first met Thurgood Marshall in the fall of 1944, when I interviewed for a job as his legal research assistant at the legal department of the NAACP. Marshall had only one full-time assistant at the time, and the office had only a few law books that were inadequate for even minimal research. Nonetheless, with virtually no full-time staff and no law library, Marshall had already convinced the Supreme Court in *Smith* v. *Allwright* to strike down barriers that had prevented blacks from participating in the Democratic Party primaries in the South. Marshall had also won a series of cases establishing the rights of black teachers to salaries equal to those of their white counterparts and had succeeded in having the convictions of several black defendants overturned on procedural due process grounds. His accomplishment of all these feats with such primitive and limited resources attests to his extraordinary talents.

I had been recommended to Marshall by William Hastie, who was his close friend and mentor; undoubtedly, Hastie's support ensured my being hired. The interview took place at the NAACP's national headquarters, then located in one of those old but sturdy structures on lower Fifth Avenue in New York City. I recall that Marshall hired me on the spot. I am not certain of this, but telling me immediately that I had the job, instead of having me sweat it out, would have been more his style.

My hiring marked the beginning of staff expansion, and within a year or so, the staff had doubled and then tripled in size. I worked closely with Marshall at the NAACP for about fifteen years, primarily as his chief assistant. Our principal agenda was to outlaw racial segregation in public transportation, housing, and education, with our focus on the last of these.

Marshall had come to the NAACP in 1936 as assistant to the Chief Counsel, Charles Houston. Houston, who graduated from Harvard Law School and later went on to become a professor and dean at Howard Law School, had begun the legal offensive against segregation in graduate and professional schools. Rather than attacking the "separate but equal" doctrine on its merits, however, Houston had asked the courts merely to require the doctrine's full implementation. When the states provided white students with educational facilities in law, medicine, journalism, and the like—so the argument went—they were required to offer similar facilities to black students in separate institutions or admit them into the existing all-white schools. Underlying this strategy was the belief that the segregation system would eventually implode—in other words, that the financial burden of having duplicate educational facilities for blacks and whites in the various professions would become so great that the states would be forced to abandon segregation altogether at the graduate and professional school level. When Houston left the NAACP after his short tenure, Marshall became Chief Counsel.

Marshall graduated in 1933 from Lincoln University, which was an all-male black college, and in 1936 from Howard Law School. The overriding theory of legal education at Howard during those years was that the United States Constitution—in particular, the Civil War Amendments—was a powerful force, heretofore virtually untapped, that should be used for social engineering in race relations. The Due Process and Equal Protection Clauses of the Fourteenth Amendment, the abolition of involuntary servitude by the Thirteenth, and the protection against disenfranchisement on the basis of race by the Fifteenth were, in effect, the guarantors of equal citizenship rights for black people. A principal objective of the faculty at Howard was to produce

lawyers capable of structuring and litigating test cases that would provide effective implementation of these guarantees on behalf of the
black community. Houston, and then Marshall, sought to inject concrete, real-life meaning into the constitutional guarantees through
NAACP-sponsored litigation. Marshall internalized Howard Law
School's teachings, especially those of Houston, and developed an un-
dying faith in the Constitution and the "rule of law," a faith that he has
never relinquished to this very day.

By the time I joined the NAACP staff, Marshall had already become
the most well-known black lawyer in the United States. Marshall's reputation and popularity among black people grew to such heights that he
was probably revered and hero-worshipped as much as Martin Luther
King, Jr. was in his heyday; the black community affectionately referred
to Marshall as "Mr. Civil Rights." Outgoing and possessing an earthy
wit, Marshall had both presence and charisma. He was most in his
element when he spoke to a crowd extemporaneously; he would bring
the audience to their feet and fill them with inspiration. He was far less
successful when he had to follow a written text. The text insulated him
from the audience, not permitting the kind of direct interplay that
occurred when he spoke without notes.

Marshall was an easy person to work for; he gave his staff considerable freedom and encouraged innovative thinking. For instance, he
gave me the freedom to develop legal strategy on my own and, as the
staff expanded, to direct others to do the same. When I became second
in command at the NAACP's legal department, Marshall expected me
to be responsible for the day-to-day running of the office and to resolve
all internal office disputes without his participation. He was always in
demand, and as our most effective fundraiser, he had to spend a great
deal of his time traveling around the country exhorting and enlarging
our constituency. Marshall had great confidence in the staff he had
chosen, and he did not believe that a senior lawyer was needed to
monitor a younger colleague's first trial. In his view, a competent lawyer could—and should—plunge in and learn to swim unassisted. Marshall rarely praised a staff member face to face, but in his public utter-
ances he was generous with kind words about the staff's skill, hard
work, and dedication.

Despite the many demands on Marshall's time, he remained the
guiding force behind the NAACP's legal strategy. We had a group of
advisors—the NAACP National Legal Committee—whom Marshall
would convene from time to time to discuss some development in staff

strategy, the articulation and defense of which Marshall usually had me assume. Marshall encouraged the NAACP staff to develop a viable theory that racial discrimination and segregation were unconstitutional per se. Consequently, I usually argued for the most aggressive position possible. Marshall would listen, ask questions, and help move the debate towards consensus. When the sessions ended, the staff position was usually accepted and endorsed as the official NAACP legal policy, with, of course, refinements and embellishments from our advisors.

Some participants or observers at these sessions have since described my role as the militant dragging Marshall along. Nothing could be further from the truth. If Marshall had not fully supported the staff position, it would not have been adopted. Although I was usually the one at these meetings who articulated and defended the staff's position and its implications, I did so with Marshall's wholehearted support. Marshall expected and encouraged me to be outspoken and uncompromising. He would surely have been disappointed had I wavered. These sessions enabled him to test the strength of a theory and to envision how we would have to hone the argument to persuade the courts. I was encouraged to play the gadfly role, positing all kinds of radical ideas, and if things ever went sour, no finger would be pointed my way. It was Marshall who would have had to take the heat on any such occasion. Even then I recognized the enormous pressure under which he was operating. Although he must have felt that the fate of the black community rested on his making the right choices, he never gave me any outward indication that such decisions were burdensome.

The closest Marshall and I came to disagreeing on strategy occurred when we were faced with a court order directing us to reveal the names of NAACP members in Alabama to the state attorney general. The Supreme Court's decisions in *Brown* v. *Board of Education* had confronted the South with the necessity of dismantling its dual school system. There was widespread resistance to doing so, of course, and a number of states resisted by striking at the NAACP. These states believed that if the NAACP were destroyed, there would be no force to prod the black community into enforcing its right to school desegregation. Some states, for example, passed laws making NAACP-sponsored litigation illegal by classifying such activity as barratry.

The attorney general of Alabama sought a more direct and faster solution. Without warning, he obtained an *ex parte* injunction in state court barring the NAACP from operating in Alabama. I went to Alabama to move for a lifting of the injunction pending a hearing, but

Judge Walter B. Jones, to whom the matter had been assigned, and the Attorney General had orchestrated the proceeding so that a more recently filed state motion to secure the NAACP membership list was heard first. Judge Jones granted the state's motion and ordered the list produced before he would hear the NAACP's motion. I refused to obey the order. Judge Jones set a hearing date and told me that if I did not produce the list, he would declare the NAACP in contempt of court and fine it $100,000. This was, as I recall, a Friday, and I had to be back in Alabama the following Monday with an answer.

Marshall and I met with Roy Wilkins, the NAACP's Executive Director, in our offices in New York on Saturday morning to determine what to do. Whatever we decided, we would expose the organization to grave risks. If we obeyed Judge Jones's order, we would be finished in Alabama and possibly in the South as a whole. If we defied the court, we would face a $100,000 fine that the organization could not pay, as well as possible public censure for refusing to obey a lawful court order. I vigorously argued that we could not give up the list, since doing so would expose our members to economic and possibly physical reprisals and finish the NAACP in Alabama. Although it was technically Wilkins's responsibility as Executive Director to make the decision, Wilkins would not have wanted to act against Marshall's advice.

Marshall was reluctant to support my position. He feared that the NAACP might appear to be advocating a refusal to comply with the law. After all, it was 1956, when the organization was insisting that the mandate of *Brown* be followed. Since we regarded this decision as critical, Wilkins and Marshall both decided to seek outside counsel. Wilkins polled the NAACP's Board members and Marshall sought the advice of members of the NAACP's National Legal Committee. Interestingly, the lawyers almost unanimously told Marshall that we should produce the list; the lay people on the Board almost unanimously told Wilkins to risk the fine. Based on this input, Marshall deferred to Wilkins, who then gave me the green light to return to Alabama and refuse to produce the list.

During the next year or so, when we were trying to surmount the various obstacles the Alabama courts erected to keep us from taking the case to the U.S. Supreme Court with a cogent First Amendment argument, Marshall worked enthusiastically on the case as if he had never had any qualms about the course the NAACP had chosen. He could have indicated to me how erroneous he felt my position had been on many occasions, but he never did. Once the decision was made, he was on the team to help produce a winner.

To be sure, the Alabama case was not the only time the NAACP's litigation strategy created controversy within the civil rights movement. In late 1949 and early 1950, opposition started to mount against the NAACP's decision to take *McLaurin* v. *Oklahoma State Regents for Higher Education* to the Supreme Court. Through *McLaurin,* we wanted to target segregation itself, not merely the full implementation of the "separate but equal" doctrine; we wanted integrated public classrooms, cafeterias, and libraries, not simply relegation to equal separate facilities. Marjorie Lawson, a columnist for an influential black newspaper called *The Pittsburgh Courier,* made the case for the opposition. She argued that it would be a strategic blunder to take the case to the High Court, because if we lost—which was a real possibility—it would be a disastrous setback. The publisher of *The Pittsburgh Courier,* by the way, was a respected member of the NAACP Board.

Marshall did not back down. Instead, he rallied support for his ambitious strategy in *McLaurin.* To build support for his cause, Marshall organized a conference at Howard University to discuss the evils of all forms of racial segregation and economic exploitation. The publicity that accompanied the conference served to blunt whatever real opposition Lawson might have generated in the black community. Through his pragmatism and political savvy, Marshall succeeded in galvanizing popular support for the NAACP's strategy in *McLaurin.* Marshall thus demonstrated that his winning talents extended well beyond the courtroom.

In 1950, at Marshall's urging, the NAACP Board endorsed a new policy of refusing to take any cases fighting school discrimination except those that attacked segregation per se. The NAACP national convention adopted a resolution that same year to the same effect. This policy was very controversial, at least among the local lawyers on whom the NAACP relied in the South. Two of these lawyers, among the NAACP's best at the time—Martin Martin and Oliver Hill—resigned from the National Legal Committee in protest. They believed that the NAACP should not abandon litigation that sought to equalize educational facilities. Although I am sure that Marshall felt sorry to lose these men, their departure did not dissuade him from pursuing the chosen course. Martin died shortly after his resignation. Fortunately, about a year later, Hill rejoined the Committee and helped litigate *Davis* v. *County School Board,* one of the five state cases disposed of in

Brown. Lawyers from the organization's national office, including Marshall himself, conducted the bulk of the NAACP's litigation. Having grown up in Maryland, Marshall had a slight Southern accent, but when our opponents were Southern lawyers, which was virtually all the time, his accent would become much more pronounced. Before and after the case was called, Marshall would joke with the opposing counsel or exchange some pleasantry, all in a Southern accent so broad that he sounded as if he had lived all his life in the deep rural South. This practice irritated me at first. The very lawyers Marshall's Southern drawl would put at ease were defending a system we detested. I saw no point in trying to be buddy-buddy with any of them. Marshall, however, was attempting to communicate to these men that, although we were on opposite sides of an emotionally charged lawsuit, we were lawyers representing our clients and had no personal quarrel with each other. Once I understood what he was doing and saw the sense of it, I too would speak cordially to my opponents when I was lead counsel on a case, albeit without the Southern drawl.

In the courtroom, Marshall was the consummate professional. I heard him make several splendid arguments before the Supreme Court. But perhaps the best courtroom performance I ever saw him give was his cross-examination of the Director of South Carolina's Educational Finance Commission in *Briggs* v. *Elliott*. The Commission was under state mandate to guarantee equal educational opportunity for all children in the state, but it opposed integrating South Carolina's public schools. The Director had testified on direct examination that public sentiment was opposed to racial mixing in the schools and that an order requiring desegregation would result in the elimination of public schools in the state.

Marshall never raised his voice. His deft cross-examination exposed the fact that there were no black members or employees of this Commission, which was supposed to provide equal educational opportunities for blacks, that the Director had no knowledge of the black community and knew no black educators personally, and that the public he referred to as opposed to racial mixing was the white community only. Finally, Marshall made the Director admit that when he warned that racial mixing would result in the elimination of public schools in South Carolina, he was not implying that a court order to desegregate would not be obeyed.

A fillip to the examination, at least for the blacks in attendance, was that the witness's name was E.R. Crow. Marshall referred to him a few times as "Mr. Crow," which brought the blacks in the courtroom to near explosion with hilarity by the time he sat down. The recent television production, "Separate but Equal," dramatized this event, but unfortunately the television rendition failed to capture the brilliance of Marshall's cross-examination, its devastating impact on the witness, and the exhilaration it inspired in the black audience who heard it in the courtroom.

The pride and dignity that Thurgood Marshall has inspired in the black community over his long career is paralleled only by the very real, enormous contribution he has made in ensuring that black Americans enjoy equality of citizenship. But the most lasting imprint he leaves is more far-reaching. Marshall's steadfast belief in the Constitution as the pillar of democratic and egalitarian principles and in law generally as the protector of the poor and powerless—and his efforts toward the realization of these ideals—reminds the American people as a whole of their vast potential for social progress.

In 1981 Stephen L. Carter clerked for Marshall Thurgood; today he is a professor of law at Yale University. In this tribute "Living Without the Judge," written for The Yale Law Journal *(November 1991), Carter recalls the accomplishments of his hero Thurgood Marshall in the field of civil rights. He remembers too the very moment an era ended—that era when the Supreme Court was "the first and best hope for curing the nation's ills."*

LIVING WITHOUT THE JUDGE

Stephen L. Carter

THURGOOD MARSHALL, I THOUGHT, WOULD ALWAYS BE THERE.

My life has been rounded by his. I was born in 1954, scant months after his advocacy led to the stunning victory in *Brown* v. *Board of Education*, and so I grew up in the world he had helped to build. I arrived at college just as the Warren Court, which he joined only near its end, began to fragment. I was privileged to serve as his law clerk at the very instant when liberalism ran into the stone wall of electoral distaste—the Reagan landslide of 1980. And now, upon his retirement, I am at last coming to grips with my partial estrangement from the liberal establishment to which Marshall has always been a hero.

Thurgood Marshall has long been my hero, too. Few black Americans would say otherwise. Not long ago, I chatted with an elderly taxi driver, a beautiful black man who popped up one day like a Greek chorus, to help me keep my head on straight. The driver explained to me that I was too young to remember what it was like in the old days. He told me that for his generation, rooting for Thurgood Marshall was like rooting for Joe Louis—the heavyweight out to battle and demolish one white hope after another. Marshall was the man to call whenever the racists struck. Marshall, the lawyer, using the white man's weapons to fight back the white man's system. Marshall, the symbol. Marshall, the hero.

John Ely, in dedicating *Democracy and Distrust* to Earl Warren, writes, "You don't need many heroes if you choose carefully." Point taken—but choosing Thurgood Marshall as my hero didn't require much care. He was simply *there*. I met him for the first time in the spring of 1978, when he came to Yale to preside over the final moot court arguments, in which I was a finalist. For me, he was already larger than life. Before attending law school, I had spent a week reading *Simple Justice*, Richard Kluger's fascinating, but flawed, history of the litigation culminating in *Brown*. Kluger writes history by locating heroes and telling their stories. Some of the heroes of his book were the individuals with the courage to stand up against the totalitarian white supremacist power structures than governing their states and communities. Some of the heroes of his book were judges. And some of the heroes were lawyers, like Charles Hamilton Houston and William Hastie, even now too often ignored in law school classrooms, and Thurgood Marshall—who would probably be ignored, despite his remarkable legal achievements, but for his elevation to the Supreme Court.

Before I read *Simple Justice*, I had only the thinnest appreciation for the achievements of the legal arm of the civil rights struggle. Although I was a history major, my courses on twentieth century American history treated *Brown* as an axiom and the civil rights movement that followed—which we *did* study in history—as what really mattered. Indeed, in the armchair radicalism of my undergraduate days, I was inclined to treat law as relatively unimportant, as a cloak for the true power relations of society. Certainly I could not imagine lawyers as heroes.

Which is why Kluger's book was an eye-opener for me. Kluger's tale has its faults—I have in mind particularly his exaltation of Earl Warren and his crediting the inner dynamics of the *Brown* Court, rather than the skill or force of the litigants before it, as well as his notion that Marshall and others in the New York office of the NAACP Legal Defense Fund had to be pushed to confront segregation directly. Later, listening eagerly at the feet of Thurgood Marshall and also of Spottswood W. Robinson, III, for whom it was my privilege to serve as law clerk at the Court of Appeals for the District of Columbia Circuit, I would hear most of the same tales, and many others, with greater nuance and complexity. But my critique would come later. At the time, it was the heroes who got to me, and Kluger's book is full of them. Kluger, much like David Halberstam, paints his principal figures as much larger than life, and as a budding lawyer, I was content, even delighted, to leave them that way. I came away from Kluger convinced that there were indeed giants roaming the earth in those days, giants who might have won the battle much earlier than they did except that the moral Lilliputians who fought them were far more numerous and held all the guns.

Very few of the Justices who have served on the Supreme Court would have been in the legal hall of fame without their careers on the Court, but Marshall was one of these. So to meet Thurgood Marshall in the flesh was, for me, to come into contact with a demigod. I had no idea what to expect, but I was worried and not a little awed. What I found, to my delight, was a great warmth, an openness, and an earthy good humor. His supreme unpretentiousness, his choice not to subject himself to the opinions of others, put me immediately at ease.

And then, in the late summer or early fall of 1979, I was astonished to be invited to serve as one of his law clerks, to join, for twelve months, his chambers family. (As an officer of the *Yale Law Journal*, I had been trained to see the Supreme Court as a sort of wholly owned subsidiary that was obliged to give us employment upon application, but the Justices did not always play their proper roles.) And for those twelve months, Justice Marshall, or the Judge, as we used to call him around the chambers, was one of the finest teachers I have ever had—at pool as well as at law. Because he was so often in dissent as the Burger Court majority chipped away at the edifice he had spent a lifetime building (an edifice the Rehnquist Court would later hit with a bulldozer), it would have been easy for the chambers to develop a bunker mentality, to see the rest of the Justices as enemies. But the Judge would have none of that. In those days, he was far too confident, far too good humored, and had far to capacious a view of human nature for those sins to turn him bitter. And for his ability to maintain his aplomb and his warmth even as the edifice began to crumble, I loved him all the more.

So, yes, Thurgood Marshall is my hero, too—but my reasons are not the same as those cited in some of the agonized commentaries on his departure. The greatness of a judge should no more be measured by the results he reaches than the greatness of a writer should be judged by the titles of her books. It is a trivialization of Marshall's importance to the Court for those on the left or the right to reduce his towering career to a series of outcomes in concrete cases.

Yes, every vote matters, and the new and relatively untested Justice Clarence Thomas makes many people nervous. One may easily make predictions about the Court without Marshall: *Roe* v. *Wade* hangs by a thread, more bizarre First Amendment decisions are sure to follow, civil rights statutes are likely to receive ever more restrictive interpretations, and the Court has lost its one member whose clients once included large numbers of those who sat on the other side of the interrogation tables in police stations.

On the other hand, many of the precedents that are said to be threatened are marked by judicial overreaching. Well before Marshall arrived to join the Warren Court in 1967, the Justices, perhaps awed by their own stellar achievements in helping to hasten the end of America's version of apartheid, occasionally began to write as though their own moral compasses were the true signposts of constitutional law. In the early 1970's, the last years of liberalism triumphant, the Court seemed to develop a "We have the votes" mentality that is always dangerous in the judicial branch—the same arrogance, as it happens, that lately seems to be infecting the Rehnquist Court, to the unfortunate glee of people on the right who ought to know better.

If President Bush, as his rhetoric suggests, wants to avoid the sin of judicial legislation, then one must hope that in appointing Clarence Thomas, he has followed Marshall with someone like Marshall—but like Marshall in a particular and rarely mentioned sense.

Thurgood Marshall's entire legal career has been marked by a strong and abiding faith in the rule of law—a faith too often absent in the antilegal cynicism of those on the left or the right who measure the success of the Supreme Court by whether it reads into the Constitution the political programs they prefer.

Just consider the fight against racial segregation. When others were sure that the only route to racial justice in America was direct action, Thurgood Marshall was out litigating—and litigating, it must be said, before a Supreme Court that included no members selected for their opposition to segregation. Marshall could do this with such confidence, such passion, only if he believed that people of good will would keep their minds open and could be persuaded if presented with clear and sensible legal arguments.

This ideal of the judge as someone amenable to reason is generally lost in today's popular clamor for the preservation of this precedent or the rejection of that one. If a President, pressured from his right flank, seeks a candidate who will vote "the right way," or if a Senate, pressured from the left, rejects a nominee who will vote "the wrong way," enormous damage is done to this ideal. Indeed, enormous damage is done to the notion of law as a guiding rather than a governing force in our democracy.

As a legal scholar, I rather unfashionably prefer that judges attempt a sharp separation of personal political and moral preferences from constitutional analysis. That judges generally seen as on the left cross that line in their quest for a better society has long been a commonplace of constitutional theory, which is probably why so much of contemporary scholarship is devoted to proving that it isn't so. But judges who are considered to be on the right do it too, with increasing frequency, most recently in the Court's restrictions of the constitutional right to seek writs of habeas corpus. Indeed, I fear that the Rehnquist Court's monument in the struggle for racial justice may prove to be its sharp departure from the original understanding of the Fourteenth Amendment in *McCleskey* v. *Kemp*. There the Justices rejected the claim that the death penalty is administered in a racially discriminatory fashion, even though statistics plainly demonstrate that capital juries value the lives of white murder victims higher than the lives of black ones; and the rejection came notwithstanding the clear concern of the authors of the Fourteenth Amendment that the criminal law would be used to protect whites but not blacks.

Critics of Thurgood Marshall have long contended that he has, at some points in his career on the Court, identified his personal moral compass with the commands of the Constitution. Certainly I do not agree with every legal position that he has taken. But if the line is going to be crossed, I think we could do far worse than have the judge who does the crossing be a person of the integrity, compassion, and commitment to individuals that the Judge has displayed throughout his career. This is not because his moral instincts are always right—whose are?—but because they are always compassionate. There are other judges of integrity and compassion, conservatives as well as liberals, and some of them are on the Court. But there is only one Thurgood Marshall.

Still, his decision to step down from the bench should not be viewed as a light going out. In the three and a half decades since *Brown*, people who describe their goals as progressive have come to rely far too much on the Court as an ally for social change; whereas, if the truth is told, it has not been a reliable ally for those on the left in two decades. (Even

Roe, fiercely defended, and as fiercely attacked, as a decision about reproductive privacy, is, if one reads it carefully, much more a quasi-administrative-law decision, deferring to the considered judgment of the medical establishment.)

In fighting for a cause, one must use the tools that are available, and in the fifties and sixties, the Court happened to be available. That the Court was on the side of the angels in the battle against segregation was simply a coincidence. It is not easy to study the fabric of social change and come away with the conclusion that had *Brown* come out the other way, the civil rights movement would have died aborning. More likely, the Court would have sunk slowly into obscurity; a vital element in the prestige the Court now enjoys comes from the rhetorical buildup it received as antisegregation intellectuals and politicians in the fifties insisted that its edicts, no matter how controversial, must be obeyed.

In that sense, it is a tragedy of our era that everyone who has a cause seems to suppose that the *Brown* litigation is necessarily the model to follow. *Brown* was wonderful, but it does not represent the whole fabric of social change. For most of human history, people have relied on themselves rather than on their courts to make vital moral judgments and to ensure human ethical progress. The skill of deciding difficult issues through public moral debate, rather than through arcane legal argument, is one that it is time for all of us to recover.

Public dialogue is risky, for one must face and persuade not a few judges, members of the ruling elite, but a broader range of people, many of them not subject to any particular conversational constraints. In other words, a tough world awaits when one leaves the courts and enters politics. Yet we live in a constitutional democracy, which means that not every moral wrong must be remedied by the creation of a constitutional right. The Constitution places some moral choices outside the political process, but most of them are—and should be—left within it. The legislatures, not the courts, are the places where most of our great moral battles should be fought.

Besides, it is simply not true that Thurgood Marshall's departure, along with that of William Brennan last year, marks the end of the era when the Court was the first and best hope for curing the nation's ills. That era ended long ago, and I can even give it a date—a date, I think, when Justices Brennan and Marshall themselves knew with certainty that the era had passed, even though, on many issues, their side still had the votes.

During my year as a law clerk for Justice Marshall, I was a witness—the only witness, I think, other than the participants—to an incident I promised myself I would never reveal until both Justices were off the Court. The incident occurred the morning after Ronald Reagan's landslide election in November 1980. Jimmy Carter's defeat was, by that time, a foregone conclusion; what stunned many observers was that the Democrats lost control of the Senate for the first time in more than two decades.

The court was sitting that day to hear oral arguments—a little thing like a presidential election could hardly disrupt the precise schedule—and, as usual, the Justices were rushing to the robing room and the law clerks to our little marble alcove off to the side of the courtroom. I left the chambers fast on the Judge's heels. In the broad, sunny corridor, Marshall encountered Brennan. From where I stood, it appeared that Brennan had tears in his eyes.

Brennan, looking unusually frail, gazed up at his old friend and ally. "Is it really true," he asked softly, "that Strom Thurmond is going to be chairman of the Judiciary Committee?" Senator Thurmond, one of Marshall's principal tormentors in his confirmation hearings, was once an ardent segregationist. The name, no doubt, was a symbol for Marshall of all that he had spent his career struggling against.

Marshall, towering over his friend, looked down, hesitated, then slipped his arm around Brennan's narrow shoulders. They walked to the robing room that way, passing in and out of the shadows where the brilliant morning sunlight struck curtains or walls. That is the moment when the era ended, as these two great soldiers of liberalism squared their shoulders and marched off to fight their battle against the new political order.

And so the old order passeth. Perhaps it was time. But we will never see their like again.

II

The Jurisprudence
of Justice Thurgood Marshall

WHEN THURGOOD MARSHALL RETIRED FROM THE UNITED STATES SU-
preme Court in 1991 after nearly a quarter century on the Court, the
country lost its most eloquent spokesman for the rights of all Americans. He is the last of the justices from the Court of Chief Justice Earl
Warren who looked to the principles of the Bill of Rights and the Civil
Rights amendments to protect the most powerless and despised among
us. The majority on the Supreme Court he left in 1991 reads those
same sources quite narrowly, striking down legislation as unconstitutional on the rare occasion where the constitutional text or history
shows that the framers of the amendments would have disapproved of
the particular law in question. Although most of the Warren Court
legacy survives, with the recent retirements of Justices Marshall and
Brennan, and their replacement by Justices Thomas and Souter, it is
likely that many Warren Court cases will be overturned or drastically
limited during the next two decades.

Why, then, are Thurgood Marshall's Supreme Court opinions, the
majority of which were dissents joined in by only one or two other
justices, so significant? First, anyone who cares deeply about individual
freedom should be familiar with Marshall's vision of the just society as
articulated in his opinions. Second, yesterday's dissent can become tomorrow's Supreme Court majority opinion as occurred with the dissents of Justices Brandeis and Holmes in the early part of this century.
Finally, even though few of his opinions are accepted by the current
Supreme Court which will sit well into the next century, there are other
forums that will be more sympathetic to his views: state supreme
courts; courts in countries that are just now developing human-rights
law such as Poland and Czechoslovakia; and legislatures, both state and
federal. In many instances in recent years, Congress has been more
sympathetic to claims of individual rights than the Supreme Court. The
Civil Rights Act of 1991, for example, overturned several Supreme
Court decisions which had narrowly read civil rights statutes. And Congress passed a bill that would have effectively overturned a 1991 Supreme Court decision holding that health-care workers in federally
subsidized clinics can be prohibited, consistent with the First Amendment, from advising their clients that abortion was an option for pregnancy.[1]

Unlike the texts of many modern bills of rights found in other coun-

---

[1] The bill, however, never became law as President Bush vetoed the legislation.

tries and in the United Nations Universal Declaration of Human Rights, the U.S. Constitution and its twenty-six amendments are quite limited in their protection of individual rights. There are no affirmative obligations placed on government to provide the basic necessities of life. Except for the Thirteenth Amendment's prohibition of slavery, there are no restraints placed on individuals or corporations, just on government. Until the Warren Court era, commencing in 1953, Supreme Court protection of individual rights through constitutional interpretation was relatively modest.

When Thurgood Marshall took his seat on the Court in 1967, he already had a distinguished career as a lawyer, winning eleven out of the fourteen cases he argued to the Court on behalf of the NAACP Legal Defense Fund, including *Brown* v. *Board of Education* in 1954; as a judge on the U.S. Court of Appeals for the Second Circuit; and as United States Solicitor General. By the time Marshall joined the Court, the landmark Warren Court cases had been decided: *Brown* v. *Board of Education*, outlawing segregated schools; *Mapp* v. *Ohio*, applying the exclusionary rule for violation of the Fourth Amendment to state courts; *Miranda* v. *Arizona*, giving criminal suspects a right to counsel in jails prior to interrogation; *Baker* v. *Carr* and *Reynolds* v. *Sims*, requiring one person–one vote in congressional and state elections; *New York Times* v. *Sullivan*, protecting the press from libel suits by public officials; and *Griswold* v. *Connecticut* establishing a right to privacy for married couples using birth control devices.

Besides Chief Justice Warren, the court Marshall joined in 1967 included Justices Brennan, Douglas, Black, and Fortas. In his first year on the Court, his position was that of a centrist, rarely dissenting and often joining his colleagues to uphold the power of the state over the individual. For example, he was in the majority in a case that upheld, for the first time, the power of the police to stop and question a person even though there was no probable cause to do so [*Terry* v. *Ohio* (1968)]. He voted to uphold a loan by the state of textbooks to students attending parochial schools, rejecting the claim that the loan violated the Establishment Clause of the First Amendment [*Board of Education* v. *Allen* (1968)]. And his was the decisive vote in the case of *Powell* v. *Texas* (1968), when he wrote the majority opinion, over four dissents, rejecting the claim of a chronic alcoholic that criminal punishment for the offense of public drunkenness was cruel and unusual in violation of the Eighth Amendment.

When Marshall joined the Warren Court, it was in its final years.

Warren Earl Burger replaced Earl Warren as Chief Justice in 1969, two years after Marshall's appointment. In the late sixties, Justice Hugo Black was no longer voting consistently to sustain claims of individual rights. Every appointment to the Court after Marshall joined it was made by Presidents whose view of the proper role of a justice was antithetical to Marshall's. Although a few of the appointees were Marshall's allies, most were not. In short, Justice Marshall's views could not count on the kind of sympathetic hearing they had received as Attorney Marshall and as time went on, the divergence in constitutional interpretation between Marshall and his colleagues became greater. From a position at the center of the Court in the sixties, retirements and new appointments pushed him to the left for the rest of his career.

With a constitutional text that did not address societal inequalities, on a Court no longer interested in aggressively protecting the powerless, Justice Marshall had an uphill battle to defend individual rights. This is the story of that fight.

AN OVERVIEW OF MARSHALL'S CONSTITUTIONAL JURISPRUDENCE

Where the constitutional text is clear, Marshall follows it, even if the results seem inconsistent with his personal views. For example, the Seventh Amendment preserves the right to a jury trial in civil cases, if that right existed "at common law." In one of the leading cases interpreting the meaning of the amendment, Marshall upheld the right to a jury trial for a white landlord in a housing discrimination suit by a black tenant, even though the tenant would have had a better chance of prevailing had the facts been determined by the federal judge without a jury. In another area of constitutional law—the taking of property clause under the Fifth Amendment—Marshall wrote an opinion requiring the government to compensate property owners for installing cable television on private property. Even though he normally took the position that the government had virtually unlimited power over private property, as opposed to liberty, Marshall found the historical meaning of the clause required a "per se" rule, stating that where the government is responsible for physical invasions of property, it must compensate the owner.

Marshall reads expansively those parts of the Bill of Rights and Civil Rights amendments that are broadly phrased—"due process," "equal protection," "freedom of speech," "cruel and unusual punishments"—finding principles that transcend narrow historical confines and apply to modern society. These provisions permit the Court to protect those outside the political mainstream—the poor, racial and political minorities, and women. Marshall is willing to let the political branches also help those on the outside, for example, upholding affirmative action programs on behalf of racial minorities from constitutional challenges of "reverse discrimination" and permitting Congress to use its powers over the national economy without judicial oversight.

Perhaps Marshall's most enduring legacy as a justice is his development of a method for deciding who is entitled to special protection under the Constitution's equal protection clause. The notion that certain kinds of persons and interests might be entitled to heightened Court attention was first made in a footnote in a 1938 Supreme Court opinion by Chief Justice Harlan Stone. Stone observed that the normal deference given by the Court to statutes passed by the legislatures might not apply where they conflict with one of the Bill of Rights; where they restrict political rights, such as the right to vote; or where they affect religious or racial minorities. Following Stone's suggestion, the Court, especially during the 1960's, would closely scrutinize legislation that interfered with certain "fundamental rights" or that discriminated on the basis of certain "suspect classifications." If a fundamental right or suspect classification was not involved, the legislation would be upheld so long as the law is rational; if a fundamental right or a suspect classification was involved, the legislation would be stricken. It was an all or nothing approach, which Marshall began criticizing soon after he arrived on the Court.

In several important opinions, Marshall expanded the kinds of persons and interests entitled to such special protection, for example, persons whose welfare benefits are arbitrarily cut in the case of *Dandridge* v. *Williams* or residents of impoverished local school districts where per pupil expenditures are substantially less than that of wealthy school districts in the case of *San Antonio School District* v. *Rodriguez*. Using the Rodriguez case as an example, Marshall's analysis focussed on both the interest affected—education—and the persons harmed by the law—residents of poor districts. He then weighed the asserted state interests in the law that were not strong enough to overcome the harm to the individual.

Although never explicitly adopted by a majority of the Court, Marshall's approach does explain many decisions of the Court. In the 1976 case of *Craig* v. *Boren,* the majority held that discrimination on the basis of gender should be subject to a third level of scrutiny, termed "intermediate," between "rational-basis" level and "strict." Marshall's advocacy that the rigid two-tier approach is untenable was finally accepted by the Court. *Craig,* however, did not incorporate Marshall's focus on both the right or interest at stake and the classification of persons in the statute. The best example of the Court taking that approach is the case of *Plyler* v. *Doe* which invalidated a Texas law denying free public education to children of illegal aliens. Justice Brennan's majority opinion weighed both the important interest involved—education—and the persons affected by the law—children who were being punished because their parents came to the United States illegally. The dissent would have retained the "rigidified approach" and used the rational basis test, since there was neither a suspect classification or fundamental right involved. In most cases, the Court rejects Marshall's sliding-scale approach but it remains available to courts in the future interested in expanding the reach of the Constitution to protect those left out of the political mainstream.

POLITICS AND THE POWERLESS

One of the major criticisms of the Warren Court's decisions was that they were an intrusion into the political process. The Burger Court, on the other hand, was much more deferential to legislative decisions. For example, in upholding as rational a state law that discriminated against large families concerning the amount of welfare assistance they received under the Aid to Families with Dependent Children program (AFDC), Justice Stewart said: "[T]he intractable economic, social, and even philosophical problems presented by public welfare assistance programs are not the business of this Court" [*Dandridge* v. *Williams* (1970)].

One of the factors behind the Court's reluctance to interfere with legislative determinations was the deserved criticism of the Supreme Court in the early 1900's when it used the due process clause to strike down economic legislation designed to improve working conditions for employees. For example, minimum-wage and maximum-hour laws were held to violate the liberty to contract of both employer and employee. Those cases were overruled when the Roosevelt appointees became a majority in the late 1930's and began upholding such laws.

Recognizing the factual difference between regulation of business and welfare programs, the *Dandridge* majority believed it was no more appropriate under the Constitution for the Court to examine welfare laws any more closely than laws regulating what employers must pay their workers.

Justice Marshall's dissent in *Dandridge* was his first opinion criticizing the Court's traditional equal-protection analysis and suggesting a sliding-scale approach. He applauded the Court's use of the rational-basis test in regulating businesses "who have more than enough power to protect themselves in the legislative halls," but unlike the majority, distinguished welfare regulation:

> This case, involving the literally vital interests of a powerless minority—poor families without breadwinners—is far removed from the area of business regulation, as the Court concedes. . . . AFDC support to need dependent children provides the stuff that sustains those children's lives: food, clothing, shelter. And this Court has already recognized several times that when a benefit, even a "gratuitous" benefit, is necessary to sustain life, stricter constitutional standards, both procedural and substantive, are applied to the deprivation of that benefit.

Unable to muster a majority for his view that politically powerless welfare recipients are entitled to greater protection from the Court when they are discriminated against in the provision of welfare benefits, Marshall raised in a footnote a more radical question: "whether or not there is a constitutional right to subsistence." Marshall obviously thought that there was no need to decide whether the Constitution required states to set up a welfare program in the first place when a majority of his colleagues was not even willing to scrutinize discrimination among recipients. On a Court more hospitable to his views, Marshall might have been willing to develop a theory by which the Constitution did place affirmative obligations on government to provide the basic necessities of life. The only obligations the Court has imposed on government have been the provision of counsel, trial transcripts, and related matters in criminal prosecutions, as well as the waiving of filing fees in divorces and the provision of counsel in some civil cases.

Marshall's view that the economically and politically powerful in society do not need protection from the Supreme Court explains his opinions permitting states to restrict campaign contributions under the First Amendment. In *Buckley* v. *Valeo* [(1976)], the majority held that the

First Amendment was violated by a law that limited the amount a candidate for office could spend from his personal funds or family funds under his control. Marshall dissented on the grounds the law was justified "in promoting the reality and appearance of equal access to the political arena."

> The perception that personal wealth wins elections may not only discourage potential candidates without significant personal wealth from entering the political arena but also undermine public confidence in the integrity of the electoral process.

More recently, he wrote for the majority that a state, under the First Amendment, could ban corporations from supporting or opposing candidates in state elections with general treasury funds [*Austin* v. *Michigan Chamber of Commerce* (1990)] because of the state's interest in reducing "the threat that huge corporate treasuries amassed with the aid of favorable state laws will be used to influence unfairly the outcome of elections."

DISCRIMINATION AGAINST THE POOR

While laws that discriminated on the basis of race were subject to strict scrutiny under equal protection, Court decisions were ambiguous on how to treat legislation that discriminated against the poor in Marshall's early years on the Court. In 1970, the majority used the rational-basis approach to uphold a California law requiring a local voter referendum whenever low-income housing is to be built *(James* v. *Valtierra)*. No such referenda were required for other types of governmentally assisted housing. Marshall dissented, believing that a classification on the basis of poverty is "a suspect classification which demands exacting judicial scrutiny."

> It is far too late in the day to contend that the Fourteenth Amendment prohibits only racial discrimination; and to me, singling out the poor to bear a burden not placed on any other class of citizens tramples the values the Fourteenth Amendment was designed to protect.

However, bowing to the realities of such decisions as *Dandridge* v. *Williams* and *San Antonio School District* v. *Rodriguez,* Marshall, in later decisions, noted that strict scrutiny was not available to legislation which disfavors the poor. However, his sliding-scale approach would protect the poor by requiring heightened judicial scrutiny of such legislation, although as the Warren Court became a dim memory, the Court refused to use any additional scrutiny beyond the rational-basis test when faced with legislation discriminating against the poor.

Marshall explained that the cases in which the Court was willing to invalidate legislation directed against the poor often involved restrictions on voting or access to the courts:

One source of these decisions, in my view, is a deep distrust of policies that specially burden the access of disadvantaged persons to the governmental institutions and processes that offer members of our society an opportunity to improve their status and better their lives. The intent of the Fourteenth Amendment was to abolish caste legislation. . . . When state action has the predictable tendency to entrap the poor and create a permanent underclass, that intent is frustrated. . . . Thus, to the extent that a law places discriminatory barriers between indigents and the basic tools and opportunities that might enable them to rise, exacting scrutiny should be applied [*Kadrmas* v. *Dickinson Public Schools* (1988)].

Justice Marshall brought to the Court a perspective of the poor which he was willing to share with his colleagues when the occasion required. In one of his most memorable dissents, [*United States* v. *Kras* (1973)], he responded to the majority's holding that a fifty-dollar filing fee for filing a bankruptcy petition was not an unconstitutional denial of access to the courts for a person who could not pay the fee. The majority noted that the fee could be paid in installments over six months, with the possibility of a three-month extension, lowering the weekly amount to $1.28, "a sum less than the payments Kras makes on his couch of negligible value in storage, and less than the price of a movie and little more than the cost of a pack or two of cigarettes."

Marshall shot back:

It may be easy for some people to think that weekly savings of less than two dollars are no burden. But no one who has had close contact with poor people can fail to understand how close to the margin of survival many of them are. A sudden illness, for example, may destroy whatever savings they may have accumulated, and by eliminating a sense of security may destroy the incentive to save in the future. A pack or two of cigarettes may be, for them, not a routine purchase but a luxury indulged in only rarely. The desperately poor almost never go to see a movie, which the majority seems to believe is an almost weekly activity. They have more important things to do with what little money they have—like attempting to provide some comforts for a gravely ill child, as Kras must do.

It is perfectly proper for judges to disagree about what the Constitution requires. But it is disgraceful for an interpretation of the Constitution to be premised upon unfounded assumptions about how people live.

Marshall was quick to challenge assumptions by the Court about the ability of the poor to protect their rights. For example, in one case, the court stated that a litigant could have used state remedies to recover her goods, but Marshall pointed out that state law required posting of a bond which the litigant could not afford. "I cannot remain silent as the Court demonstrates, not for the first time, an attitude of callous indifference to the realities of life for the poor." [*Flagg Bros. Inc.*, v. *Brooks* (1978).]

Marshall's belief that the Constitution protects the rights of everyone was never more eloquently expressed than in the case of *Wyman* v. *James* (1971). The majority held that the Fourth Amendment's prohibition of unreasonable searches and seizures was not violated by the termination of a welfare recipient's benefits because she refused to permit her caseworker to make a home visit, even though she was willing to meet with the caseworker outside her home. Distinguishing this case from other cases involving home searches, the majority noted that the caseworker was not a sleuth, but a friend to one in need; that the recipient could refuse entry with no risk of criminal penalty, just a termination of welfare benefits; and that there were important reasons for such home visits, including detection of child abuse.

Marshall took the offensive in dissent:

Would the majority sanction, in the absence of probable cause, compulsory visits to all American homes for the purpose of discovering child abuse? Or is this Court prepared to hold as a matter of constitutional law that a mother, merely because she is poor, is substantially more likely to injure or exploit her children? Such a categorical approach to an entire class of citizens would be dangerously at odds with the tenets of our democracy.

In deciding that the homes of AFDC recipients are not entitled to protection from warrantless searches by welfare caseworkers, the Court declines to follow prior case law and employs a rationale that, if applied to the claims of all citizens, would threaten the vitality of the Fourth Amendment. This Court has occasionally pushed beyond established constitutional contours to protect the vulnerable and to further basic human values. I find no little irony in the fact that the burden of today's departure from principled adjudication is placed upon the lowly poor. Perhaps the majority has explained why a commercial warehouse deserves more protection than does this poor woman's home. I am not convinced . . .

EXPANDING THE REACH OF THE CONSTITUTION

A. State Action

Except for the Thirteenth Amendment's prohibition of slavery, the Constitution's guarantees of individual rights only protect persons from action by governmental officials, not private persons, corporations, etc. The line between "state action" and private action, however, is not always clear. For example, Thurgood Marshall argued successfully on behalf of the NAACP Legal Defense Fund that the Texas Democratic party's establishing an all-white primary constituted state action and violated the Fifteenth Amendment's prohibition of racial discrimination by the state in voting [*Smith* v. *Allwright* (1944)].

From the outset of his tenure on the Court, Justice Marshall pushed for an expansion of the state-action doctrine. In his first term, he wrote for the majority that a privately owned shopping center is subject to constitutional constraints and could therefore not ban peaceful labor picketing of a store in the mall [*Food Employees* v. *Logan Valley Plaza* (1968)]. Marshall relied on an earlier Supreme Court decision, *Marsh* v. *Alabama* (1946)], which held that a company-owned town could not stop leafletting in the business district, equating the malls to the business district in Marsh. He worried that permitting shopping malls to stop such activities would create a "cordon sanitaire" around suburban stores, immunizing themselves from such protest activities as "workers seeking to challenge substandard working conditions, consumers protesting shoddy or overpriced merchandise, and minority groups seeking nondiscriminatory hiring policies." He distinguished shopping centers from the home where privacy interests are at stake.

The Court in Logan Valley left open the question of whether picketing on an issue not directly related to the use to which the property is put could be banned. In that case, labor picketing was directly related to the property. Four years later, the Court held in *Lloyd Corp.* v. *Tanner* [(1972)], that picketing on a privately owned shopping center to protest the Vietnam War could be banned, deciding the issue left open in Logan Valley. Marshall dissented, believing that when balancing freedom of speech and freedom of a private property owned to control his property, the balance is to be struck in favor of speech.

> For many persons who do not have easy access to television, radio, the major newspapers, and the other forms of mass media, the only way they can express themselves to a broad range of citizens on issues of general public concern is to picket, or to handbill, or to utilize other free or relatively inexpensive means of communication. The only hope that these people have to be able to communicate effectively is to be permitted to speak in these areas in which most of their fellow citizens can be found.

Marshall worried that in the future, with more and more government activities taken over by the private sector, it would become "harder and harder for citizens to find means to communicate with other citizens. Only the wealthy may find effective communication possible . . . When there are no effective means of communication, free speech is a mere shibboleth."

In *Lloyd Corp.*, Marshall suspected that the majority wanted to overrule *Logan Valley* but hesitated to do so since the decision was only four years old. He noted that "the composition of this Court has radically changed in four years." His worry became reality in 1976 when the Court overruled *Logan Valley* in the case of *Hudgens* v. *NLRB*. In his dissent, Marshall noted that he recognized the legitimacy of the values of privacy and autonomy associated with private property, but "property that is privately owned is not always held for private use, and when a property owner opens his property to public use the force of those values diminishes." Although now in dissent, he continued to believe that "the shopping center owner has assumed the traditional role of the state in its control of historical First Amendment forums."

The final chapter on the shopping-center cases was written in 1980 when the Court decided *PruneYard Shopping Center* v. *Robins*. The California Supreme Court interpreted the California Constitution to protect free-speech rights on shopping centers. The shopping center owner claimed that the state was depriving it of its property rights to exclude expressive activities of others. The U.S. Supreme Court rejected that claim. Marshall, concurring, applauded the state court's decision to adopt under its constitution Marshall's reading of the U.S. Constitution in the earlier cases, noting that the state court's action "is a part of a very healthy trend of affording state constitutional provisions a more expansive interpretation than this Court has given to the Federal Constitution," citing Justice Brennan's Law Review article on state constitutions and the protection of individual rights.

Justice Marshall has objected to the Court's narrowing of the state-action doctrine in areas outside shopping centers. In *Jackson* v. *Metropolitan Edison Co.* (1974), the Court held that a private electric utility company—the only one in town—was not subject to constitutional restrictions of due process when it cut off service to a customer without a hearing. Marshall's dissent stressed the monopoly position held by the utility, that its extensive regulation by the state and the essential public service it performs should constitute state action. The implications of the decision were particularly troubling:

> [T]he majority's analysis would seemingly apply as well to a [private utility] company that refused to extend service to Negroes, welfare recipients, or any other group that the company preferred, for its own reasons, not to serve. I cannot believe that this Court would hold that the State's involvement with the utility company was not sufficient to impose upon the company an obligation to meet the constitutional mandate of a nondiscrimination. Yet nothing in the analysis of the majority opinion suggests otherwise.

Even where the state heavily regulates and provides virtually all the funds to a private school to fulfill the state's statutory duty to educate children with special needs, the Court has found no state action in a suit brought by teachers who were discharged for criticizing school policies. Marshall's dissent characterized the Court's decision as "a return to empty formalism in state sanction doctrine . . . I believe that the state-action requirement must be given a more sensitive and flexible interpretation than the majority offers."

B. Standing

The question of who should be able to raise constitutional claims in court raises the issue of standing. A finding that a party has no standing means that the constitutional issue is not reached. In 1972, Marshall wrote one of the leading opinions for the Court when he held that only a person directly injured by a law has standing to challenge it [*Linda R. S.* v. *Richard D.*].

More frequently, Marshall dissented from the Burger and Rehnquist Courts denial of standing. For example, he believed that a group, Reservists to Stop the War, had standing to sue congressmen who were members of the Armed Forces Reserves on the grounds that it violated the Incompatibility Clause of the Constitution for members of Congress to hold another federal office. Without reaching the merits of the claim, the majority denied standing [*Schlesinger* v. *Reservists to Stop the War* (1974)]. In his dissent, Marshall noted the irony that the Court had given standing to persons in an environmental case for interference with aesthetic appreciation of natural resources, "while one who contends that a violation of a specific provision of the United States Constitution has interfered with the effectiveness of expression protected by the First Amendment is turned away without a hearing on the merits of his claim."

In 1980, the Court held that a person whose property is seized does not automatically have standing to claim that the search and seizure violates the Fourth Amendment. Rather, there must be a legitimate expectation of privacy in the place searched for a person to be able to raise the constitutional claim [*Rawlings* v. *Kentucky* (1980)]. Marshall dissented, noting that the text and history of the Fourth Amendment protects both the place searched and the property seized. He believed that hostility to the Fourth Amendment was responsible for their decision:

Today, a majority of the Court has substantially cut back the protection afforded by the Fourth Amendment and the ability of the people to claim that protection, apparently out of concern lest the government's ability to obtain criminal convictions be impeded. A slow and steady erosion of the ability of victims of unconstitutional searches and seizures to obtain a remedy for the invasion of their rights saps the constitutional guarantee of its life just as surely as would a substantive limitation. Because we are called on to decide whether evidence should be excluded only when a search has been "successful," it is easy to forget that the standards we announce determine what government conduct is reasonable in searches and seizures directed at persons who turn out to be innocent as well as those who are guilty. I continue to believe that ungrudging application of the Fourth Amendment is indispensable to preserving the liberties of a democratic society.

EQUALIZING THE BALANCE BETWEEN THE STATE AND THE INDIVIDUAL

With twenty-five years' experience as a lawyer fighting for justice for the poor and racial minorities in courts across the country, Justice Marshall brought to the Court a unique perspective on the importance of fair legal processes. He insisted that constitutional rights be respected at every stage, from a person's initial confrontation with law-enforcement officers all the way up to the U.S. Supreme Court. Our system of justice should strive to have individuals know their rights, to provide representation at all stages by knowledgeable counsel and to have courts available for trial, appeal, and postconviction relief. Although Marshall was able to persuade his colleagues in some cases, most of the time he wrote dissents from the Court's refusal to even the balance between the individual and the state.

A. Rights of the Suspect

In 1965, U.S. Solicitor General Thurgood Marshall appeared before the Supreme Court to argue one of the companion cases to *Miranda* v. *Arizona* which held that a suspect who is interrogated in police custody must be given certain warnings, including the right to have counsel paid for by the state during interrogation. As Solicitor General, he argued against requiring the state to pay for the suspect's lawyer, but as a justice, he was the strongest supporter of *Miranda* on the Court. He was critical of his colleagues who were willing to uphold warnings that were ambiguous. "The recipients of police warnings are often frightened suspects unlettered in the law, not lawyers or judges or others schooled in interpreting legal or semantic nuance." [*Duckworth* v. *Eagan* (1989)] He similarly chided the majority for holding that a suspect's question—"What is going to happen to me now?"—indicated a willingness to talk about the crime. "If [the suspect's] question had been posed by Jean-Paul Sartre before a class of philosophy students, it might well have evinced a desire for a 'generalized' discussion. But under the circumstances of this case, it is plain that [his] only 'desire' was to find out where the police were going to take him" [*Oregon* v. *Bradshaw* (1983)].

As the Court began to carve out exceptions to *Miranda,* Marshall decried the nibbling away at *Miranda*'s foundations. For example, the Court created an exception permitting the police to question without warnings when public safety so requires, [*New York* v. *Quarles* (1984)], prompting Marshall to state that, by permitting questions without warnings, the Court was admitting compelled testimony in violation of the Fifth Amendment. He objected to the Court's cost-benefit analysis of weighing the rights of the individual against the need for public safety:

> The majority should not be permitted to elude the Amendment's absolute prohibition simply by calculating special costs that arise when the public's safety is at issue. Indeed, were constitutional adjudication always conducted in such an ad hoc manner, the Bill of Rights would be a most unreliable protector of individual liberties.

In a case in which the majority held that an undercover police officer, pretending to be a cellmate, need not give warnings when questioning the suspect [*Illinois* v. *Perkins* (1990)], Marshall objected that such an exception "complicates a previously clear and straightforward doctrine" and could lead to "a proliferation of departmental policies to encourage police officers to conduct interrogations of confined suspects through undercover agents, thereby circumventing the need to administer *Miranda* warnings." And to the majority's creation of another exception for "routine booking questions," Marshall observed that these exceptions, "undermine *Miranda*'s fundamental principle that the doctrine should be clear so that it can be easily applied by both police and courts" [*Pennsylvania* v. *Muniz* (1990)].

* * *

In 1973, the Court faced a Miranda-type problem involving a different amendment: Must the police advise a suspect that he has the right to refuse a police request to search his property under the Fourth Amendment? The majority held that there was no such right; so long as consent is voluntarily given, the search is valid. Marshall, in dissent, asked: How can a person give up a right without knowing of its existence? He would require the police to advise the suspect of his right to refuse consent, which the majority refused to require because of "practicality." Marshall responded:

> [W]hen the Court speaks of practicality, what it really is talking of is the continued ability of the police to capitalize on the ignorance of citizens so as to accomplish by subterfuge what they could not achieve by relying only on the knowing relinquishment of constitutional rights. Of course it would be "practical" for the police to ignore the commands of the Fourth Amendment, if by practicality we mean that mere criminals will be apprehended, even though the constitutional rights of innocent people also go by the board. But such a practical advantage is achieved only by the cost of permitting the police to disregard the limitations that the Constitution places on this behavior, a cost that a constitutional democracy cannot long absorb.

Marshall believed that the Court's holding would mean that only the "sophisticated, the knowledgeable, and . . . the few" would be capable of refusing consent, and that the Court's holding was solely for the convenience of the police:

> The framers of the Fourth Amendment struck the balance against this sort of convenience and in favor of certain basic civil rights. It is not for the Court to restrike that balance because of its own views of the needs of law-enforcement officers.

B. Obligation of Prosecutors

Prosecutors have a dual role in the criminal process: to be the advocate for the state in presenting the case against the defendant and to ensure that a fair verdict is reached. To fulfill that latter role, the Court held in 1963 that due process requires the prosecution to give to defense counsel any favorable evidence that is material with respect to guilt or punishment, thereby giving counsel the opportunity to introduce the favorable evidence to the jury. Marshall's explanation of why the Court recognized this obligation to disclose, which is inconsistent with the prosecutor's adversarial role, reveals his view of the real world of criminal justice administration:

> This recognition no doubt stems in part from the frequently considerable imbalance in resources between most criminal defendants and most prosecutors' offices. Many, perhaps most, criminal defendants in the United States are represented by appointed counsel, who often are paid minimal wages and operate on shoestring budgets. In addition, unlike police, defense counsel generally is not present at the scene of the crime, or at the time of arrest, but instead comes into the case late. Moreover, unlike the government, defense counsel is not in the position to make deals with witnesses to gain evidence. Thus, an inexperienced, unskilled, or unaggressive attorney often is unable to amass the factual support necessary to a reasonable defense.[2]

Marshall wrote that the due process clause speaks "to the balance of forces between the accused and his accuser" in striking down a state law which required the defendant to turn over information to the prosecutor, without a reciprocal obligation that the prosecutor turn over information it had to the defendant [*Wardius* v. *Oregon* (1973)]. Under Oregon's procedure of pretrial discovery, defendants were required to inform the prosecutor of their intention to introduce an alibi defense at trial. There was no requirement that the state give any information it had, for example, witnesses who would refute the alibi defense. Marshall wrote for the Court that, in general, discovery was a two-way street:

> The State may not insist that trials be run as a "search for truth" so far as defense witnesses are concerned, while maintaining "poker game" secrecy for its own witnesses. It is fundamentally unfair to require a defendant to divulge the details of his own case while at the same time subjecting him to the hazard of surprise concerning refutation of the very pieces of evidence which he disclosed to the State.

[2] This statement came in a dissent [*United States* v. *Bagley* (1985)] where the majority held that failure to disclose would not require a new trial unless there is a reasonable probability the jury would have decided differently with that evidence. Marshall argued for a tougher standard ordering a new trial unless it was clear beyond a reasonable doubt the outcome would have been the same.

C. Access to Competent Counsel

In 1963, the Court held in the Gideon case that the Sixth Amendment entitles a defendant to counsel to represent him in felony trials at no cost to the defendant. Later cases extended the right to counsel to misdemeanors and any other case in which the defendant is sentenced to jail. Defendants are entitled to "effective assistance of counsel," but it was not until 1984 that the Court addressed the question: what level of attorney competence is required to satisfy the requirement of "effective assistance?" In *Strickland* v. *Washington,* the Court held that counsel's performance was inadequate if it "fell below an objective standard of reasonableness," and in such a case, the conviction is to be reversed only if "there is a reasonable probability that, but for counsel's unprofessional errors, the result of the proceeding would have been different."

Marshall dissented from both parts of the Court's holding. First, the majority failed to define what it meant by "reasonableness," and therefore it would provide no guidance to lower courts. Second, the requirement that there is a reasonable probability of a different outcome would be difficult for defendants to prove. Moreover,

> [T]he assumption on which the Court's holding rests is that the only purpose of the constitutional guarantee of effective assistance of counsel is to reduce the chance that innocent persons will be convicted. In my view, the guarantee also functions to ensure that convictions are obtained only through fundamentally fair procedures. The majority contends that the Sixth Amendment is not violated when a manifestly guilty defendant is convicted after a trial in which he was represented by a manifestly ineffective attorney. I cannot agree. Every defendant is entitled to a trial in which his interests are vigorously and conscientiously advocated by an able lawyer. A proceeding in which the defendant does not receive meaningful assistance in meeting the forces of the State does not, in my opinion, constitute due process.

Marshall's worry that Strickland would provide no help to badly represented defendants was reiterated in a dissent from the Court's refusal to hear an ineffective assistance claim in a case involving capital punishment [*Mitchell* v. *Kemp.* (1987)]. In this case, defendant pleaded guilty to murder. At the sentencing proceeding, defense counsel called no witnesses and presented no mitigating evidence, relying on a legal defense that was without merit. He interviewed no witnesses concerning mitigation even though there were many such witnesses available. This prompted Justice Marshall to write:

> In light of the importance that this Court has placed upon the role mitigating evidence in capital-sentencing decisions, I cannot believe the *Strickland* was intended to permit a defendant to be sentenced to death solely on the basis of the State's evidence, when a powerful defense easily could have been marshaled on his behalf. Any reasonable standard of professionalism governing the conduct of a capital defense must impose upon the attorney, at a minimum, the obligation to explore the aspects of his clients' character that might persuade the sentencer to spare his life. Without even this effort by the defense, the adversarial process breaks down. By denying certiorari in this compelling case, the Court has refused to apply *Strickland* in a manner that gives meaning to the constitutional values from which it was derived.

Marshall was well aware that the mistakes of counsel are visited, literally, on the heads of defendants. For that reason, he believed that

> an attorney must consult with the client fully on matters of constitutional magnitude. Without such consultation, the representation of criminal defendants becomes only another method of manipulating persons in situations where their control over their lives is precisely what is at stake [*Tollett* v. *Henderson* (1973)].

D. Right to Confer with Counsel

For Justice Marshall, prosecutorial spying by an undercover agent on attorney-client communications is automatic grounds for reversal of a criminal conviction because it undermines the adversarial process and because it threatens the right to effective assistance of counsel. In *Weatherford* v. *Bursey* (1977), the majority held that reversal is required only if the information is communicated to the prosecutor or if the witness testified against the defendant. Marshall's dissent stressed that "the precious constitutional rights at stake here . . . need 'breathing space to survive' . . . and a prophylactic prohibition on all intrusions of this sort is therefore essential." Broad protection of constitutional rights was a repetitive theme in Marshall's jurisprudence.

E. Beyond the Right to Counsel

Marshall wrote for the majority in holding for the first time that due process requires the state to provide an indigent defendant with access to a psychiatrist where the defendant's sanity at the time of the offense is likely to be a significant factor at the trial [*Ake* v. *Oklahoma* (1985)]. Marshall stated that this decision was in line with earlier decisions whose theme was meaningful access to justice to assure the proper functioning of the adversary process. "[A] criminal trial is fundamentally unfair if the State proceeds against an indigent defendant without making certain that he has access to the raw materials integral to the building of an effective defense." Marshall was not only concerned about the rights of defendants to help in their trial and appeals but also about the rights of a person who has been convicted and wants to challenge his conviction once in prison. Writing for or a majority, Marshall held that "the fundamental constitutional right of access to the courts requires prison authorities to assist inmates in the preparation and filing of meaningful legal papers by providing prisoners with adequate law libraries or adequate assistance from persons trained in the law" [*Bounds* v. *Smith* (1977)].

FAIR PROCESS FOR PERSONS ACCUSED OF CRIME

Our Government is the potent, the omnipresent teacher. For good or for ill, it teaches the whole people by its example. Crime is contagious. If the Government becomes a lawbreaker, it breeds contempt for law; it invites every man to become a law unto himself; it invites anarchy. To declare that in the administration of the criminal law the end justifies the means—to declare that the Government may commit crimes in order to secure the conviction of a private criminal—would bring terrible retribution. Against that pernicious doctrine this Court should resolutely set its face.

Brandeis, J. dissenting in *Olmstead* v. *United States,* (1928)

A. Ends and Means

Justice Brandeis ended his dissenting opinion in *Olmstead* v. *United States* with what has become the most famous judicial statement on the need for controlling governmental misconduct. That quote well summarizes Justice Marshall's own views on the necessity of lawful behavior by law enforcement officials in the administration of the criminal law. It was used to conclude his concurring opinion in *Brewer* v. *Williams* (1977) which he wrote in response to three dissenting opinions which strongly criticized the majority for upholding defendant's claim that his confession was obtained in an unconstitutional manner. The dissenters, said Marshall, have "lost sight of the fundamental constitutional backbone of our criminal law" in finding that the detective's actions in obtaining the confession were examples of good police work.

> In my view, good police work is something far different from catching the criminal at any price. It is equally important that the police, as guardians of the law, fulfill their responsibility to obey its command scrupulously. For "in the end life and liberty can be as much endangered from illegal methods used to convict those thought to be criminals as from the actual criminals themselves."

Marshall then summarized the detective's conduct which resulted in obtaining the confession as intentional police misconduct—not good police practice—that the Court rightly condemns.

> The heinous nature of the crime is no excuse, as the dissenters would have it, for condoning knowing and intentional police transgression of the constitutional rights of a defendant. If Williams is to go free . . . [i]t will be because Detective Leaming, knowing full well that he risked reversal of Williams's conviction, intentionally denied Williams the right of *every* American under the Sixth Amendment to have the protective shield of a lawyer between himself and the awesome power of the State.

B. Judicial Integrity

In addition to excluding evidence obtained in a violation of the Constitution, as in *Brewer,* Marshall would exclude evidence obtained in violation of federal regulations, something a majority of the Court is reluctant to do in recent cases. For example, electronic monitoring of face-to-face conversations by government agents and an individual has been held by the Court not to violate the Fourth Amendment because a person has no reasonable expectation that such conversations will remain private. Although the IRS had enacted regulations restricting such surveillance, the Court held that violation of the regulations should not result in excluding those conversations from evidence at the defendant's trial for bribing the agent [*United States* v. *Caceres* (1979)]. Marshall dissented, first finding that due process was violated by agency violation of its own regulations, then going on to say that, even if there was no constitutional violation, the evidence should be excluded:

> [T]here are significant values served by a rule that excludes evidence secured by lawless enforcement of the law. Denying an agency the fruits of noncompliance gives credibility to the due process and privacy interest implicated by its conduct. Also, and perhaps more significantly, exclusion reaffirms the Judiciary's commitment to those values. Preservation of judicial integrity demands that unlawful intrusions on privacy should "find no sanction in the judgments of the courts." . . . Today's holding necessarily confers upon the Judiciary a "taint of partnership in official lawlessness."

The Court's unwillingness to use its power to supervise federal criminal trials by excluding illegally seized evidence prompted a vehement dissent by Marshall in the case of *United States* v. *Payner* (1980). In that case, IRS agents intentionally violated the Fourth Amendment rights of an individual by having a paid informant enter his apartment and steal his briefcase, photograph four hundred documents taken from the briefcase and later steal a Rolodex file from his office. The evidence obtained was used against other persons, who did not have "standing" to object the constitutional violations because the Court has held that only persons whose own Fourth Amendment rights are violated can complain.

Although the Court had in the past used a "supervisory power" rationale by which nonconstitutional claims can be raised, it refused to use that theory in *Payner,* holding that the same rules of standing for constitutional violations also apply to a person claiming supervisory power violations. Marshall's dissent noted that this case was particularly appropriate for use of the supervisory power "to prevent the federal courts from becoming accomplices to such misconduct." Citing Brandeis's dissent in *Olmstead* as perhaps the best expression of the need for the use of the supervisory power, Marshall said that the court should not lend its aid in the enforcement of the criminal law when the government itself was guilty of misconduct. By admitting the evidence, "the judiciary has given full effect to the deliberate wrongdoings of the Government. . . . Such a pollution of the federal courts should not be permitted."

C. Presumption of Innocence

In the Bail Reform Act of 1984, Congress authorized the pretrial detention of persons who have been indicted on federal charges if the judge finds by clear and convincing evidence that the person poses a danger to others or to the community. In *United States* v. *Salerno* (1987), the Supreme Court upheld the Act despite claims that it violated due process of the Fifth Amendment and violated the Eighth Amendment's prohibition of excessive bail. Marshall's dissent characterized such statutes as "consistent with the usages of tyranny and the excesses of what bitter experience teaches us to call the police state" which "have long been thought incompatible with the fundamental human rights protected by our Constitution." He stated that the proposition "innocent until proven guilty" is established by the due process clause, although the Court has never explicitly held that the presumption is part of due process. Marshall admits that honoring the presumption is difficult: "Sometimes we must pay substantial social costs as a result of our commitment to the values we espouse."

> But at the end of the day the presumption of innocence protects the innocent; the shortcuts we take with those whom we believe to be guilty injure only those wrongfully accused and, ultimately, ourselves.

> Throughout the world today there are men, women, and children interned indefinitely, awaiting trials which may never come or which may be a mockery of the word, because their governments believe them to be "dangerous." Our Constitution, whose construction began two centuries ago, can shelter us forever from the evils of such unchecked power. Over two hundred years it has slowly, through our efforts, grown more durable, more expansive, and more just. But it cannot protect us if we lack the courage, and the self-restraint, to protect ourselves. Today a majority of the Court applies itself to an ominous exercise in demolition. Theirs is truly a decision which will go forth without authority, and come back without respect.

D. Capital Punishment

In the 1972 case of *Furman* v. *Georgia,* the Court by a 5–4 vote held that the imposition and carrying out of the death penalty in the three cases before the Court—one involving murder, two involving rape—

constituted cruel and unusual punishment in violation of the Eighth Amendment. Each justice wrote his own opinion. In his concurring opinion, Marshall noted that the fate of almost six hundred other persons on death row depended on the Court's decision.

Marshall found the most important principle in determining whether a punishment was cruel and unusual was that it evolved over time: "a penalty that was permissible at one time in our Nation's history is not necessarily permissible today." For capital punishment to be unconstitutional, it must be found "to be excessive or unnecessary, or because it is abhorrent to currently existing moral values."

Marshall first found that the death penalty was excessive and unnecessary. There was no evidence that capital punishment was a greater deterrent to crime than life imprisonment. If its only purpose was retribution or vengeance, that would not justify its existence:

> At times a cry is heard that morality requires vengeance to evidence society's abhorrence of the act. But the Eighth Amendment is our insulation from our baser selves. The "cruel and unusual" language limits the avenues through which vengeance can be channeled. Were this not so, the language would be empty and a return to the rack and other tortures would be possible in a given case.

The dissenters argued that in a democracy, legislators make policy choices such as the wisdom of capital punishment. Marshall argued since there was little if any evidence that capital punishment served no legitimate purpose life imprisonment did not also serve.

> The point has now been reached at which deference to the legislatures is tantamount to abdication of our judicial roles as fact-finders, judges, and ultimate arbiters of the Constitution. We know that at some point the presumption of constitutionality accorded legislative acts gives way to a realistic assessment of those acts. This point comes where there is sufficient evidence available so that judges can determine, not whether the legislature acted wisely, but whether it had any rational basis whatsoever for acting. We have this evidence before us now. There is no rational basis for concluding that capital punishment is not excessive.

Even if not excessive, Marshall argued that capital punishment is unconstitutional "because it is morally unacceptable to the people of the United States at this time in their history." First, he believed that the people would not support capital punishment if informed that its sole purpose was "purposeless vengeance." Further disapproval would come if the people realized that it is imposed discriminatorily against certain groups, such as blacks, has been imposed against innocent people, and "wreaks havoc with our entire criminal justice system." With respect to its imposition on certain groups, Marshall wrote:

> It also is evidence that the burden of capital punishment falls upon the poor, the ignorant, and the underprivileged members of society. It is the poor, and the members of minority groups who are least able to voice their complaints against capital punishment. Their impotence leaves them victims of a sanction that the wealthier, better-represented, just-as-guilty person can escape. So long as the capital sanction is used only against the forlorn, easily forgotten members of society, legislators are content to maintain the status quo, because change would draw attention to the problem and concern might develop. Ignorance is perpetuated and apathy soon becomes its mate, and we have today's situation.

Marshall stated that if all the facts of capital punishment were known, "the average citizen would . . . find it shocking to his conscience and sense of justice." Other justices found this conclusion speculative, but Marshall countered that "the people of this country would care" if they learned that "it is only the poor, the ignorant, the racial minorities, and the hapless in our society" who are executed "for no real reason other than to satisfy some vague notion of society's cry for vengeance":

> I cannot agree that the American people have been so hardened, so embittered that they want to take the life of one who performs even the basest criminal act knowing that the execution is nothing more than bloodlust. This has not been my experience with my fellow citizens. Rather, I have found that they earnestly desire their system of punishments to make sense in order that it can be a morally justifiable system.

Marshall knew that the Court's decision to invalidate the death penalty statutes was a controversial one and he closed his opinion with a ringing defense of the Court's action:

> At a time in our history when the streets of the Nation's cities inspire fear and despair, rather than pride and hope, it is difficult

to maintain objectivity and concern for our fellow citizens. But, the measure of a country's greatness is its ability to retain compassion in time of crisis. No nation in the recorded history of man has a greater tradition of revering justice and fair treatment for all its citizens in times of turmoil, confusion, and tension than ours. This is a country which stands tallest in troubled times, a country that clings to fundamental principles, cherishes its constitutional heritage, and rejects simple solutions that compromise the values that lie at the roots of our democratic system.

In striking down capital punishment, this Court does not malign our system of government. On the contrary, it pays homage to it. Only in a free society could right triumph in difficult times, and could civilization record its magnificent advancement. In recognizing the humanity of our fellow beings, we pay ourselves the highest tribute. We achieve "a major milestone, in the long road up from barbarism: and join the approximately seventy other jurisdictions in the world which celebrate their regard for civilization and humanity by shunning capital punishment.

In the years after *Furman,* many states rewrote their death penalty statutes to address the concerns of some of the justices who concurred in the Furman decision. In 1976, a majority of the Court upheld the imposition of the death penalty, with Marshall dissenting [*Gregg* v. *Georgia*]. He admitted that the fact thirty-five states had rewritten their death penalty laws cast doubt on his assertion in Furman that the death penalty was morally unacceptable to the American people, although he still believed that if citizens were truly informed about capital punishment, they would oppose it. Aside from that argument, however, he still believed that the death penalty was unconstitutional because it was excessive. A new study on the deterrent effect of capital punishment did not change Marshall's mind on that aspect of the death penalty. What disturbed him most was that several members of the Court's majority approved retribution as a legitimate reason for imposing the death penalty, reasoning that it prevents people from forming lynch mobs. Marshall countered: "It simply defies belief to suggest that the death penalty is necessary to prevent the American people from taking the law into their own hands."

Another argument made by some of the justices in the majority was that retribution for its own sake justified capital punishment because the community demands it. But, concluded Marshall, "the taking of life 'because the wrongdoer deserves it' surely must fall, for such a punishment has as its very basis the total denial of the wrongdoer's dignity and worth," which is the goal of the Eighth Amendment to respect.

Although Marshall was unable to persuade a majority of his colleagues that the death penalty is always cruel and unusual punishment, he continued to make that argument in dissent. He also wrote some majority opinions invalidating particular death penalty statutes, for example, holding that it is cruel and unusual punishment to execute an insane person [*Ford* v. *Wainwright* (1986)].

FAIRNESS IN CIVIL PROCEEDINGS

A. Judicial Proceedings

Since 1878, the Court has been deciding the question of when it is fair, as a matter of due process, to require persons who are not residents of a state to come to the state to appear in courts as defendants in civil lawsuits. Of the three most important decisions in the Court's history in dealing with this question, called personal jurisdiction, Marshall wrote one of them, *Shaffer* v. *Heitner,* in 1977. If there is no jurisdiction over the nonresident defendant, the plaintiff usually has no other choice but to sue the defendant in his home state.

Prior to Shaffer, the Court had developed a "minimum contacts" test, that is, the nonresident defendant must have certain minimum contacts with a state "such that the maintenance of the suit does not offend 'traditional notions of fair play and substantial justice.' " But that test did not apply if the defendant happened to have property in the state: in that case, the property could be brought to court and the plaintiff could proceed against that property to satisfy the claim. The nonresident, if he did not want to lose the property, would have to show up in court, even if there was no jurisdiction over him. If he did not appear, the plaintiff would be able to satisfy the claim against the property.

What Marshall did in Shaffer was to extend the minimum contacts test to cases involving the defendant's property, overruling that part of the 1878 case which permitted suits against the property. Marshall admitted that this long history suggests the practice met due process but that history is not decisive:

Traditional notions of fair play and substantial justice" can be as readily offended by the perpetuation of ancient forms that are no longer justified as by the adoption of new procedures that are inconsistent with the basic values of our constitutional heritage . . . the fiction that an assertion of jurisdiction over property is anything but an assertion of jurisdiction over the owner of the property supports an ancient form without substantial modern justification. Its continued acceptance would serve only to allow state-court jurisdiction that is fundamentally unfair to the defendant.

The minimum contacts test requires a judge to balance several factors, and Marshall's experience as a lawyer before joining the Court undoubtedly helped in his ability to apply the test to specific fact situations. As he observed in another case he wrote for the majority, the determination of reasonableness and minimum contacts are not subject to mechanical application. In that case, *Kulko* v. *Superior Court* (1978), the California courts had upheld jurisdiction in a suit by the mother for increased child support against the father, who was a nonresident of the state. The state reasoned that the father consented to letting his daughter live with her mother during the school year, sent her to California for that purpose, and received a financial benefit by having her daughter live in California. Marshall disagreed, noting that the father's single act of acquiescence in his child's preference is not one "that a reasonable parent would expect to result in the substantial financial burden and personal strain of litigating a child-support suit in a forum three thousand miles away."

[T]he mere act of sending a child to California to live with her mother is not a commercial act and connotes no intent to obtain or expectancy of receiving a corresponding benefit in the State that would make fair the assertion of that State's judicial jurisdiction.

In contrast to the domestic-relations setting of *Kulko,* Marshall would have upheld personal jurisdiction in a products liability case, *World-Wide Volkswagen Corp.* v. *Woodson* (1980). A car, purchased by the plaintiffs in New York, was involved in an accident in Oklahoma. The question was whether there was jurisdiction over the New York automobile dealer and regional distributor, who had no contacts with Oklahoma other than the vehicle involved in the accident. The Supreme Court, relying on *Kulko,* held there was no jurisdiction. Marshall dissented, noting that *Kulko* did not involve commercial transactions in interstate commerce:

> Commercial activity is more likely to cause effects in a larger sphere, and the actor derives an economic benefit from the activity that makes it fair to require him to answer for his conduct where its effects are felt. The profits may be used to pay the costs of suit, and knowing that the activity is likely to have effects in other States the defendant can readily ensure against the cost of those effects, thereby sparing himself much of the inconvenience of defending in a distant forum.

B. Administrative Proceedings

Marshall took three major approaches to protect individuals from arbitrary action by administrative agencies. First, he wrote an important opinion for the Court which established that courts should review an agency's action to ensure that the agency acted with care in reaching a decision concerning alternative policy choice. [*Citizens to Preserve Overton Park, Inc.* v. *Volpe, 401 (1971).*] The court is not making the decision; its role is to make sure the agency operates in a reasonable way. Second, Marshall believed that the Constitution itself established broad rights of liberty and property in the due process clauses of the Fifth and Fourteenth Amendments. In most cases, Marshall was in the dissent since the majority of the Court believed that unless state law or federal statutes established the right, no such right existed under the Constitution. For example, Marshall believed that every applicant for a government job had a "property" right to the job that could not be denied without some reason [*Board of Regents (1972)*]. The final way that Marshall sought to protect the individual from arbitrary agency action was through ensuring that the agency use fair procedure, such as an adversary hearing, before taking action against the individual. For example, he wrote in dissent that a discharged federal employee should be given the chance to cross-examine witnesses against him and bring in witnesses to testify in his own behalf [*Arnett* v. *Kennedy (1974)*].

PRIVACY

The makers of our Constitution undertook to secure conditions favorable to the pursuit of happiness. They recognized the significance of man's spiritual nature, of his feelings and of his intellect. They knew that only a part of the aim, pleasure, and satisfactions of life are to be found in material things. They sought to protect Americans in their beliefs, their thoughts, their emotions and their sensations. They conferred, as against the government, the right to be let alone—the most comprehensive of rights and the rights most valued by civilized man.

> —Brandeis, J., dissenting in *Olmstead* v. *United States* (1928)

Agreeing wholeheartedly with Brandeis's famous statement of the fundamental importance of privacy, Marshall utilized that quote in one of his most famous decisions, *Stanley* v. *Georgia* (1969), overturning a conviction of a person for possessing obscene materials in his home. In *Stanley*, two constitutional rights converged: free speech and privacy of the home:

> If the First Amendment means anything, it means that a State has no business telling a man, sitting alone in his own house, what books he may read of what films he may watch. Our whole constitutional heritage rebels at the thought of giving government the power to control men's minds.

The state argued that it had the right to protect the individual's mind from the effects of obscenity which Marshall interpreted to mean an "assertion that the State has the right to control the moral content of a person's thoughts." That, said Marshall, is inconsistent with the First Amendment.

Most of Marshall's privacy opinions area were dissents, just as Brandeis's opinion was in *Olmstead*.

A. Privacy of Place

Marshall believed that how a person wished to associate in his living arrangements was entirely his own business. In *Belle Terre* v. *Boraas* (1973), he wrote alone in dissent, objecting to the majority's deference in upholding as constitutional a village's ordinance that prohibited groups of more than two unrelated persons from living together. Marshall chided the author of the majority opinion, Justice Douglas, for abandoning his approach in an earlier case that struck down governmental interference with living arrangements. Marshall believed that two constitutional norms were violated: the First Amendment right of freedom of association and the Fourteenth Amendment's right to privacy, which he found are often inextricably entwined. Relying on earlier cases protecting associational rights of union members for their social and economic benefit, Marshall believed that "the selection of one's living companions involves similar choices as to the emotional, social, or economic benefits to be derived from alternative living arrangements."

> The choice of household companions—of whether a person's "intellectual and emotional needs" are best met by living with family, friends, professional associates, or others—involves deeply personal considerations as to the kind and quality of intimate relationships within the home. That decision surely falls within the ambit of the right to privacy protected by the Constitution.

Marshall believed that the village had acted "to fence out those individuals whose choice of lifestyle differs from that of its current residents."

B. Appearance

Marshall has been the only justice to have spoken at length about the right of a citizen to decide on issues regarding his own personal appearance. In the one Supreme Court case which raised the issue [*Kelley* v. *Johnson* (1976)], the majority merely assumed, without deciding, that matters of personal appearance are constitutionally protected and then went on to uphold as rational a county regulation that regulated the length of a policeman's hair. Believing that the regulation was irrational, Marshall's dissent reasoned that one's interest in dressing according to one's own taste was a liberty interest protected by the Constitution because

> [an] individual's personal appearance may reflect, sustain, and nourish his personality and may well be used as a means of expressing his attitude and lifestyle. In taking control over a citizen's personal appearance, the government forces him to sacrifice substantial elements of his integrity and identity as well. To say that the liberty guarantee of the Fourteenth Amendment does not encompass matters of personal appearance would be fundamentally inconsistent with the values of privacy, self-identity, autonomy, and personal integrity that I have always assumed the Constitution was designed to protect.

Noting that governments in other countries have regulated the personal appearance of their citizens, Marshall concluded:

> In an increasingly crowded society in which it is already extremely difficult to maintain one's identity and personal integrity, it would be distressing, to say the least, if the government could regulate our personal appearance unconfined by any constitutional strictures whatsoever.

C. Marriage

Although earlier cases had implicitly found that marriage was a fundamental privacy right protected by the Constitution, Marshall wrote the first opinion for the Court to explicitly so hold, *Zablocki* v. *Redhail* (1978). He invalidated a state law that prohibited a person from receiving a marriage license if the person had failed to pay child support or if the child is likely to go on public assistance. Noting that the woman whom Redhail sought to marry was pregnant and had a fundamental right to seek an abortion, Marshall said:

> Surely, a decision to marry and raise the child in a traditional family setting must receive equivalent protection. And, if [Redhail's] right to procreate means anything at all, it must imply some right to enter the only relationship in which the State of Wisconsin allows sexual relations legally to take place.

Realizing that there are many state regulations of marriage, Marshall stated that they would not be at risk of judicial invalidation by limiting rigorous judicial scrutiny to only those regulations which "significantly interfere" with the marital relationship.

D. Unconventional Personal Relationships

The Court has not yet decided a case involving state laws prohibiting fornication or adultery. It refused to hear a case in 1978 [*Hollenbaugh* v. *Carnegie Free Library*], in which two public employees, one of whom was married to someone else, were fired by their employer, a public library, for living together after the woman became pregnant. The reason for the firing was that some members of the community disapproved of their lifestyle; there was no evidence that the employees were not performing their jobs well or that members of the community used the library less frequently. The lower court upheld the dismissals using the very deferential rational-basis test. Dissenting from the Court's refusal to hear the case, Justice Marshall noted that the state had repealed its law prohibiting fornication and adultery and that the dismissals were because the employees were living together in a state of "open adultery." Marshall was particularly troubled by the library's discriminatory treatment: It was apparently willing to retain the employees, so long as they saw each other furtively.

Marshall believed that the Court's earlier privacy cases, encompassing matters of marriage and family life, similarly protected the choice of the employees to live together openly and rear their child together. "That the [employees'] arrangement was unconventional or socially disapproved does not negate the resemblance . . . particularly in the absence of a judgment that the arrangement so offends social norms as to evoke criminal sanctions." He chided the majority for giving only token protection to choices concerning individuals' private lives and said that whether or not the Court approves of those choices should be irrelevant.

E. Right to an Abortion

1. Refusal to Fund Abortions for Indigents

In the 1973 case of *Roe* v. *Wade,* the Court held that a woman's constitutional right to privacy includes the decision, with her physician, to have an abortion. At later stages of pregnancy, the state's interest in the life of the fetus becomes compelling, but a woman can still choose an abortion to protect her life or health. Marshall voted with the majority in *Roe* and in subsequent cases protecting the right of a woman to choose abortion. His opinions argued for extension of these rights to minors and indigent women.

In 1977, four years after *Roe,* the Court held that states could constitutionally choose to pay for childbirth yet refuse to fund nontherapeutic abortions under their Medicaid program for indigents [*Beal* v. *Doe*]. The Court reasoned that no fundamental right was involved because there was no unduly burdensome interference with a woman's right to choose an abortion since she was still free to obtain an abortion. Using the rational-basis test, the state could rationally have a policy which favored childbirth.

Marshall criticized the Court for its deference to state legislators when enacting laws involving those outside the political process:

The impact of the regulations here falls tragically upon those among us least able to help or defend themselves. As the Court well knows, these regulations inevitably will have the practical effect of preventing nearly all poor women from obtaining safe and legal abortion. . . . The enactments challenged here brutally coerce poor women to bear children whom society will scorn for every day of their lives.

Noting that many of these children will live in foster homes and attend segregated schools with little chance to grow up in a decent environment, Marshall was "appalled at the ethical bankruptcy of those who preach a 'right to life' that means, under present social policies, a bare existence in utter misery for so many poor women and their children." He concluded his dissent with a strong criticism of the majority: "When elected leaders cower before public pressure, this Court, more than ever, must not shirk its duty to enforce the Constitution for the benefit of the poor and powerless."

In 1980, the Court was faced with a federal law—the Hyde Amendment—that prohibited the use of federal funds for some therapeutic abortions as distinguished from the nontherapeutic abortions in the 1977 cases. The Court upheld the law in *Harris* v. *McRae*. Marshall once again criticized the Court for its unwillingness to use a different level of scrutiny given legislation "whose cruel impact falls exclusively on indigent pregnant women" from other legislation "that makes distinctions between economic interests more than able to protect themselves in the political process." Moreover, since minority women obtain abortions at twice the rate as white women, that racial impact ought also to be relevant. The impact of the Court's decision would be that indigent women would carry the fetus to term, even though that could result in injury or death to the mother and fetus, or resort to self-help or illegal abortions. Marshall concluded:

One category of medically necessary expenditure has been singled out for exclusion, and the sole basis for the exclusion is a premise repudiated for purposes of constitutional law in *Roe* v. *Wade*. The consequence is a devastating impact on the lives and health of poor women. I do not believe that a Constitution committed to the equal protection of the laws can tolerate this result.

2. Right of Minors to an Abortion

Marshall dissented in a 1990 case, *Hodgson* v. *Minnesota*, which upheld a state law requiring parental notification of a minor's intent to obtain an abortion. The specific provision of the law required the minor to notify one or both parents and wait forty-eight hours before obtaining the abortion; if she did not want to notify her parents, she had the option of requesting a judge to grant permission to have the abortion. If the judge determined that the minor was mature enough to make her own decision, or if immature, it was still in her best interests not to notify her parents, he could authorize the abortion.

Marshall objected to the parental notification because it forced the pregnant minor to disclose a deeply personal matter which could have traumatic effects on the young woman depending on her relationship with her parents. It is possible she could be physically or psychologically harmed by her parents upon notification. As Marshall wrote in a similar dissent in a 1981 case, the parental notification may cause "actual obstruction of the abortion decision," and the threat of parental notice "may cause some minor women to delay past the first trimester of pregnancy, after which the health risks increase significantly." In addition, the minor might attempt to self-abort or seek an illegal abortion, while others "may bear an unwanted child" [*H.L.* v. *Matheson*].

The majority of the Court upheld the law because there was a judicial bypass procedure for the minor who did not want to notify her parents. Marshall, however, believed that *Roe* v. *Wade* controlled and prevented a judge from intruding into that decision: "No person may veto *any* minor's decision, made in consultation with her physician, to terminate her pregnancy. An "immature" minor has no less right to make decisions regarding her own body than a mature adult." Marshall did not believe a judge could really determine what was in the young woman's best interests.

> It is difficult to conceive of any reason, aside from a judge's personal opposition to abortion, that would justify a finding that any immature woman's best interests would be served by forcing her to endure pregnancy and childbirth against her will.

Marshall's "vehement dissent" concluded with the following assessment of the law:

> This scheme forces a young woman in an already dire situation to choose between two fundamentally unacceptable alternatives: no-

tifying a possibly dictatorial or even abusive parent and justifying her profoundly personal decision in an intimidating judicial proceeding to a black-robed stranger. For such a woman, this dilemma is more likely to result in trauma and pain than in an informed and voluntary decision.

F. Freedom from Unreasonable Searches and Seizures

1. Marshall's Early Years on the Court

The majority of Marshall's privacy opinions involved Fourth Amendment protections from unreasonable searches and seizures by law-enforcement officers. In most Fourth Amendment cases, the question for the Court to determine is whether evidence seized without a warrant or without probable cause is nonetheless admissible in the defendant's trial.

In his early years on the Court, Marshall was sometimes willing to permit such seizures. For example, he joined Chief Justice Warren's majority opinion in the famous case of *Terry* v. *Ohio* in 1968 permitting the police to "stop and frisk" a suspect, that is, to briefly detain and frisk a person where there is reasonable suspicion the person is about to commit a crime with a weapon. Only Justice Douglas dissented, on the grounds that there was no probable cause, but only an inkling of possible criminality. And in 1973 Marshall wrote an opinion concurring with the majority's approval of a suspect's detention and warrantless seizure of easily destructible evidence—scrapings from the suspect's fingernails—yet his unease was apparent [*Cupp* v. *Murphy*]:

> I realize that exceptions to the warrant requirement may be established because of 'powerful hydraulic pressures . . . that bear heavily on the Court to water down constitutional guarantees,' *Terry* v. *Ohio* . . . (Douglas, J., dissenting), and that those same pressures may lead to later expansion of the exceptions beyond the narrow confines of the cases in which they are established. *Adams* v. *Williams* . . . (Marshall, J., dissenting). But I cannot say that, in the precise circumstances of this case, the police violated the Fourth Amendment in detaining Murphy for the limited purpose of scraping his fingernails.

Marshall's 1972 dissent in *Adams* v. *Williams,* a case which upheld a warrantless stop and frisk on the basis of unreliable information from an informant, indicated that he now regretted he went along with the majority in *Terry:*

> While I took the position [in *Terry*] that we were not watering down rights, but were hesitantly and cautiously striking a necessary balance between the rights of American citizens to be free from government intrusion into their privacy and their government's urgent need for narrow exception to the warrant requirement of the Fourth Amendment, today's decision demonstrates just how prescient Mr. Justice Douglas was.

> It seems that the delicate balance that *Terry* struck was simply too delicate, too susceptible to the "hydraulic pressures" of the day. As a result of today's decision, the balance struck in *Terry* is now heavily weighted in favor of the government. And the Fourth Amendment, which was included in the Bill of Rights to prevent the kind of arbitrary and oppressive police action involved herein, is dealt a serious blow. Today's decision invokes the specter of a society in which innocent citizens may be stopped, searched, and arrested at the whim of police officers who have only the slightest suspicion of improper conduct.

Since the Burger and Rehnquist Courts could not "delicately balance" citizens' privacy and government needs, Marshall abandoned his approach in *Terry* and *Cupp* and thereafter resisted all attempts to make new exceptions to the warrant and probable cause requirements. This meant, for the most part, writing dissenting opinions on behalf of privacy rights of citizens.

2. The War on Drugs . . . or on the Constitution?

Although *Terry* v. *Ohio* involved persons suspected of being armed and dangerous, the greatest number of cases reaching the Court since *Terry* has involved stops without probable cause of persons in airports suspected of smuggling drugs. Marshall did not approve of the use of "drug-courier profiles" by Drug Enforcement Agents and dissented from the majority's opinion that such information could be used by an agent to establish reasonable suspicion [*U.S.* v. *Sokolow* (1989)]. Marshall began his opinion with a reminder:

> Because the strongest advocates of Fourth Amendment rights are frequently criminals, it is easy to forget that our interpretations of

such rights apply to the innocent and the guilty alike. . . . [I]n sustaining this conviction . . . the Court diminishes the rights of *all* citizens to "be secure in their persons, "U.S. Const., Amdt. IV, as they traverse the Nation's airports.

Marshall disagreed that the following activities gave the agent reasonable suspicion to stop Sokolow as a drug courier: he was nervous, took a brief trip to a resort city, brought only carry-on luggage, came from Miami, a "source city" for drugs, had his phone listed in another person's name (his roommate's), paid for his tickets in cash, was dressed in a black jumpsuit, and wore gold jewelry. On this last point, Marshall believed that:

> For law-enforcement officers to base a search, even in part, on a pop guess that persons dressed in a particular fashion are likely to commit crimes not only stretches the concept of reasonable suspicion beyond recognition, but also is inimical to the self-expression which the choice of wardrobe may provide.

His explanation for the majority's finding of reasonable suspicion is "its willingness, when drug crimes or anti-drug policies are at issue, to give short shrift to constitutional rights."

In 1991, Marshall's last year on the Court, the majority approved of another law-enforcement practice aimed at drug carriers: police sweeps on interstate and intrastate buses without any suspicion that a particular person possesses drugs, *Florida* v. *Bostick* (1991). Marshall dissented:

> Our Nation, we are told, is engaged in a "war on drugs." No one disputes that it is the job of law-enforcement officials to devise effective weapons for fighting this war. But the effectiveness of a law-enforcement technique is not proof of its constitutionality.

He reminded his colleagues that historically, the general warrant was an effective method of law enforcement, yet "it was one of the primary aims of the Fourth Amendment to protect citizens from the tyranny of being singled out for search and seizure without particularized suspicion *notwithstanding* the effectiveness of this method."

Marshall's most stinging dissent came in a case involving drug testing of public employees for administrative purposes rather than criminal prosecution. The majority upheld compelled blood and urine testing of railroad employees in safety-sensitive jobs who were involved in an accident, without a warrant or suspicion that a particular employee was using drugs or alcohol.

"The issue in this case," Marshall began, "is not whether declaring a war on illegal drugs is good public policy. The importance of ridding our society of such drugs is, by now, apparent to all.

> Rather, the issue here is whether the Government's deployment in that war of a particularly draconian weapon—the compulsory collection and chemical testing of railroad workers' blood and urine —comports with the Fourth Amendment. Precisely because the need for action against the drug scourge is manifest, the need for vigilance against unconstitutional excess is great. History teaches that grave threats to liberty often come in times of urgency, when constitutional rights seem too extravagant to endure.

Marshall then cited as examples of constitutional excesses the World War II Japanese relocation-camp cases and the Red Scare and McCarthy-era internal subversion cases in which the Court upheld the government claims against constitutional rights of individuals. "[W]hen we allow fundamental freedoms to be sacrificed in the name of real or perceived exigency, we invariably come to regret it." The Court, felt Marshall, was making a similar mistake by its decision: "The majority's acceptance of dragnet blood and urine testing ensures that the first, and worst, casualty of the war on drugs will be the precious liberties of our citizens."

The majority found that the government's interest in deterring drug and alcohol use by the workers outweighed the minimal intrusion on the employees' privacy. Marshall, on the other hand, believed that forcibly taking blood, requiring urine tests, and analyzing the samples were intrusive invasions of privacy and therefore probable cause, or at least individualized suspicion, is constitutionally required. He admitted that invalidating the program "may hinder the Government's attempts to make rail transit as safe as humanly possible.

> But constitutional rights have their consequences, and one is that efforts to maximize the public welfare, no matter how well intentioned, must always be pursued within constitutional boundaries. Were the police freed from the constraints of the Fourth Amend-

ment for just one day to seek out evidence of criminal wrongdoing, the resulting convictions and incarcerations would probably prevent thousands of fatalities. Our refusal to tolerate this spectra reflects our shared belief that even beneficent governmental power —whether exercised to save money, save lives, or make the trains run on time—must always yield to "a resolute loyalty to constitutional safeguards."

Marshall ended his opinion quoting Justice Oliver Wendell Holmes's first dissent that "Great cases, like hard cases, make bad law." Such cases are called great, said Holmes "because of some accident of immediate overwhelming interest which appeals to the feelings and distorts the judgment," creating a kind of "hydraulic pressure which makes what previously was clear seem doubtful, and before which even well-settled principles of law will bend." Marshall believed that the majority had succumbed to popular pressure to stop the scourge of illegal drugs, bending Fourth Amendment principles in the process.

I believe the Framers would be appalled by the vision of mass governmental intrusions upon the integrity of the human body that the majority allows to become reality. The immediate victims of the majority's constitutional timorousness will be those railroad workers whose bodily fluids the Government may now forcibly collect and analyze. But ultimately, today's decision will reduce the privacy all citizens may enjoy, for, as Justice Holmes understood, principles of law, once bent, do not snap back easily.

3. Searches of Homes

The great concern Justice Marshall had for privacy in the home, as reflected in cases like *Stanley* and *Wyman,* was also reflected in his opinions concerning searches of the home for criminal evidence. For example, the broadly read congressional statutes concerning entries into homes for law-enforcement purposes, holding that merely because the front door was unlocked did not mean the officers could open it without knocking and announcing their purpose for being there [*Sabbath* v. *United States* (1968). He believed that nighttime searches of the home required a showing of additional justification beyond mere probable cause. [*Gooding* v. *United States* (1974)].

[T]here is no expectation of privacy more reasonable and more demanding of constitutional protection than our right to expect that we will be let alone in the privacy of our homes during the night. The idea of the police unnecessarily forcing their way into the home in the middle of the night—frequently, in narcotics cases, without knocking and announcing their purpose—rousing the resident out of their beds, and forcing them to stand by in indignity in their night clothes while the police rummage through their belongings does indeed smack of a " 'police state' lacking in the respect for the right of privacy dictated by the U.S. Constitution."

The Court has held that an arrest warrant must be obtained to arrest a person in his own home, unless there are exigent circumstances. If no warrant was obtained, any evidence seized is inadmissible in the person's trial. In a more recent case, the Court said that a statement given by a person arrested in his home without a warrant need not be excluded from his trial if the statement is given outside the home [*New York* v. *Harris* (1990)]. Marshall objected to allowing the fruits of the illegal arrest to be used because of potential abuse: "The Court . . . creates powerful incentives for police officers to violate the Fourth Amendment. In the context of our constitutional rights and the sanctity of our homes, we cannot afford to presume that officers will be entirely impervious to those incentives."

Marshall's 1981 opinion for the majority in *Steagald* v. *United States* held, for the first time, that in order to arrest a suspect in another person's home, the police must have first obtained a search warrant from a judge who must first find that the person is probably at that location. If the police only had an arrest warrant, feared Marshall, they "could search all the homes of that individual's friends and acquaintances." Although obtaining a search warrant may to some extent impede the police, "the right protected—that of presumptively innocent people to be secure in their homes from unjustified, forcible intrusions by the Government—is weighty."

4. Who Decides the Reasonableness of Searches, Judges or the Police?

The trend on the Court during the Burger and Rehnquist years has been to let the police have more authority to conduct searches and seizures of property and arrest of persons without judicial oversight.

Justice Marshall consistently opposed this diminished role for the courts because of its impact on privacy.

In *United States* v. *Robinson* (1973), the defendant was arrested for operating a motor vehicle after his permit had been revoked. He was searched and in a crumpled cigarette package, drugs were found which were used in his trial for possession of illegal drugs. The majority upheld the warrantless search under an exception to the normal requirement that the police must have a warrant before they can search. That exception—a search can be made without a warrant when it is incident to an arrest—was developed in order to protect police from hidden weapons and the destruction or concealment of evidence that might occur if a warrant was required. Even though neither of the reasons was present in Robinson's case, since it involved an arrest for a traffic violation, the majority said that it was not necessary to establish any justification other than the arrest because it did not want courts overruling the "quick ad hoc judgment" of the police.

Marshall dissented, stating that it is the very function of the Fourth Amendment "to ensure that the quick ad hoc judgments of police officers are subject to review and control by the judiciary." It was the role of the courts, not the police, "to delimit the scope of exceptions to the warrant requirement." He believed the majority was abandoning its tradition of the judiciary evaluating the reasonableness of searches on a case-by-case basis. Merely because there had been an arrest "should be no justification, in and of itself, for invading the privacy of the individual's personal effects." And Marshall rejected the government's argument that Robinson had no legitimate expectation of privacy in his cigarette pack:

> One wonders if the result in this case would have been the same were [Robinson] a businessman who was lawfully taken into custody for driving without a license and whose wallet was taken from him by the police. . . . Or suppose a lawyer lawfully arrested for a traffic offense if found to have a sealed envelope on his person. Would it be permissible for the arresting officer to tear open the envelope in order to make sure that it did not contain a clandestine weapon—perhaps a pin or a razor blade?

Marshall could not draw principled distinctions among these cases and therefore would have held the search by the officer of the cigarette pack to be unreasonable "since it went far beyond what was reasonably necessary to protect him from harm or to ensure that [Robinson] would not effect an escape from custody."

Marshall similarly objected to the majority's acceptance of routine inventory searches as reasonable whenever a car is impounded for traffic violations and searched pursuant to standardized procedures. Marshall would permit such searches only when the owner of the car consented, or when there were particular reasons to search. Among the reasons for the majority's holding were that it could protect the police from claims that property was removed from the car and prevent items from being stolen from the car. Marshall noted that the Court's result "elevates the conservation of property interests—indeed mere possibilities of property interests—above the privacy and security interests" of the individual [*South Dakota* v. *Opperman* (1976)].

The normal rule is that a warrant is to be obtained prior to a *search,* with a few, though growing number of, exceptions. Marshall would have applied that same presumption, that a warrant is to be obtained, to the law of *arrests.* The majority, however, in *United States* v. *Watson* (1976), held that no warrant was needed to arrest a person in public where the officer has probable cause to believe the person had committed a felony, even if it would be easy to obtain a warrant. The majority relied on historical practice as well as state and federal laws authorizing such warrantless arrests.

Marshall, in dissent, observed that the Court's role is more than merely determining past practices: "Our function in constitutional cases is weightier than the Court today suggests: where reasoned analysis shows a practice to be constitutionally deficient, our obligation is to the Constitution, not the Congress." Marshall could see no reason for requiring warrants in searches of property, while permitting warrantless seizures—arrests—of persons. "Indeed, an unjustified arrest that forces the individual temporarily to forfeit his right to control his person and movements and interrupts the course of his daily business may be more intrusive than an unjustified search." The reason the Fourth Amendment requires judges to issue warrants is to minimize unjustified intrusions into privacy: Judges are presumed to be neutral, while the job of the police is to catch criminals and they will be less able therefore to fairly determine whether there is probable cause: "Surely there is no reason to place greater trust in the partisan assessment of a police officer that there is probable cause for an arrest than in his determination that probable cause exists for a search."

*   *   *

Although the Court has always indicated it wants to encourage the police to use both arrest warrants and search warrants, Marshall noted the consequences of the decision in *Watson:*

> By its holding today, the preference for an arrest warrant, which the Court has conceded is the optimal method to protect our citizens from the affront of an unlawful arrest, will remain only an ideal, one that the Court will espouse but not enforce.

Marshall believed that his colleagues went about interpreting the Fourth Amendment in too narrow a fashion. For example, the majority upheld as reasonable a warrantless police search of private property, even though the defendant had posted No Trespassing signs on the property [*Oliver* v. *United States* (1984)]. The Court held that the words of the Amendment—"persons, houses, papers, and effects"—did not include open fields. Marshall disagreed with this narrow construction of the Amendment:

> The Fourth Amendment, like the other central provisions of the Bill of Rights that loom large in our modern jurisprudence, was designed, not to prescribe with "precision" permissible and impermissible activities, but to identify a fundamental human liberty that should be shielded forever from government intrusion. We do not construe constitutional provisions of this sort the way we do statutes, whose drafters can be expected to indicate with some comprehensiveness and exactitude the conduct they wish to forbid or control and to change those prescriptions when they become obsolete. Rather, we strive, when interpreting these seminal constitutional provisions, to effectuate their purposes—to lend them meanings that ensure that the liberties the Framers sought to protect are not undermined by the changing activities of government officials."

5. What is a "Reasonable Expectation of Privacy"?

The most important Fourth Amendment decision of the Warren Court was *Katz* v. *United States* decided in 1967, which held that the Fourth Amendment "protects people—and not simply areas." Since that case, the Court has used the test of whether a defendant had a reasonable expectation of privacy to determine whether the Fourth Amendment's protections apply. Although it was thought that Katz would usher in an era of decisions protecting privacy, that has not occurred because the Court often finds that a person's expectation of privacy was not reasonable. Marshall consistently objected to this weakening of the right to privacy.

The Court has held that permitting others to have access to certain information, such as bank checks and deposits, causes a person to lose any reasonable expectation of privacy in that information. "The fact that one has disclosed private papers to the bank, for a limited purpose, within the context of a confidential customer-bank relationship," objected Marshall, "does not mean that one has waived all right to the privacy of the papers" [*California Bankers Association* v. *Shultz* (1974)]. He similarly objected to the Court's decision that a person has no expectation of privacy from the government enlisting the phone company's assistance in monitoring the phone numbers dialed from a person's home because the homeowner assumes the risk of disclosure [*Smith* v. *Maryland* (1979)].

> In my view, whether privacy expectations are legitimate within the meaning of *Katz* depends not on the risks an individual can be presumed to accept when imparting information to third parties, but on the risks he should be forced to assume in a free and open society. . . . Privacy in placing calls is of value not only to those engaged in criminal activity. The prospect of unregulated governmental monitoring will undoubtedly prove disturbing even to those with nothing illicit to hide. Many individuals, including members of unpopular political organizations or journalists with confidential sources, may legitimately wish to avoid disclosure of their personal contacts. Permitting governmental access to telephone records on less than probable cause may thus impede certain forms of political affiliation and journalistic endeavor that are the hallmark of a truly free society.

Marshall similarly objected to the majority's decision that a person has no constitutional privacy in his fields or woods, even though marked with No Trespassing signs [*Oliver* v. *United States* (1984)].

> Privately owned woods and fields that are not exposed to public view regularly employed in a variety of ways that society acknowledges deserve privacy. Many landowners like to take solitary walks on their property, confident that they will not be confronted in their rambles by strangers or policemen. Others conduct agricul-

tural businesses on their property. Some landowners use their secluded spaces to meet lovers, others to gather together with fellow worshippers, still others to engage in sustained creative endeavor. Private land is sometimes used as a refuge for wildlife, where flora and fauna are protected from human intervention of any kind.

DISCRIMINATION AND THE CONSTITUTION

A. What Interests and Groups are Protected by the Constitution from Discrimination?

The Fourteenth Amendment prohibits a state from denying to any person within its boundaries the equal protection of the laws. Although this provision was written to protect blacks from discriminatory legislation, the Court included as protected classifications national origin, alienage, illegitimacy, and gender. More controversially, in the 1960's, the Warren Court began to use the equal protection clause to protect not only groups but also certain fundamental interests for example, the right to vote in state elections and the right to travel. If laws were directed at "suspect" classifications, such as race, or "fundamental" rights, such as voting, the Court would apply the "strict scrutiny" test and almost always invalidate the law. If the classification was not suspect and the right not fundamental, the Court would virtually always uphold the law as being rational. Marshall objected to this two-tier equal protection methodology:

> It cannot be gainsaid that there remain rights, not now classified as "fundamental," that remain vital to the flourishing of a free society, and classes, not now classified as "suspect," that are unfairly burdened by invidious discrimination unrelated to the individual worth of their members. Whatever we call these rights and classes, we simply cannot forgo all judicial protection against discriminatory legislation bearing upon them, but for the rare instances when the legislative choice can be termed "wholly irrelevant" to the legislative goal.

Marshall would replace the "all or nothing" model with a much more finely tuned, sliding-scale approach, evaluating both the interest affected and the classification used in the statute to determine the importance of the interest and the legitimacy of the classification. If the interest involved is important and the classification involved largely irrelevant to legitimate lawmaking, the statute should be closely examined by the Court, using heightened scrutiny but not automatically invalidated as under the strict scrutiny test.

The majority of the Court never explicitly adopted Marshall's approach, although it occasionally did so implicitly. Marshall was pleased that "the Court's deeds have not matched its words" but concerned that its refusal to say what it was doing was confusing to the litigants and the lower courts and unpredictable in its application.

1. Expanding Constitutionally Protected Interests

In *Dunn* v. *Blumstein* (1972), Tennessee limited the right to vote to persons who had resided in the state for at least one year and in the county for at least three months prior to the election. Even though neither the right to travel nor the right to vote is specifically protected in the text of the Constitution, Marshall found that earlier cases had established that both rights were fundamental and that the residence requirements did not meet "the exacting standards of precision we require of statutes affecting constitutional rights."

Marshall also wrote the majority opinion striking down Arizona's restriction of nonemergency medical care at county hospitals to persons who had resided in the county for at least one year [*Memorial Hospital* v. *Maricopa County* (1974)]. Recognizing that some durational resident requirements had been upheld by the Court, such as lower tuition at state institutions, while others had been disapproved, such as welfare benefits, which were considered "a basic necessity of life," Marshall found the denial of medical care to be more like welfare.

> It would be odd, indeed, to find that the State of Arizona was required to afford [the individual] welfare assistance to keep him from discomfort of inadequate housing or the pangs of hunger but could deny him the medical care necessary to relieve him from the wheezing and gasping for breath that attend his illness. . . . The denial of medical care is all the more cruel in this context, falling as it does on indigents who are often without the means to obtain alternative treatment.

Marshall was unable to persuade his colleagues that a law restricting the right to file for a divorce to persons who had resided in the state for one year violated equal protection [*Sosna* v. *Iowa* (1975)]. He believed that the right to seek a divorce, so closely related to the right to marry, is of such fundamental importance that its denial penalizes the right to travel in the same way that denial of welfare benefits, medical care, and voting does.

Marshall's most forceful argument for broadening the list of fundamental constitutional rights was contained in his dissenting opinion in a 1973 case, *San Antonio Independent School District* v. *Rodriguez.* That case raised the questions of whether education was a fundamental constitutional right and whether discrimination on the basis of group wealth was to be a protected classification.

The *Rodriguez* majority found that education was not a fundamental right because it was neither implicitly nor explicitly to be found in the text of the Constitution. Marshall rejected that approach as inconsistent with earlier Supreme Court cases which found as fundamental the right to vote in state elections, the right of access to the criminal appellate process, and the right to procreate, even though none of these interests were explicitly or implicitly found in the Constitution's text. Those interests were considered fundamental, according to Marshall, because they were "firmly rooted in the text of the Constitution." The question in every case is to determine "the extent to which constitutionally guaranteed rights are dependent on interests not mentioned in the Constitution."

Education, said Marshall, is firmly rooted in the Constitution because it affects a child's ability to exercise First Amendment rights of free speech and association and instills an appreciation for principles of government and the political process. He quoted Chief Justice Warren's opinion in *Brown* v. *Board of Education,* a case which Attorney Thurgood Marshall successfully argued:

> Today, education is perhaps the most important function of state and local governments. Compulsory school attendance laws and the great expenditures for education both demonstrate our recognition of the importance of education to our democratic society. It is required in the performance of our most basic public responsibilities, even service in the armed forces. It is the very foundation of good citizenship. Today it is a principal instrument in awakening the child to cultural values, in preparing him for later professional training, and in helping him to adjust normally to his environment.

Marshall was aware of the criticism that protecting nonconstitutional interests had no stopping place, and that the claim would be made that food, welfare, or housing was a constitutional right. Although Marshall had sidestepped the question of whether welfare was a constitutional right four years earlier in the *Dandridge* case, he was apparently conceding the point in order to make the case for education as a fundamental right:

> Whatever the severity of the impact of insufficient food or inadequate housing on a person's life, they have never been considered to bear the same direct and immediate relationship to constitutional concerns for free speech and for our political processes as education has long been recognized to bear. Perhaps the best evidence of this fact is the unique status which has been accorded public education as the single public service nearly unanimously guaranteed in the constitutions of our States. . . . Education, in terms of constitutional values, is much more analogous in my judgment, to the right to vote in state elections than to public welfare or public housing. Indeed, it is not without significance that we have long recognized education as an essential step in providing the disadvantaged with the tools necessary to achieve economic self-sufficiency.

Yet, in later opinions, it was evident that he believed legislative deprivations of the necessities of life deserved constitutional protection. The majority of the Court upheld congressional restrictions of food stamp benefits to related families living together [*Lyng* v. *Castillo* (1986)]. In his dissent, Marshall noted that the regulation not only affected the privacy interest in living arrangements, "but the even more vital interest in survival." The regulation "threatens their lives and health by denying them the minimal benefits provided to all other families of similar income and needs." He similarly dissented from the Court's decision upholding as constitutional the denial of food stamps to strikers and their families [*Lyng* v. *Automobile Workers* (1988)]. One justification given for the law was that food stamps should be reserved for those persons most " 'genuinely in need.' " Marshall noted that such persons were as financially needy as others who did qualify since the law denied benefits even after counting strike-fund payments as household income. Marshall was most disturbed by the effect on the striker's children:

> Their need for nourishment is in no logical way diminished by the striker's action. The denial to these children of what is often the only buffer between them and malnourishment and disease cannot

be justified as a targeting of the most needy: they *are* the most needy. The record below bears witness to this point in a heart-breaking fashion.

2. Expanding Constitutionally Protected Groups

In *City of Cleburne, Tex.* v. *Cleburne Living Center* (1985), Marshall articulated his views on what groups are entitled to special judicial consideration. The *Cleburne* case involved a zoning ordinance requiring a special use permit to operate group homes for the mentally retarded, even though no such permit was required for other types of group homes. Although the majority found the city's action unconstitutional, it held that, unlike race or sex, mental retardation was not a classification deserving special treatment by the Court. Marshall objected to the Court's refusal to expand the classifications requiring heightened Court scrutiny and explained his approach for determining when a legislative classification is constitutionally vulnerable:

No single talisman can define those groups likely to be the target of classification offensive to the Fourteenth Amendment and therefore warranting heightened or strict scrutiny; experience, not abstract logic, must be the primary guide. The "political power-lessness" of a group may be relevant . . . but that factor is neither necessary, as the gender cases demonstrate, nor sufficient, as the example of minors illustrates. Minors cannot vote and thus might be considered politically powerless to an extreme degree. Nonetheless, we see few statutes reflecting prejudice or indifference to minors, and I am not aware of any suggestion that legislation affecting them be viewed with the suspicion of heightened scrutiny. Similarly, immutability of the trait at issue may be relevant, but many immutable characteristics, such as height or blindness, are valid bases of governmental action and classifications under a variety of circumstances.

The political powerlessness of a group and the immutability of its defining trait are relevant insofar as they point to a social and cultural isolation that gives the majority little reason to respect or be concerned with the group's interests and needs. Statutes discriminating against the young have not been common nor need be feared because those who do vote and legislate were once themselves young, typically have children of their own, and certainly interact regularly with minors. Their social integration means that minors, unlike discrete and insular minorities, tend to be treated in legislative arenas with full concern and respect, despite their formal and complete exclusion from the electoral process.

The discreteness and insularity warranting a "more searching judicial inquiry" . . . must therefore be viewed from a social and cultural perspective as well as a political one. To the task judges are well suited, for the lessons of history and experience are surely the best guide as to when, and with respect to what interests, society is likely to stigmatize individuals as members of an inferior caste or view them as not belonging to the community. Because prejudice spawns prejudice, and stereotypes on which they are based, a history of unequal treatment requires sensitivity to the prospect that its vestiges endure. In separating those groups that are discrete and insular from those that are not, as in many important legal distinctions, "a page of history is worth a volume of logic."

For Marshall, the mentally retarded shared characteristics of other groups that had received heightened scrutiny from the Court. Most important, "lengthy and continuing isolation of the retarded has perpetuated the ignorance, irrational fears, and stereotyping that long have plagued" the mentally retarded. But the majority refused to treat the retarded with heightened scrutiny despite the history of discrimination because some recent legislation was benevolent. Marshall countered:

For the retarded, just as for Negroes and women, much has changed in recent years, but much remains the same; outdated statutes are still on the books, and irrational fears or ignorance, traceable to the prolonged social and cultural isolation of the retarded, continue to stymie recognition of the dignity and individuality of retarded people. Heightened judicial scrutiny of action appearing to impose unnecessary barriers to the retarded is required in light of increasing recognition that such barriers are inconsistent with evolving principles of equality embedded in the Fourteenth Amendment.

Marshall's approach would not invalidate all legislation concerning the mentally retarded: "Heightened scrutiny does not allow courts to second-guess reasoned legislative or professional judgments tailored to the unique needs of a group like the retarded." That approach, however, "does seek to assure that the hostility or thoughtlessness with which there is reason to be concerned has not carried the day . . . and compels lower courts to recognize that a group may well be the target of the sort of prejudiced, thoughtless, or stereotyped action that offends principles of equality. . . ."

B. What Constitutes Discrimination under the Constitution?

One of the major questions facing the Court in the past twenty years is whether a law or governmental practice which has the *effect* of discriminating against certain groups even though there is no *intent* to discriminate violates the Constitution. A majority of the Court has held in several decisions since 1976 that only intentional discrimination is prohibited, prompting several vigorous dissents by Justice Marshall.

The Court has upheld a state's welfare law which gave smaller benefits to persons in one program—Aid to Families with Dependent Children (AFDC)—even though that program had many more members of minority groups [*Jefferson* v. *Hackney* (1972)]. The Court also approved a Massachusetts law that reserved the highest paying civil service laws to veterans, the overwhelming majority of whom were male, on the grounds the law was enacted *in spite of* the impact on women, not *because of* that impact [*Personnel Administrator of Massachusetts* v. *Feeney* (1979)]. And the Court upheld a method for selecting members of a city council which had the effect, but not the intent, of excluding blacks from being elected [*Mobile* v. *Bolden* (1980)].

In the welfare case, one of the earliest cases to reject impact as constituting proof of discrimination, Marshall said in dissent that "at some point a showing that state action has a devastating impact on the lives of minority racial groups must be relevant." In the civil service case, Marshall believed that "since reliable evidence of subjective intentions is seldom obtainable, resort to inference based on objective factors is generally unavoidable." He did not believe that the judiciary was capable of ascertaining the sole or dominant purpose of a statute. Finally, in the voting case, *Mobile* v. *Bolden,* Marshall was adamant that where constitutional rights, like voting, are involved, impact alone constitutes discrimination under both the Fourteenth Amendment's equal protection clause and the Fifteenth Amendment's prohibition of racial discrimination in voting. He was again concerned about the practical problems of proof if intent was required:

It is beyond dispute that a standard based solely upon the motives of official decisionmakers creates significant problems of proof for plaintiffs and forces the inquiring court to undertake an unguided, tortuous look into the minds of officials in the hope of guessing why certain policies were adopted and others rejected.

Moreover, requiring intent invites subterfuge by government officials:

An approach based on motivation creates the risk that officials will be able to adopt policies that are the products of discriminatory intent so long as they sufficiently mask their motives through the use of subtlety and illusion.

Finally, Marshall was deeply worried about the consequences of the Court's approach to discrimination in voting which he said indicated "an indifference to the plight of minorities who through no fault of their own have suffered diminution of the right preservative of all other rights." Freezing minorities out of the political process can only result in "the frustration of minority desires, the stigmatization of the minority as second-class citizens, and the perpetuation of inhumanity." And the Court's approach makes it an "accessory to the perpetuation of racial discrimination." Marshall despaired of the future:

The plurality's requirement of proof of intentional discrimination, so inappropriate in today's cases, may represent an attempt to bury the legitimate concerns of the minority beneath the soil of a doctrine almost as impermeable as it is specious. If so, the superficial tranquility created by such measures can be but short-lived. If this Court refuses to honor our long-recognized principle that the Constitution "nullifies sophisticated as well as simple-minded modes of discrimination" . . . it cannot expect the victims of discrimination to respect political channels of seeking redress.

On the same day Marshall wrote these words in dissent, he authored an opinion for a majority of the Court in *City of Rome* v. *United States* which in 1980 upheld the federal Voting Rights Act prohibiting voting procedures which have the effect, but not the intent, of discriminating on the basis of race. Marshall held that under Section 2 of the Fifteenth Amendment, which gives Congress the power to enforce the Fifteenth Amendment "by appropriate legislation," Congress, by statute, could outlaw such discrimination, even if the Amendment itself only prohibits intentional discrimination. "Congress could rationally have concluded that, because electoral changes by jurisdictions with a demonstrable history of intentional racial discrimination in voting creates the risk of purposeful discrimination, it was proper to prohibit changes that have a discriminatory impact." The dissenters objected that under Section 2, Congress could only remedy a constitutional violation, and impact discrimination, under the *Mobile* case, is not such a violation.

C. Are Government Affirmative Action Programs Constitutional?

The other major issue concerning discrimination while Marshall was on the Court was whether affirmative action programs, undertaken by the government *to help* racial minorities and women, is measured by a different standard than discriminatory action by government *against* racial minorities or women. Prior to 1989, agreement on how to measure such programs, said Marshall, had "eluded this Court every time the issue" came before them. On one side were justices who believed that such programs unconstitutionally denied the rights of innocent whites who would not be able to get a government job or would not be admitted to a professional school at a state university. On the other were justices, like Marshall, who believed that the use of racial preferences could be justified. Others were somewhere in the middle.

The first affirmative action case was decided by the Court in 1978, *University of California Regents* v. *Bakke,* involving a medical school admissions program which reserved a certain percentage of seats to racial minorities. The particular program was invalidated by five members of the Court while Marshall and the three other justices co-authored an opinion which would have upheld the program. They noted that discrimination against minorities has been disfavored by the Court because of their disabilities—political powerlessness and a history of being discriminated against—which did not burden the white majority. Yet they also noted that such programs could claim to be benign legislation when in fact they merely perpetuated past stereotypes about minorities. For these reasons, their opinion struck a middle ground between never allowing government to adopt affirmative action programs and always upholding such programs.

Marshall wrote a separate opinion in *Bakke* which set forth the history of how the legal system has treated blacks in America.

[T]he racism of our society has been so pervasive that none, regardless of wealth or position, has managed to escape its impact.

The experience of Negroes in America has been different in kind, not just in degree, from that of other ethnic groups. It is not merely the history of slavery alone but also that a whole people were marked as inferior by the law. And that mark has endured. The dream of America as the great melting pot has not been realized for the Negro; because of his skin color he never even made it into the pot.

These differences in the experience of the Negro make it difficult for me to accept that Negroes cannot be afforded greater protection under the Fourteenth Amendment where it is necessary to remedy the effect of past discrimination.

To those who argue that Justice Harlan's statement in the 1898 case of *Plessy* v. *Ferguson* that the "Constitution is colorblind," Marshall noted that Harlan said that as the lone dissenter. "The majority of the Court rejected the principle of color blindness, and for the next sixty years, from *Plessy* to *Brown* v. *Board of Education,* ours was a nation where, by law, an individual could be given 'special' treatment based on the color of his skin."

It is because of a legacy of unequal treatment that we now must permit the institutions of this society to give consideration to race in making decisions about who will hold the positions of influence, affluence, and prestige in America. For far too long, the doors to those positions have been shut to Negroes. If we are ever to become a fully integrated society, one in which the color of a person's skin will not determine the opportunities available to him or her, we must be willing to take steps to open those doors. I do not believe that anyone can truly look into America's past and still find that a remedy for the effects of that past is impermissible.

The next affirmative action case reaching the Court involved a federal program that set aside a certain percentage of construction work on federally funded projects for minority business enterprises [*Fullilove* v. *Klutznick* (1980)]. This time, the Court upheld the set-aside, prompting Justice Marshall to write in an opinion concurring in the judgment:

Today, by upholding this race-conscious remedy, the Court accords Congress the authority necessary to undertake the task of moving our society toward a state of meaningful equality of opportunity, not an abstract version of equality in which the effects of past discrimination would be forever frozen into our social fabric.

In the third major affirmative action case, *Wygant* v. *Jackson Board of Education,* the Court in 1986 held unconstitutional a portion of a collective bargaining agreement designed to preserve the effects of an affirmative hiring policy. The agreement protected some minority teachers from layoffs even though they had less seniority than nonminority teachers. "I, too," said Marshall "believe that layoffs are unfair. But unfairness ought not to be confused with constitutional injury."

[T]his case calls for calm, dispassionate reflection upon exactly what has been done, to whom, and why. . . . when an elected school board and a teachers' union collectively bargain a layoff provisions designed to preserve the effects of a valid minority recruitment plan by apportioning layoffs between two racial groups, as a result of a settlement achieved under the auspices of a supervisory state agency charged with protecting the civil rights of all citizens, that provisions should not be upset by this Court on constitutional grounds.

Not until the 1989 case of *Richmond* v. *J. A. Croson Co.* did a majority of the Court agree that state or local affirmative action plans should be subject to the same degree of judicial scrutiny as governmental action directed against minorities. Since action directed against minorities virtually guarantee a holding of unconstitutionality, affirmative actions are likely to have the same fate; in Croson, the Court invalidated the City of Richmond's set-aside plan for minority contractors.

Marshall lamented the Court's treating all race-based legislation the same:

A profound difference separates governmental actions that themselves are racist and governmental actions that seek to remedy the effects of prior racism to prevent neutral governmental activity from perpetuating the effects of such racism.

Where government action is taken for reasons such as race hatred, it is subject to strict judicial scrutiny because those reasons are irrelevant to any legitimate government purpose:

By contrast, racial classifications drawn for the purpose of remedying the effects of discrimination that itself was race based have highly pertinent basis: the tragic and indelible fact that discrimination against blacks and other racial minorities in this Nation has pervaded our Nation's history and continues to scar our society.

Marshall viewed the majority's action as indicating that racial discrimination is no longer a real problem in today's society:

> I, however, do not believe this Nation is anywhere close to eradicating racial discrimination or its vestiges. In constitutionalizing its wishful thinking, the majority today does a grave disservice not only to those victims of past and present racial discrimination in this Nation whom government has sought to assist but also this Court's long tradition of approaching issues of race with the utmost sensitivity.

> The majority today sounds a full-scale retreat from the Court's longstanding solicitude to race-conscious remedial efforts "directed toward deliverance of the century-old promise of equality of economic opportunity. . . . The new and restrictive tests it applies scuttle one city's effort to surmount its discriminatory past, and imperil those of dozens more localities. I, however, profoundly disagree with the cramped vision of the Equal Protection Clause which the majority offers today and with its application of that vision to Richmond, Virginia's, laudable set-aside plan. The battle against pernicious racial discrimination or its effects is nowhere near won.

D. School Desegregation Remedies

After a lifetime of fighting for desegregation of the public schools, both as a lawyer and Supreme Court justice, Marshall was disheartened by the Court's retreat from fully implementing the promises of *Brown* v. *Board of Education*. The first time the Court after *Brown* disapproved of a lower court remedy in a school desegregation case was in *Milliken* v. *Bradley* (1974), a case seeking to desegregate an urban school district—the City of Detroit—by involving suburban school districts. The majority disapproved of such an interdistrict remedy since it had not been shown that the suburban districts had contributed to the segregation in Detroit. Marshall, in dissent, decried what he perceived as the Court's retreat from Brown:

> Desegregation is not and was never expected to be an easy task. Racial attitudes ingrained in our Nation's childhood and adoles-

cence are not quickly thrown aside in its middle years. But just as the inconvenience of some cannot be allowed to stand in the way of the rights of others, so public opposition, no matter how strident, cannot be permitted to divert this Court from the enforcement of the constitutional principles at issue in this case. Today's holding, I fear, is more a reflection of a perceived public mood that we have gone far enough in enforcing the Constitution's guarantee of equal justice than it is the product of neutral principles of law. In the short run, it may seem to be the easier course to allow our great metropolitan areas to be divided up each into two cities —one white, the other black—but it is a course, I predict, our people will ultimately regret.

FIRST AMENDMENT

Compared to his opinions in the topics discussed earlier where he was usually writing in dissent, Marshall wrote more frequently for the majority in the area of the First Amendment, particularly in his earlier years on the Court. Marshall was a strong believer in protecting First Amendment rights, usually finding that the First Amendment takes precedence over other individual rights that he cared deeply about, including privacy, fair trials for persons accused of crime, and racial integration.

A. Rights in Conflict

When both the First Amendment and another constitutional right of the individual were infringed by a state law, such as privacy in the home as in the *Stanley* case discussed earlier, Marshall wrote a powerful opinion on behalf of both constitutional rights: "If the First Amendment means anything, it means that a State has no business telling a man, sitting alone in his own house, what books he may read of what films he may watch."

When another individual right was in conflict with the First Amendment, however, he often sought to accommodate both rights. For example, in dissent from an opinion in *Rosenbloom* v. *Metromedia* (1971), written by Justice Brennan, his usual ally on the Court, Marshall sought to protect both the reputation of a private individual about whom falsehoods are written and the right of the press to report, since they are "two essential and fundamental values." Believing that Brennan's approach gave too much protection to the press and not enough to the private individual, Marshall would permit recovery for the defamed individual if he could prove the press was negligent in its reporting, an easier standard of proof than Brennan required. But concerned about huge punitive damage awards against the press which could endanger their very existence, Marshall limited the individual's recovery to actual damages. Marshall's approach was eventually followed by the Court in later years.

In a 1989 case, *Florida Star* v. *B.J.F.,* state law prohibited the publication by the mass media of the name of a victim of a sexual offense. Even though the information was truthful, the state wanted to protect such persons from an invasion of privacy by having their names published in the mass media. The issue facing the Court was whether a civil damage award in favor of a rape victim against the newspaper for publishing her name in violation of the law was permissible under the First Amendment. The newspaper requested that the Court hold that the press can never be punished for publishing the truth; the individual asked that publication of a rape victim's name is never protected by the First Amendment. Just as he did in his *Rosenbloom* opinion, Marshall, writing for the majority, was keenly aware that two important interests were at stake and that neither of the extreme positions was acceptable:

> We continue to believe that the sensitivity and significance of the interests presented in clashes between First Amendment and privacy rights counsel relying on limited principles that sweep no more broadly than the appropriate context of the instant case.

Among the factors leading Marshall to conclude that the damage award must be reversed were that the newspaper obtained the victim's name from a publicly released report issued by the local police department. Under different circumstances, he indicated that truthful publication of the name of the victim of a sexual offense could be constitutionally punished.

Sometimes the rights in conflict were both First Amendment rights as in a case involving a congressional act requiring public high schools to give equal access to students who want to hold meetings with a religious, political, philosophical, or other content. Although Marshall agreed with the majority that the law did not violate the Establishment Clause by permitting access for religious meetings, he filed a separate opinion in which he tried to accommodate the two competing constitutional rights when religious speech is introduced into the schools: the Free Speech Clause and the Establishment Clause. For Marshall, the Establishment Clause would be violated if the school appeared to endorse the goals of religious clubs. He was particularly worried about peer pressure if a school had only one advocacy-oriented club—the religious club—and a substantial number of the students belonged to the club.

> [I]t is precisely in a school without such a forum that intolerance for different religious and other views would be most dangerous and that a student who does not share the religious beliefs of his classmates would perceive "that religion or a particular religious belief is favored or preferred."

The school cannot claim that the peer pressure is not of its own making: "The state has structured an environment in which students holding mainstream views may be able to coerce adherents of minority religions to attend club meetings or to adhere to club beliefs." Accordingly, Marshall would require that schools affirmatively disassociate themselves from any endorsement of religious clubs.

Marshall consistently rejected First Amendment claims in those cases where he believed extending such protection would actually undermine constitutional interests. As discussed earlier, he would uphold limits on the amount a candidate for public office could contribute to his own campaign as well as state laws banning corporations from supporting or opposing candidates from general corporate treasuries. In both cases, he was concerned about the undue influence massive amounts of money would have in the electoral process, including discouraging persons from running and unfairly influencing elections.

He also rejected First Amendment claims of nonunion members that they should not have to pay for various expenses of the union chosen by a majority of the employees [*Lehnert* v. *Ferris Faculty Ass'n.* (1991)]. He believed that such dissenters were getting a "free ride," that is, getting the benefits of the union's actions in their behalf without having to pay for it. Taken to its extreme, the free rider problem could undermine the rights of union members to associate by weakening the financial strength of the union.

Finally, Marshall refused to hold that the Free Exercise and Establishment Clauses of the First Amendment were violated by a federal law that exempted a person from military service "who, by reason of religious training and belief, is conscientiously opposed to participation in war in any form" [*Gillette* v. *United States* (1971)]. In rejecting the argument that the law was unconstitutional as applied to a person who opposed only unjust wars, not all war, Marshall was concerned about the potential difficulty of an administrative body determining a person's claim that a particular war was unjust and that "the objector would succeed who is more articulate, better educated, or better counseled." Further, there could be religious discrimination, "a danger that a claim's chances of success would be greater the more familiar or salient the claim's connection with conventional religiosity could be made to appear."

B. Freedom of Speech

Marshall's most important decision concerning free speech was *Police Department of Chicago* v. *Mosley* written in 1972 for a Court majority. That case established the principle that government may not enact laws that discriminate on the basis of content. Since the case involved discrimination—Chicago prohibited all picketing next to a school, except peaceful labor picketing—it was decided under the Equal Protection Clause, although First Amendment interests were "closely intertwined." In a phrase to be repeated many times in later cases, Marshall said: "[A]bove all else, the First Amendment means that government has no power to restrict expression because of its messages, its ideas, its subject matter, or its content."

In explaining why the government cannot pass such laws, Marshall articulated what, for him, are the central purposes of free speech:

To permit the continued building of our politics and culture, and to assure self-fulfillment for each individual, our people are guaranteed the right to express any thought, free from government censorship. The essence of this forbidden censorship is content control.

He then addressed the problem of discrimination apparent in the ordinance:

[U]nder the Equal Protection Clause, not to mention the First Amendment itself, government may not grant the use of a forum to people whose views it finds acceptable, but deny use to those wishing to express less favored or more controversial views. And it may not select which issues are worth discussing or debating in public facilities. There is an "equality of status in the field of ideas," and government must afford all points of view an equal opportunity to be heard. Once a forum is opened up to assembly or speaking by some groups, government may not prohibit others from assembling or speaking on the basis of what they intend to say. Selective exclusions from a public forum may not be based on content alone, and may not be justified by reference to content alone.

Even where the government seeks to regulate the content of speech for a good reason, the First Amendment stands in the way. In *Linmark Associates, Inc.* v. *Willingboro* (1977), a city banned For Sale signs because of the fear that such signs induced whites to engage in "panic selling" with a reduction in property values. Noting that the Court and Congress recognized the importance of integrated neighborhoods, Marshall wrote for the Court that the effect of the ordinance was to keep important information from being disseminated to residents about one of the most important decisions they have to make: "where to live and raise their families." The First Amendment prohibits that result.

If dissemination of this information can be restricted, then every locality in the country can suppress any facts that reflect poorly on the locality, so long as a plausible claim can be made that disclosure would cause the recipients of the information to act "irrationally."

Marshall wrote opinions for the Court striking down attempts to punish speech of public employees by dismissing them from employment. In an important 1968 case involving public school teachers, *Pickering* v. *Board of Education,* a teacher was dismissed for writing a letter critical of the school board in connection with a proposed tax increase for educational purposes that failed to pass. Marshall wrote that teachers, when commenting on matters of public importance only tangentially related to their employment, have the same rights of free speech as members of the general public. An informed electorate needs the input of teachers on such matters, said Marshall:

Teachers are, as a class, the members of a community most likely to have informed and definite opinions as to how funds alloted to the operation of the schools should be spent. Accordingly, it is essential that they be able to speak out freely on such questions without fear of dismissal.

The test Marshall developed balanced "the interests of the [employee] as a citizen, in commenting upon matters of public concern and the interest of the State, as an employer, in promoting the efficiency of the public services it performs through its employees."

A more controversial decision involving free speech rights of public employees involved the dismissal of a clerical employee in a county constable's office [*Rankin* v. *McPherson* (1987)]. During a private conversation by the employee with a co-worker, she said, in reference to the attempt on the President's life in 1981, "If they go for him again, I hope they get him." Another co-worker overheard the remark and reported it to the constable, who then fired the employee. Once again, Marshall balanced the interests, noting that vigilance "is necessary to ensure that public employers do not use authority over employees to silence discourse, not because it hampers public functions but simply because superiors disagree with the content of employees' speech." Finding that the comment did not constitute a threat, Marshall said it did concern matters of public concern even though the statement might be controversial or inappropriate. Turning to the state's interest, there was no showing it interfered with smooth running of the office nor made to discredit the office as it might had the remark been made in public. Finally, the low-level nature of the job lessened the impact her remark would have on the functioning of the office.

Although the Court continues to disapprove of content-based discrimination, it has been quite tolerant of content-neutral regulations. Marshall believed that even those regulations need close judicial scrutiny because the "consistent imposition of silence upon all may fulfill the dictates of an evenhanded content-neutrality." For example, he dissented in a case that upheld a National Park Service regulation prohibiting camping in certain parks, including Lafayette Park, across from the White House. Demonstrators sought to sleep in the park to draw attention to the problem of homelessness [*Clark* v. *Community for Creative Non-Violence* (1984)]. Although content-neutral—the regulation prohibited everyone from camping—its effects were felt most strongly "upon relatively poor speakers and the points of view that such speakers typically espouse."

A disquieting feature about the disposition of this case is that it lends credence to the charge that judicial administration of the

First Amendment, in conjunction with a social order marked by large disparities in wealth and other sources of power, tends systematically to discriminate against efforts by the relatively disadvantaged to convey their political ideas.

Marshall criticized the Court for being so deferential to public officials who draft content-neutral regulations because they have "strong incentives to overregulate even in the absence of an intent to censor particular views" by acting in behalf of the political power of the general public rather than the interests of those who want to use a particular forum for First Amendment activities. Pointing to evidence in the record that the Park Service had, in fact, enacted the regulations in response to "political" rather than administrative concerns, Marshall concluded:

[G]overnment agencies by their very nature are driven to overregulate public forums to the detriment of First Amendment rights [(and)] facial neutrality is no shield against unnecessary restrictions on unpopular ideas or modes of expression.

The same day Marshall wrote *Mosley,* he also wrote for the majority what is probably his second most influential free speech opinion, *Grayned* v. *City of Rockford* (1971). In that case, Marshall upheld an ordinance prohibiting the willful making of noise adjacent to a school while in session. The ordinance was challenged under the First Amendment by a person who was convicted while engaging in a civil rights demonstration in front of a school. In considering the constitutionality of the ordinance, Marshall reviewed earlier Court cases involving First Amendment activities at various places, such as libraries, streets, and parks, and set forth a test that the Court still uses: "The crucial question is whether the manner of expression is basically incompatible with the normal activity of a particular place at a particular time." Since the antinoise ordinance did not prohibit all picketing but only noisy picketing while schools were in session, he found it consistent with the First Amendment since "it represents a considered and specific legislative judgment that some kinds of expressive activity should be restricted at a particular time and place, here in order to protect the schools."

In cases after *Grayned,* Marshall found himself dissenting as the majority upheld with a minimum of scrutiny First Amendment restrictions on military bases [*Greer* v. *Spock* (1971)] and the use of homeowners' mailboxes for communications by civic organizations [*U.S. Postal Service* v. *Greenburgh Civic Assns.* (1981)]. Marshall would put a much heavier burden on the government to justify restrictions on where First Amendment activities may take place. And in a case which dealt with government efforts to restrict the volume of sound at a bandshell in a public park, Marshall accused the majority of deferring too readily to public officials. In *Ward* v. *Rock Against Racism* (1989), a city regulation required all users of the bandshell to use city-supplied sound-amplification equipment and sound technicians. The majority upheld the regulation without first determining if there were other alternatives that would permit the performers to use their own equipment. Marshall believed that such deference was inconsistent with previous decisions of the Court and concluded:

> Today's decision has significance far beyond the world of rock music. Governments no longer need balance the effectiveness of regulation with the burdens on free speech. After today, government need only assert that it is most effective to control speech in advance of its expressions. Because such a result eviscerates the First Amendment, I dissent.

C. Freedom of the Press

Marshall was a strong advocate of the right of the press to publish and was particularly critical of efforts of the government to put restraints on the press prior to publication. He concurred in the Court's decision to refuse to permit enjoining publication of the Pentagon Papers, noting that Congress had specifically refused to enact a law permitting such injunctions [*New York Times Co.* v. *United States* (1971)]. Where trial judges close criminal trials to the press and public in such preliminary proceedings as jury selection in order to protect the privacy rights of jurors and fair trial rights of defendants, Marshall finds the First Amendment violated in almost all cases [*Press-Enterprise Co.* v. *Superior Court of Cal.* (1984)]. And when CNN was enjoined from broadcasting taped telephone conversations between Manuel Noriega and his counsel, Marshall dissented from the Court's refusal to hear the case which he believed "is of extraordinary consequence for freedom of the press" [*Cable News Network, Inc.* v. *Noriega* (1990)]. He was particularly disturbed by the trial court's decision that it need not find suppression of the broadcast was necessary to protect Noriega's right to a fair trial until CNN handed over the tapes to the Court for its inspection. Said Marshall: "I do not see how the prior restraint imposed in this case can be reconciled with" Supreme Court precedent.

Aside from prior restraint concerns, Marshall was concerned about state laws which selectively taxed the press. He relied on his opinion in *Mosely* in writing a majority opinion striking down an Arkansas law which taxed some, but not all, magazines. "[T]he basis on which Arkansas differentiates between magazines is particularly repugnant to First Amendment principles: a magazine's tax status depends entirely on its *content*" [*Arkansas Writers' Project, Inc.* v. *Ragland* (1987)]. He dissented in a case where the majority upheld a state law that taxed one medium—cable television—more heavily than others [*Leathers* v. *Medlock*, (1991)]. Marshall believed that permitting heavier taxation of one information medium risked covert censorship by government since it could favor one outlet over another. "Under the First Amendment, government simply has no business interfering with the process by which citizens' preferences for information formats evolve."

D. Establishment Clause

Believing that the Establishment Clause prohibited subsidizing religious education, whether directly or indirectly, Marshall dissented from the majority's decision upholding a state law permitting parents to take tax deductions for the cost of their children's tuition, including the costs of attending parochial schools, as well as deductions for the cost of books and other materials [*Mueller* v. *Allen* (1983)]. Joined by three others in dissent, Marshall pointed out that the fact there was a secular purpose behind the law is irrelevant since the result was also to subsidize religious instruction through taxes:

> For the first time, the Court has upheld financial support for religious schools without any reason at all to assume that the support will be restricted to the secular functions of those schools and will not be used to support religious instruction. This result is flatly at odds with the fundamental principle that a State may provide no financial support whatsoever to promote religion.

CONCLUSION

Marshall was committed to upholding the Supreme Court as an institution as well as protecting the constitutional rights of citizens. When those two goals were in conflict, Marshall felt the tension keenly. For example, when the question of the legality of the bombing of Cambodia came before him as Circuit Justice while the Court was in summer recess, Marshall posed the dilemma facing him in this way:

> [I]f the decision were mine alone, I might well conclude on the merits that continued American military operations in Cambodia are unconstitutional. But the Supreme Court is a collegial institution, and its decisions reflect the views of a majority of the sitting Justices. It follows that when I sit in my capacity as a Circuit Justice, I act not for myself alone but as a surrogate for the entire Court, from whence my ultimate authority in these matters derives. A Circuit Justice therefore bears a heavy responsibility to conscientiously reflect the views of his Brethren as best he perceives them . . . and this responsibility is particularly pressing when, as now, the Court is not in session.

He observed that the bombing of Cambodia might be judged to be "not only unwise but also unlawful":

> But the proper response to an arguably illegal action is not lawlessness by judges charged with interpreting and enforcing the laws. Down that road lies tyranny and repression. We have a government of limited powers, and those limits pertain to the Justices of the Court as well as to Congress and the Executive. Our Constitution assures that the law will ultimately prevail, but it also requires that the law be applied in accordance with lawful procedures.

Marshall's profound respect for the Court's traditions was reiterated in a dissenting opinion issued on June 27, 1991, the same day he announced his retirement from the Court. In the case of *Payne* v. *Tennessee,* the majority overruled two Supreme Court cases—*Booth* v. *Maryland* and *South Carolina* v. *Gathers*—decided a few years earlier. Those cases had prohibited a prosecutor from mentioning the worth of a victim's life in death penalty cases. Marshall was troubled by the Court's willingness to ignore the doctrine of *stare decisis*—respect for precedent. The majority indicated that this doctrine was less important in cases involving individual constitutional liberties than those involving commercial interests. The majority's decision undermined not only institutional concerns—respect for precedent—but also individual liberties. Marshall did not mince any words:

> Power, not reason, is the new currency of this Court's decision-making. . . . Neither the law nor the facts supporting *Booth* and *Gathers* underwent any change in the last four years. Only the personnel of this Court did.

> The majority today sends a clear signal that scores of established constitutional liberties are now ripe for reconsideration, thereby inviting the very type of open defiance of our precedents that the majority rewards in this case.

> The truncation of the Court's duty to stand by its own precedents is astonishing. By limiting full protection of the doctrine of *stare decisis* to "cases involving property and contract rights. . . . the majority sends a clear signal that essentially *all* decisions implementing the personal liberties protected by the Bill of Rights and the Fourteenth Amendment are open to reexamination.

> In my view, this impoverished conception of *stare decisis* cannot possibly be reconciled with the values that inform the proper judicial function. . . . *[S]tare decisis* is important . . . because fidelity to precedent is part and parcel of a conception of the "judiciary as a source of impersonal and reasoned judgments.". . . . Indeed, this function of *stare decisis* is in many respects even *more* critical in adjudication involving constitutional liberties than in adjudication involving commercial entitlements. Because enforcement of the Bill of Rights and the Fourteenth Amendment frequently requires this Court to rein in the forces of democratic politics, this Court can legitimately lay claim to compliance with its direct view only if the public understands the Court to be implementing "principles . . . founded in the law rather than in the proclivities of individuals."

> If this Court shows so little respect for its own precedents, it can hardly expect them to be treated more respectfully by the state actors whom these decisions are supposed to bind.

His concluding words captured his despair for the future of the Court as well as highlighted his most important role on the Court spanning four decades—to remind the Court, and the country, that there is no justice unless there is justice for all:

[T]he overruling of *Booth* and *Gathers* is but a preview of an even broader and more far-reaching assault upon this Court's precedents. Cast aside today are those condemned to face society's ultimate penalty. Tomorrow's victims may be minorities, women, or the indigent. Inevitably, this campaign to resurrect yesterday's "spirited dissents" will squander the authority and legitimacy of this Court as a protector of the powerless.

III

The Opinions of Justice Thurgood Marshall

ROBERT ELI STANLEY, Appellant,
versus
State of GEORGIA.

Argued Jan. 14 and 15, 1969
Decided April 7, 1969

Defendant was convicted in the Superior Court, Fulton County, Georgia, of possessing obscene matter and he appealed. The Supreme Court of Georgia affirmed. On appeal, the Supreme Court, Mr. Justice Marshall, held that First and Fourteenth Amendments prohibit making mere private possession of obscene material a crime.

Reversed and remanded with directions.

Mr. Justice MARSHALL delivered the opinion of the Court.

An investigation of appellant's alleged bookmaking activities led to the issuance of a search warrant for appellant's home. Under authority of this warrant, federal and state agents secured entrance. They found very little evidence of bookmaking activity, but while looking through a desk drawer in an upstairs bedroom, one of the federal agents, accompanied by a state officer, found three reels of eight-millimeter film. Using a projector and screen found in an upstairs living room, they viewed the films. The state officer concluded that they were obscene and seized them. Since a further examination of the bedroom indicated that appellant occupied it, he was charged with possession of obscene matter and placed under arrest. He was later indicted for "knowingly having possession of obscene matter" in violation of Georgia law. Appellant was tried before a jury and convicted. The Supreme Court of Georgia affirmed. Stanley v. State (1968). We noted probable jurisdiction of an appeal brought under 28 U.S.C. 1257(2) (1968).

Appellant raises several challenges to the validity of his conviction. We find it necessary to consider only one. Appellant argues here, and argued below, that the Georgia obscenity statute, insofar as it punishes mere private possession of obscene matter, violates the First Amendment, as made applicable to the States by the Fourteenth Amendment. For reasons set forth below, we agree that the mere private possession of obscene matter cannot constitutionally be made a crime.

The court below saw no valid constitutional objection to the Georgia statute, even though it extends further than the typical statute forbidding commercial sales of obscene material. It held that "[i]t is not essential to an indictment charging one with possession of obscene matter that it be alleged that such possession was 'with intent to sell, expose or circulate the same.'" Stanley v. State. The State and appellant both agree that the question here before us is whether "a statute imposing criminal sanctions upon the mere [knowing] possession of obscene matter" is constitutional. In this context, Georgia concedes that the present case appears to be one of the "first impression on this exact point," but contends that since "obscenity is not within the area of constitutionally protected speech or press," Roth v. United States (1957), the States are free, subject to the limits of other provisions of the Constitution, see, e.g., Ginsberg v. New York (1968), to deal with it any way deemed necessary, just as they may deal with possession of other things thought to be detrimental to the welfare of their citizens. If the State can protect the body of a citizen, may it not, argues Georgia, protect his mind?

It is true that *Roth* does declare, seemingly without qualification, that obscenity is not protected by the First Amendment. That statement has been repeated in various forms in subsequent cases. See, e.g., Smith v. California (1959); Jacobellis v. Ohio (1964) (opinion of Brennan, J.); Ginsberg v. New York. However, neither *Roth* nor any subsequent decision of this Court dealt with the precise problem involved in the present case. Roth was convicted of mailing obscene circulars and advertising, and an obscene book, in violation of a federal obscenity statute. The defendant in a companion case, Alberts v. California (1957), was convicted of "lewdly keeping for sale obscene and indecent books, and [of] writing, composing and publishing an obscene advertisement of them." None of the statements cited by the Court in *Roth* stood for the proposition that "this Court has always assumed that obscenity is not protected by the freedoms of speech and press" were made in the context of a statute punishing more private possession of obscene material; the cases cited deal for the most part with use of the mails to distribute objectionable material or with some form of public distribution or dissemination. Moreover, none of this Court's decisions subsequent to *Roth* involved prosecution for private possession of obscene materials. Those cases dealt with the power of the State and Federal Governments to prohibit or regulate certain public actions taken or intended to be taken with respect to obscene matter. Indeed, with one exception, we have been unable to discover any case in which the issue in the present case has been fully considered.

In this context, we do not believe that this case can be decided simply by citing *Roth*. *Roth* and its progeny certainly do mean that the First and Fourteenth Amendments recognize a valid governmental interest in dealing with the problem of obscenity. But the assertion of that interest cannot, in every context, be insulated from all constitutional protections. Neither *Roth* nor any other decision of this Court reaches that far. As the Court said in *Roth* itself, "[c]easeless vigilance is the watchword to prevent erosion [of First Amendment rights] by Congress or by the States. The door barring federal and state intrusion into this area cannot be left ajar; it must be kept tightly closed and opened only the slightest crack necessary to prevent encroachment upon more important interests." *Roth* and the cases following it discerned such an "important interest" in the regulation of commercial distribution of obscene material. That holding cannot foreclose an examination of the constitutional implications of a statute forbidding mere private possession of such material.

It is now well established that the Constitution protects the right to receive information and ideas. "This freedom [of speech and press] necessarily protects the right to receive" Martin v. City of Struthers (1943). This right to receive information and ideas, regardless of their social worth, see Winters v. New York, (1948), is fundamental to our free society. Moreover, in the context of this case—a prosecution for mere possession of printed or filmed material in the privacy of a person's own home—that right takes on an added dimension. For also fundamental is the right to be free, except in very limited circumstances, from unwanted governmental intrusions into one's privacy.

"The makers of our Constitution undertook to secure conditions favorable to the pursuit of happiness. They recognized the significance of man's spiritual nature, of his feelings and of his intellect. They knew that only a part of the pain, pleasure and satisfactions of life are to be found in material things. They sought to protect Americans in their beliefs, their thoughts, their emotions and their sensations. They conferred, as against the government, the right to be let alone—the most comprehensive of rights and the right most valued by civilized man." Olmstead v. United States (1928).

These are the rights that appellant is asserting in the case before us. He is asserting the right to read or observe what he pleases—the right to satisfy his intellectual and emotional needs in the privacy of his own home. He is asserting the right to be free from state inquiry into the contents of his library. Georgia contends that appellant does not have these rights, that there are certain types of materials that the individual may not read or even possess. Georgia justifies this assertion by arguing that the films in the present case are obscene. But we think that mere categorization of these films as "obscene" is insufficient justification for such a drastic invasion of personal liberties guaranteed by the First and Fourteenth Amendments. Whatever may be the justifications for other statutes regulating obscenity, we do not think they reach into the privacy of one's own home. If the First Amendment means anything, it means that a State has no business telling a man, sitting alone in his own house, what books he may read or what films he may watch. Our whole constitutional heritage rebels at the thought of giving government the power to control men's minds.

And yet, in the face of these traditional notions of individual liberty, Georgia asserts the right to protect the individual's mind from the effects of obscenity. We are not certain that this argument amounts to anything more than the assertion that the State has the right to control the moral content of a person's thoughts. To some, this may be a noble purpose, but it is wholly inconsistent with the philosophy of the First Amendment. As the Court said in Kingsley International Pictures Corp. v. Regents (1959), "[t]his argument misconceives what it is that the Constitution protects. Its guarantee is not confined to the expression of ideas that are conventional or shared by a majority. And in the realm of ideas it protects expression which is eloquent no less than that which is unconvincing." (1952). Nor is it relevant that obscene materials in general, or the particular films before the Court, are arguably devoid of any ideological content. The line between the transmission of ideas and mere entertainment is much too elusive for this Court to draw, if indeed such a line can be drawn at all. See Winters v. New York. Whatever the power of the state to control public dissemination of ideas inimical to the public morality, it cannot constitutionally premise legislation on the desirability of controlling a person's private thoughts.

Perhaps recognizing this, Georgia asserts that exposure to obscene materials may lead to deviant sexual behavior or crimes of sexual violence. There appears to be little empirical basis for that assertion. But more important, if the State is only concerned about printed or filmed materials inducing antisocial conduct, we believe that in the context of private consumption of ideas and information we should adhere to the view that "[a]mong free men, the deterrents ordinarily to be applied to prevent crime are education and punishment for violations of the law." Whitney v. California (1927) (Brandeis, J., concurring). (1963). Given the present state of knowledge, the State may no more prohibit mere possession of obscene matter on the ground that it may lead to antisocial conduct than it may prohibit possession of chemistry books on the ground that they may lead to the manufacture of homemade spirits.

It is true that in *Roth* this Court rejected the necessity of proving that exposure to obscene material would create a clear and present danger of antisocial conduct or would probably induce its recipients to such conduct. But that case dealt with public distribution of obscene materials and such distribution is subject to different objections. For example, there is always the danger that obscene material might fall into the hands of children, see Ginsberg v. New York, *supra,* or that it might intrude upon the sensibilities or privacy of the general public. See Redrup v. New York (1967). No such dangers are present in this case.

Finally, we are faced with argument that prohibition of possession of obscene materials is a necessary incident to statutory schemes prohibiting distribution. That argument is based on alleged difficulties of proving an intent to distribute or in producing evidence of actual distribution. We are not convinced that such difficulties exist, but even if they did we do not think that they would justify infringement of the individual's right to read or observe what he pleases. Because that right is so fundamental to our scheme of individual liberty, its restriction may not be justified by the need to ease the administration of otherwise valid criminal laws. See Smith v. California (1959).

We hold that the First and Fourteenth Amendments prohibit mere private possession of obscene material a crime. *Roth* and the cases following that decision are not impaired by today's holding. As we have said, States retain broad power to regulate obscenity; that power simply does not extend to mere possession by the individual in the privacy of his own home. Accordingly, the judgment of the court below is reversed and the case is remanded for proceedings not inconsistent with this opinion.

It is so ordered.

Judgment reversed and case remanded.

GRAYNED
versus
CITY OF ROCKFORD
APPEAL FROM THE SUPREME COURT OF ILLINOIS

Argued January 19, 1972
Decided June 26, 1972

1. Antipicketing ordinance, virtually identical with one invalidated as violative of equal protection in *Police Department of Chicago* v. *Mosley,* is likewise invalid.
2. Antinoise ordinance prohibiting a person while on grounds adjacent to a building in which a school is in session from willfully making a noise or diversion that disturbs or tends to disturb the peace or good order of the school session is not unconstitutionally vague or overbroad. The ordinance is not vague since, with fair warning, it prohibits only actual or imminent, and willful, interference with normal school activity, and is not a broad invitation to discriminatory enforcement. *Cox* v. *Louisiana, Coates* v. *Cincinnati,* distinguished. The ordinance is not overbroad as unduly interfering with First Amendment rights since expressive activity is prohibited only if it "materially disrupts classwork." *Tinker* v. *Des Moines School District,* affirmed in part and reversed in part.

MARSHALL, J., delivered the opinion of the Court, in which BURGER, C. J., and BRENNAN, STEWART, WHITE, POWELL, and REHNQUIST, JJ., joined. BLACKMUN, J., filed a statement joining in the judgment and in Part I of the Court's opinion and concurring in the result as to Part II of the opinion, DOUGLAS, J., filed an opinion dissenting in part and joining in Part I of the Court's opinion.

MR. JUSTICE MARSHALL delivered the opinion of the Court.
Appellant Richard Grayned was convicted for his part in a demon-

stration in front of West Senior High School in Rockford, Illinois. Negro students at the school had first presented their grievances to school administrators. When the principal took no action on crucial complaints, a more public demonstration of protest was planned. On April 25, 1969, approximately 200 people—students, their family members, and friends—gathered next to the school grounds. Appellant, whose brother and twin sisters were attending the school, was part of this group. The demonstrators marched around on a sidewalk about 100 feet from the school building, which was set back from the street. Many carried signs which summarized the grievances: "Black cheerleaders to cheer too"; "Black history with black teachers"; "Equal rights, Negro counselors." Others, without placards, made the "power to the people" sign with their upraised and clenched fists.

In other respects, the evidence at appellant's trial was sharply contradictory. Government witnesses reported that the demonstrators repeatedly cheered, chanted, baited policemen, and made other noise that was audible in the school; that hundreds of students were distracted from their school activities and lined the classroom windows to watch the demonstration; that some demonstrators successfully yelled to their friends to leave the school building and join the demonstration; that uncontrolled latenesses after period changes in the school were far greater than usual, with late students admitting that they had been watching the demonstration; and that, in general, orderly school procedure was disrupted. Defense witnesses claimed that the demonstrators were at all times quiet and orderly; that they did not seek to violate the law, but only to "make a point"; that the only noise was made by policemen using loudspeakers; that almost no students were noticeable at the schoolhouse windows; and that orderly school procedure was not disrupted.

After warning the demonstrators, the police arrested 40 of them, including appellant. For participating in the demonstration, Grayned was tried and convicted of violating two Rockford ordinances, hereinafter referred to as the "antipicketing" ordinance and the "antinoise" ordinance. A $25 fine was imposed for each violation. Since Grayned challenged the constitutionality of each ordinance, he appealed directly to the Supreme Court of Illinois. Ill. Sup. Ct. Rule 302. He claimed that the ordinances were invalid on their face, but did not urge that, as applied to him, the ordinances had punished constitutionally protected activity. The Supreme Court of Illinois held that both ordinances were constitutional on their face. (1970). We noted probable jurisdiction, 404

U. S. 820 (1971). We conclude that the antipicketing ordinance is unconstitutional, but affirm the court below with respect to the antinoise ordinance.

I

At the time of appellant's arrest and conviction, Rockford's antipicketing ordinance provided that

"A person commits disorderly conduct when he knowingly:

"(i) Pickets or demonstrates on a public way within 150 feet of any primary or secondary school building while the school is in session and one-half hour before the school is in session and one-half hour after the school session has been concluded, provided that this subsection does not prohibit the peaceful picketing of any school involved in a labor dispute. . . ." Code of Ordinances, c. 28, § 18.1 (i).

This ordinance is identical to the Chicago disorderly conduct ordinance we have today considered in *Police Department of Chicago* v. *Mosley.* For the reasons given in *Mosley,* we agree with dissenting Justice Schaefer below, and hold that § 18.1 (i) violates the Equal Protection Clause of the Fourteenth Amendment. Appellant's conviction under this invalid ordinance must be reversed

II

The antinoise ordinance reads, in pertinent part, as follows:

"[N]o person, while on public or private grounds adjacent to any building in which a school or any class thereof is in session, shall willfully make or assist in the making of any noise or diversion which disturbs or tends to disturb the peace or good order of such school session or class thereof. . . ." Code of Ordinances, c. 28, § 19.2 (a).

Appellant claims that, on its face, this ordinance is both vague and overbroad, and therefore unconstitutional. We conclude, however, that the ordinance suffers from neither of these related infirmities.

A. Vagueness

It is a basic principle of due process that an enactment is void for vagueness if its prohibitions are not clearly defined. Vague laws offend several important values. First, because we assume that man is free to steer between lawful and unlawful conduct, we insist that laws give the person of ordinary intelligence a reasonable opportunity to know what is prohibited, so that he may act accordingly. Vague laws may trap the innocent by not providing fair warning. Second, if arbitrary and discriminatory enforcement is to be prevented, laws must provide explicit standards for those who apply them. A vague law impermissibly delegates basic policy matters to policemen, judges, and juries for resolution on an *ad hoc* and subjective basis, with the attendant dangers of arbitrary and discriminatory application. Third, but related, where a vague statute "abut[s] upon sensitive areas of basic First Amendment freedoms," it "operates to inhibit the exercise of [those] freedoms." Uncertain meanings inevitably lead citizens to " 'steer far wider of the unlawful zone' . . . than if the boundaries of the forbidden areas were clearly marked."

Although the question is close, we conclude that the antinoise ordinance is not impermissibly vague. The court below rejected appellant's arguments "that proscribed conduct was not sufficiently specified and that police were given too broad a discretion in determining whether conduct was proscribed." Although it referred to other, similar statutes it had recently construed and upheld, the court below did not elaborate on the meaning of the antinoise ordinance. In this situation, as Mr. Justice Frankfurter put it, we must "extrapolate its allowable meaning." Here, we are "relegated . . . to the words of the ordinance itself," to the interpretations the court below has given to analogous statutes, and, perhaps to some degree, to the interpretation of the statute given by those charged with enforcing it. "Extrapolation," of course, is a delicate task, for it is not within our power to construe and narrow state laws.

With that warning, we find no unconstitutional vagueness in the antinoise ordinance. Condemned to the use of words, we can never expect mathematical certainty from our language. The words of the Rockford ordinance are marked by "flexibility and reasonable breadth, rather than meticulous specificity," *Esteban* v. *Central Missouri State College* (CA8 1969) (Blackmun, J.), cert. denied, (1970), but we think it is clear what the ordinance as a whole prohibits. Designed, according to its preamble, "for the protection of Schools," the ordinance forbids deliberately noisy or diversionary activity that disrupts or is about to disrupt normal school activities. It forbids this willful activity at fixed times—when school is in session—and at a sufficiently fixed place—"adjacent" to the school. Were we left with just the words of the ordinance, we might be troubled by the imprecision of the phrase "tends to disturb." However, in *Chicago* v. *Meyer* (1969), and *Chicago* v. *Gregory* (1968), reversed on other grounds, (1969), the Supreme Court of Illinois construed a Chicago ordinance prohibiting, *inter alia,* a "diversion tending to disturb the peace," and held that it permitted conviction only where there was *"imminent* threat of violence." (Emphasis supplied.) See *Gregory* v. *Chicago* (1969) (Black, J., concurring). Since *Meyer* was specifically cited in the opinion below, and it in turn drew heavily on *Gregory,* we think it proper to conclude that the Supreme Court of Illinois would interpret the Rockford ordinance to prohibit only actual or imminent interference with the "peace or good order" of the school.

Although the prohibited quantum of disturbance is not specified in the ordinance, it is apparent from the statute's announced purpose that the measure is whether normal school activity has been or is about to be disrupted. We do not have here a vague, general "breach of the peace" ordinance, but a statute written specifically for the school context, where the prohibited disturbances are easily measured by their impact on the normal activities of the school. Given this "particular context," the ordinance gives "fair notice to those to whom [it] is directed." Although the Rockford ordinance may not be as precise as the statute we upheld in *Cameron* v. *Johnson* (1968)—which prohibited picketing "in such a manner as to obstruct or unreasonably interfere with free ingress or egress to and from" any courthouse—we think that, as in *Cameron,* the ordinance here clearly "delineates its reach in words of common understanding."

Cox v. *Louisiana* (1965), and *Coates* v. *Cincinnati* (1971), on which appellant particularly relies, presented completely different situations. In *Cox,* a general breach of the peace ordinance had been construed by state courts to mean "to agitate, to arouse from a state of repose, to molest, to interrupt, to hinder, to disquiet." The Court correctly concluded that, as construed, the ordinance permitted persons to be punished for merely expressing unpopular views. In *Coates,* the ordinance punished the sidewalk assembly of three or more persons who "conduct themselves in a manner annoying to persons passing by. . . ." We held, in part, that the ordinance was impermissibly vague because enforcement depended on the completely subjective standard of "annoyance."

In contrast, Rockford's antinoise ordinance does not permit punishment for the expression of an unpopular point of view, and it contains no broad invitation to subjective or discriminatory enforcement. Rockford does not claim the broad power to punish all "noises" and "diversions." The vagueness of these terms, by themselves, is dispelled by the ordinance's requirements that (1) the "noise or diversion" be actually incompatible with normal school activity; (2) there be a demonstrated causality between the disruption that occurs and the "noise or diversion"; and (3) the acts be "willfully" done. "Undesirables" or their "annoying" conduct may not be punished. The ordinance does not permit people to "stand on a public sidewalk . . . only at the whim of any police officer." Rather, there must be demonstrated interference with school activities. As always, enforcement requires the exercise of some degree of police judgment, but, as confined, that degree of judgment here is permissible. The Rockford City Council has made the basic policy choices, and has given fair warning as to what is prohibited. "[T]he ordinance defines boundaries sufficiently distinct" for citizens, policemen, juries, and appellate judges. It is not impermissibly vague.

B. Overbreadth

A clear and precise enactment may nevertheless be "overbroad" if in its reach it prohibits constitutionally protected conduct. Although appellant does not claim that, as applied to him, the antinoise ordinance has punished protected expressive activity, he claims that the ordinance is overbroad on its face. Because overbroad laws, like vague ones, deter privileged activity, our cases firmly establish appellant's standing to raise an overbreadth challenge. The crucial question, then, is whether the ordinance sweeps within its prohibitions what may not be punished under the First and Fourteenth Amendments. Specifically, appellant contends that the Rockford ordinance unduly interferes with First and Fourteenth Amendment rights to picket on a public sidewalk near a school. We disagree.

"In considering the right of a municipality to control the use of public streets for the expression of religious [or political] views, we start with the words of Mr. Justice Roberts that 'Wherever the title of streets and parks may rest, they have immemorially been held in trust for the use of the public and, time out of mind, have been used for purposes of assembly, communicating thoughts between citizens, and discussing public questions.' *Hague* v. *CIO* (1939)." *Kunz* v. *New York* (1951). See *Shuttlesworth* v. *Birmingham* (1969). The right to use a public place for expressive activity may be restricted only for weighty reasons.

Clearly, government has no power to restrict such activity because of its message. Our cases make equally clear, however, that reasonable "time, place and manner" regulations may be necessary to further significant governmental interests, and are permitted. For example, two parades cannot march on the same street simultaneously, and government may allow only one. *Cox* v. *New Hampshire* (1941). A demonstration or parade on a large street during rush hour might put an intolerable burden on the essential flow of traffic, and for that reason could be prohibited. *Cox* v. *Louisiana.* If overamplified loudspeakers assault the citizenry, government may turn them down. *Kovacs* v. *Cooper* (1949); *Saia* v. *New York* (1948). Subject to such reasonable regulation, however, peaceful demonstrations in public places are protected by the First Amendment. Of course, where demonstrations turn violent, they lose their protected quality as expression under the First Amendment.

The nature of a place, "the pattern of its normal activities, dictate the kinds of regulations of time, place, and manner that are reasonable." Although a silent vigil may not unduly interfere with a public library, *Brown* v. *Louisiana* (1966), making a speech in the reading room almost certainly would. That same speech should be perfectly appropriate in a park. The crucial question is whether the manner of expression is basically incompatible with the normal activity of a particular place at a particular time. Our cases make clear that in assessing the reasonableness of a regulation, we must weigh heavily the fact that communication is involved; the regulation must be narrowly tailored to further the State's legitimate interest. Access to the "streets, sidewalks, parks, and other similar public places . . . for the purpose of exercising [First Amendment rights] cannot constitutionally be denied broadly. . . ." Free expression "must not, in the guise of regulation, be abridged or denied."

In light of these general principles, we do not think that Rockford's ordinance is an unconstitutional regulation of activity around a school. Our touchstone is *Tinker* v. *Des Moines School District* (1969), in which we considered the question of how to accommodate First Amendment rights with the "special characteristics of the school environment." *Tinker* held that the Des Moines School District could not punish students for wearing black armbands to school in protest of the Vietnam war. Recognizing that " 'wide exposure to . . . robust exchange of ideas' " is an "important part of the educational process" and should be nurtured, we concluded that free expression could not be barred from the school campus. We made clear that "undifferentiated fear or apprehension of disturbance is not enough to overcome the right to freedom of expression," and that particular expressive activity could not be prohibited because of a "mere desire to avoid the discomfort and unpleasantness that always accompany an unpopular viewpoint." But we nowhere suggested that students, teachers, or anyone else has an absolute constitutional right to use all parts of a school building or its immediate environs for his unlimited expressive purposes. Expressive activity could certainly be restricted, but only if the forbidden conduct "materially disrupts classwork or involves substantial disorder or invasion of the rights of others." The wearing of armbands was protected in *Tinker* because the students "neither interrupted school activities nor sought to intrude in the school affairs or the lives of others. They caused discussion outside of the classrooms, but no interference with work and no disorder." Compare *Burnside* v. *Byars* (CA5 1966), and *Butts* v. *Dallas Ind. School District* (CA5 1971), with *Blackwell* v. *Issaquena County Board of Education* (CA5 1966).

Just as *Tinker* made clear that school property may not be declared off limits for expressive activity by students, we think it clear that the public sidewalk adjacent to school grounds may not be declared off limits for expressive activity by members of the public. But in each case, expressive activity may be prohibited if it "materially disrupts classwork or involves substantial disorder or invasion of the rights of others." *Tinker* v. *Des Moines School District.*

We would be ignoring reality if we did not recognize that the public schools in a community are important institutions, and are often the focus of significant grievances. Without interfering with normal school activities, daytime picketing and handbilling on public grounds near a school can effectively publicize those grievances to pedestrians, school visitors, and deliverymen, as well as to teachers, administrators, and students. Some picketing to that end will be quiet and peaceful, and will in no way disturb the normal functioning of the school. For example, it would be highly unusual if the classic expressive gesture of the solitary picket disrupts anything related to the school, at least on a public sidewalk open to pedestrians. On the other hand, schools could hardly tolerate boisterous demonstrators who drown out classroom conversation, make studying impossible, block entrances, or incite children to leave the schoolhouse.

Rockford's antinoise ordinance goes no further than *Tinker* says a municipality may go to prevent interference with its schools. It is narrowly tailored to further Rockford's compelling interest in having an undisrupted school session conducive to the students' learning, and does not unnecessarily interfere with First Amendment rights. Far from having an impermissibly broad prophylactic ordinance, Rockford punishes only conduct which disrupts or is about to disrupt normal school activities. That decision is made, as it should be, on an individualized basis, given the particular fact situation. Peaceful picketing which does not interfere with the ordinary functioning of the school is permitted. And the ordinance gives no license to punish anyone because of what he is saying.

We recognize that the ordinance prohibits some picketing that is neither violent nor physically obstructive. Noisy demonstrations that disrupt or are incompatible with normal school activities are obviously within the ordinance's reach. Such expressive conduct may be constitutionally protected at other places or other times, cf. *Edwards* v. *South Carolina* (1963); *Cox* v. *Louisiana* (1965), but next to a school, while classes are in session, it may be prohibited. The antinoise ordinance imposes no such restriction on expressive activity before or after the school session, while the student/faculty "audience" enters and leaves the school.

In *Cox* v. *Louisiana* (1965), this Court indicated that, because of the special nature of the place, persons could be constitutionally prohibited from picketing "in or near" a courthouse "with the intent of interfering with, obstructing, or impeding the administration of justice." Likewise, in *Cameron* v. *Johnson* (1968), we upheld a statute prohibiting picketing "in such a manner as to obstruct or unreasonably interfere with free ingress or egress to and from any . . . county . . . courthouses." As in those two cases, Rockford's modest restriction on some peaceful picketing represents a considered and specific legislative judgment that some kinds of expressive activity should be restricted at a particular time and place, here in order to protect the schools. Such a reasonable regulation is not inconsistent with the First and Fourteenth Amendments. The antinoise ordinance is not invalid on its face.

The judgment is

Affirmed in part and reversed in part.

CLARK, SECRETARY OF THE INTERIOR, ET AL.
versus
COMMUNITY FOR CREATIVE NON-VIOLENCE, ET AL.

Argued March 21, 1984
Decided June 29, 1984

In 1982, the National Park Service issued a permit to respondent Community for Creative Non-Violence (CCNV) to conduct a demonstration in Lafayette Park and the Mall, which are National Parks in the heart of Washington, D.C. The purpose of the demonstration was to call attention to the plight of the homeless, and the permit authorized the erection of two symbolic tent cities. However, the Park Service, relying on its regulations—particularly one that permits "camping" (defined as including sleeping activities) only in designated campgrounds, no campgrounds ever having been designated in Lafayette Park or the Mall—denied CCNV's request that demonstrators be permitted to sleep in the symbolic tents. CCNV and the individual respondents then filed an action in Federal District Court, alleging that application of the regulations to prevent sleeping in the tents violated the First Amendment. The District Court granted summary judgment for the Park Service, but the Court of Appeals reversed.

Held: The challenged application of the Park Service regulations does not violate the First Amendment.

(a) Assuming that overnight sleeping in connection with the demonstration is expressive conduct protected to some extent by the First Amendment, the regulation forbidding sleeping meets the requirements for a reasonable time, place, or manner restriction of expression, whether oral, written, or symbolized by conduct. The regulation is neutral with regard to the message presented, and leaves open ample alternative methods of communicating the intended message concerning the plight of the homeless. Moreover, the regulation narrowly focuses on the Government's substantial interest in maintaining the parks in the heart of the Capital in an attractive and intact condition, readily available to the millions of people who wish to see and enjoy them by their presence. To permit camping would be totally inimical to these purposes. The validity of the regulation need not be judged solely by reference to the demonstration at hand, and none of its provisions are unrelated to the ends that it was designed to serve.

(b) Similarly, the challenged regulation is also sustainable as meeting the standards for a valid regulation of expressive conduct. Aside from its impact on speech, a rule against camping or overnight sleeping in public parks is not beyond the constitutional power of the Government to enforce. And as noted above, there is a substantial Government interest, unrelated to suppression of expression, in conserving park property that is served by the proscription of sleeping.

Reversed.

White, J. delivered the opinion of the Court, in which BURGER, C.J., and BLACKMUN, POWELL, REHNQUIST, STEVENS, and O'CONNER, JJ., joined. BURGER, C.J., filed a concurring opinion, post. MARSHALL, J., filed a dissenting opinion, in which BRENNAN, J., joined, post.

JUSTICE MARSHALL, with whom JUSTICE BRENNAN joins, dissenting.

The Court's disposition of this case is marked by two related failings. First, the majority is either unwilling or unable to take seriously the First Amendment claims advanced by respondents. Contrary to the impression given by the majority, respondents are not supplicants seeking to wheedle an undeserved favor from the Government. They are citizens raising issues of profound public importance who have properly turned to the courts from the vindication of their constitutional rights. Second, the majority misapplies the test for ascertaining whether a restraint on speech qualifies as a reasonable time, place, and manner regulation. In determining what constitutes a sustainable regulation, the majority fails to subject the alleged interests of the Government to the degree of scrutiny required to ensure that expressive activity protected by the First Amendment remains free of unnecessary limitations.

I

The proper starting point for analysis of this case is a recognition that the activity in which respondents seek to engage—sleeping in a highly public place, outside, in the winter for the purpose of protesting homelessness—is symbolic speech protected by the First Amendment. The majority assumes, without deciding, that the respondents' conduct is entitled to constitutional protection. The problem with this assumption is that the Court thereby avoids examining closely the reality of respondents' planned expression. The majority's approach denatures respondents' asserted right and thus makes all too easy identification of a Government interest sufficient to warrant its abridgment. A realistic appraisal of the competing interests at stake in this case requires a closer look at the nature of the expressive conduct at issue and the context in which that conduct would be displayed.

In late autumn of 1982, respondents sought permission to conduct a round-the-clock demonstration in Lafayette Park and on the Mall. Part of the demonstration would include homeless persons sleeping outside in tents without any other amenities. Respondents sought to begin their demonstration on a date full of ominous meaning to any homeless person: the first day of winter. Respondents were similarly purposeful in choosing demonstration sites. The Court portrays these sites—the Mall and Lafayette Park—in a peculiar fashion. According to the Court:

> "Lafayette Park and the Mall . . . are unique resources that the Federal Government holds in trust for the American people. Lafayette Park is a roughly seven-acre square located across Pennsylvania Avenue from the White House. Although originally part of the White House grounds, President Jefferson set it aside as a park for the use of residents and visitors. It is a 'garden park with a . . . formal landscaping of flowers and trees, with fountains, walks and benches.' . . . The Mall is a stretch of land running westward from the Capitol to the Lincoln Memorial some two miles away. It includes the Washington Monument, a series of reflecting pools, trees, lawns, and other greenery. It is bordered by, inter alia, the Smithsonian Institution and the National Gallery of Art. Both the Park and the Mall were included in Major Pierre L'Enfant's original plan for the Capital. Both are visited by vast numbers of visitors from around the country, as well as by large numbers of residents of the Washington metropolitan area."

Missing from the majority's description is any inkling that Lafayette Park and the Mall have served as the sites for some of the most rousing political demonstrations in the nation's history. It is interesting to learn, I suppose, that Lafayette Park and the Mall were both part of Major Pierre L'Enfant's original plan for the Capital. Far more pertinent, however, is that these areas constitute, in the Government's words, "a fitting and powerful forum for political expression and political protest."

The primary purpose for making sleep an integral part of the demonstration was "to reenact the central reality of homelessness" and to impress upon public consciousness, in as dramatic a way as possible, that homelessness is a widespread problem, often ignored, that confronts its victims with life-threatening deprivations. As one of the homeless men seeking to demonstrate explained: "Sleeping in Lafayette Park or on the Mall, for me, is to show people that conditions are so poor for the homeless and poor in this city that we would actually sleep outside in the winter to get the point across."

In a long line of cases, this Court has afforded First Amendment protection to expressive conduct that qualifies as symbolic speech. See, e.g., *Tinker* v. *Des Moines School Dist.* (1969) (black armband worn by students in public school as protest against United States policy in Vietnam war); *Brown* v. *Louisiana* (1966) (sit-in by Negro students in "whites only" library to protest segregation); *Stromberg* v. *California* (1931) (flying red flag as gesture of support for communism). In light of the surrounding contest, respondents' proposed activity meets the qualifications. The Court has previously acknowledged the importance of context in determining whether an act can properly be denominated as "speech" for First Amendment purposes and has provided guidance concerning the way in which courts should "read" a context in making this determination. The leading case is *Spence* v. *Washington* (1974), where this Court held that displaying a United States flag with a peace symbol attached to it was conduct protected by the First Amendment. The Court looked first to the intent of the speaker—whether there was an "intent to convey a particularized message"—and second to the perception of the audience—whether "the likelihood was great that the message would be understood by those who viewed it." Here respondents clearly intended to protest the reality of homelessness by sleeping outdoors in the winter in the near vicinity of the magisterial residence of the President of the United States. In addition to accentuating the political character of their protest by their choice of location and mode of communication, respondents also intended to underline the meaning of their protest by giving their demonstration satirical names. Respondents planned to name the demonstration on the Mall "Congressional Village," and the demonstration in Lafayette Park, "Reaganville II."

Nor can there be any doubt that in the surrounding circumstances the likelihood was great that the political significance of sleeping in the parks would be understood by those who viewed it. Certainly the news media understood the significance of respondents' proposed activity; newspapers and magazines from around the nation reported their previous sleep-in and their planned display. Ordinary citizens, too, would likely understand the political message intended by respondents. This likelihood stems from the remarkably apt fit between the activity in which respondents seek to engage and the social problem they seek to highlight. By using sleep as an integral part of their mode of protest, respondents "can express with their bodies the poignancy of their plight. They can physically demonstrate the neglect from which they suffer with an articulateness even Dickens could not match" [*Community for Creative Non-Violence* v. *Watt* (1983); (Edwards, J., concurring)].

It is true that we all go to sleep as part of our daily regimen and that, for the most part, sleep represents a physical necessity and not a vehicle for expression. But these characteristics need not prevent an activity that is normally devoid of expressive purpose from being used as a novel mode of communication. Sitting or standing in a library is a commonplace activity necessary to facilitate ends usually having nothing to do with making a statement. Moreover, sitting or standing is not conduct that an observer would normally construe as expressive conduct. However, for Negroes to stand or sit in a "whites only" library in Louisiana in 1965 was powerfully expressive; in that particular context, those acts became "monuments of protest" against segregation. *Brown* v. *Louisiana, supra.*

The Government contends that a forseeable difficulty of administration counsels against recognizing sleep as a mode of expression protected by the First Amendment. The predicament the Government envisions can be termed "the imposter problem": the problem of distinguishing bona fide protesters from imposters whose requests for permission to sleep in Lafayette Park or the Mall on First Amendment grounds would mask ulterior designs—the simple desire, for example, to avoid the expense of hotel lodgings. The Government maintains that such distinctions cannot be made without inquiring into the sincerity of demonstrators and that such an inquiry would itself pose dangers to First Amendment values because it would necessarily be content-sensitive. I find this argument unpersuasive. First, a variety of circumstances already require government agencies to engage in the delicate task of inquiring into the sincerity of claimants asserting First Amendment rights. See, *e.g., Wisconsin* v. *Yoder* (1972), (exception of members of religious group from compulsory education statute justified by group's adherence to deep religious conviction rather than subjective secular values); *Welsh* v. *United States* (1970), (eligibility for exemption from military service as conscientious objector status justified by sincere religious beliefs). It is thus incorrect to imply that any scrutiny of the asserted purpose of persons seeking a permit to display sleeping as a form of symbolic speech would import something altogether new and disturbing into our First Amendment jurisprudence. Second, the administrative difficulty the Government envisions is now nothing more than a vague apprehension. If permitting sleep to be used as a form of protected First Amendment activity actually created the administrative problems the Government now envisions, there would emerge a clear factual basis upon which to establish the necessity for the limitation the Government advocates.

The Government's final argument against granting respondents proposed activity any degree of First Amendment protection is that the contextual analysis upon which respondents rely is fatally flawed by overinclusiveness. The Government contends that the Spence approach is overinclusive because it accords First Amendment status to a wide variety of acts that, although expressive, are obviously subject to prohibition. As the Government notes, "[a]ctions such as assassination of political figures and the bombing of government buildings can fairly be characterized as intended to convey a message that is readily perceived by the public." The Government's argument would pose a difficult problem were the determination whether an act constitutes "speech" the end of First Amendment analysis. But such a determination is not the end. If an act is defined as speech, it must still be balanced against countervailing government interests. The balancing which the First Amendment requires would doom any argument seeking to protect antisocial acts such as assassination or destruction of government property from government interference because compelling interests would outweigh the expressive value of such conduct.

II

Although sleep in the context of this case is symbolic speech protected by the First Amendment, it is nonetheless subject to reasonable time, place, and manner restrictions. I agree with the standard enunciated by the majority: "[R]estrictions of this kind are valid provided that they are justified without reference to the content of the regulated speech, that they are narrowly tailored to serve a significant governmental interest, and that they leave open ample alternative channels for communication of the information." I conclude, however, that the regulations at issue in this case, as applied to respondents, fail to satisfy this standard.

According to the majority, the significant Government interest advanced by denying respondents' request to engage in sleep-speech is the interest in "maintaining the parks in the heart of our Capital in an attractive and intact condition, readily available to the millions of people who wish to see and enjoy them by their presence." That interest is indeed significant. However, neither the Government nor the majority adequately explains how prohibiting respondents' planned activity will substantially further that interest.

The majority's attempted explanation begins with the curious statement that it seriously doubts that the First Amendment requires the Park Service to permit a demonstration in Lafayette Park and the Mall involving a twenty-four-hour vigil and the erection of tents to accommodate a hundred and fifty people. I cannot perceive why the Court should have "serious doubts" regarding this matter, and it provides no explanation for its uncertainty. Furthermore, even if the majority's doubts were well founded, I cannot see how such doubts relate to the problem at hand. The issue posed by this case is not whether the Government is constitutionally compelled to permit the erection of tents and the staging of a continuous twenty-four-hour vigil; rather, the issue is whether any substantial Government interest is served by banning sleep that is part of a political demonstration.

What the Court may be suggesting is that if the tents and the twenty-four-hour vigil are permitted, but not constitutionally required to be permitted, then respondents have no constitutional right to engage in expressive conduct that supplements these activities. Put in arithmetical terms, the Court appears to contend that if X is permitted by grace rather than by constitutional compulsion, X + 1 can be denied without regard to the requirements the Government must normally satisfy in order to restrain protected activity. This notion, however, represents a misguided conception of the First Amendment. The First Amendment requires the Government to justify every instance of abridgment. That requirement stems from our oft-stated recognition that the First

Amendment was designed to secure "the widest possible dissemination of information from diverse and antagonistic sources," [*Associated Press* v. *United States*] (1945), and "to assure unfettered interchange of ideas for the bringing about of political and social changes desired by the people" [*Roth* v. *United States* (1957)]. See also *Buckley* v. *Valeo* (1976); *New York Times Co.* v. *Sullivan* (1964); *Whitney* v. *California* (1927) (Brandeis, J., concurring). Moreover, the stringency of that requirement is not diminished simply because of the activity the Government may have permitted out of grace but was not constitutionally compelled to allow. If the Government cannot adequately justify abridgment of protected expression, there is no reason why citizens should be prevented from exercising the first of the rights safeguarded by our Bill of Rights.

The majority's second argument is comprised of the suggestion that, although sleeping contains an element of expression, "its major value to [respondents'] demonstration would have been facilitative." While this observation does provide a hint of the weight the Court attached to respondents' First Amendment claims, it is utterly irrelevant to whether the Government's ban on sleeping advances a substantial Government interest.

The majority's third argument is based upon two claims. The first is that the ban on sleeping relieves the Government of an administrative burden because, without the flat ban, the process of issuing and denying permits to other demonstrators asserting First Amendment rights to sleep in the parks "would present difficult problems for the Park Service." The second is that the ban on sleeping will increase the probability that "some around-the-clock demonstrations for days on end will not materialize, [that] others will be limited in size and duration, and that the purpose of the regulation will thus be materially served," that purpose being "to limit the wear and tear on park properties."

The flaw in these two contentions is that neither is supported by a factual showing that evinces a real, as opposed to a merely speculative, problem. The majority fails to offer any evidence indicating that the absence of an absolute ban on sleeping would present administrative problems to the Park Service that are substantially more difficult than those it ordinarily confronts. A mere apprehension of difficulties should not be enough to overcome the right to free expression. See *United States* v. *Grace* (1983); *Tinker* v. *Des Moines School Dist.* Moreover, if the Government's interest in avoiding administrative difficulties were truly "substantial," one would expect the agency most involved in administering the parks at least to allude to such an interest. Here, however, the perceived difficulty of administering requests from other demonstrators seeking to convey messages through sleeping was not among the reasons underlying the Park Service regulations. Nor was it mentioned by the Park Service in its rejection of respondents' particular request.

The Court's erroneous application of the standard for ascertaining a reasonable time, place, and manner restriction is also revealed by the majority's conclusion that a substantial governmental interest is served by the sleeping ban because it will discourage "around-the-clock demonstrations for days" and thus further the regulation's purpose "to limit wear and tear on park properties." The majority cites no evidence indicating that sleeping engaged in as symbolic speech will cause substantial wear and tear on park property. Furthermore, the Government's application of the sleeping ban in the circumstances of this case is strikingly underinclusive. The majority acknowledges that a proper time, place, and manner restriction must be "narrowly tailored." Here, however, the tailoring requirement is virtually forsaken inasmuch as the Government offers no justification for applying its absolute ban on sleeping yet is willing to allow respondents to engage in activities—such as feigned sleeping—that are no less burdensome.

In short, there are no substantial Government interests advanced by the Government's regulations as applied to respondents. All that the Court's decision advances are the prerogatives of a bureaucracy that over the years has shown an implacable hostility toward citizens' exercise of First Amendment rights.

III

The disposition of this case impels me to make two additional observations. First, in this case, as in some others involving time, place, and manner restrictions, the Court has dramatically lowered its scrutiny of governmental regulations once it has determined that such regulations are content-neutral. The result has been the creation of a two-tiered approach to First Amendment cases: While regulations that turn on the content of the expression are subjected to a strict form of judicial review, regulations that are aimed at matters other than expression receive only a minimal level of scrutiny. The minimal scrutiny prong of this two-tiered approach has led to an unfortunate diminution of First Amendment protection. By narrowly limiting its concern to whether a given regulation creates a content-based distinction, the Court has seemingly overlooked the fact that content-neutral restrictions are also capable of unnecessarily restricting protected expressive activity. To be sure, the general prohibition against content-based regulations is an essential tool of First Amendment analysis. It helps to put into operation the well-established principle that "government may not grant the use of a forum to people whose views it finds acceptable, but deny use to those wishing to express less favored or more controversial views." *Police Department of Chicago* v. *Mosley* (1972). The Court, however, has transformed the ban against content distinctions from a floor that offers all persons at least equal liberty under the First Amendment into a ceiling that restricts persons to the protection of First Amendment equality—but nothing more. The consistent imposition of silence upon all may fulfill the dictates of an evenhanded content-neutrality. But it offends our "profound national commitment to the principle that debate on public issues should be uninhibited, robust, and wide-open" *New York Times Co.* v. *Sullivan.*

Second, the disposition of this case reveals a mistaken assumption regarding the motives and behavior of Government officials who create and administer content-neutral regulations. The Court's salutary skepticism of governmental decisionmaking in First Amendment matters suddenly dissipates once it determines that a restriction is not content-based. The Court evidently assumes that the balance struck by officials is deserving of deference so long as it does not appear to be tainted by content discrimination. What the Court fails to recognize is that public officials have strong incentives to overregulate even in the absence of an intent to censor particular views. This incentive stems from the fact that of the two groups whose interests officials must accommodate—on the one hand, the interests of the general public and, on the other, the interests of those who seek to use a particular forum for First Amendment activity—the political power of the former is likely to be far greater than that of the latter. The political dynamics likely to lead officials to a disproportionate sensitivity to regulatory as opposed to First Amendment interests can be discerned in the background of this case. Although the Park Service appears to have applied the revised regulations consistently, there are facts in the record of this case that raise a substantial possibility that the impetus behind the revision may have derived less from concerns about administrative difficulties and wear and tear on the park facilities than from other, more "political," concerns. The alleged need for more restrictive regulations stemmed from a court decision favoring the same First Amendment claimants that are parties to this case. Moreover, in response both to the Park Service's announcement that it was considering changing its rules and the respondents' expressive activities, at least one powerful group urged the Service to tighten its regulations. The point of these observations is not to impugn the integrity of the National Park Service. Rather, my intention is to illustrate concretely that government agencies by their very nature are driven to overregulate public forums to the detriment of First Amendment rights, that facial viewpoint-neutrality is no shield against unnecessary restrictions on unpopular ideas or modes of expression, and that in this case in particular there was evidence readily available that should have impelled the Court to subject the Government's restrictive policy to something more than minimal scrutiny.

For the foregoing reasons, I respectfully dissent.

THE FLORIDA STAR, APPELLANT,
versus
B.J.F.

Argued March 21, 1989
Decided June 21, 1989

Appellant, *The Florida Star,* is a newspaper which publishes a "Police Reports" section containing brief articles describing local criminal incidents under police investigation. After appellee B.J.F. reported to the Sheriff's Department that she had been robbed and sexually assaulted, the Department prepared a report, which identified B.J.F. by her full name, and placed it in the Department's press room. The Department does not restrict access to the room or to the reports available there. A *Star* reporter-trainee sent to the press room copied the police report verbatim, including B.J.F.'s full name. Consequently, her name was included in a "Police Reports" story in the paper, in violation of the *Star*'s internal policy. Florida Stat. § 794.03 makes it unlawful to "print, publish, or broadcast . . . in any instrument of mass communication" the name of the victim of a sexual offense. B.J.F. filed suit in a Florida court alleging that the *Star* had negligently violated § 794.03. The trial court denied the *Star*'s motion to dismiss, which claimed, among other things, that imposing civil sanctions on the newspaper pursuant to § 794.03 violated the First Amendment. However, it granted B.J.F.'s motion for a directed verdict on the issue of negligence, finding the *Star* *per se* negligent based on its violation of § 794.03. The jury then awarded B.J.F. both compensatory and punitive damages. The verdict was upheld on appeal.

Held: Imposing damages on the *Star* for publishing B.J.F.'s name violates the First Amendment.

(a) The sensitivity and significance of the interests presented in clashes between First Amendment and privacy rights counsels the Court to rely on limited principles that sweep no more broadly than the appropriate context of the instant case, rather than to accept invitations to hold broadly that truthful publication may never be punished consistent with the First Amendment or that publication of a rape victim's name never enjoys constitutional protection. One such principle is that "if a newspaper lawfully obtains truthful information about a matter of public significance then state officials may not constitutionally punish publication of the information, absent a need to further a state interest of the highest order." *Smith* v. *Daily Mail Publishing Co.* Applied to the instant case, the *Daily Mail* principle commands reversal.

(b) The *Star* "lawfully obtain[ed] truthful information." The actual news article was accurate and the *Star* lawfully obtained B.J.F.'s name from the government. The fact that state officials are not required to disclose such reports or that the Sheriff's Department apparently failed to fulfill its § 794.03 obligation not to cause or allow B.J.F.'s name to be published does not make it unlawful for the *Star* to have received the information, and Florida has taken no steps to proscribe such receipt. The government has ample means to safeguard the information that are less drastic than punishing truthful publication. Furthermore, it is clear that the news article generally, as opposed to the specific identity contained in it, involved "a matter of public significance": the commission, and investigation, of a violent crime that had been reported to authorities.

(c) Imposing liability on the *Star* does not serve "a need to further a state interest of the highest order." Although the interests in protecting the privacy and safety of sexual assault victims and in encouraging them to report offenses without fear of exposure are highly significant, imposing liability on the *Star* in this case is too precipitous a means of advancing those interests. Since the *Star* obtained the information because the Sheriff's Department failed to abide by § 794.03's policy, the imposition of damages can hardly be said to be a narrowly tailored means of safeguarding anonymity. Self-censorship is especially likely to result from imposition of liability when a newspaper gains access to the information from a government news release. Moreover, the negligence *per se* standard adopted by the courts below does not permit case-by-case findings that the disclosure was one a reasonable person would find offensive and does not have a scienter requirement of any kind. In addition, § 794.03's facial underinclusiveness—which prohibits publication only by an "instrument of mass communication" and does not prohibit the spread of victims' names by other means—raises serious doubts about whether Florida is serving the interests specified by

B.J.F. A State must demonstrate its commitment to the extraordinary measure of punishing truthful publication in the name of privacy by applying its prohibition evenhandedly to both the smalltime disseminator and the media giant.

(Fla. App. 1986), reversed.

MARSHALL, J., delivered the opinion of the Court.

Justice MARSHALL delivered the opinion of the Court.

Florida Stat. § § 794.03 (1987) makes it unlawful to "print, publish, or broadcast . . . in any instrument of mass communication" the name of the victim of a sexual offense. Pursuant to this statute, appellant *The Florida Star* was found civilly liable for publishing the name of a rape victim which it had obtained from a publicly released police report. The issue presented here is whether this result comports with the First Amendment. We hold that it does not.

I

The Florida Star is a weekly newspaper which serves the community of Jacksonville, Florida, and which has an average circulation of approximately 18,000 copies. A regular feature of the newspaper is its "Police Reports" section. That section, typically two to three pages in length, contains brief articles describing local criminal incidents under police investigation.

On October 20, 1983, appellee B.J.F. reported to the Duval County, Florida, Sheriff's Department (the Department) that she had been robbed and sexually assaulted by an unknown assailant. The Department prepared a report on the incident which identified B.J.F. by her full name. The Department then placed the report in its press room. The Department does not restrict access either to the press room or to the reports made available therein.

A *Florida Star* reporter-trainee sent to the press room copied the police report verbatim, including B.J.F.'s full name, on a blank duplicate of the Department's forms. A *Florida Star* reporter then prepared a one-paragraph article about the crime, derived entirely from the trainee's copy of the police report. The article included B.J.F.'s full name. It appeared in the "Robberies" subsection of the "Police Reports" section on October 29, 1983, one of fifty-four police blotter stories in that day's edition. The article read:

"[B.J.F.] reported on Thursday, October 20, she was crossing Brentwood Park, which is in the 500 block of Golfair Boulevard, enroute to her bus stop, when an unknown black man ran up behind the lady and placed a knife to her neck and told her not to yell. The suspect then undressed the lady and had sexual intercourse with her before fleeing the scene with her 60 cents, Timex watch, and gold necklace. Patrol efforts have been suspended concerning this incident because of lack of evidence."

In printing B.J.F.'s full name, *The Florida Star* violated its internal policy of not publishing the names of sexual offense victims.

On September 26, 1984, B.J.F. filed suit in the Circuit Court of Duval County against the Department and *The Florida Star,* alleging that these parties negligently violated § 794.03. Before trial, the Department settled with B.J.F. for $2,500. *The Florida Star* moved to dismiss, claiming that imposing civil sanctions on the newspaper pursuant to § 794.03 violated the First Amendment. The trial judge rejected the motion.

At the close of B.J.F.'s case, and again at the close of its defense, *The Florida Star* moved for a directed verdict. On both occasions, the trial judge denied these motions. He ruled from the bench that § 794.03 was constitutional because it reflected a proper balance between the First Amendment and privacy rights, as it applied only to a narrow set of "rather sensitive . . . criminal offenses." At the close of newspaper's defense, the judge granted B.J.F.'s motion for a directed verdict on the issue of negligence, finding the newspaper *per se* negligent based upon its violation of § 794.03. This ruling left the jury to consider only the questions of causation and damages. The judge instructed the jury that it could award B.J.F. punitive damages if it found that the newspaper had "acted with reckless indifference to the rights of others." The jury awarded B.J.F. $75,000 in compensatory damages and $25,000 in punitive damages. Against the actual damage award, the judge set off B.J.F.'s settlement with the Department.

The First District Court of Appeals affirmed in a three-paragraph opinion. In the paragraph devoted to *The Florida Star*'s First Amendment claim, the court stated that the directed verdict for B.J.F. had been properly entered because, under § 794.03, a rape victim's name is "of a private nature and not to be published as a matter of law," citing *Doe* v. *Sarasota-Brandenton Florida Television Co., Inc.* (Fla. App. 1983). The Supreme Court of Florida denied discretionary review.

The Florida Star appealed to this Court. We noted probable jurisdiction (1988), and now reverse.

II

The tension between the right which the First Amendment accords to a free press, on the one hand, and the protections which various statutes and common-law doctrines accord to personal privacy against the publication of truthful information, on the other, is a subject we have addressed several times in recent years. Our decisions in cases involving government attempts to sanction the accurate dissemination of information as invasive privacy, have not, however, exhaustively considered this conflict. On the contrary, although our decisions have without exception upheld the press's right to publish, we have emphasized each time that we were resolving this conflict only as it arose in a discrete factual context.

The parties to this case frame their contentions in light of a trilogy of cases which have presented, in different contexts, the conflict between truthful reporting and state-protected privacy interests. In *Cox Broadcasting Corp* v. *Cohn* (1975), we found unconstitutional a civil damages award entered against a television station for broadcasting the name of a rape-murder victim which the station had obtained from courthouse records. In *Oklahoma Publishing Co.* v. *District Court* (1977), we found unconstitutional a state court's pretrial order enjoining the media from publishing the name or photograph of an eleven-year-old boy in connection with a juvenile proceeding involving that child which reporters had attended. Finally, in *Smith* v. *Daily Mail Publishing Co.* (1979), we found unconstitutional the indictment of two newspapers for violating a state statute forbidding newspapers to publish, without written approval of the juvenile court, the name of any youth charged as a juvenile offender. The papers had learned about a shooting by monitoring a police band radio frequency, and had obtained the name of the alleged juvenile assailant from witnesses, the police, and a local prosecutor.

Appellant takes the position that this case is indistinguishable from *Cox Broadcasting*. Alternatively, it urges that our decisions in the above trilogy, and in other cases in which we have held that the right of the press to publish truth overcame asserted interests other than personal privacy, can be distilled to yield a broader First Amendment principle that the press may never be punished, civilly or criminally, for publishing the truth. Appellee counters that the privacy trilogy is inapposite, because in each case the private information already appeared on a "public record" and because the privacy interests at stake were far less profound than in the present case. In the alternative, appellee urges that *Cox Broadcasting* be overruled and replaced with a categorical rule that publication of the name of a rape victim never enjoys constitutional protection.

[1] We conclude that imposing damages on appellant for publishing B.J.F.'s name violated the First Amendment, although not for either of the reasons appellant urges. Despite the strong resemblance this case bears to *Cox Broadcasting*, that case cannot fairly be read as controlling here. The name of the rape victim in that case was obtained from courthouse records that were open to public inspection, a fact which Justice WHITE's opinion for the Court repeatedly noted (noting "special protected nature of accurate reports of *judicial* proceedings"). Significantly, one of the reasons we gave in *Cox Broadcasting* for invalidating the challenged damages award was the important role the press plays in subjecting trials to public scrutiny and thereby helping guarantee their fairness. That role is not directly compromised where, as here, the information in question comes from a police report prepared and disseminated at a time at which not only had no adversarial criminal proceedings begun, but no suspect had been identified.

Nor need we accept appellant's invitation to hold broadly that truthful publication may never be punished consistent with the First Amendment. Our cases have carefully eschewed reaching this ultimate question, mindful that the future may bring scenarios which prudence counsels our not resolving anticipatorily. See, *e.g., Near* v. *Minnesota ex rel. Olson* (1931) (hypothesizing "publication of the sailing dates of transports or the number and location of troops"); see also *Garrison* v. *Louisiana* (1964) (endorsing absolute defense of truth "where discussion of public affairs is concerned," but leaving unsettled the constitutional implications of truthfulness "in the discrete area of purely private libels. Indeed, in *Cox Broadcasting*, we pointedly refused to answer even the less sweeping question "whether truthful publications may ever be subjected to civil or criminal liability" for invading "an area of privacy" defined by the State. Respecting the fact that press freedom and privacy rights are both "plainly rooted in the traditions and significant concerns of our society," we instead focused on the less sweeping issue of "whether the State may impose sanctions on the accurate publication of the name of a rape victim obtained from public records— more specifically, from judicial records which are maintained in connection with a public prosecution and which themselves are open to public inspections." We continue to believe that the sensitivity and significance of the interests presented in clashes between First Amendment and privacy rights counsel relying on limited principles that sweep no more broadly than the appropriate context of the instant case.

In our view, this case is appropriately analyzed with reference to such a limited First Amendment principle. It is the one, in fact, which we articulated in *Daily Mail* in our synthesis of prior cases involving attempts to punish truthful publication: "[I]f a newspaper lawfully obtains truthful information about a matter of public significance then state officials may not constitutionally punish publication of the information, absent a need to further a state interest of the highest order." According the press the ample protection provided by that principle is supported by at least three separate considerations, in addition to, of course, the overarching " 'public interest, secured by the Constitution, in the dissemination of truth.' " *Cox Broadcasting,* quoting *Garrison.* The cases on which the *Daily Mail* synthesis relied demonstrate these considerations.

First, because the *Daily Mail* formulation only protects the publication of information which a newspaper has "lawfully obtain[ed]," the government retains ample means of safeguarding significant interests upon which publication may impinge, including protecting a rape victim's anonymity. To the extent sensitive information rests in private hands, the government may under some circumstances forbid its nonconsensual acquisition, thereby bringing outside of the *Daily Mail* principle the publication of any information so acquired. To the extent sensitive information is in the government's custody, it has even greater power to forestall or mitigate the injury caused by its release. The government may classify certain information, establish and enforce procedures ensuring its redacted release, and extend a damages remedy against the government or its officials where the government's mishandling of sensitive information leads to its dissemination. Where information is entrusted to the government, a less drastic means than punishing truthful publication almost always exists for guarding against the dissemination of private facts. See, *e.g., Landmark Communications,* "much of the risk [from disclosure of sensitive information regarding judicial disciplinary proceedings] can be eliminated through careful internal procedures to protect the confidentiality of Commission proceedings"); *Oklahoma Publishing* (noting trial judge's failure to avail himself of the opportunity, provided by a state statute, to close juvenile hearing to the public, including members of the press, who later broadcast juvenile defendant's name); *Cox Broadcasting* ("If there are privacy interests to be protected in judicial proceedings, the States must respond by means which avoid public documentation or other exposure of private information").

A second consideration undergirding the *Daily Mail* principle is the fact that punishing the press for its dissemination of information which is already publicly available is relatively unlikely to advance the interests in the service of which the State seeks to act. It is not, of course, always the case that information lawfully acquired by the press is known, or accessible, to others. But where the government has made certain information publicly available, it is highly anomalous to sanction persons other than the source of its release. We noted this anomaly in *Cox Broadcasting:* "By placing the information in the public domain on official court records, the State must be presumed to have concluded that the public interest was thereby being served." The *Daily Mail* formulation reflects the fact that it is a limited set of cases indeed where, despite the accessibility of the public to certain information, a meaningful public interest is served by restricting its further release by other entities, like the press. As *Daily Mail* observed in its summary of *Oklahoma Publishing,* "once the truthful information was 'publicly revealed' or 'in the public domain' the court could not constitutionally restrain its dissemination."

A third and final consideration is the "timidity and self-censorship" which may result from allowing the media to be punished for publishing certain truthful information. *Cox Broadcasting* noted this concern with overdeterrence in the context of information made public through official court records, but the fear of excessive media self-suppression is applicable as well to other information released, without qualification, by the government. A contrary rule, depriving protection to those who rely on the government's implied representations of the lawfulness of dissemination, would force upon the media the onerous obligation of sifting through government press releases, reports, and pronouncements to prune out material arguably unlawful for publication. This situation could inhere even where the newspaper's sole object was to reproduce, with no substantial change, the government's rendition of the event in question.

Applied to the instant case, the *Daily Mail* principle clearly commands reversal. The first inquiry is whether the newspaper "lawfully obtain[ed] truthful information about a matter of public significance." It is undisputed that the news article describing the assault on B.J.F. was accurate. In addition, appellant lawfully obtained B.J.F.'s name.

Appellee's argument to the contrary is based on the fact that under Florida law, police reports which reveal the identity of the victim of a sexual offense are not among the matters of "public record" which the public, by law, is entitled to inspect. But the fact that state officials are not required to disclose such reports does not make it unlawful for a newspaper to receive them when furnished by the government. Nor does the fact that the Department apparently failed to fulfill its obligation under § 794.03 not to "cause or allow to be . . . published" the name of a sexual offense victim make the newspaper's ensuing receipt of this information unlawful. Even assuming the Constitution permitted a State to *proscribe* receipt of information, Florida has not taken this step. It is clear, furthermore, that the news article concerned "a matter of public significance," in the sense in which the Daily Mail synthesis of prior cases used that term. That is, the article generally, as opposed to the specific identity contained within it, involved a matter of paramount public import: the commission, and investigation, of a violent crime which had been reported to authorities. See *Cox Broadcasting, supra* (article identifying victim of rape-murder) *Oklahoma Publishing Co.* v. *District Court* (1977) (article identifying juvenile alleged to have committed murder); *Daily Mail, supra* (same); cf. *Landmark Communications, Inc.* v. *Virginia.*

The second inquiry is whether imposing liability on appellant pursuant to § 794.03 serves "a need to further a state interest of the highest order." *Daily Mail.* Appellee argues that a rule punishing publication furthers three closely related interests: the privacy of victims of sexual offenses; the physical safety of such victims, who may be targeted for retaliation if their names become known to their assailants; and the goal of encouraging victims of such crimes to report these offenses without fear of exposure.

At a time in which we are daily reminded of the tragic reality of rape, it is undeniable that these are highly significant interests, a fact underscored by the Florida Legislature's explicit attempt to protect these interests by enacting a criminal statute prohibiting much dissemination of victim identities. We accordingly do not rule out the possibility that, in a proper case, imposing civil sanctions for publication of the name of a rape victim might be so overwhelmingly necessary to advance these interests as to satisfy the *Daily Mail* standard. For three independent reasons, however, imposing liability for publication under the circumstances of this case is too precipitous a means of advancing these interests to convince us that there is a "need" within the meaning of the

Daily Mail formulation for Florida to take this extreme step. Cf. *Landmark Communications, supra* (invalidating penalty on publication despite State's expressed interest in nondissemination, reflected in statute prohibiting unauthorized divulging of names of judges under investigation).

First is the manner in which appellant obtained the identifying information in question. As we have noted, where the government itself provides information to the media, it is more appropriate to assume that the government had, but failed to utilize, far more limited means of guarding against dissemination than the extreme step of punishing truthful speech. That assumption is richly borne out in this case. B.J.F.'s identity would never have come to light were it not for the erroneous, if inadvertent, inclusion by the Department of her full name in an accident report made available in a press room open to the public. Florida's policy against disclosure of rape victims' identities, reflected in § 794.03, was undercut by the Department's failure to abide by this policy. Where, as here, the government has failed to police itself in disseminating information, it is clear under *Cox Broadcasting, Oklahoma Publishing,* and *Landmark Communications* that the imposition of damages against the press for its subsequent publication can hardly be said to be a narrowly tailored means of safeguarding anonymity. Once the government has placed such information in the public domain, "reliance must rest upon the judgment of those who decide what to publish or broadcast," *Cox Broadcasting,* and hopes for restitution must rest upon the willingness of the government to compensate victims for their loss of privacy and to protect them from the other consequences of its mishandling of the information which these victims provided in confidence.

That appellant gained access to the information in question through a government news release makes it especially likely that, if liability were to be imposed, self-censorship would result. Reliance on a news release is a paradigmatically "routine newspaper reporting techniqu[e]." *Daily Mail.* The government's issuance of such a release, without qualification, can only convey to recipients that the government considered dissemination lawful, and indeed expected the recipients to disseminate the information further. Had appellant merely reproduced the news release prepared and released by the Department, imposing civil damages would surely violate the First Amendment. The fact that appellant converted the police report into a news story by adding the linguistic connecting tissue necessary to transform the report's facts into full sentences cannot change this result.

A second problem with Florida's imposition of liability for publication is the broad sweep of the negligence *per se* standard applied under the civil cause of action implied from § 794.03. Unlike claims based on the common law tort of invasion of privacy, civil actions based on § 794.03 require no case-by-case findings that the disclosure of a fact about a person's private life was one that a reasonable person would find highly offensive. On the contrary, under the *per se* theory of negligence adopted by the courts below, liability follows automatically from publication. This is so regardless of whether the identity of the victim is already known throughout the community; whether the victim has voluntarily called public attention to the offense; or whether the identity of the victim has otherwise become a reasonable subject of public concern—because perhaps, questions have arisen whether the victim fabricated an assault by a particular person. Nor is there a scienter requirement of any kind under § 794.03, engendering the perverse result that truthful publications challenged pursuant to this cause of action are less protected by the First Amendment than even the least protected defamatory falsehoods: those involving purely private figures, where liability is evaluated under a standard, usually applied by a jury, of ordinary negligence. See *Gertz* v. *Robert Welch, Inc.* (1974). We have previously noted the impermissibility of categorical prohibitions upon media access where important First Amendment interests are at stake. See *Globe Newspaper Co.* v. *Superior Court* (1982) (invalidating state statute providing for the categorical exclusion of the public from trials of sexual offenses involving juvenile victims). More individualized adjudication is no less indispensable where the State, seeking to safeguard the anonymity of crime victims, sets its face against publication of their names.

Third, and finally, the facial underinclusiveness of § 794.03 raises serious doubts about whether Florida is, in fact, serving, with this statute, the significant interests which appellee invokes in support of affirmance. Section § 794.03 prohibits the publication of identifying information only if this information appears in an "instrument of mass communication," a term the statute does not define. Section § 794.03 does not prohibit the spread by other means of the identities of victims of sexual offenses. An individual who maliciously spreads word of the identity of a rape victim is thus not covered, despite the fact that the communication of such information to persons who live near, or work with, the victim may have consequences equally devastating as the exposure of her name to large numbers of strangers. (Appellee acknowledges that § 794.03 would not apply to "the backyard gossip who tells fifty people that don't have to know.")

When a State attempts the extraordinary measure of punishing truthful publication in the name of privacy, it must demonstrate its commitment to advancing this interest by applying its prohibition evenhandedly, to the smalltime disseminator as well as the media giant. Where important First Amendment interests are at stake, the mass scope of disclosure is not an acceptable surrogate for injury. A ban on disclosures effected by "instrument[s] of mass communication" simply cannot be defended on the ground that partial prohibitions may effect partial relief. See *Daily Mail* (statute is insufficiently tailored to interest in protecting anonymity where it restricted only newspapers, not the electronic media or other forms of publication, from identifying juvenile defendants). Without more careful and inclusive forms of precautions against alternative forms of dissemination, we cannot conclude that Florida's selective ban on publication by the mass media satisfactorily accomplishes its state purpose.

III

[2] Our holding today is limited. We do not hold that truthful publication is automatically constitutionally protected, or that there is no zone of personal privacy within which the State may protect the individual from intrusion by the press, or even that a State may never punish publication of the name of a victim of a sexual offense. We hold only that where a newspaper publishes truthful information which it has lawfully obtained, punishment may lawfully be imposed, if at all, only when narrowly tailored to a state interest of the highest order, and that no such interest is satisfactorily served by imposing liability under § 794.03 to appellant under the facts of this case. The decision below is therefore

Reversed.

SCHNECKLOTH, CONSERVATION CENTER SUPERINTENDENT
versus
BUSTAMONTE

CERTIORARI TO THE UNITED STATES COURT OF APPEALS

FOR THE NINTH CIRCUIT

Argued October 10, 1972
Decided May 29, 1973

During the course of a consent search of a car that had been stopped by officers for traffic violations, evidence was discovered that was used to convict respondent of unlawfully possessing a check. In a habeas corpus proceeding, the Court of Appeals, reversing the District Court, held that the prosecution had failed to prove that consent to the search had been made with the understanding that it could freely be withheld. *Held:* When the subject of a search is not in custody and the State would justify a search on the basis of his consent, the Fourth and Fourteenth Amendments require that it demonstrate that the consent was in fact voluntary; voluntariness is to be determined from the totality of the surrounding circumstances. While knowledge of a right to refuse consent is a factor to be taken into account, the State need not prove that the one giving permission to search knew that he had a right to withhold his consent.
448 F. 2d 699, reversed.

STEWART, J., delivered the opinion of the Court, in which BURGER, C. J., and WHITE, BLACKMUN, POWELL, and REHNQUIST, JJ., joined. BLACKMUN, J., filed a concurring opinion. POWELL, J., filed a concurring opinion, in which BURGER, C. J., and REHNQUIST, J., joined. DOUGLAS, J., BRENNAN, J., and MARSHALL, J., filed dissenting opinions.

MR. JUSTICE MARSHALL, dissenting.
Several years ago, MR. JUSTICE STEWART reminded us that "[t]he Con-

stitution guarantees . . . a society of free choice. Such a society pre-
supposes the capacity of its members to choose." *Ginsberg* v. *New York*
(1968) (concurring in result). I would have thought that the capacity to
choose necessarily depends upon knowledge that there is a choice to be
made. But today the Court reaches the curious result that one can
choose to relinquish a constitutional right—the right to be free of unreasonable searches—without knowing that he has the alternative of
refusing to accede to a police request to search. I cannot agree, and
therefore dissent.

I believe that the Court misstates the true issue in this case. That
issue is not, as the Court suggests, whether the police overbore Alcala's
will in eliciting his consent, but rather, whether a simple statement of
assent to search, without more, should be sufficient to permit the police
to search and thus act as a relinquishment of Alcala's constitutional
right to exclude the police. This Court has always scrutinized with great
care claims that a person has forgone the opportunity to assert constitutional rights. See, *e.g., Fuentes* v. *Shevin* (1972); *D. H. Overmyer Co.* v.
Frick Co., (1972). I see no reason to give the claim that a person consented to a search any less rigorous scrutiny. Every case in this Court
involving this kind of search has heretofore spoken of consent as a
waiver. See, *e.g., Amos* v. *United States* (1921). Perhaps one skilled in
linguistics or epistemology can disregard those comments, but I find
them hard to ignore.

To begin, it is important to understand that the opinion of the Court
is misleading in its treatment of the issue here in three ways. First, it
derives its criterion for determining when a verbal statement of assent
to search operates as a relinquishment of a person's right to preclude
entry from a justification of consent searches that is inconsistent with
our treatment in earlier cases of exceptions to the requirements of the
Fourth Amendment, and that is not responsive to the unique nature of
the consent-search exception. Second, it applies a standard of voluntariness that was developed in a very different context, where the standard was based on policies different from those involved in this case.
Third, it mischaracterizes our prior cases involving consent searches.

A

The Court assumes that the issue in this case is: what are the standards by which courts are to determine that consent is voluntarily
given? It then imports into the law of search and seizure standards

developed to decide entirely different questions about coerced confessions.

The Fifth Amendment, in terms, provides that no person "shall be compelled in any criminal case to be a witness against himself." Nor is the interest protected by the Due Process Clause of the Fourteenth Amendment any different. The inquiry in a case where a confession is challenged as having been elicited in an unconstitutional manner is, therefore, whether the behavior of the police amounted to compulsion of the defendant. Because of the nature of the right to be free of compulsion, it would be pointless to ask whether a defendant knew of it before he made a statement; no sane person would knowingly relinquish a right to be free of compulsion. Thus, the questions of compulsion and of violation of the right itself are inextricably intertwined. The cases involving coerced confessions, therefore, pass over the question of knowledge of that right as irrelevant, and turn directly to the question of compulsion.

Miranda v. *Arizona* (1966), confirms this analysis. There the Court held that certain warnings must be given to suspects prior to their interrogation so that the inherently coercive nature of in-custody questioning would be diminished by the suspect's knowledge that he could remain silent. But, although those warnings, of course, convey information about various rights of the accused, the information is intended only to protect the suspect against acceding to the other coercive aspects of police interrogation. While we would not ordinarily think that a suspect could waive his right to be free of coercion, for example, we do permit suspects to waive the rights they are informed of by police warnings, on the belief that such information in itself sufficiently decreases the chance that a statement would be elicited by compulsion. Thus, nothing the defendant did in the cases involving coerced confessions was taken to operate as a relinquishment of his rights; certainly the fact that the defendant made a statement was never taken to be a relinquishment of the right to be free of coercion.

B

In contrast, this case deals not with "coercion," but with "consent," a subtly different concept to which different standards have been applied in the past. Freedom from coercion is a substantive right, guaranteed by the Fifth and Fourteenth Amendments. Consent, however, is a mechanism by which substantive requirements otherwise applicable, are avoided. In the context of the Fourth Amendment, the relevant substantive requirements are that searches be conducted only after evidence justifying them has been submitted to an impartial magistrate for a determination of probable cause. There are, of course, exceptions to these requirements based on a variety of exigent circumstances that make it impractical to invalidate a search simply because the police failed to get a warrant. But none of the exceptions relating to the overriding needs of law enforcement are applicable when a search is justified solely by consent. On the contrary, the needs of law enforcement are significantly more attenuated, for probable cause to search may be lacking but a search permitted if the subject's consent has been obtained. Thus, consent searches are permitted, not because such an exception to the requirements of probable cause and warrant is essential to proper law enforcement, but because we permit our citizens to choose whether or not they wish to exercise their constitutional rights. Our prior decisions simply do not support the view that a meaningful choice has been made solely because no coercion was brought to bear on the subject.

For example, in *Bumper* v. *North Carolina* (1968), four law enforcement officers went to the home of Bumper's grandmother. They announced that they had a search warrant, and she permitted them to enter. Subsequently, the prosecutor chose not to rely on the warrant, but attempted to justify the search by the woman's consent. We held that consent could not be established "by showing no more than acquiescence to a claim of lawful authority." We did not there inquire into all the circumstances, but focused on a single fact, the claim of authority, even though the grandmother testified that no threats were made. It may be that, on the facts of that case, her consent was under all the circumstances involuntary, but it is plain that we did not apply the test adopted by the Court today. And, whatever the posture of the case when it reached this Court, it could not be said that the police in *Bumper* acted in a threatening or coercive manner, for they did have the warrant they said they had; the decision not to rely on it was made long after the search, when the case came into court.

That case makes it clear that police officers may not courteously order the subject of a search simply to stand aside while the officers carry out a search they have settled on. Yet there would be no coercion or brutality in giving that order. No interests that the Court today recognizes would be damaged in such a search. Thus, all the police must do is conduct what will inevitably be a charade of asking for consent. If they display any firmness at all, a verbal expression of assent will undoubtedly be forthcoming. I cannot believe that the protections of the Constitution mean so little.

I

My approach to the case is straightforward and, to me, obviously required by the notion of consent as a relinquishment of Fourth Amendment rights. I am at a loss to understand why consent "cannot be taken literally to mean a 'knowing' choice." In fact, I have difficulty in comprehending how a decision made without knowledge of available alternatives can be treated as a choice at all.

If consent to search means that a person has chosen to forgo his right to exclude the police from the place they seek to search, it follows that his consent cannot be considered a meaningful choice unless he knew that he could in fact exclude the police. The Court appears, however, to reject even the modest proposition that, if the subject of a search convinces the trier of fact that he did not know of his right to refuse assent to a police request for permission to search, the search must be held unconstitutional. For it says only that "knowledge of the right to refuse consent is one factor to be taken into account." I find this incomprehensible. I can think of no other situation in which we would say that a person agreed to some course of action if he convinced us that he did not know that there was some other course he might have pursued. I would therefore hold, at a minimum, that the prosecution may not rely on a purported consent to search if the subject of the search did not know that he could refuse to give consent. That, I think, is the import of *Bumper* v. *North Carolina, supra.* Where the police claim authority to search yet in fact lack such authority, the subject does not know that he may permissibly refuse them entry, and it is this lack of knowledge that invalidates the consent.

If one accepts this view, the question then is a simple one: must the Government show that the subject knew of his rights, or must the subject show that he lacked such knowledge?

I think that any fair allocation of the burden would require that it be placed on the prosecution. On this question, the Court indulges in what might be called the "straw man" method of adjudication. The Court responds to this suggestion by overinflating the burden. And, when it is suggested that the *prosecution's* burden of proof could be easily satisfied if the police informed the subject of his rights, the Court responds by refusing to require the *police* to make a "detailed" inquiry. If the Court candidly faced the real question of allocating the burden of proof, neither of these maneuvers would be available to it.

If the burden is placed on the defendant, all the subject can do is to testify that he did not know of his rights. And I doubt that many trial judges will find for the defendant simply on the basis of that testimony. Precisely because the evidence is very hard to come by, courts have traditionally been reluctant to require a party to prove negatives such as the lack of knowledge.

In contrast, there are several ways by which the subject's knowledge of his rights may be shown. The subject may affirmatively demonstrate such knowledge by his responses at the time the search took place, as in *United States* v. *Curiale,* 744 (CA2 1969). Where, as in this case, the person giving consent is someone other than the defendant, the prosecution may require him to testify under oath. Denials of knowledge may be disproved by establishing that the subject had, in the recent past, demonstrated his knowledge of his rights, for example, by refusing entry when it was requested by the police. The prior experience or training of the subject might in some cases support an inference that he knew of his right to exclude the police.

The burden on the prosecutor would disappear, of course, if the police, at the time they requested consent to search, also told the subject that he had a right to refuse consent and that his decision to refuse would be respected. The Court's assertions to the contrary notwithstanding, there is nothing impractical about this method of satisfying the prosecution's burden of proof. It must be emphasized that the decision about informing the subject of his rights would lie with the officers seeking consent. If they believed that providing such information would impede their investigation, they might simply ask for consent, taking the risk that at some later date the prosecutor would be unable to prove that the subject knew of his rights or that some other basis for the search existed.

The Court contends that if an officer paused to inform the subject of his rights, the informality of the exchange would be destroyed. I doubt that a simple statement by an officer of an individual's right to refuse consent would do much to alter the informality of the exchange, except to alert the subject to a fact that he surely is entitled to know. It is not without significance that for many years the agents of the Federal Bureau of Investigation have routinely informed subjects of their right to refuse consent, when they request consent to search. The reported cases in which the police have informed subjects of their right to refuse consent show, also, that the information can be given without disrupting the casual flow of events. See, *e.g., United States* v. *Miller* (CA7 1968). What evidence there is, then, rather strongly suggests that nothing disastrous would happen if the police, before requesting consent, informed the subject that he had a right to refuse consent and that his refusal would be respected.

I must conclude, with some reluctance, that when the Court speaks of practicality, what it really is talking of is the continued ability of the police to capitalize on the ignorance of citizens so as to accomplish by subterfuge what they could not achieve by relying only on the knowing relinquishment of constitutional rights. Of course it would be "practical" for the police to ignore the commands of the Fourth Amendment, if by practicality we mean that more criminals will be apprehended, even though the constitutional rights of innocent people also go by the board. But such a practical advantage is achieved only at the cost of permitting the police to disregard the limitations that the Constitution places on their behavior, a cost that a constitutional democracy cannot long absorb.

I find nothing in the opinion of the Court to dispel my belief that, in such a case, as the Court of Appeals for the Ninth Circuit said, "[u]nder many circumstances a reasonable person might read an officer's 'May I' as the courteous expression of a demand backed by force of law." Most cases, in my view, are akin to *Bumper* v. *North Carolina* (1968): consent is ordinarily given as acquiescence in an implicit claim of authority to search. Permitting searches in such circumstances, without any assurance at all that the subject of the search knew that, by his consent, he was relinquishing his constitutional rights, is something that I cannot believe is sanctioned by the Constitution.

II

The proper resolution of this case turns, I believe, on a realistic assessment of the nature of the interchange between citizens and the police, and of the practical import of allocating the burden of proof in one way rather than another. The Court seeks to escape such assessments by escalating its rhetoric to unwarranted heights, but no matter how forceful the adjectives the Court uses, it cannot avoid being judged by how well its image of these interchanges accords with reality. Although the Court says without real elaboration that it "cannot agree," the holding today confines the protection of the Fourth Amendment against searches conducted without probable cause to the sophisticated, the knowledgeable, and, I might add, the few. In the final analysis, the Court now sanctions a game of blindman's buff, in which the police always have the upper hand, for the sake of nothing more than the convenience of the police. But the guarantees of the Fourth Amendment were never intended to shrink before such an ephemeral and changeable interest. The Framers of the Fourth Amendment struck the balance against this sort of convenience and in favor of certain basic civil rights. It is not for this Court to restrike that balance because of its own views of the needs of law enforcement officers. I fear that that is the effect of the Court's decision today.

It is regrettable that the obsession with validating searches like that conducted in this case, so evident in the Court's hyperbole, has obscured the Court's vision of how the Fourth Amendment was designed to govern the relationship between police and citizen in our society. I believe that experience and careful reflection show how narrow and inaccurate that vision is, and I respectfully dissent.

NEW YORK
versus
QUARLES

Argued January 18, 1984
Decided June 12, 1984

Respondent was charged in a New York State court with criminal possession of a weapon. The record showed that a woman approached two police officers who were on road patrol, told them that she had just been raped, described her assailant, and told them that the man had just entered a nearby supermarket and was carrying a gun. While one of the officers radioed for assistance, the other [Officer Kraft] entered the store and spotted respondent, who matched the description given by the woman. Respondent ran toward the rear of the store, and Officer Kraft pursued him with a drawn gun but lost sight of him for several seconds. Upon regaining sight of respondent, Officer Kraft ordered him to stop and put his hands over his head; frisked him and discovered that he was wearing an empty shoulder holster; and, after handcuffing him, asked him where the gun was. Respondent nodded toward some empty cartons and responded that "the gun is over there." Officer Kraft then retrieved the gun from one of the cartons, formally arrested respondent, and read him his rights under *Miranda* v. *Arizona.* Respondent indicated that he would answer questions without an attorney being present and admitted that he owned the gun and had purchased it in Florida. The trial court excluded respondent's initial statment and the gun because the respondent had not yet been given the *Miranda* warnings, and also excluded respondent's other statements as evidence tainted by the *Miranda* violation. Both the Appellate Division of the New York Supreme Court and the New York Court of Appeals affirmed.

Held: The Court of Appeals erred in affirming the exclusion of respondent's initial statement and the gun because of Officer Kraft's failure to read respondent his *Miranda* rights before attempting to locate the weapon. Accordingly, it also erred in affirming the exclusion of respondent's subsequent statements as illegal fruits of the *Miranda* violation. This case presents a situation where concern for public safety must be paramount to adherence to the literal language of the prophylactic rules enunciated in *Miranda*.

(a) Although respondent was in police custody when he made his statements and the facts come within the ambit of *Miranda*, nevertheless on these facts there is a "public safety" exception to the requirement that *Miranda* warnings be given before a suspect's answers may be admitted into evidence, and the availability of that exception does not depend upon the motivation of the individual officers involved. The doctrinal underpinnings of *Miranda* do not require that it be applied in all its rigor to a situation in which police officers ask questions reasonably prompted by a concern for the public safety. In this case, so long as the gun was concealed somewhere in the supermarket, it posed more than one danger to the public safety: an accomplice might make use of it, or a customer or employee might later come upon it.

(b) Procedural safeguards that deter a suspect from responding, and increase the possibility of fewer convictions, were deemed acceptable in *Miranda* in order to protect the Fifth Amendment privilege against compulsory self-incrimination. However, if *Miranda* warnings had deterred responses to Officer Kraft's question about the whereabouts of the gun, the cost would have been something more than merely the failure to obtain evidence useful in convicting respondent. An answer was needed to ensure that future danger to the public did not result from the concealment of the gun in a public area.

(c) The narrow exception to the *Miranda* rule recognized here will to some degree lessen the desirable clarity of that rule. However, the exception will not be difficult for police officers to apply because in each case it will be circumscribed by the exigency which justifies it. Police officers can and will distinguish almost instinctively between questions necessary to secure their own safety or the safety of the public and questions designed solely to elicit testimonial evidence from a suspect.

Reversed and remanded.

* * *

Rehnquist, J., delivered the opinion of the Court, in which Burger, C.J., and White, Blackmun, and Powell, JJ., joined. O'Connor, J., filed an opinion concurring in the judgment in part and dissenting in part. Marshall, J., filed a dissenting opinion, in which Brennan and Stevens, JJ., joined.

JUSTICE MARSHALL, with whom JUSTICE BRENNAN and JUSTICE STEVENS join, dissenting.

The police in this case arrested a man suspected of possessing a firearm in violation of New York law. Once the suspect was in custody and found to be unarmed, the arresting officer initiated an interrogation. Without being advised of his right not to respond, the suspect incriminated himself by locating the gun. The majority concludes that the State may rely on this incriminating statement to convict the suspect of possessing a weapon. I disagree. The arresting officers had no legitimate reason to interrogate the suspect without advising him of his rights to remain silent and to obtain assistance of counsel. By finding on these facts justification for unconsented interrogation, the majority abandons the clear guidelines enunciated in *Miranda* v. *Arizona* (1966), and condemns the American judiciary to a new era of *post hoc* inquiry into the propriety of custodial interrogations. More significantly and in direct conflict with this Court's longstanding interpretation of the Fifth Amendment, the majority has endorsed the introduction of coerced self-incriminating statements in criminal prosecutions. I dissent.

I

Shortly after midnight on September 11, 1980, Officer Kraft and three other policemen entered an A & P supermarket in search of respondent Quarles, a rape suspect who was reportedly armed. After a brief chase, the officers cornered Quarles in the back of the store. As the other officers trained their guns on the suspect, Officer Kraft frisked Quarles and discovered an empty shoulder holster. Officer Kraft then handcuffed Quarles, and the other officers holstered their guns. With Quarles' hands manacled behind his back and the other officers standing close by, Officer Kraft questioned Quarles: "Where is the gun?" Gesturing towards a stack of liquid-soap cartons a few feet away, Quarles responded: "The gun is over there." Behind the cartons, the police found a loaded revolver. The State of New York subsequently failed to prosecute the alleged rape, and charged Quarles on a solitary count of criminal possession of a weapon in the third degree. As proof of the critical element of the offense, the State sought to introduce Quarles' response to Officer Kraft's question as well as the revolver found behind the cartons. The Criminal Term of the Supreme Court of the State of New York ordered both Quarles' statement and the gun suppressed. The suppression order was affirmed first by the Appellate Division (1981), and again by the New York Court of Appeals (1982).

The majority's entire analysis rests on the factual assumption that the public was at risk during Quarles' interrogation. This assumption is completely in conflict with the facts as found by New York's highest court. Before the interrogation began, Quarles had been "reduced to a condition of physical powerlessness." Contrary to the majority's speculations, *ante,* at 657, Quarles was not believed to have, nor did he in fact have, an accomplice to come to his rescue. When the questioning began, the arresting officers were sufficiently confident of their safety to put away their guns. As Officer Kraft acknowledged at the suppression hearing, "the situation was under control." Based on Officer Kraft's own testimony, the New York Court of Appeals found: "Nothing suggests that any of the officers was by that time concerned for his own physical safety." The Court of Appeals also determined that there was no evidence that the interrogation was prompted by the arresting officers' concern for the public's safety.

The majority attempts to slip away from these unambiguous findings of New York's highest court by proposing that danger be measured by objective facts rather than the subjective intentions of arresting officers. Though clever, this ploy was anticipated by the New York Court of Appeals: "[T]here is no evidence in the record before us that there were exigent circumstances posing a risk to the public safety. . . ."

The New York court's conclusion that neither Quarles nor his missing gun posed a threat to the public's safety is amply supported by the evidence presented at the suppression hearing. Again contrary to the majority's intimations, no customers or employees were wandering about the store in danger of coming across Quarles' discarded weapon. Although the supermarket was open to the public, Quarles' arrest took place during the middle of the night when the store was apparently deserted except for the clerks at the check-out counter. The police could easily have cordoned off the store and searched for the missing gun. Had they done so, they would have found the gun forthwith. The police were well aware that Quarles had discarded his weapon somewhere near the scene of the arrest. As the State acknowledged before the New York Court of Appeals: "After Officer Kraft had handcuffed and frisked the defendant in the supermarket, *he knew with a high degree of certainty that the defendant's gun was within the immediate vicinity of the encounter.* He undoubtedly would have searched for it in the carton a few feet away without the defendant having looked in that direction and saying that it was there."

Earlier this Term, four Members of the majority joined an opinion stating: "[Q]uestions of historical fact . . . must be determined, in the first instance, by state courts and deferred to, in the absence of 'convincing evidence' to the contrary, by the federal courts." *Rushen* v. *Spain.* In this case, there was convincing, indeed almost overwhelming, evidence to support the New York court's conclusion that Quarles' hidden weapon did not pose a risk either to the arresting officers or to the public. The majority ignores this evidence and sets aside the factual findings of the New York Court of Appeals. More cynical observers might well conclude that a state court's findings of fact "deserv[e] a 'high measure of deference,' " [(quoting *Sumner* v. *Mata* (1982)], only when deference works against the interests of a criminal defendant.

II

The majority's treatment of the legal issues presented in this case is no less troubling than its abuse of the facts. Before today's opinion, the Court had twice concluded that, under *Miranda* v. *Arizona* (1966), police officers conducting custodial interrogations must advise suspects of their rights before any questions concerning the whereabouts of incriminating weapons can be asked. *Rhode Island* v. *Innis* (1980), *Orozco* v. *Texas* (1969). Now the majority departs from these cases and rules that police may withhold *Miranda* warnings whenever custodial interrogations concern matters of public safety.

The majority contends that the law, as it currently stands, places police officers in a dilemma whenever they interrogate a suspect who appears to know of some threat to the public's safety. If the police interrogate the suspect without advising him of his rights, the suspect may reveal information that the authorities can use to defuse the threat, but the suspect's statements will be inadmissible at trial. If, on the other hand, the police advise the suspect of his rights, the suspect may be deterred from responding to the police's questions, and the risk to the public may continue unabated. According to the majority, the police must now choose between establishing the suspect's guilt and safeguarding the public from danger.

The majority proposes to eliminate this dilemma by creating an exception to *Miranda* v. *Arizona* for custodial interrogations concerning matters of public safety. Under the majority's exception, police would be permitted to interrogate suspects about such matters before the suspects have been advised of their constitutional rights. Without being "deterred" by the knowledge that they have a constitutional right not to respond, these suspects will be likely to answer the questions. Should the answers also be incriminating, the State would be free to introduce them as evidence in a criminal prosecution. Through this "narrow exception to the *Miranda* rule," the majority proposes to protect the public's safety without jeopardizing the prosecution of criminal defendants. I find in this reasoning an unwise and unprincipled departure from our Fifth Amendment precedents.

Before today's opinion, the procedures established in *Miranda* v. *Arizona* had "the virtue of informing police and prosecutors with specificity as to what they may do in conducting custodial interrogation, and of informing courts under what circumstances statements obtained during such interrogation are not admissible." *Fare* v. *Michael C.* (1979); *Harryman* v. *Estelle* (CA5 1980) (1980). In a chimerical quest for public safety, the majority has abandoned the rule that brought 18 years of doctrinal tranquility to the field of custodial interrogations. As the majority candidly concedes, a public-safety exception destroys forever the clarity of *Miranda* for both law enforcement officers and members of the judiciary. The Court's candor cannot mask what a serious loss the administration of justice has incurred.

This case is illustrative of the chaos the "public-safety" exception will unleash. The circumstances of Quarles' arrest have never been in dispute. After the benefit of briefing and oral argument, the New York Court of Appeals, as previously noted, concluded that there was "no evidence in the record before us that there were exigent circumstances posing a risk to the public safety." Upon reviewing the same facts and hearing the same arguments, a majority of this Court has come to precisely the opposite conclusion: "So long as the gun was concealed somewhere in the supermarket, with its actual whereabouts unknown, it obviously posed more than one danger to the public safety. . . ."

If after plenary review two appellate courts so fundamentally differ over the threat to public safety presented by the simple and uncontested facts of this case, one must seriously question how law enforcement officers will respond to the majority's new rule in the confusion and haste of the real world. As THE CHIEF JUSTICE wrote in a similar context: "Few, if any, police officers are competent to make the kind of evaluation seemingly contemplated. . . ." *Rhode Island* v. *Innis.* Not only will police officers have to decide whether the objective facts of an arrest justify an unconsented custodial interrogation, they will also have to remember to interrupt the interrogation and read the suspect his *Miranda* warnings once the focus of the inquiry shifts from protecting the public's safety to ascertaining the suspect's guilt. Disagreements of the scope of the "public-safety" exception and mistakes in its application are inevitable.

The end result, as JUSTICE O'CONNOR predicts, will be "a finespun new doctrine on public safety exigencies incident to custodial interrogation, complete with the hair-splitting distinctions that currently plague our Fourth Amendment jurisprudence." In the meantime, the courts will have to dedicate themselves to spinning this new web of doctrines, and the country's law enforcement agencies will have to suffer patiently through the frustrations of another period of constitutional uncertainty.

III

Though unfortunate, the difficulty of administering the "public-safety" exception is not the most profound flaw in the majority's decision. The majority has lost sight of the fact that *Miranda* v. *Arizona* and our earlier custodial-interrogation cases all implemented a constitutional privilege against self-incrimination. The rules established in these cases were designed to protect criminal defendants against prosecutions based on coerced self-incriminating statements. The majority today turns its back on these constitutional considerations, and invites the government to prosecute through the use of what necessarily are coerced statements.

A

The majority's error stems from a serious misunderstanding of *Miranda* v. *Arizona* and of the Fifth Amendment upon which that decision was based. The majority implies that *Miranda* consisted of no more than a judicial balancing act in which the benefits of "enlarged protection for the Fifth Amendment privilege" were weighed against "the cost to society in terms of fewer convictions of guilty suspects." Supposedly because the scales tipped in favor of the privilege against self-incrimination, the *Miranda* Court erected a prophylactic barrier around statements made during custodial interrogations. The majority now proposes to return to the scales of social utility to calculate whether *Miranda*'s prophylactic rule remains cost-effective when threats to the public's safety are added to the balance. The results of the majority's "test" are announced with pseudoscientific precision:

> "We conclude that the need for answers to questions in a situation posing a threat to the public safety outweighs the need for the prophylactic rule protecting the Fifth Amendment's privilege against self-incrimination."

The majority misreads *Miranda.* Though the *Miranda* dissent prophesized dire consequences, the *Miranda* Court refused to allow such concerns to weaken the protections of the Constitution:

> "A recurrent argument made in these cases is that society's need for interrogation outweighs the privilege. This argument is not unfamiliar to this Court. The whole thrust of our foregoing discussion demonstrates that the Constitution has prescribed the rights of the individual when confronted with the power of government when it provided in the Fifth Amendment that an individual cannot be compelled to be a witness against himself. That right cannot be abridged."

Whether society would be better off if the police warned suspects of their rights before beginning an interrogation or whether the advantages of giving such warnings would outweigh their costs did not inform the *Miranda* decision. On the contrary, the *Miranda* Court was concerned with the proscriptions of the Fifth Amendment, and, in particular, whether the Self-Incrimination Clause permits the government to prosecute individuals based on statements made in the course of custodial interrogations.

Miranda v. *Arizona* was the culmination of a century-long inquiry into how this Court should deal with confessions made during custodial interrogations. Long before *Miranda,* the Court had recognized that the Federal Government was prohibited from introducing at criminal trials compelled confessions, including confessions compelled in the course of custodial interrogations. In 1924, Justice Brandeis was reciting settled law when he wrote: "[A] confession obtained by compulsion must be excluded whatever may have been the character of the compulsion, and whether the compulsion was applied in a judicial proceeding or otherwise." *Wan* v. *United States* [(citing *Bram* v. *United States* (1897)].

Prosecutors in state courts were subject to similar constitutional restrictions. Even before *Malloy* v. *Hogan* (1964), formally applied the Self-Incrimination Clause of the Fifth Amendment to the States, the Due Process Clause constrained the States from extorting confessions from criminal defendants. *Chambers* v. *Florida* (1940); *Brown* v. *Mississippi* (1936). Indeed, by the time of *Malloy*, the constraints of the Due Process Clause were almost as stringent as the requirements of the Fifth Amendment itself. *Haynes* v. *Washington* (1963).

When *Miranda* reached this Court, it was undisputed that both the States and the Federal Government were constitutionally prohibited from prosecuting defendants with confessions coerced during custodial interrogations. As a theoretical matter, the law was clear. In practice, however, the courts found it exceedingly difficult to determine whether a given confession had been coerced. Difficulties of proof and subtleties of interrogation technique made it impossible in most cases for the judiciary to decide with confidence whether the defendant had voluntarily confessed his guilt or whether his testimony had been unconstitutionally compelled. Courts around the country were spending countless hours reviewing the facts of individual custodial interrogations.

Miranda dealt with these practical problems. After a detailed examination of police practices and a review of its previous decisions in the area, the Court in *Miranda* determined that custodial interrogations are inherently coercive. The Court therefore created a constitutional presumption that statements made during custodial interrogations are compelled in violation of the Fifth Amendment and are thus inadmissible in criminal prosecutions. As a result of the Court's decision in *Miranda*, a statement made during a custodial interrogation may be introduced as proof of a defendant's guilt only if the prosecution demonstrates that the defendant knowingly and intelligently waived his constitutional rights before making the statement. The now-familiar *Miranda* warnings offer law enforcement authorities a clear, easily administered device for ensuring that criminal suspects understand their constitutional rights well enough to waive them and to engage in consensual custodial interrogation.

In fashioning its "public-safety" exception to *Miranda*, the majority makes no attempt to deal with the constitutional presumption established by that case. The majority does not argue that police questioning about issues of public safety is any less coercive than custodial interrogations into other matters. The majority's only contention is that police officers could more easily protect the public if *Miranda* did not apply to custodial interrogations concerning the public's safety. But *Miranda* was not a decision about public safety; it was a decision about coerced confessions. Without establishing that interrogations concerning the public's safety are less likely to be coercive than other interrogations, the majority cannot endorse the "public-safety" exception and remain faithful to the logic of *Miranda* v. *Arizona.*

B

The majority's avoidance of the issue of coercion may not have been inadvertent. It would strain credulity to contend that Officer Kraft's questioning of respondent Quarles was not coercive. In the middle of the night and in the back of an empty supermarket, Quarles was surrounded by four armed police officers. His hands were handcuffed behind his back. The first words out of the mouth of the arresting officer were: "Where is the gun?" In the majority's phrase, the situation was "kaleidoscopic." Police and suspect were acting on instinct. Officer Kraft's abrupt and pointed question pressured Quarles in precisely the way that the *Miranda* Court feared the custodial interrogations would coerce self-incriminating testimony.

That the application of the "public-safety" exception in this case entailed coercion is no happenstance. The majority's *ratio decidendi* is that interrogating suspects about matters of public safety *will* be coercive. In its cost-benefit analysis, the Court's strongest argument in favor of a "public-safety" exception to *Miranda* is that the police would be better able to protect the public's safety if they were not always required to give suspects their *Miranda* warnings. The crux of this argument is that, by deliberately withholding *Miranda* warnings, the police can get information out of suspects who would refuse to respond to police questioning were they advised of their constitutional rights. The "public-safety" exception is efficacious precisely because it permits police officers to coerce criminal defendants into making involuntary statements.

Indeed, in the efficacy of the "public-safety" exception lies a fundamental and constitutional defect. Until today, this Court could truthfully state that the Fifth Amendment is given "broad scope" "[w]here there has been genuine compulsion of testimony." *Michigan* v. *Tucker*

(1974). Coerced confessions were simply inadmissible in criminal prosecutions. The "public-safety" exception departs from this principle by expressly inviting police officers to coerce defendants into making incriminating statements, and then permitting prosecutors to introduce those statements at trial. Though the majority's opinion is cloaked in the beguiling language of utilitarianism, the Court has sanctioned *sub silentio* criminal prosecutions based on compelled self-incriminating statements. I find this result in direct conflict with the Fifth Amendment's dictate that "[n]o person . . . shall be compelled in any criminal case to be a witness against himself."

The irony of the majority's decision is that the public's safety can be perfectly well protected without abridging the Fifth Amendment. If a bomb is about to explode or the public is otherwise imminently imperiled, the police are free to interrogate suspects without advising them of their constitutional rights. Such unconsented questioning may take place not only when police officers act on instinct but also when higher faculties lead them to believe that advising a suspect of his constitutional rights might decrease the likelihood that the suspect would reveal life-saving information. If trickery is necessary to protect the public, then the police may trick a suspect into confessing. While the Fourteenth Amendment sets limits on such behavior, nothing in the Fifth Amendment or our decision in *Miranda* v. *Arizona* proscribes this sort of emergency questioning. All the Fifth Amendment forbids is the introduction of coerced statements at trial. Cf. *Weatherford* v. *Bursey* (1977) (Sixth Amendment violated only if trial affected).

To a limited degree, the majority is correct that there is a cost associated with the Fifth Amendment's ban on introducing coerced self-incriminating statements at trial. Without a "public-safety" exception, there would be occasions when a defendant incriminated himself by revealing a threat to the public, and the State was unable to prosecute because the defendant retracted his statement after consulting with counsel and the police cannot find independent proof of guilt. Such occasions would not, however, be common. The prosecution does not always lose the use of incriminating information revealed in these situations. After consulting with counsel, a suspect may well volunteer to repeat his statement in hopes of gaining a favorable plea bargain or more lenient sentence. The majority thus overstates its case when it suggests that a police officer must necessarily choose between public safety and admissibility.

But however frequently or infrequently such cases arise, their regularity is irrelevant. The Fifth Amendment prohibits compelled self-incrimination. As the Court has explained on numerous occasions, this prohibition is the mainstay of our adversarial system of criminal justice. Not only does it protect us against the inherent unreliability of compelled testimony, but it also ensures that criminal investigations will be conducted with integrity and that the judiciary will avoid the taint of official lawlessness. See *Murphy* v. *Waterfront Comm'n* (1964). The policies underlying the Fifth Amendment's privilege against self-incrimination are not diminished simply because testimony is compelled to protect the public's safety. The majority should not be permitted to elude the Amendment's absolute prohibition simply by calculating special costs that arise when the public's safety is at issue. Indeed, were constitutional adjudication always conducted in such an ad hoc manner, the Bill of Rights would be a most unreliable protector of individual liberties.

IV

Having determined that the Fifth Amendment renders inadmissible Quarles' response to Officer Kraft's questioning, I have no doubt that our precedents require that the gun discovered as a direct result of Quarles' statement must be presumed inadmissible as well. The gun was the direct product of a coercive custodial interrogation. In *Silverthorne Lumber Co.* v. *United States* (1920), and *Wong Sun* v. *United States* (1963), this Court held that the Government may not introduce incriminating evidence derived from an illegally obtained source. This Court recently explained the extent of the *Wong Sun* rule:

> "Although *Silverthorne* and *Wong Sun* involved violations of the Fourth Amendment, the 'fruit of the poisonous tree' doctrine has not been limited to cases in which there has been a Fourth Amendment violation. The Court has applied the doctrine where the violations were of the Sixth Amendment, see *United States* v. *Wade* (1967), as well as of the Fifth Amendment." *Nix* v. *Williams.*

Accord, *United States* v. *Crews* (1980). When they ruled on the issue, the New York courts were entirely correct in deciding that Quarles' gun was the tainted fruit of a nonconsensual interrogation and therefore was inadmissible under our precedents.

However, since the New York Court of Appeals issued its opinion, the scope of the *Wong Sun* doctrine has changed. In *Nix* v. *Williams, supra,* this Court construed *Wong Sun* to permit the introduction into evidence of constitutionally tainted "fruits" that inevitably would have been discovered by the government. In its briefs before this Court and before the New York courts, petitioner has argued that the "inevitable-discovery" rule, if applied to this case, would permit the admission of Quarles' gun. Although I have not joined the Court's opinion in *Nix,* and although I am not wholly persuaded that New York law would permit the application of the "inevitable-discovery" rule to this case, I believe that the proper disposition of the matter is to vacate the order of the New York Court of Appeals to the extent that it suppressed Quarles' gun and remand the matter to the New York Court of Appeals for further consideration in light of *Nix* v. *Williams.*

Accordingly, I would affirm the order of the Court of Appeals to the extent that it found Quarles' incriminating statement inadmissible under the Fifth Amendment, would vacate the order to the extent that it suppressed Quarles' gun, and would remand the matter for reconsideration in light of *Nix* v. *Williams.*

POWELL
versus
TEXAS

APPEAL FROM THE COUNTY COURT AT LAW NO. 1
of travis county, texas.

Argued March 7, 1968
Decided June 17, 1968

Appellant was arrested and charged with being found in a state of intoxication in a public place, in violation of Art. 477 of the Texas Penal Code. He was tried in the Corporation Court of Austin, and found guilty. He appealed to the County Court of Travis County, and after a trial *de novo,* he was again found guilty. That court made the following "findings of fact": (1) chronic alcoholism is a disease which destroys the afflicted person's will power to resist the constant, excessive use of alcohol, (2) a chronic alcoholic does not appear in public by his own volition but under a compulsion symptomatic of the disease of chronic alcoholism, and (3) appellant is a chronic alcoholic who is afflicted by the disease of chronic alcoholism; but ruled as a matter of law that chronic alcoholism was not a defense to the charge. The principal testimony was that of a psychiatrist, who testified that appellant, a man with a long history of arrests for drunkenness, was a "chronic alcoholic" and was subject to a "compulsion" which was "not completely overpowering," but which was "an exceedingly strong influence." *Held:* The judgment is affirmed.

Mr. Justice Marshall, joined by The Chief Justice, Mr. Justice Black, and Mr. Justice Harlan, concluded that:
1. The lower court's "findings of fact" were not such in any recognizable, traditional sense, but were merely premises of a syllogism

designed to bring this case within the scope of *Robinson* v. *California* (1962).

2. The record here is utterly inadequate to permit the informed adjudication needed to support an important and wide-ranging new constitutional principle.

3. There is no agreement among medical experts as to what it means to say that "alcoholism" is a "disease," or upon the "manifestations of alcoholism," or on the nature of a "compulsion."

4. Faced with the reality that there is no known generally effective method of treatment or adequate facilities or manpower for a full-scale attack on the enormous problem of alcoholics, it cannot be asserted that the use of the criminal process to deal with the public aspects of problem drinking can never be defended as rational.

5. Appellant's conviction on the record in this case does not violate the Cruel and Unusual Punishment Clause of the Eighth Amendment.

(a) Appellant was convicted, not for being a chronic alcoholic, but for being in public while drunk on a particular occasion, and thus, as distinguished from *Robinson* v. *California, supra,* was not being punished for a mere status.

(b) It cannot be concluded, on this record and the current state of medical knowledge, that appellant suffers from such an irresistible compulsion to drink and to get drunk in public that he cannot control his performance of these acts and thus cannot be deterred from public intoxication. In any event, this Court has never articulated a general constitutional doctrine of *mens rea,* as the development of the doctrine and its adjustment to changing conditions has been thought to be the province of the States.

Mr. Justice Black, joined by Mr. Justice Harlan, concluded:

1. Public drunkenness, which has been a crime throughout our history, is an offense in every State, and this Court certainly cannot strike down a State's criminal law because of the heavy burden of enforcing it.

2. Criminal punishment provides some form of treatment, protects alcoholics from causing harm or being harmed by removing them from the streets, and serves some deterrent functions; and States should not be barred from using the criminal process in attempting to cope with the problem.

3. Medical decisions based on clinical problems of diagnosis and treatment bear no necessary correspondence to the legal decision

whether the overall objectives of criminal law can be furthered by imposing punishment; and States should not be constitutionally required to inquire as to what part of a defendant's personality is responsible for his actions and to excuse anyone whose action was the result of a "compulsion."

4. Crimes which require the State to prove that the defendant actually committed some proscribed act do not come within the scope of *Robinson* v. *California, supra,* which is properly limited to pure status crimes.

5. Appellant's argument that it is cruel and unusual to punish a person who is not morally blameworthy goes beyond the Eighth Amendment's limits on the use of criminal sanctions and would create confusion and uncertainty in areas of criminal law where our understanding is not complete.

6. Appellant's proposed constitutional rule is not only revolutionary but it departs from the premise that experience in making local laws by local people is the safest guide for our Nation to follow.

MR. JUSTICE WHITE concluded:

While *Robinson* v. *California, supra,* would support the view that a chronic alcoholic with an irresistible urge to consume alcohol should not be punishable for drinking or being drunk, appellant's conviction was for the different crime of being drunk in a public place; and though appellant showed that he was to some degree compelled to drink and that he was drunk at the time of his arrest, he made no showing that he was unable to stay off the streets at that time.

MR. JUSTICE MARSHALL announced the judgment of the Court and delivered an opinion in which THE CHIEF JUSTICE, MR. JUSTICE BLACK, and MR. JUSTICE HARLAN join.

In late December 1966, appellant was arrested and charged with being found in a state of intoxication in a public place, in violation of Texas Penal Code, Art. 477 (1952), which reads as follows:

"Whoever shall get drunk or be found in a state of intoxication in any public place, or at any private house except his own, shall be fined not exceeding one hundred dollars."

Appellant was tried in the Corporation Court of Austin, Texas, found guilty, and fined $20. He appealed to the County Court at Law No. 1 of Travis County, Texas, where a trial *de novo* was held. His counsel urged that appellant was "afflicted with the disease of chronic alcoholism," that "his appearance in public [while drunk was] . . . not of his own volition," and therefore that to punish him criminally for that conduct would be cruel and unusual, in violation of the Eighth and Fourteenth Amendments to the United States Constitution.

The trial judge in the county court, sitting without a jury, made certain findings of fact, but ruled as a matter of law that chronic alcoholism was not a defense to the charge. He found appellant guilty, and fined him $50. There being no further right to appeal within the Texas judicial system, appellant appealed to this Court; we noted probable jurisdiction (1967).

I

The principal testimony was that of Dr. David Wade, a Fellow of the American Medical Association, duly certificated in psychiatry. His testimony consumed a total of 17 pages in the trial transcript. Five of those pages were taken up with a recitation of Dr. Wade's qualifications. In the next 12 pages Dr. Wade was examined by appellant's counsel, cross-examined by the State, and reexamined by the defense, and those 12 pages contain virtually all the material developed at trial which is relevant to the constitutional issue we face here. Dr. Wade sketched the outlines of the "disease" concept of alcoholism; noted that there is no generally accepted definition of "alcoholism"; alluded to the ongoing debate within the medical profession over whether alcohol is actually physically "addicting" or merely psychologically "habituating"; and concluded that in either case a "chronic alcoholic" is an "involuntary drinker," who is "powerless not to drink," and who "loses his self-control over his drinking." He testified that he had examined appellant, and that appellant is a "chronic alcoholic," who "by the time he has reached [the state of intoxication] . . . is not able to control his behavior, and [who] . . . has reached this point because he has an uncontrollable compulsion to drink." Dr. Wade also responded in the negative to the question whether appellant has "the willpower to resist the constant excessive consumption of alcohol." He added that in his opinion jailing appellant without medical attention would operate neither to rehabilitate him nor to lessen his desire for alcohol.

On cross-examination, Dr. Wade admitted that when appellant was sober he knew the difference between right and wrong, and he responded affirmatively to the question whether appellant's act of taking the first drink in any given instance when he was sober was a "voluntary exercise of his will." Qualifying his answer, Dr. Wade stated that "these individuals have a compulsion, and this compulsion, while not completely overpowering, is a very strong influence, an exceedingly strong influence, and this compulsion coupled with the firm belief in their mind that they are going to be able to handle it from now on causes their judgment to be somewhat clouded."

Appellant testified concerning the history of his drinking problem. He reviewed his many arrests for drunkenness; testified that he was unable to stop drinking; stated that when he was intoxicated he had no control over his actions and could not remember them later, but that he did not become violent; and admitted that he did not remember his arrest on the occasion for which he was being tried. On cross-examination, appellant admitted that he had had one drink on the morning of the trial and had been able to discontinue drinking. In relevant part, the cross-examination went as follows:

"Q. You took that one at eight o'clock because you wanted to drink?

"A. Yes, sir.

"Q. And you knew that if you drank it, you could keep on drinking and get drunk?

"A. Well, I was supposed to be here on trial, and I didn't take but that one drink.

"Q. You knew you had to be here this afternoon, but this morning you took one drink and then you knew that you couldn't afford to drink any more and come to court; is that right?

"A. Yes, sir, that's right.

"Q. So you exercised your willpower and kept from drinking anything today except that one drink?

"A. Yes, sir, that's right.

"Q. Because you knew what you would do if you kept drinking, that you would finally pass out or be picked up?

"A. Yes, sir.

"Q. And you didn't want that to happen to you today?

"A. No, sir.

"Q. Not today?

"A. No, sir.

"Q. So you only had one drink today?

"A. Yes, sir."

On redirect examination, appellant's lawyer elicited the following:

"Q. Leroy, isn't the real reason why you just had one drink today because you just had enough money to buy one drink?

"A. Well, that was just give to me.

"Q. In other words, you didn't have any money with which you could buy any drinks yourself?

"A. No, sir, that was give to me.

"Q. And that's really what controlled the amount you drank this morning, isn't it?

"A. Yes, sir.

"Q. Leroy, when you start drinking, do you have any control over how many drinks you can take?

"A. No, sir."

Evidence in the case then closed. The State made no effort to obtain expert psychiatric testimony of its own, or even to explore with appellant's witness the question of appellant's power to control the frequency, timing, and location of his drinking bouts, or the substantial disagreement within the medical profession concerning the nature of the disease, the efficacy of treatment and the prerequisites for effective treatment. It did nothing to examine or illuminate what Dr. Wade might have meant by his reference to a "compulsion" which was "not completely overpowering," but which was "an exceedingly strong influence," or to inquire into the question of the proper role of such a "compulsion" in constitutional adjudication. Instead, the State contented itself with a brief argument that appellant had no defense to the charge because he "is legally sane and knows the difference between right and wrong."

Following this abbreviated exposition of the problem before it, the trial court indicated its intention to disallow appellant's claimed defense of "chronic alcoholism." Thereupon defense counsel submitted, and the trial court entered, the following "findings of fact":

"(1) That chronic alcoholism is a disease which destroys the afflicted person's willpower to resist the constant, excessive consumption of alcohol.

"(2) That a chronic alcoholic does not appear in public by his own volition but under a compulsion symptomatic of the disease of chronic alcoholism.

"(3) That Leroy Powell, defendant herein, is a chronic alcoholic who is afflicted with the disease of chronic alcoholism."

Whatever else may be said of them, those are not "findings of fact" in any recognizable, traditional sense in which that term has been used in a court of law; they are the premises of a syllogism transparently designed to bring this case within the scope of this Court's opinion in *Robinson* v. *California* (1962). Nonetheless, the dissent would have us adopt these "findings" without critical examination; it would use them as the basis for a constitutional holding that "a person may not be punished if the condition essential to constitute the defined crime is part of the pattern of his disease and is occasioned by a compulsion symptomatic of the disease."

The difficulty with that position, as we shall show, is that it goes much too far on the basis of too little knowledge. In the first place, the record in this case is utterly inadequate to permit the sort of informed and responsible adjudication which alone can support the announcement of an important and wide-ranging new constitutional principle. We know very little about the circumstances surrounding the drinking bout which resulted in this conviction, or about Leroy Powell's drinking problem, or indeed about alcoholism itself. The trial hardly reflects the sharp legal and evidentiary clash between fully prepared adversary litigants which is traditionally expected in major constitutional cases. The State put on only one witness, the arresting officer. The defense put on three—a policeman who testified to appellant's long history of arrests for public drunkenness, the psychiatrist, and appellant himself.

Furthermore, the inescapable fact is that there is no agreement among members of the medical profession about what it means to say that "alcoholism" is a "disease." One of the principal works in this field states that the major difficulty in articulating a "disease concept of alcoholism" is that "alcoholism has too many definitions and disease has practically none." This same author concludes that *"a disease is what the medical profession recognizes as such."* In other words, there is widespread agreement today that "alcoholism" is a "disease," for the simple reason that the medical profession has concluded that it should attempt to treat those who have drinking problems. There the agreement stops. Debate rages within the medical profession as to whether "alcoholism" is a separate "disease" in any meaningful biochemical, physiological or psychological sense, or whether it represents one peculiar manifestation in some individuals of underlying psychiatric disorders.

Nor is there any substantial consensus as to the "manifestations of alcoholism." E. M. Jellinek, one of the outstanding authorities on the subject, identifies five different types of alcoholics which predominate in the United States, and these types display a broad range of different and occasionally inconsistent symptoms. Moreover, wholly distinct types, relatively rare in this country, predominate in nations with different cultural attitudes regarding the consumption of alcohol. Even if we limit our consideration to the range of alcoholic symptoms more typically found in this country, there is substantial disagreement as to the manifestations of the "disease" called "alcoholism." Jellinek, for example, considers that only two of his five alcoholic types can truly be said to be suffering from "alcoholism" as a "disease," because only these two types attain what he believes to be the requisite degree of physiological dependence on alcohol. He applies the label "gamma alcoholism" to "that species of alcoholism in which (1) acquired increased tissue tolerance to alcohol, (2) adaptive cell metabolism . . . , (3) withdrawal symptoms and 'craving,' i. e., physical dependence, and (4) loss of control are involved." A "delta" alcoholic, on the other hand, "shows the first three characteristics of gamma alcoholism as well as a less marked form of the fourth characteristic—that is, instead of loss of control there is inability to abstain." Other authorities approach the problems of classification in an entirely different manner and, taking account of the large role which psycho-social factors seem to play in "problem drinking," define the "disease" in terms of the earliest identifiable manifestations of any sort of abnormality in drinking patterns.

Dr. Wade appears to have testified about appellant's "chronic alcoholism" in terms similar to Jellinek's "gamma" and "delta" types, for these types are largely defined, in their later stages, in terms of a strong compulsion to drink, physiological dependence and an inability to abstain from drinking. No attempt was made in the court below, of course, to determine whether Leroy Powell could in fact properly be diagnosed as a "gamma" or "delta" alcoholic in Jellinek's terms. The focus at the trial, and in the dissent here, has been exclusively upon the factors of loss of control and inability to abstain. Assuming that it makes sense to compartmentalize in this manner the diagnosis of such a formless "disease," tremendous gaps in our knowledge remain, which the record in this case does nothing to fill.

The trial court's "finding" that Powell "is afflicted with the disease of chronic alcoholism," which "destroys the afflicted person's willpower to resist the constant, excessive consumption of alcohol" covers a multitude of sins. Dr. Wade's testimony that appellant suffered from a compulsion which was an "exceedingly strong influence," but which was "not completely overpowering" is at least more carefully stated, if no less mystifying. Jellinek insists that conceptual clarity can only be achieved by distinguishing carefully between "loss of control" once an individual has commenced to drink and "inability to abstain" from drinking in the first place. Presumably a person would have to display both characteristics in order to make out a constitutional defense, should one be recognized. Yet the "findings" of the trial court utterly fail to make this crucial distinction, and there is serious question whether the record can be read to support a finding of either loss of control or inability to abstain.

Dr. Wade did testify that once appellant began drinking he appeared to have no control over the amount of alcohol he finally ingested. Appellant's own testimony concerning his drinking on the day of the trial would certainly appear, however, to cast doubt upon the conclusion that he was without control over his consumption of alcohol when he had sufficiently important reasons to exercise such control. However that may be, there are more serious factual and conceptual difficulties with reading this record to show that appellant was unable to abstain from drinking. Dr. Wade testified that when appellant was sober, the act of taking the first drink was a "voluntary exercise of his will," but that this exercise of will was undertaken under the "exceedingly strong influence" of a "compulsion" which was "not completely overpowering." Such concepts, when juxtaposed in this fashion, have little meaning.

Moreover, Jellinek asserts that it cannot accurately be said that a person is truly unable to abstain from drinking unless he is suffering the physical symptoms of withdrawal. There is no testimony in this record that Leroy Powell underwent withdrawal symptoms either before he began the drinking spree which resulted in the conviction under review here, or at any other time. In attempting to deal with the alcoholic's desire for drink in the absence of withdrawal symptoms, Jellinek is reduced to unintelligible distinctions between a "compulsion" (a "psychopathological phenomenon" which can apparently serve in some instances as the functional equivalent of a "craving" or symptom of withdrawal) and an "impulse" (something which differs from a loss of control, a craving or a compulsion, and to which Jellinek attributes the start of a new drinking bout for a "gamma" alcoholic). Other scholars are equally unhelpful in articulating the nature of a "compulsion."

It is one thing to say that if a man is deprived of alcohol his hands will begin to shake, he will suffer agonizing pains and ultimately he will have hallucinations; it is quite another to say that a man has a "compulsion" to take a drink, but that he also retains a certain amount of "free will" with which to resist. It is simply impossible, in the present state of our knowledge, to ascribe a useful meaning to the latter statement. This definitional confusion reflects, of course, not merely the undeveloped state of the psychiatric art but also the conceptual difficulties inevitably attendant upon the importation of scientific and medical models into a legal system generally predicated upon a different set of assumptions.

II

Despite the comparatively primitive state of our knowledge on the subject, it cannot be denied that the destructive use of alcoholic beverages is one of our principal social and public health problems. The lowest current informed estimate places the number of "alcoholics" in America (definitional problems aside) at 4,000,000 and most authorities are inclined to put the figure considerably higher. The problem is compounded by the fact that a very large percentage of the alcoholics in this country are "invisible"—they possess the means to keep their drinking problems secret, and the traditionally uncharitable attitude of our society toward alcoholics causes many of them to refrain from seeking treatment from any source. Nor can it be gainsaid that the legislative response to this enormous problem has in general been inadequate.

There is as yet no known generally effective method for treating the vast number of alcoholics in our society. Some individual alcoholics have responded to particular forms of therapy with remissions of their symptomatic dependence upon the drug. But just as there is no agreement among doctors and social workers with respect to the causes of alcoholism, there is no consensus as to why particular treatments have been effective in particular cases and there is no generally agreed-upon approach to the problem of treatment on a large scale. Most psychiatrists are apparently of the opinion that alcoholism is far more difficult to treat than other forms of behavioral disorders, and some believe it is impossible to cure by means of psychotherapy; indeed, the medical

profession as a whole, and psychiatrists in particular, have been severely criticized for the prevailing reluctance to undertake the treatment of drinking problems. Thus it is entirely possible that, even were
the manpower and facilities available for a full-scale attack upon
chronic alcoholism, we would find ourselves unable to help the vast
bulk of our "visible"—let alone our "invisible"—alcoholic population.

However, facilities for the attempted treatment of indigent alcoholics are woefully lacking throughout the country. It would be tragic
to return large numbers of helpless, sometimes dangerous and frequently unsanitary inebriates to the streets of our cities without even
the opportunity to sober up adequately which a brief jail term provides.
Presumably no State or city will tolerate such a state of affairs. Yet the
medical profession cannot, and does not, tell us with any assurance
that, even if the buildings, equipment and trained personnel were made
available, it could provide anything more than slightly higher-class jails
for our indigent habitual inebriates. Thus we run the grave risk that
nothing will be accomplished beyond the hanging of a new sign—reading "hospital"—over one wing of the jailhouse.

One virtue of the criminal process is, at least, that the duration of
penal incarceration typically has some outside statutory limit; this is
universally true in the case of petty offenses, such as public drunkenness, where jail terms are quite short on the whole. "Therapeutic civil
commitment" lacks this feature; one is typically committed until one is
"cured." Thus, to do otherwise than affirm might subject indigent alcoholics to the risk that they may be locked up for an indefinite period
of time under the same conditions as before, with no more hope than
before of receiving effective treatment and no prospect of periodic
"freedom."

Faced with this unpleasant reality, we are unable to assert that the
use of the criminal process as a means of dealing with the public aspects of problem drinking can never be defended as rational. The picture of the penniless drunk propelled aimlessly and endlessly through
the law's "revolving door" of arrest, incarceration, release and re-arrest
is not a pretty one. But before we condemn the present practice across-
the-board, perhaps we ought to be able to point to some clear promise
of a better world for these unfortunate people. Unfortunately, no such
promise has yet been forthcoming. If, in addition to the absence of a
coherent approach to the problem of treatment, we consider the almost
complete absence of facilities and manpower for the implementation of
a rehabilitation program, it is difficult to say in the present context that

the criminal process is utterly lacking in social value. This Court has never held that anything in the Constitution requires that penal sanctions be designed solely to achieve therapeutic or rehabilitative effects, and it can hardly be said with assurance that incarceration serves such purposes any better for the general run of criminals than it does for public drunks.

Ignorance likewise impedes our assessment of the deterrent effect of criminal sanctions for public drunkenness. The fact that a high percentage of American alcoholics conceal their drinking problems, not merely by avoiding public displays of intoxication but also by shunning all forms of treatment, is indicative that some powerful deterrent operates to inhibit the public revelation of the existence of alcoholism. Quite probably this deterrent effect can be largely attributed to the harsh moral attitude which our society has traditionally taken toward intoxication and the shame which we have associated with alcoholism. Criminal conviction represents the degrading public revelation of what Anglo-American society has long condemned as a moral defect, and the existence of criminal sanctions may serve to reinforce this cultural taboo, just as we presume it serves to reinforce other, stronger feelings against murder, rape, theft, and other forms of antisocial conduct.

Obviously, chronic alcoholics have not been deterred from drinking to excess by the existence of criminal sanctions against public drunkenness. But all those who violate penal laws of any kind are by definition undeterred. The long-standing and still raging debate over the validity of the deterrence justification for penal sanctions has not reached any sufficiently clear conclusions to permit it to be said that such sanctions are ineffective in any particular context or for any particular group of people who are able to appreciate the consequences of their acts. Certainly no effort was made at the trial of this case, beyond a monosyllabic answer to a perfunctory one-line question, to determine the effectiveness of penal sanctions in deterring Leroy Powell in particular or chronic alcoholics in general from drinking at all or from getting drunk in particular places or at particular times.

III

Appellant claims that his conviction on the facts of this case would violate the Cruel and Unusual Punishment Clause of the Eighth Amendment as applied to the States through the Fourteenth Amendment. The primary purpose of that clause has always been considered, and properly so, to be directed at the method or kind of punishment imposed for the violation of criminal statutes; the nature of the conduct made criminal is ordinarily relevant only to the fitness of the punishment imposed. See, *e.g., Trop* v. *Dulles* (1958); *Louisiana ex rel. Francis* v. *Resweber* (1947); *Weems* v. *United States* (1910).

Appellant, however, seeks to come within the application of the Cruel and Unusual Punishment Clause announced in *Robinson* v. *California* (1962), which involved a state statute making it a crime to "be addicted to the use of narcotics." This Court held there that "a state law which imprisons a person thus afflicted [with narcotic addiction] as a criminal, even though he has never touched any narcotic drug within the State or been guilty of any irregular behavior there, inflicts a cruel and unusual punishment. . . ."

On its face the present case does not fall within that holding, since appellant was convicted, not for being a chronic alcoholic, but for being in public while drunk on a particular occasion. The State of Texas thus has not sought to punish a mere status, as California did in *Robinson;* nor has it attempted to regulate appellant's behavior in the privacy of his own home. Rather, it has imposed upon appellant a criminal sanction for public behavior which may create substantial health and safety hazards, both for appellant and for members of the general public, and which offends the moral and esthetic sensibilities of a large segment of the community. This seems a far cry from convicting one for being an addict, being a chronic alcoholic, being "mentally ill, or a leper. . . ."

Robinson so viewed brings this Court but a very small way into the substantive criminal law. And unless *Robinson* is so viewed it is difficult to see any limiting principle that would serve to prevent this Court from becoming, under the aegis of the Cruel and Unusual Punishment Clause, the ultimate arbiter of the standards of criminal responsibility, in diverse areas of the criminal law, throughout the country.

It is suggested in dissent that *Robinson* stands for the "simple" but "subtle" principle that "[c]riminal penalties may not be inflicted upon a person for being in a condition he is powerless to change." In that view, appellant's "condition" of public intoxication was "occasioned by a compulsion symptomatic of the disease" of chronic alcoholism, and thus, apparently, his behavior lacked the critical element of *mens rea*. Whatever may be the merits of such a doctrine of criminal responsibility, it surely cannot be said to follow from *Robinson*. The entire thrust of *Robinson*'s interpretation of the Cruel and Unusual Punishment Clause is that criminal penalties may be inflicted only if the accused has committed some act, has engaged in some behavior, which society has an interest in preventing, or perhaps in historical common law terms, has committed some *actus reus.* It thus does not deal with the question of whether certain conduct cannot constitutionally be punished because it is, in some sense, "involuntary" or "occasioned by a compulsion."

Likewise, as the dissent acknowledges, there is a substantial definitional distinction between a "status," as in *Robinson,* and a "condition," which is said to be involved in this case. Whatever may be the merits of an attempt to distinguish between behavior and a condition, it is perfectly clear that the crucial element in this case, so far as the dissent is concerned, is whether or not appellant can legally be held responsible for his appearance in public in a state of intoxication. The only relevance of *Robinson* to this issue is that because the Court interpreted the statute there involved as making a "status" criminal, it was able to suggest that the statute would cover even a situation in which addiction had been acquired involuntarily. That this factor was not determinative in the case is shown by the fact that there was no indication of how Robinson himself had become an addict.

Ultimately, then, the most troubling aspects of this case, were *Robinson* to be extended to meet it, would be the scope and content of what could only be a constitutional doctrine of criminal responsibility. In dissent it is urged that the decision could be limited to conduct which is "a characteristic and involuntary part of the pattern of the disease as it afflicts" the particular individual, and that "[i]t is not foreseeable" that it would be applied "in the case of offenses such as driving a car while intoxicated, assault, theft, or robbery." That is limitation by fiat. In the first place, nothing in the logic of the dissent would limit its application to chronic alcoholics. If Leroy Powell cannot be convicted of public intoxication, it is difficult to see how a State can convict an individual for murder, if that individual, while exhibiting normal behavior in all other respects, suffers from a "compulsion" to kill, which is an "exceedingly strong influence," but "not completely overpowering." Even if we limit our consideration to chronic alcoholics, it would seem impossible to confine the principle within the arbitrary bounds which the dissent seems to envision.

It is not difficult to imagine a case involving psychiatric testimony to the effect that an individual suffers from some aggressive neurosis which he is able to control when sober; that very little alcohol suffices to remove the inhibitions which normally contain these aggressions, with the result that the individual engages in assaultive behavior without becoming actually intoxicated; and that the individual suffers from a very strong desire to drink, which is an "exceedingly strong influence" but "not completely overpowering." Without being untrue to the rationale of this case, should the principles advanced in dissent be accepted here, the Court could not avoid holding such an individual constitutionally unaccountable for his assaultive behavior.

Traditional common-law concepts of personal accountability and essential considerations of federalism lead us to disagree with appellant. We are unable to conclude, on the state of this record or on the current state of medical knowledge, that chronic alcoholics in general, and Leroy Powell in particular, suffer from such an irresistible compulsion to drink and to get drunk in public that they are utterly unable to control their performance of either or both of these acts and thus cannot be deterred at all from public intoxication. And in any event this Court has never articulated a general constitutional doctrine of *mens rea*.

We cannot cast aside the centuries-long evolution of the collection of interlocking and overlapping concepts which the common law has utilized to assess the moral accountability of an individual for his antisocial deeds. The doctrines of *actus reus, mens rea,* insanity, mistake, justification, and duress have historically provided the tools for a constantly shifting adjustment of the tension between the evolving aims of the criminal law and changing religious, moral, philosophical, and medical views of the nature of man. This process of adjustment has always been thought to be the province of the States.

Nothing could be less fruitful than for this Court to be impelled into defining some sort of insanity test in constitutional terms. Yet, that task would seem to follow inexorably from an extension of *Robinson* to this case. If a person in the "condition" of being a chronic alcoholic cannot be criminally punished as a constitutional matter for being drunk in public, it would seem to follow that a person who contends that, in terms of one test, "his unlawful act was the product of mental disease or mental defect," *Durham* v. *United States* (1954), would state an issue of constitutional dimension with regard to his criminal responsibility had he been tried under some different and perhaps lesser standard, *e.g.,* the right-wrong test of *M'Naghten's Case*. The experimentation of one jurisdiction in that field alone indicates the magnitude of the problem. See, *e.g., Carter* v. *United States* (1957). But formulating a constitutional rule would reduce, if not eliminate, that fruitful experimentation, and freeze the developing productive dialogue between law and psychiatry into a rigid constitutional mold. It is simply not yet the time to write into the Constitution formulas cast in terms whose meaning, let alone relevance, is not yet clear either to doctors or to lawyers.

Affirmed.

Argued January 17, 1972
Decided June 29, 1972

Imposition and carrying out of death penalty in these cases to constitute cruel and unusual punishment in violation of Eighth and Fourteenth Amendments.

Reversed and remanded.

Petitioner No. 69-5003 was convicted of murder in Georgia and was sentenced to death pursuant to Ga. Code Ann. § 26-1005 (1971) (1969). Petitioner No. 69-5030 was convicted of rape in Georgia and was sentenced to death pursuant to Ga. Code Ann. § 26-1302. Petitioner was convicted of rape in Texas and was sentenced to death pursuant to Tex. Penal Code, Art. 1189 (1961). Certiorari was granted limited to the following question: "Does the imposition and carrying out of the death penalty in [these cases] constitute cruel and unusual punishment in violation of the Eighth and Fourteenth Amendments?" (1971). The Court holds that the imposition and carrying out of the death penalty in these cases constitute cruel and unusual punishment in violation of the Eighth and Fourteenth Amendments. The judgment in each case is therefore reversed insofar as it leaves undisturbed the death sentence imposed, and the cases are remanded for further proceedings.

So ordered.

Mr. Justice Marshall, concurring.

These three cases present the question whether the death penalty is a cruel and unusual punishment prohibited by the Eighth Amendment to the United States Constitution.

In No. 69-5003, Furman was convicted of murder for shooting the father of five children when he discovered that Furman had broken into his home early one morning. Nos. 69-5030 and 69-5031 involve state convictions for forcible rape. Jackson was found guilty of rape during the course of a robbery in the victim's home. The rape was accomplished as he held the pointed ends of scissors at the victim's throat. Branch also was convicted of a rape committed in the victim's home. No weapon was utilized, but physical force and threats of physical force were employed.

The criminal acts with which we are confronted are ugly, vicious, reprehensible acts. Their sheer brutality cannot and should not be minimized. But, we are not called upon to condone the penalized conduct; we are asked only to examine the penalty imposed on each of the petitioners and to determine whether or not it violates the Eighth Amendment. The question then is not whether we condone rape or murder, for surely we do not; it is whether capital punishment is "a punishment no longer consistent with our own self-respect" and, therefore, violative of the Eighth Amendment.

The elasticity of the constitutional provision under consideration presents dangers of too little or too much self-restraint. Hence, we must proceed with caution to answer the question presented. By first examining the historical derivation of the Eighth Amendment and the construction given it in the past by this Court, and then exploring the history and attributes of capital punishment in this country, we can answer the question presented with objectivity and a proper measure of self-restraint.

Candor is critical to such an inquiry. All relevant material must be marshaled and sorted and forthrightly examined. We must not only be precise as to the standards of judgment that we are utilizing, but exacting in examining the relevant material in light of those standards.

Candor compels me to confess that I am not oblivious to the fact that this is truly a matter of life and death. Not only does it involve the lives of these three petitioners, but those of the almost 600 other condemned men and women in this country currently awaiting execution. While this fact cannot affect our ultimate decision, it necessitates that the decision be free from any possibility of error.

I

The Eighth Amendment's ban against cruel and unusual punishments derives from English law. In 1583, John Whitgift, Archbishop of

Canterbury, turned the High Commission into a permanent ecclesiastical court, and the Commission began to use torture to extract confessions from persons suspected of various offenses. Sir Robert Beale protested that cruel and barbarous torture violated Magna Carta, but his protests were made in vain.

Cruel punishments were not confined to those accused of crimes, but were notoriously applied with even greater relish to those who were convicted. Blackstone described in ghastly detail the myriad of inhumane forms of punishment imposed on persons found guilty of any of a large number of offenses. Death, of course, was the usual result.

The treason trials of 1685—the "Bloody Assizes"—which followed an abortive rebellion by the Duke of Monmouth, marked the culmination of the parade of horrors, and most historians believe that it was this event that finally spurred the adoption of the English Bill of Rights containing the progenitor of our prohibition against cruel and unusual punishments. The conduct of Lord Chief Justice Jeffreys at those trials has been described as an "insane lust for cruelty" which was "stimulated by orders from the King" (James II). The assizes received wide publicity from Puritan pamphleteers and doubtless had some influence on the adoption of a cruel and unusual punishments clause. But, the legislative history of the English Bill of Rights of 1689 indicates that the assizes may not have been as critical to the adoption of the clause as is widely thought. After William and Mary of Orange crossed the channel to invade England, James II fled. Parliament was summoned into session and a committee was appointed to draft general statements containing "such things as are absolutely necessary to be considered for the better securing of our religion, laws and liberties." An initial draft of the Bill of Rights prohibited "illegal" punishments, but a later draft referred to the infliction by James II of "illegal and cruel" punishments, and declared "cruel and unusual" punishments to be prohibited. The use of the word "unusual" in the final draft appears to be inadvertent.

This legislative history has led at least one legal historian to conclude "that the cruel and unusual punishments clause of the Bill of Rights of 1689 was, first, an objection to the imposition of punishments that were unauthorized by statute and outside the jurisdiction of the sentencing court, and second, a reiteration of the English policy against disproportionate penalties," and not primarily a reaction to the torture of the High Commission, harsh sentences, or the assizes.

Whether the English Bill of Rights prohibition against cruel and unusual punishments is properly read as a response to excessive or illegal punishments, as a reaction to barbaric and objectionable modes of punishment, or as both, there is no doubt whatever that in borrowing the language and in including it in the Eighth Amendment, our Founding Fathers intended to outlaw torture and other cruel punishments.

The precise language used in the Eighth Amendment first appeared in America on June 12, 1776, in Virginia's "Declaration of Rights," § 9 of which read: "That excessive bail ought not to be required, nor excessive fines imposed, nor cruel and unusual punishments inflicted." This language was drawn verbatim from the English Bill of Rights of 1689. Other States adopted similar clauses, and there is evidence in the debates of the various state conventions that were called upon to ratify the Constitution of great concern for the omission of any prohibition against torture or other cruel punishments.

The Virginia Convention offers some clues as to what the Founding Fathers had in mind in prohibiting cruel and unusual punishments. At one point George Mason advocated the adoption of a Bill of Rights, and Patrick Henry concurred, stating:

> "By this Constitution, some of the best barriers of human rights are thrown away. Is there not an additional reason to have a bill of rights? . . . Congress, from their general powers, may fully go into business of human legislation. They may legislate, in criminal cases, from treason to the lowest offence—petty larceny. They may define crimes and prescribe punishments. In the definition of crimes, I trust they will be directed by what wise representatives ought to be governed by. But when we come to punishments, no latitude ought to be left, nor dependence put on the virtue of representatives. What says our bill of rights?—'that excessive bail ought not to be required, nor excessive fines imposed, nor cruel and unusual punishments inflicted.' Are you not, therefore, now calling on those gentlemen who are to compose Congress, to prescribe trials and define punishments without this control? Will they find sentiments there similar to this bill of rights? You let them loose; you do more—you depart from the genius of your country. . . .
>
> "In this business of legislation, your members of Congress will loose the restriction of not imposing excessive fines, demanding excessive bail, and inflicting cruel and unusual punishments. These are prohibited by your declaration of rights. What has distin-

guished our ancestors?—That they would not admit of tortures, or cruel and barbarous punishment. But Congress may introduce the practice of the civil law, in preference to that of the common law. They may introduce the practice of France, Spain, and Germany—of torturing, to extort a confession of the crime. They will say that they might as well draw examples from those countries as from Great Britain, and they will tell you that there is such a necessity of strengthening the arm of government, that they must have a criminal equity, and extort confession by torture, in order to punish with still more relentless severity. We are then lost and undone."

Henry's statement indicates that he wished to ensure that "relentless severity" would be prohibited by the Constitution. Other expressions with respect to the proposed Eighth Amendment by Members of the First Congress indicate that they shared Henry's view of the need for and purpose of the Cruel and Unusual Punishments Clause.

Thus, the history of the clause clearly establishes that it was intended to prohibit cruel punishments. We must now turn to the case law to discover the manner in which courts have given meaning to the term "cruel."

II

This Court did not squarely face the task of interpreting the cruel and unusual punishments language for the first time until *Wilkerson* v. *Utah* (1879), although the language received a cursory examination in several prior cases. See, *e.g., Pervear* v. *Commonwealth* (1867). In *Wilkerson,* the Court unanimously upheld a sentence of public execution by shooting imposed pursuant to a conviction for premeditated murder. In his opinion for the Court, Mr. Justice Clifford wrote:

"Difficulty would attend the effort to define with exactness the extent of the constitutional provision which provides that cruel and unusual punishments shall not be inflicted; but it is safe to affirm that punishments of torture . . . and all others in the same line of unnecessary cruelty, are forbidden by that amendment to the Constitution."

Thus, the Court found that unnecessary cruelty was no more permissible than torture. To determine whether the punishment under attack was unnecessarily cruel, the Court examined the history of the Utah Territory and the then-current writings on capital punishment, and compared this Nation's practices with those of other countries. It is apparent that the Court felt it could not dispose of the question simply by referring to traditional practices; instead, it felt bound to examine developing thought.

Eleven years passed before the Court again faced a challenge to a specific punishment under the Eighth Amendment. In the case of *In re Kemmler* (1890), Chief Justice Fuller wrote an opinion for a unanimous Court upholding electrocution as a permissible mode of punishment. While the Court ostensibly held that the Eighth Amendment did not apply to the States, it is very apparent that the nature of the punishment involved was examined under the Due Process Clause of the Fourteenth Amendment. The Court held that the punishment was not objectionable. Today, *Kemmler* stands primarily for the proposition that a punishment is not necessarily unconstitutional simply because it is unusual, so long as the legislature has a humane purpose in selecting it.

Two years later in *O'Neil* v. *Vermont* (1892), the Court reaffirmed that the Eighth Amendment was not applicable to the States. O'Neil was found guilty on 307 counts of selling liquor in violation of Vermont law. A fine of $6,140 ($20 for each offense) and the costs of prosecution ($497.96) were imposed. O'Neil was committed to prison until the fine and the costs were paid; and the court provided that if they were not paid before a specified date, O'Neil was to be confined in the house of corrections for 19,914 days (approximately 54 years) at hard labor. Three Justices—Field, Harlan, and Brewer—dissented. They maintained not only that the Cruel and Unusual Punishments Clause was applicable to the States, but that in O'Neil's case it had been violated. Mr. Justice Field wrote:

> "That designation [cruel and unusual], it is true, is usually applied to punishments which inflict torture, such as the rack, the thumbscrew, the iron boot, the stretching of limbs and the like, which are attended with acute pain and suffering. . . . The inhibition is directed, not only against punishments of the character mentioned, but against all punishments which by their excessive length or severity are greatly disproportioned to the offences charged. The whole inhibition is against that which is excessive. . . ."

In *Howard* v. *Fleming* (1903), the Court, in essence, followed the approach advocated by the dissenters in *O'Neil*. In rejecting the claim that 10-year sentences for conspiracy to defraud were cruel and unusual, the Court (per Mr. Justice Brewer) considered the nature of the crime, the purpose of the law, and the length of the sentence imposed.

The Court used the same approach seven years later in the landmark case of *Weems* v. *United States* (1910). Weems, an officer of the Bureau of Coast Guard and Transportation of the United States Government of the Philippine Islands, was convicted of falsifying a "public and official document." He was sentenced to 15 years' incarceration at hard labor with chains on his ankles, to an unusual loss of his civil rights, and to perpetual surveillance. Called upon to determine whether this was a cruel and unusual punishment, the Court found that it was. The Court emphasized that the Constitution was not an "ephemeral" enactment, or one "designed to meet passing occasions." Recognizing that "[t]ime works changes, [and] brings into existence new conditions and purposes," the Court commented that "[i]n the application of a constitution . . . our contemplation cannot be only of what has been but of what may be."

In striking down the penalty imposed on Weems, the Court examined the punishment in relation to the offense, compared the punishment to those inflicted for other crimes and to those imposed in other jurisdictions, and concluded that the punishment was excessive. Justices White and Holmes dissented and argued that the cruel and unusual prohibition was meant to prohibit only those things that were objectionable at the time the Constitution was adopted.

Weems is a landmark case because it represents the first time that the Court invalidated a penalty prescribed by a legislature for a particular offense. The Court made it plain beyond any reasonable doubt that excessive punishments were as objectionable as those that were inherently cruel. Thus, it is apparent that the dissenters' position in *O'Neil* had become the opinion of the Court in *Weems*.

Weems was followed by two cases that added little to our knowledge of the scope of the cruel and unusual language, *Badders* v. *United States* (1916), and *United States ex rel. Milwaukee Social Democratic Publishing Co.* v. *Burleson* (1921). Then came another landmark case, *Louisiana ex rel. Francis* v. *Resweber* (1947).

Francis had been convicted of murder and sentenced to be electrocuted. The first time the current passed through him, there was a mechanical failure and he did not die. Thereafter, Francis sought to prevent a second electrocution on the ground that it would be a cruel and unusual punishment. Eight members of the Court assumed the applicability of the Eighth Amendment to the States. The Court was virtually unanimous in agreeing that "[t]he traditional humanity of modern An-glo-American law forbids the infliction of unnecessary pain," but split 5–4 on whether Francis would, under the circumstances, be forced to undergo any excessive pain. Five members of the Court treated the case like *In re Kemmler* and held that the legislature adopted electrocu-tion for a humane purpose, and that its will should not be thwarted because, in its desire to reduce pain and suffering in most cases, it may have inadvertently increased suffering in one particular case. The four dissenters felt that the case should be remanded for further facts.

As in *Weems,* the Court was concerned with excessive punishments. *Resweber* is perhaps most significant because the analysis of cruel and unusual punishment questions first advocated by the dissenters in *O'Neil* was at last firmly entrenched in the minds of an entire Court.

Trop v. *Dulles* (1958), marked the next major cruel and unusual pun-ishment case in this Court. Trop, a native-born American, was declared to have lost his citizenship by reason of a conviction by court-martial for wartime desertion. Writing for himself and Justices Black, Douglas, and Whittaker, Chief Justice Warren concluded that loss of citizenship amounted to a cruel and unusual punishment that violated the Eighth Amendment.

Emphasizing the flexibility inherent in the words "cruel and un-usual," the Chief Justice wrote that "[t]he Amendment must draw its meaning from the evolving standards of decency that mark the progress of a maturing society." His approach to the problem was that utilized by the Court in *Weems:* he scrutinized the severity of the penalty in relation to the offense, examined the practices of other civilized nations of the world, and concluded that involuntary statelessness was an exces-sive and, therefore, an unconstitutional punishment. Justice Frank-furter, dissenting, urged that expatriation was not punishment, and that even if it were, it was not excessive. While he criticized the conclusion arrived at by the Chief Justice, his approach to the Eighth Amendment question was identical.

Whereas in *Trop* a majority of the Court failed to agree on whether loss of citizenship was a cruel and unusual punishment, four years later a majority did agree in *Robinson* v. *California* (1962), that a sentence of 90 days' imprisonment for violation of a California statute making it a crime to "be addicted to the use of narcotics" was cruel and unusual. Mr. Justice Stewart, writing the opinion of the Court, reiterated what the Court had said in *Weems* and what Chief Justice Warren wrote in *Trop*—that the cruel and unusual punishment clause was not a static concept, but one that must be continually re-examined "in the light of contemporary human knowledge." The fact that the penalty under attack was only 90 days evidences the Court's willingness to carefully examine the possible excessiveness of punishment in a given case even where what is involved is a penalty that is familiar and widely accepted.

We distinguished *Robinson* in *Powell* v. *Texas* (1968), where we sustained a conviction for drunkenness in a public place and a fine of $20. Four Justices dissented on the ground that *Robinson* was controlling. The analysis in both cases was the same; only the conclusion as to whether or not the punishment was excessive differed. *Powell* marked the last time prior to today's decision that the Court has had occasion to construe the meaning of the term "cruel and unusual" punishment.

Several principles emerge from these prior cases and serve as a beacon to an enlightened decision in the instant cases.

III

Perhaps the most important principle in analyzing "cruel and unusual" punishment questions is one that is reiterated again and again in the prior opinions of the Court: *i.e.*, the cruel and unusual language "must draw its meaning from the evolving standards of decency that mark the progress of a maturing society." Thus, a penalty that was permissible at one time in our Nation's history is not necessarily permissible today.

The fact, therefore, that the Court, or individual Justices, may have in the past expressed an opinion that the death penalty is constitutional is not now binding on us. A fair reading of *Wilkerson* v. *Utah, In re Kemmler,* and *Louisiana ex rel. Francis* v. *Resweber,* would certainly indicate an acceptance *sub silentio* of capital punishment as constitutionally permissible. Several Justices have also expressed their individual opinions that the death penalty is constitutional. Yet, some of these same Justices and others have at times expressed concern over capital punishment. There is no holding directly in point, and the very nature of the Eighth Amendment would dictate that unless a very recent decision existed, *stare decisis* would bow to changing values, and the question of the constitutionality of capital punishment at a given moment in history would remain open.

Faced with an open question, we must establish our standards for decision. The decisions discussed in the previous section imply that a punishment may be deemed cruel and unusual for any one of four distinct reasons.

First, there are certain punishments that inherently involve so much physical pain and suffering that civilized people cannot tolerate them— *e.g.*, use of the rack, the thumbscrew, or other modes of torture. See *O'Neil* v. *Vermont* (Field, J., dissenting). Regardless of public sentiment with respect to imposition of one of these punishments in a particular case or at any one moment in history, the Constitution prohibits it. These are punishments that have been barred since the adoption of the Bill of Rights.

Second, there are punishments that are unusual, signifying that they were previously unknown as penalties for a given offense. Cf. *United States ex rel. Milwaukee Social Democratic Publishing Co.* v. *Burleson* (Brandeis, J., dissenting). If these punishments are intended to serve a humane purpose, they may be constitutionally permissible. *In re Kemmler, Louisiana ex rel. Francis v. Resweber.* Prior decisions leave open the question of just how much the word "unusual" adds to the word "cruel." I have previously indicated that use of the word "unusual" in the English Bill of Rights of 1689 was inadvertent, and there is nothing in the history of the Eighth Amendment to give flesh to its intended meaning. In light of the meager history that does exist, one would suppose that an innovative punishment would probably be constitutional if no more cruel than that punishment which it superseded. We need not decide this question here, however, for capital punishment is certainly not a recent phenomenon.

Third, a penalty may be cruel and unusual because it is excessive and serves no valid legislative purpose. *Weems* v. *United States, supra.* The decisions previously discussed are replete with assertions that one of the primary functions of the cruel and unusual punishments clause is to prevent excessive or unnecessary penalties, *e.g., Wilkerson* v. *Utah; O'Neil* v. *Vermont* (Field, J., dissenting); *Weems* v. *United States; Louisiana ex rel. Francis v. Resweber, supra;* these punishments are unconstitutional even though popular sentiment may favor them. Both THE CHIEF JUSTICE and MR. JUSTICE POWELL seek to ignore or to minimize this aspect of the Court's prior decisions. But, since Mr. Justice Field first suggested that "[t]he whole inhibition [of the prohibition against cruel and unusual punishments] is against that which is excessive," *O'Neil* v. *Vermont,* this Court has steadfastly maintained that a penalty is unconstitutional whenever it is unnecessarily harsh or cruel. This is what the Founders of this country intended; this is what their fellow citizens

believed the Eighth Amendment provided; and this was the basis for
our decision in *Robinson* v. *California, supra,* for the plurality opinion
by Mr. Chief Justice Warren in *Trop* v. *Dulles,* and for the Court's
decision in *Weems* v. *United States.* It should also be noted that the
"cruel and unusual" language of the Eighth Amendment immediately
follows language that prohibits *excessive* bail and *excessive* fines. The
entire thrust of the Eighth Amendment is, in short, against "that which
is excessive."

Fourth, where a punishment is not excessive and serves a valid legislative purpose, it still may be invalid if popular sentiment abhors it. For
example, if the evidence clearly demonstrated that capital punishment
served valid legislative purposes, such punishment would, nevertheless,
be unconstitutional if citizens found it to be morally unacceptable. A
general abhorrence on the part of the public would, in effect, equate a
modern punishment with those barred since the adoption of the Eighth
Amendment. There are no prior cases in this Court striking down a
penalty on this ground, but the very notion of changing values requires
that we recognize its existence.

It is immediately obvious, then, that since capital punishment is not a
recent phenomenon, if it violates the Constitution, it does so because it
is excessive or unnecessary, or because it is abhorrent to currently existing moral values.

We must proceed to the history of capital punishment in the United
States.

IV

Capital punishment has been used to penalize various forms of conduct by members of society since the beginnings of civilization. Its precise origins are difficult to perceive, but there is some evidence that its
roots lie in violent retaliation by members of a tribe or group, or by the
tribe or group itself, against persons committing hostile acts toward
group members. Thus, infliction of death as a penalty for objectionable
conduct appears to have its beginnings in private vengeance.

As individuals gradually ceded their personal prerogatives to a sovereign power, the sovereign accepted the authority to punish wrongdoing
as part of its "divine right" to rule. Individual vengeance gave way to
the vengeance of the state, and capital punishment became a public
function. Capital punishment worked its way into the laws of various
countries and was inflicted in a variety of macabre and horrific ways.

It was during the reign of Henry II (1154–1189) that English law first recognized that crime was more than a personal affair between the victim and the perpetrator. The early history of capital punishment in England is set forth in *McGautha* v. *California* (1971), and need not be repeated here.

By 1500, English law recognized eight major capital crimes: treason, petty treason (killing of husband by his wife), murder, larceny, robbery, burglary, rape, and arson. Tudor and Stuart kings added many more crimes to the list of those punishable by death, and by 1688 there were nearly 50. George II (1727–1760) added nearly 36 more, and George III (1760–1820) increased the number by 60.

By shortly after 1800, capital offenses numbered more than 200 and not only included crimes against person and property, but even some against the public peace. While England may, in retrospect, look particularly brutal, Blackstone points out that England was fairly civilized when compared to the rest of Europe.

Capital punishment was not as common a penalty in the American Colonies. "The Capitall Lawes of NewEngland," dating from 1636, were drawn by the Massachusetts Bay Colony and are the first written expression of capital offenses known to exist in this country. These laws make the following crimes capital offenses: idolatry, witchcraft, blasphemy, murder, assault in sudden anger, sodomy, buggery, adultery, statutory rape, rape, manstealing, perjury in a capital trial, and rebellion. Each crime is accompanied by a reference to the Old Testament to indicate its source. It is not known with any certainty exactly when, or even if, these laws were enacted as drafted; and, if so, just how vigorously these laws were enforced. We do know that the other Colonies had a variety of laws that spanned the spectrum of severity.

By the 18th century, the list of crimes became much less theocratic and much more secular. In the average colony, there were 12 capital crimes. This was far fewer than existed in England, and part of the reason was that there was a scarcity of labor in the Colonies. Still, there were many executions, because "[w]ith county jails inadequate and insecure, the criminal population seemed best controlled by death, mutilation, and fines."

Even in the 17th century, there was some opposition to capital punishment in some of the colonies. In his "Great Act" of 1682, William Penn prescribed death only for premeditated murder and treason, although his reform was not long lived.

In 1776 the Philadelphia Society for Relieving Distressed Prisoners organized, and it was followed 11 years later by the Philadelphia Society for Alleviating the Miseries of Public Prisons. These groups pressured for reform of all penal laws, including capital offenses. Dr. Benjamin Rush soon drafted America's first reasoned argument against capital punishment, entitled An Enquiry into the Effects of Public Punishments upon Criminals and upon Society. In 1793, William Bradford, the Attorney General of Pennsylvania and later Attorney General of the United States, conducted "An Enquiry How Far the Punishment of Death is Necessary in Pennsylvania." He concluded that it was doubtful whether capital punishment was at all necessary, and that until more information could be obtained, it should be immediately eliminated for all offenses except high treason and murder.

The "Enquiries" of Rush and Bradford and the Pennsylvania movement toward abolition of the death penalty had little immediate impact on the practices of other States. But in the early 1800's, Governors George and DeWitt Clinton and Daniel Tompkins unsuccessfully urged the New York Legislature to modify or end capital punishment. During this same period, Edward Livingston, and American lawyer who later became Secretary of State and Minister to France under President Andrew Jackson, was appointed by the Louisiana Legislature to draft a new penal code. At the center of his proposal was "the total abolition of capital punishment." His Introductory Report to the System of Penal Law Prepared for the State of Louisiana contained a systematic rebuttal of all arguments favoring capital punishment. Drafted in 1824, it was not published until 1833. This work was a tremendous impetus to the abolition movement for the next half century.

During the 1830's, there was a rising tide of sentiment against capital punishment. In 1834, Pennsylvania abolished public executions, and two years later, The Report on Capital Punishment Made to the Maine Legislature was published. It led to a law that prohibited the executive from issuing a warrant for execution within one year after a criminal was sentenced by the courts. The totally discretionary character of the law was at odds with almost all prior practices. The "Maine Law" resulted in little enforcement of the death penalty, which was not surprising since the legislature's idea in passing the law was that the affirmative burden placed on the governor to issue a warrant one full year or more after a trial would be an effective deterrent to exercise of his power. The law spread throughout New England and led to Michigan's being the first State to abolish capital punishment in 1846.

Anti-capital-punishment feeling grew in the 1840's as the literature of the period pointed out the agony of the condemned man and expressed the philosophy that repentance atoned for the worst crimes, and that true repentance derived, not from fear, but from harmony with nature.

By 1850, societies for abolition existed in Massachusetts, New York, Pennsylvania, Tennessee, Ohio, Alabama, Louisiana, Indiana, and Iowa. New York, Massachusetts, and Pennsylvania constantly had abolition bills before their legislatures. In 1852, Rhode Island followed in the footsteps of Michigan and partially abolished capital punishment. Wisconsin totally abolished the death penalty the following year. Those States that did not abolish the death penalty greatly reduced its scope, and "[f]ew states outside the South had more than one or two . . . capital offenses" in addition to treason and murder.

But the Civil War halted much of the abolition furor. One historian has said that "[a]fter the Civil War, men's finer sensibilities, which had once been revolted by the execution of a fellow being, seemed hardened and blunted." Some of the attention previously given to abolition was diverted to prison reform. An abolitionist movement still existed, however. Maine abolished the death penalty in 1876, restored it in 1883, and abolished it again in 1887; Iowa abolished capital punishment from 1872–1878; Colorado began an erratic period of *de facto* abolition and revival in 1872; and Kansas also abolished it *de facto* in 1872, and by law in 1907.

One great success of the abolitionist movement in the period from 1830–1900 was almost complete elimination of mandatory capital punishment. Before the legislatures formally gave juries discretion to refrain from imposing the death penalty, the phenomenon of "jury nullification," in which juries refused to convict in cases in which they believed that death was an inappropriate penalty, was experienced. Tennessee was the first State to give juries discretion, Tenn. Laws 1837–1838, but other States quickly followed suit. Then, Rep. Curtis of New York introduced a federal bill that ultimately became law in 1897 which reduced the number of federal capital offenses from 60 to 3 (treason, murder, and rape) and gave the jury sentencing discretion in murder and rape cases.

By 1917 12 States had become abolitionist jurisdictions. But, under the nervous tension of World War I, four of these States reinstituted capital punishment and promising movements in other States came grinding to a halt. During the period following the First World War, the abolitionist movement never regained its momentum.

It is not easy to ascertain why the movement lost its vigor. Certainly, much attention was diverted from penal reform during the economic crisis of the depression and the exhausting years of struggle during World War II. Also, executions, which had once been frequent public spectacles, became infrequent private affairs. The manner of inflicting death changed, and the horrors of the punishment were, therefore, somewhat diminished in the minds of the general public.

In recent years there has been renewed interest in modifying capital punishment. New York has moved toward abolition, as have several other States. In 1967, a bill was introduced in the Senate to abolish capital punishment for all federal crimes, but it died in committee.

At the present time, 41 States, the District of Columbia, and other federal jurisdictions authorize the death penalty for at least one crime. It would be fruitless to attempt here to categorize the approach to capital punishment taken by the various States. It is sufficient to note that murder is the crime most often punished by death, followed by kidnaping and treason. Rape is a capital offense in 16 States and the federal system.

The foregoing history demonstrates that capital punishment was carried from Europe to America but, once here, was tempered considerably. At times in our history, strong abolitionist movements have existed. But, they have never been completely successful, as no more than one-quarter of the States of the Union have, at any one time, abolished the death penalty. They have had partial success, however, especially in reducing the number of capital crimes, replacing mandatory death sentences with jury discretion, and developing more humane methods of conducting executions.

This is where our historical foray leads. The question now to be faced is whether American society has reached a point where abolition is not dependent on a successful grass roots movement in particular jurisdictions, but is demanded by the Eighth Amendment. To answer this question, we must first examine whether or not the death penalty is today tantamount to excessive punishment.

V

In order to assess whether or not death is an excessive or unnecessary penalty, it is necessary to consider the reasons why a legislature might select it as punishment for one or more offenses, and examine whether less severe penalties would satisfy the legitimate legislative wants as well as capital punishment. If they would, then the death penalty is unnecessary cruelty, and, therefore, unconstitutional.

There are six purposes conceivably served by capital punishment: retribution, deterrence, prevention of repetitive criminal acts, encouragement of guilty pleas and confessions, eugenics, and economy. These are considered *seriatim* below.

A. The concept of retribution is one of the most misunderstood in all of our criminal jurisprudence. The principal source of confusion derives from the fact that, in dealing with the concept, most people confuse the question "why do men in fact punish?" with the question "what justifies men in punishing?" Men may punish for any number of reasons, but the one reason that punishment is morally good or morally justifiable is that someone has broken the law. Thus, it can correctly be said that breaking the law is the *sine qua non* of punishment, or, in other words, that we only tolerate punishment as it is imposed on one who deviates from the norm established by the criminal law.

The fact that the State may seek retribution against those who have broken its laws does not mean that retribution may then become the State's sole end in punishing. Our jurisprudence has always accepted deterrence in general, deterrence of individual recidivism, isolation of dangerous persons, and rehabilitation as proper goals of punishment. See *Trop* v. *Dulles* (BRENNAN, J., concurring). Retaliation, vengeance, and retribution have been roundly condemned as intolerable aspirations for a government in a free society.

Punishment as retribution has been condemned by scholars for centuries, and the Eighth Amendment itself was adopted to prevent punishment from becoming synonymous with vengeance.

In *Weems* v. *United States,* the Court, in the course of holding that Weems' punishment violated the Eighth Amendment, contrasted it with penalties provided for other offenses and concluded:

> "[T]his contrast shows more than different exercises of legislative judgment. It is greater than that. It condemns the sentence in this case as cruel and unusual. It exhibits a difference between unrestrained power and that which is exercised under the spirit of constitutional limitations formed to establish justice. The State thereby suffers nothing and loses no power. *The purpose of punishment is fulfilled, crime is repressed by penalties of just, not tormenting, severity, its repetition is prevented, and hope is given for the reformation of the criminal.*"

It is plain that the view of the *Weems Court* was that punishment for the sake of retribution was not permissible under the Eighth Amendment. This is the only view that the Court could have taken if the "cruel and unusual" language were to be given any meaning. Retribution surely underlies the imposition of some punishment on one who commits a criminal act. But, the fact that *some* punishment may be imposed does not mean that *any* punishment is permissible. If retribution alone could serve as a justification for any particular penalty, then all penalties selected by the legislature would by definition be acceptable means for designating society's moral approbation of a particular act. The "cruel and unusual" language would thus be read out of the Constitution and the fears of Patrick Henry and the other Founding Fathers would become realities.

To preserve the integrity of the Eighth Amendment, the Court has consistently denigrated retribution as a permissible goal of punishment. It is undoubtedly correct that there is a demand for vengeance on the part of many persons in a community against one who is convicted of a particularly offensive act. At times a cry is heard that morality requires vengeance to evidence society's abhorrence of the act. But the Eighth Amendment is our insulation from our baser selves. The "cruel and unusual" language limits the avenues through which vengeance can be channeled. Were this not so, the language would be empty and a return to the rack and other tortures would be possible in a given case.

Mr. Justice Story wrote that the Eighth Amendment's limitation on punishment "would seem to be wholly unnecessary in a free government, since it is scarcely possible that any department of such a government should authorize or justify such atrocious conduct."

I would reach an opposite conclusion—that only in a free society would men recognize their inherent weaknesses and seek to compensate for them by means of a Constitution.

The history of the Eighth Amendment supports only the conclusion that retribution for its own sake is improper.

B. The most hotly contested issue regarding capital punishment is whether it is better than life imprisonment as a deterrent to crime.

While the contrary position has been argued, it is my firm opinion that the death penalty is a more severe sanction than life imprisonment. Admittedly, there are some persons who would rather die than languish in prison for a lifetime. But, whether or not they should be able to choose death as an alternative is a far different question from that presented here—*i.e.,* whether the State can impose death as a punishment. Death is irrevocable; life imprisonment is not. Death, of course, makes rehabilitation impossible; life imprisonment does not. In short, death has always been viewed as the ultimate sanction, and it seems perfectly reasonable to continue to view it as such.

It must be kept in mind, then, that the question to be considered is not simply whether capital punishment is a deterrent, but whether it is a better deterrent than life imprisonment.

There is no more complex problem than determining the deterrent efficacy of the death penalty. "Capital punishment has obviously failed as a deterrent when a murder is committed. We can number its failures. But we cannot number its successes. No one can ever know how many people have refrained from murder because of the fear of being hanged." This is the nub of the problem and it is exacerbated by the paucity of useful data. The United States is more fortunate than most countries, however, in that it has what are generally considered to be the world's most reliable statistics.

The two strongest arguments in favor of capital punishment as a deterrent are both logical hypotheses devoid of evidentiary support, but persuasive nonetheless. The first proposition was best stated by Sir James Stephen in 1864:

"No other punishment deters men so effectually from committing crimes as the punishment of death. This is one of those propositions which it is difficult to prove, simply because they are in themselves more obvious than any proof can make them. It is possible to display ingenuity in arguing against it, but that is all. The whole experience of mankind is in the other direction. The threat of instant death is the one to which resort has always been made when there was an absolute necessity for producing some result. . . . No one goes to certain inevitable death except by compulsion. Put the matter the other way. Was there ever yet a criminal who, when sentenced to death and brought out to die, would refuse the offer of a commutation of his sentence for the severest secondary punishment? Surely not. Why is this? It can only be because 'All that a man has will he give for his life.' In any secondary punishment, however terrible, there is hope; but death is death; its terrors cannot be described more forcibly."

This hypothesis relates to the use of capital punishment as a deterrent for any crime. The second proposition is that "if life imprisonment is the maximum penalty for a crime such as murder, an offender who is serving a life sentence cannot then be deterred from murdering a fellow inmate or a prison officer." This hypothesis advocates a limited deterrent effect under particular circumstances.

Abolitionists attempt to disprove these hypotheses by amassing statistical evidence to demonstrate that there is no correlation between criminal activity and the existence or nonexistence of a capital sanction. Almost all of the evidence involves the crime of murder, since murder is punishable by death in more jurisdictions than are other offenses, and almost 90% of all executions since 1930 have been pursuant to murder convictions.

Thorsten Sellin, one of the leading authorities on capital punishment, has urged that if the death penalty deters prospective murderers, the following hypotheses should be true:

"(a) Murders should be less frequent in states that have the death penalty than in those that have abolished it, other factors being equal. Comparisons of this nature must be made among states that are as alike as possible in all other respects—character of population, social and economic condition, etc.—in order not to introduce factors known to influence murder rates in a serious manner but present in only one of these states.

"(b) Murders should increase when the death penalty is abolished and should decline when it is restored.

"(c) The deterrent effect should be greatest and should therefore affect murder rates most powerfully in those communities where the crime occurred and its consequences are most strongly brought home to the population.

"(d) Law enforcement officers would be safer from murderous attacks in states that have the death penalty than in those without it."

Sellin's evidence indicates that not one of these propositions is true. This evidence has its problems, however. One is that there are no accurate figures for capital murders; there are only figures on homicides and they, of course, include noncapital killings. A second problem is that certain murders undoubtedly are misinterpreted as accidental deaths or suicides, and there is no way of estimating the number of such undetected crimes. A third problem is that not all homicides are reported. Despite these difficulties, most authorities have assumed that the proportion of capital murders in a State's or Nation's homicide statistics remains reasonably constant, and that the homicide statistics are therefore useful.

Sellin's statistics demonstrate that there is no correlation between the murder rate and the presence or absence of the capital sanction. He compares States that have similar characteristics and finds that irrespective of their position on capital punishment, they have similar murder rates. In the New England States, for example, there is no correlation between executions and homicide rates. The same is true for Midwestern States, and for all others studied. Both the United Nations and Great Britain have acknowledged the validity of Sellin's statistics.

Sellin also concludes that abolition and/or reintroduction of the death penalty had no effect on the homicide rates of the various States involved. This conclusion is borne out by others who have made similar inquiries and by the experience of other countries. Despite problems with the statistics, Sellin's evidence has been relied upon in international studies of capital punishment.

Statistics also show that the deterrent effect of capital punishment is no greater in those communities where executions take place than in other communities. In fact, there is some evidence that imposition of capital punishment may actually encourage crime, rather than deter it. And, while police and law enforcement officers are the strongest advocates of capital punishment, the evidence is overwhelming that police are no safer in communities that retain the sanction than in those that have abolished it.

There is also a substantial body of data showing that the existence of the death penalty has virtually no effect on the homicide rate in prisons. Most of the persons sentenced to death are murderers, and murderers tend to be model prisoners.

In sum, the only support for the theory that capital punishment is an effective deterrent is found in the hypotheses with which we began and the occasional stories about a specific individual being deterred from doing a contemplated criminal act. These claims of specific deterrence are often spurious, however, and may be more than counterbalanced by the tendency of capital punishment to incite certain crimes.

The United Nations Committee that studied capital punishment found that "[i]t is generally agreed between the retentionists and abolitionists, whatever their opinions about the validity of comparative studies of deterrence, that the data which now exist show no correlation between the existence of capital punishment and lower rates of capital crime."

Despite the fact that abolitionists have not proved non-deterrence beyond a reasonable doubt, they have succeeded in showing by clear and convincing evidence that capital punishment is not necessary as a deterrent to crime in our society. This is all that they must do. We would shirk our judicial responsibilities if we failed to accept the presently existing statistics and demanded more proof. It may be that we now possess all the proof that anyone could ever hope to assemble on the subject. But, even if further proof were to be forthcoming, I believe there is more than enough evidence presently available for a decision in this case.

In 1793 William Bradford studied the utility of the death penalty in Pennsylvania and found that it probably had no deterrent effect but that more evidence was needed. Edward Livingston reached a similar conclusion with respect to deterrence in 1833 upon completion of his study for Louisiana. Virtually every study that has since been undertaken has reached the same result.

In light of the massive amount of evidence before us, I see no alternative but to conclude that capital punishment cannot be justified on the basis of its deterrent effect.

C. Much of what must be said about the death penalty as a device to prevent recidivism is obvious—if a murderer is executed, he cannot possibly commit another offense. The fact is, however, that murderers are extremely unlikely to commit other crimes either in prison or upon their release. For the most part, they are first offenders, and when released from prison they are known to become model citizens. Furthermore, most persons who commit capital crimes are not executed. With respect to those who are sentenced to die, it is critical to note that the jury is never asked to determine whether they are likely to be recidivists. In light of these facts, if capital punishment were justified purely on the basis of preventing recidivism, it would have to be considered to be excessive; no general need to obliterate all capital offenders could have been demonstrated, nor any specific need in individual cases.

D. The three final purposes which may underlie utilization of a capital sanction—encouraging guilty pleas and confessions, eugenics, and reducing state expenditures—may be dealt with quickly. If the death penalty is used to encourage guilty pleas and thus to deter suspects from exercising their rights under the Sixth Amendment to jury trials, it is unconstitutional. *United States* v. *Jackson* (1968). Its elimination would do little to impair the State's bargaining position in criminal cases, since life imprisonment remains a severe sanction which can be used as leverage for bargaining for pleas or confessions in exchange either for charges of lesser offenses or recommendations of leniency.

Moreover, to the extent that capital punishment is used to encourage confessions and guilty pleas, it is not being used for punishment purposes. A State that justifies capital punishment on its utility as part of the conviction process could not profess to rely on capital punishment as a deterrent. Such a State's system would be structured with twin goals only: obtaining guilty pleas and confessions and imposing *imprisonment* as the maximum sanction. Since life imprisonment is sufficient for bargaining purposes, the death penalty is excessive if used for the same purposes.

In light of the previous discussion on deterrence, any suggestions concerning the eugenic benefits of capital punishment are obviously meritless. As I pointed out above, there is not even any attempt made to discover which capital offenders are likely to be recidivists, let alone which are positively incurable. No test or procedure presently exists by which incurables can be screened from those who would benefit from treatment. On the one hand, due process would seem to require that we have some procedure to demonstrate incurability before execution; and, on the other hand, equal protection would then seemingly require that all incurables be executed, cf. *Skinner* v. *Oklahoma* (1942). In addition, the "cruel and unusual" language would require that life imprisonment, treatment, and sterilization be inadequate for eugenic purposes. More importantly, this Nation has never formally professed eugenic goals, and the history of the world does not look kindly on them. If eugenics is one of our purposes, then the legislatures should say so forthrightly and design procedures to serve this goal. Until such time, I can only conclude, as has virtually everyone else who has looked at the problem that capital punishment cannot be defended on the basis of any eugenic purposes.

As for the argument that it is cheaper to execute a capital offender than to imprison him for life, even assuming that such an argument, if true, would support a capital sanction, it is simply incorrect. A disproportionate amount of money spent on prisons is attributable to death row. Condemned men are not productive members of the prison community, although they could be, and executions are expensive. Appeals are often automatic, and courts admittedly spend more time with death cases.

At trial, the selection of jurors is likely to become a costly, time-consuming problem in a capital case, and defense counsel will reasonably exhaust every possible means to save his client from execution, no matter how long the trial takes.

During the period between conviction and execution, there are an inordinate number of collateral attacks on the conviction and attempts to obtain executive clemency, all of which exhaust the time, money, and effort of the State. There are also continual assertions that the condemned prisoner has gone insane. Because there is a formally established policy of not executing insane persons, great sums of money may be spent on detecting and curing mental illness in order to perform the execution. Since no one wants the responsibility for the execution, the condemned man is likely to be passed back and forth from doctors to custodial officials to courts like a ping-pong ball. The entire process is very costly.

When all is said and done, there can be no doubt that it costs more to execute a man than to keep him in prison for life.

E. There is but one conclusion that can be drawn from all of this—*i.e.,* the death penalty is an excessive and unnecessary punishment that violates the Eighth Amendment. The statistical evidence is not convincing beyond all doubt, but it is persuasive. It is not improper at this point to take judicial notice of the fact that for more than 200 years men have labored to demonstrate that capital punishment serves no purpose that life imprisonment could not serve equally well. And they have done so with great success. Little, if any, evidence has been adduced to prove the contrary. The point has now been reached at which deference to the legislatures is tantamount to abdication of our judicial roles as factfinders, judges, and ultimate arbiters of the Constitution. We know that at some point the presumption of constitutionality accorded legislative acts gives way to a realistic assessment of those acts. This point comes when there is sufficient evidence available so that judges can determine, not whether the legislature acted wisely, but whether it had any *rational basis* whatsoever for acting. We have this evidence before us now. There is no rational basis for concluding that capital punishment is not excessive. It therefore violates the Eighth Amendment.

VI

In addition, even if capital punishment is not excessive, it nonetheless violates the Eighth Amendment because it is morally unacceptable to the people of the United States at this time in their history.

In judging whether or not a given penalty is morally acceptable, most courts have said that the punishment is valid unless "it shocks the conscience and sense of justice of the people."

Judge Frank once noted the problems inherent in the use of such a measuring stick:

"[The court,] before it reduces a sentence as 'cruel and unusual,' must have reasonably good assurances that the sentence offends the 'common conscience.' And, in any context, such a standard— the community's attitude—is usually an unknowable. It resembles a slithery shadow, since one can seldom learn, at all accurately, what the community, or a majority, actually feels. Even a carefully-taken 'public opinion poll' would be inconclusive in a case like this."

While a public opinion poll obviously is of some assistance in indicating public acceptance or rejection of a specific penalty, its utility cannot be very great. This is because whether or not a punishment is cruel and unusual depends, not on whether its mere mention "shocks the conscience and sense of justice of the people," but on whether people who were fully informed as to the purposes of the penalty and its liabilities would find the penalty shocking, unjust, and unacceptable.

In other words, the question with which we must deal is not whether a substantial proportion of American citizens would today, if polled, opine that capital punishment is barbarously cruel, but whether they would find it to be so in the light of all information presently available.

This is not to suggest that with respect to this test of unconstitutionality people are required to act rationally; they are not. With respect to this judgment, a violation of the Eighth Amendment is totally dependent on the predictable subjective, emotional reactions of informed citizens.

It has often been noted that American citizens know almost nothing about capital punishment. Some of the conclusions arrived at in the preceding section and the supporting evidence would be critical to an informed judgment on the morality of the death penalty: *e.g.,* that the death penalty is no more effective a deterrent than life imprisonment, that convicted murderers are rarely executed, but are usually sentenced to a term in prison; that convicted murderers usually are model prisoners, and that they almost always become law-abiding citizens upon their release from prison; that the costs of executing a capital offender exceed the costs of imprisoning him for life; that while in prison, a convict under sentence of death performs none of the useful functions that life prisoners perform; that no attempt is made in the sentencing process to ferret out likely recidivists for execution; and that the death penalty may actually stimulate criminal activity.

This information would almost surely convince the average citizen that the death penalty was unwise, but a problem arises as to whether it would convince him that the penalty was morally reprehensible. This problem arises from the fact that the public's desire for retribution, even though this is a goal that the legislature cannot constitutionally pursue as its sole justification for capital punishment, might influence the citizenry's view of the morality of capital punishment. The solution to the problem lies in the fact that no one has ever seriously advanced retribution as a legitimate goal of our society. Defenses of capital punishment are always mounted on deterrent or other similar theories. This should not be surprising. It is the people of this country who have urged in the past that prisons rehabilitate as well as isolate offenders, and it is the people who have injected a sense of purpose into our penology. I cannot believe that at this stage in our history, the American people would ever knowingly support purposeless vengeance. Thus, I believe that the great mass of citizens would conclude on the basis of the material already considered that the death penalty is immoral and therefore unconstitutional.

But, if this information needs supplementing, I believe that the following facts would serve to convince even the most hesitant of citizens to condemn death as a sanction: capital punishment is imposed discriminatorily against certain identifiable classes of people; there is evidence that innocent people have been executed before their innocence can be proved; and the death penalty wreaks havoc with our entire criminal justice system. Each of these facts is considered briefly below.

Regarding discrimination, it has been said that "[i]t is usually the poor, the illiterate, the underprivileged, the member of the minority group—the man who, because he is without means, and is defended by a court-appointed attorney—who becomes society's sacrificial lamb. . . ." Indeed, a look at the bare statistics regarding executions is enough to betray much of the discrimination. A total of 3,859 persons have been executed since 1930, of whom 1,751 were white and 2,066 were Negro. Of the executions, 3,334 were for murder; 1,664 of the executed murderers were white and 1,630 were Negro; 455 persons, including 48 whites and 405 Negroes, were executed for rape. It is immediately apparent that Negroes were executed far more often than whites in proportion to their percentage of the population. Studies indicate that while the higher rate of execution among Negroes is partially due to a higher rate of crime, there is evidence of racial discrimination. Racial or other discriminations should not be surprising. In *McGautha* v. *California,* this Court held "that committing to the untrammeled discretion of the jury the power to pronounce life or death in capital cases is [not] offensive to anything in the Constitution." This was an open invitation to discrimination.

There is also overwhelming evidence that the death penalty is employed against men and not women. Only 32 women have been executed since 1930, while 3,827 men have met a similar fate. It is difficult to understand why women have received such favored treatment since the purposes allegedly served by capital punishment seemingly are equally applicable to both sexes.

It also is evident that the burden of capital punishment falls upon the poor, the ignorant, and the underprivileged members of society. It is the poor, and the members of minority groups who are least able to voice their complaints against capital punishment. Their impotence leaves them victims of a sanction that the wealthier, better-represented, just-as-guilty person can escape. So long as the capital sanction is used only against the forlorn, easily forgotten members of society, legislators are content to maintain the status quo, because change would draw attention to the problem and concern might develop. Ignorance is perpetuated and apathy soon becomes its mate, and we have today's situation.

Just as Americans know little about who is executed and why, they are unaware of the potential dangers of executing an innocent man. Our "beyond a reasonable doubt" burden of proof in criminal cases is intended to protect the innocent, but we know it is not fool-proof. Various studies have shown that people whose innocence is later convincingly established are convicted and sentenced to death.

Proving one's innocence after a jury finding of guilt is almost impossible. While reviewing courts are willing to entertain all kinds of collateral attacks where a sentence of death is involved, they very rarely dispute the jury's interpretation of the evidence. This is, perhaps, as it should be. But, if an innocent man has been found guilty, he must then depend on the good faith of the prosecutor's office to help him establish his innocence. There is evidence, however, that prosecutors do not welcome the idea of having convictions, which they labored hard to secure, overturned, and that their cooperation is highly unlikely.

No matter how careful courts are, the possibility of perjured testimony, mistaken honest testimony, and human error remain all too real. We have no way of judging how many innocent persons have been executed but we can be certain that there were some. Whether there were many is an open question made difficult by the loss of those who were most knowledgeable about the crime for which they were convicted. Surely there will be more as long as capital punishment remains part of our penal law.

While it is difficult to ascertain with certainty the degree to which the death penalty is discriminatorily imposed or the number of innocent persons sentenced to die, there is one conclusion about the penalty that is universally accepted—*i.e.,* it "tends to distort the course of the criminal law." As Mr. Justice Frankfurter said:

> "I am strongly against capital punishment. . . . When life is at hazard in a trial, it sensationalizes the whole thing almost unwittingly; the effect on juries, the Bar, the public, the Judiciary, I regard as very bad. I think scientifically the claim of deterrence is not worth much. Whatever proof there may be in my judgment does not outweigh the social loss due to the inherent sensationalism of a trial for life."

The deleterious effects of the death penalty are also felt otherwise than at trial. For example, its very existence "inevitably sabotages a social or institutional program of reformation." In short "[t]he presence of the death penalty as the keystone of our penal system bedevils the administration of criminal justice all the way down the line and is the stumbling block in the path of general reform and of the treatment of crime and criminals."

Assuming knowledge of all the facts presently available regarding capital punishment, the average citizen would, in my opinion, find it shocking to his conscience and sense of justice. For this reason alone capital punishment cannot stand.

VII

To arrive at the conclusion that the death penalty violates the Eighth Amendment, we have had to engage in a long and tedious journey. The amount of information that we have assembled and sorted is enormous. Yet, I firmly believe that we have not deviated in the slightest from the principles with which we began.

At a time in our history when the streets of the Nation's cities inspire fear and despair, rather than pride and hope, it is difficult to maintain objectivity and concern for our fellow citizens. But, the measure of a country's greatness is its ability to retain compassion in time of crisis. No nation in the recorded history of man has a greater tradition of revering justice and fair treatment for all its citizens in times of turmoil, confusion, and tension than ours. This is a country which stands tallest in troubled times, a country that clings to fundamental principles, cherishes its constitutional heritage, and rejects simple solutions that compromise the values that lie at the roots of our democratic system.

In striking down capital punishment, this Court does not malign our system of government. On the contrary, it pays homage to it. Only in a free society could right triumph in difficult times, and could civilization record its magnificent advancement. In recognizing the humanity of our fellow beings, we pay ourselves the highest tribute. We achieve "a major milestone in the long road up from barbarism" and join the approximately 70 other jurisdictions in the world which celebrate their regard for civilization and humanity by shunning capital punishment.

I concur in the judgments of the Court.

[Appendices I, II, and III follow.]

APPENDIX I TO OPINION OF MARSHALL, J., CONCURRING

(States are listed according to year most recent action was taken)

State	Year of partial abolition	Year of complete abolition	Year of restoration	Year of reabolition
New York	1965[1]	—	—	—
Vermont	1965[2]	—	—	—
West Virginia	—	1965	—	—
Iowa	—	1872	1878	1965
Oregon	—	1914	1920	1964
Michigan	1847[3]	1963	—	—
Delaware	—	1958	1961	—
Alaska	—	1957	—	—
Hawaii	—	1957	—	—
South Dakota	—	1915	1939	—
Kansas	—	1907	1935	—
Missouri	—	1917	1919	—
Tennessee	1915[4]	—	1919	—
Washington	—	1913	1919	—
Arizona	1916[5]	—	1918	—
North Dakota	1915[6]	—	—	—
Minnesota	—	1911	—	—
Colorado	—	1897	1901	—
Maine	—	1876	1883	1887
Wisconsin	—	1853	—	—
Rhode Island	1852[7]	—	—	—

[1] Death penalty retained for persons found guilty of killing a peace officer who is acting in line of duty, and for prisoners under a life sentence who murder a guard or inmate while in confinement or while escaping from confinement.

[2] Death penalty retained for persons convicted of first-degree murder who commit a second "unrelated" murder, and for the first-degree murder of any law enforcement officer or prison employee who is in the performance of the duties of his office.

[3] Death penalty retained for treason. Partial abolition was voted in 1846, but was not put into effect until 1847.

[4] Death penalty retained for rape.

[5] Death penalty retained for treason.

[6] Death penalty retained for treason, and for first-degree murder committed by a prisoner who is serving a life sentence for first-degree murder.

[7] Death penalty retained for persons convicted of committing murder while serving a life sentence for any offense.

Based on National Prisoner Statistics No. 45, Capital Punishment 1930–1968, p. 30 (Aug. 1969).

APPENDIX II TO OPINION OF MARSHALL, J., CONCURRING

CRUDE HOMICIDE DEATH RATES, PER 100,000
POPULATION, AND NUMBER OF EXECUTIONS IN CERTAIN
AMERICAN STATES: 1920–1955

Year	Maine* Rates	N. H. Rates	N. H. Exec.	Vt. Rates	Vt. Exec.	Mass. Rates	Mass. Exec.	R. I.* Rates	Conn. Rates	Conn. Exec.
1920	1.4	1.8		2.3		2.1	1	1.8	3.9	1
1921	2.2	2.2		1.7		2.8		3.1	2.9	2
1922	1.7	1.6		1.1		2.6		2.2	2.9	1
1923	1.7	2.7		1.4		2.8	1	3.5	3.1	
1924	1.5	1.5		.6		2.7	1	2.0	3.5	
1925	2.2	1.3		.6		2.7		1.8	3.7	
1926	1.1	.9		2.2		2.0	1	3.2	2.9	1
1927	1.9	.7		.8		2.1	6	2.7	2.3	2
1928	1.6	1.3		1.4		1.9	3	2.7	2.7	
1929	1.0	1.5		1.4		1.7	6	2.3	2.6	1
1930	1.8	.9		1.4		1.8		2.0	3.2	2
1931	1.4	2.1		1.1	1	2.0	2	2.2	2.7	
1932	2.0	.2		1.1		2.1	1	1.6	2.9	
1933	3.3	2.7		1.6		2.5		1.9	1.8	
1934	1.1	1.4		1.9		2.2	4	1.8	2.4	
1935	1.4	1.0		.3		1.8	4	1.6	1.9	
1936	2.2	1.0		2.1		1.6	2	1.2	2.7	1
1937	1.4	1.8		1.8		1.9		2.3	2.0	1
1938	1.5	1.8		1.3		1.3	3	1.2	2.1	1
1939	1.2	2.3	1	.8		1.4	2	1.6	1.3	
1940	1.5	1.4		.8		1.5		1.4	1.8	2
1941	1.1	.4		2.2		1.3	1	.8	2.2	
1942	1.7	.2		.9		1.3	2	1.2	2.5	
1943	1.7	.9		.6		.9	3	1.5	1.6	2
1944	1.5	1.1		.3		1.4		.6	1.9	1
1945	.9	.7		2.9		1.5		1.1	1.5	1
1946	1.4	.8		1.7		1.4	1	1.5	1.6	3
1947	1.2	.6		1.1	1	1.6	2	1.5	1.9	
1948	1.7	1.0		.8		1.4		2.7	1.7	1
1949	1.7	1.5		.5		1.1		.5	1.8	
1950	1.5	1.3		.5		1.3		1.5	1.4	
1951	2.3	.6		.5		1.0		.9	2.0	
1952	1.0	1.5		.5		1.0		1.5	1.7	
1953	1.4	.9		.3		1.0		.6	1.5	
1954	1.7	.5		1.6	2	1.0		1.3	1.3	
1955	1.2	1.1		.5		1.2		1.7	1.3	3

* Maine has totally abolished the death penalty, and Rhode Island has severely limited its imposition. Based on ALI, *supra*, n. 98, at 25.

APPENDIX III TO OPINION OF MARSHALL, J., CONCURRING

CRUDE HOMICIDE DEATH RATES, PER 100,000
POPULATION, AND NUMBER OF EXECUTIONS IN CERTAIN
AMERICAN STATES: 1920–1955

Year	Mich.* Rate	Ohio Rate	Ex.	Ind. Rate	Ex.	Minn.* Rate	Iowa Rate	Ex.	Wis.* Rate	N.D.*	S.D. Rate	Ex.	Neb. Rate	Ex.
1920	5.5	6.9	3	4.7	2	3.1	**		1.7	**	**	***	4.2	
1921	4.7	7.9	10	6.4		4.4			2.2				4.9	
1922	4.3	7.3	12	5.7	2	3.6		3	1.8				4.5	
1923	6.1	7.8	10	6.1		2.9	2.1	2	2.2				4.1	
1924	7.1	6.9	10	7.3		3.2	2.7	1	1.8	2.1			4.4	
1925	7.4	8.1	13	6.6	1	3.8	2.7	2	2.3	2.0			4.0	
1926	10.4	8.6	7	5.8	3	2.2	2.3		2.6	1.8			2.7	
1927	8.2	8.6	8	6.3	1	2.6	2.4		2.6	1.6			3.5	
1928	7.0	8.2	7	7.0	1	2.8	2.3		2.1	1.0			3.7	
1929	8.2	8.3	5	7.0	1	2.2	2.6		2.3	1.2			3.0	
1930	6.7	9.3	8	6.4	1	3.8	3.2		3.1	3.5	1.9		3.5	
1931	6.2	9.0	10	6.5	1	2.9	2.5	1	3.6	2.0	2.3		3.6	
1932	5.7	8.1	7	6.7	2	2.9	2.9		2.8	1.2	1.6		3.7	
1933	5.1	8.2	11	5.6	3	3.5	2.9		1.9	1.2	1.7		3.2	
1934	4.2	7.7	7	7.1	4	3.4	2.3		2.4	1.6	3.0		4.4	
1935	4.2	7.1	10	4.4	2	2.6	2.0	3	1.4	2.3	2.0		3.4	
1936	4.0	6.6	6	5.2	2	2.3	1.8		1.7	2.0	1.2		2.5	
1937	4.6	5.7	1	4.7	5	1.6	2.2		2.2	1.6	.1		2.0	
1938	3.4	5.1	12	4.4	8	1.6	1.4	4	2.0	2.4	.9		1.6	
1939	3.1	4.8	10	3.8	3	1.6	1.8		1.4	1.2	2.8		2.1	
1940	3.0	4.6	2	3.3		1.2	1.3	1	1.3	1.4	2.2		1.0	
1941	3.2	4.2	4	3.1	1	1.7	1.3	1	1.4	2.3	1.0		2.1	
1942	3.2	4.6	2	3.2	1	1.7	1.2		1.6	1.4	.9		1.8	
1943	3.3	4.4	5	2.8		1.2	1.0		1.1	.6	1.4		2.4	
1944	3.3	3.9	2	2.8		1.4	1.7	1	.9	.9	1.6		1.3	
1945	3.7	4.9	7	4.0	1	1.9	1.6	1	1.6	1.0	2.0		1.2	1
1946	3.2	5.2	2	3.9	1	1.6	1.8	2	.9	1.5	1.1		2.1	
1947	3.8	4.9	5	3.8		1.2	1.9		1.4	.4	1.0	1	2.2	
1948	3.4	4.5	7	4.2		1.9	1.4		.9	.9	2.0		2.5	1
1949	3.5	4.4	15	3.2	3	1.1	.9	1	1.3	.7	2.3		1.8	
1950	3.9	4.1	4	3.6	1	1.2	1.3		1.1	.5	1.1		2.9	
1951	3.7	3.8	4	3.9	1	1.3	1.5		1.1	.5	.9		1.0	
1952	3.3	4.0	4	3.8		1.3	1.5	1	1.6	.8	2.3		1.6	1
1953	4.6	3.6	4	4.0		1.5	1.1		1.2	1.1	1.1		2.0	
1954	3.3	3.4	4	3.2		1.0	1.0		1.1	.5	1.5		2.3	
1955	3.3	3.1		3.1		1.1	1.2		1.1	.8	1.8		1.3	

* Michigan, Minnesota, and Wisconsin have completely abolished capital punishment. North Dakota has severely restricted its use.

** Iowa, North Dakota, and South Dakota were not admitted to the national death registration area until 1923, 1924, and 1930 respectively.

*** South Dakota introduced the death penalty in 1939.

Based on ALI, *supra*, n. 98, at 28. See also *id.*, at 32–34.

BOUNDS, CORRECTION COMMISSIONER, ET AL.
versus
SMITH, ET AL.

CERTIORARI TO THE UNITED STATES COURT OF APPEALS
FOR THE FOURTH CIRCUIT

Argued November 1, 1976
Decided April 27, 1977

The fundamental constitutional right of access to the courts *held* to require prison authorities to assist inmates in the preparation and filing of meaningful legal papers by providing prisoners with adequate law libraries or adequate assistance from persons trained in the law. *Younger* v. *Gilmore,* affirmed.

MARSHALL, J., delivered the opinion of the Court, in which BRENNAN, WHITE, BLACKMUN, POWELL, and STEVENS, JJ., joined. POWELL, J., filed a concurring opinion. BURGER, C. J., filed a dissenting opinion. STEWART, J., and REHNQUIST, J., filed dissenting opinions, in which BURGER, C. J., joined.

MR. JUSTICE MARSHALL delivered the opinion of the Court.
The issue in this case is whether States must protect the right of prisoners to access to the courts by providing them with law libraries or alternative sources of legal knowledge. In *Younger* v. *Gilmore,* (1971), we held that such services are constitutionally mandated. Petitioners, officials of the State of North Carolina, ask us to overrule that recent case, but for reasons explained below, we decline the invitation and reaffirm our previous decision.

I

Respondents are inmates incarcerated in correctional facilities of the Division of Prisons of the North Carolina Department of Correction. They filed three separate actions under 42 U.S.C. § 1983, all eventually consolidated in the District Court for the Eastern District of North Carolina. Respondents alleged, in pertinent part, that they were denied access to the courts in violation of their Fourteenth Amendment rights by the State's failure to provide legal research facilities.

The District Court granted respondents' motion for summary judgment on this claim, finding that the sole prison library in the State was "severely inadequate" and that there was no other legal assistance available to inmates. It held on the basis of *Younger* v. *Gilmore* that respondents' rights to access to the courts and equal protection of the laws had been violated because there was "no indication of any assistance at the initial stage of preparation of writs and petitions." The court recognized, however, that determining the "appropriate relief to be ordered . . . presents a difficult problem," in view of North Carolina's decentralized prison system. Rather than attempting "to dictate precisely what course the State should follow," the court "charge[d] the Department of Correction with the task of devising a Constitutionally sound program" to assure inmate access to the courts. It left to the State the choice of what alternative would "most easily and economically" fulfill this duty, suggesting that a program to make available lawyers, law students, or public defenders might serve the purpose at least as well as the provision of law libraries.

The State responded by proposing the establishment of seven libraries in institutions located across the State chosen so as to serve best all prison units. In addition, the State planned to set up smaller libraries in the Central Prison segregation unit and the Women's Prison. Under the plan, inmates desiring to use a library would request appointments. They would be given transportation and housing, if necessary, for a full day's library work. In addition to its collection of lawbooks, each library would stock legal forms and writing paper and have typewriters and use of copying machines. The State proposed to train inmates as research assistants and typists to aid fellow prisoners. It was estimated that ultimately some 350 inmates per week could use the libraries, although inmates not facing court deadlines might have to wait three or four weeks for their turn at a library. Respondents protested that the plan was totally inadequate and sought establishment of a library at every prison.

The District Court rejected respondents' objections, finding the State's plan "both economically feasible and practicable," and one that, fairly and efficiently run, would "insure each inmate the time to prepare his petitions." Further briefing was ordered on whether the State was required to provide independent legal advisors for inmates in addition to the library facilities.

In its final decision, the District Court held that petitioners were not constitutionally required to provide legal assistance as well as libraries. It found that the library plan was sufficient to give inmates reasonable access to the courts and that our decision in *Ross* v. *Moffitt* (1974), while not directly in point, supported the State's claim that it need not furnish attorneys to bring habeas corpus and civil rights actions for prisoners.

After the District Court approved the library plan, the State submitted an application to the Federal Law Enforcement Assistance Administration (LEAA) for a grant to cover 90% of the cost of setting up the libraries and training a librarian and inmate clerks. The State represented to LEAA that the library project would benefit all inmates in the State by giving them "meaningful and effective access to the court[s]. . . . [T]he ultimate result . . . should be a diminution in the number of groundless petitions and complaints filed. . . . The inmate himself will be able to determine to a greater extent whether or not his rights have been violated" and judicial evaluation of the petitions will be facilitated.

Both sides appealed from those portions of the District Court orders adverse to them. The Court of Appeals for the Fourth Circuit affirmed in all respects save one. It found that the library plan denied women prisoners the same access rights as men to research facilities. Since there was no justification for this discrimination, the Court of Appeals ordered it eliminated. The State petitioned for review and we granted certiorari. (1976) We affirm.

II

A. It is now established beyond doubt that prisoners have a constitutional right of access to the courts. This Court recognized that right more than 35 years ago when it struck down a regulation prohibiting state prisoners from filing petitions for habeas corpus unless they were found " 'properly drawn' " by the " 'legal investigator' " for the parole board. *Ex parte Hull* (1941). We held this violated the principle that "the state and its officers may not abridge or impair petitioner's right to apply to a federal court for a writ of habeas corpus." See also *Cochran* v. *Kansas* (1942).

More recent decisions have struck down restrictions and required remedial measures to ensure that inmate access to the courts is adequate, effective, and meaningful. Thus, in order to prevent "effectively foreclosed access," indigent prisoners must be allowed to file appeals and habeas corpus petitions without payment of docket fees. *Burns* v. *Ohio* (1959); *Smith* v. *Bennett* (1961). Because we recognized that "adequate and effective appellate review" is impossible without a trial transcript or adequate substitute, we held that States must provide trial records to inmates unable to buy them. *Griffin* v. *Illinois* (1956). Similarly, counsel must be appointed to give indigent inmates "a meaningful appeal" from their convictions. *Douglas* v. *California* (1963).

Essentially the same standards of access were applied in *Johnson* v. *Avery* (1969), which struck down a regulation prohibiting prisoners from assisting each other with habeas corpus applications and other legal matters. Since inmates had no alternative form of legal assistance available to them, we reasoned that this ban on jailhouse lawyers effectively prevented prisoners who were "unable themselves, with reasonable adequacy, to prepare their petitions," from challenging the legality of their confinements. *Johnson* was unanimously extended to cover assistance in civil rights actions in *Wolff* v. *McDonnell* (1974). And even as it rejected a claim that indigent defendants have a constitutional right to appointed counsel for discretionary appeals, the Court reaffirmed that States must "assure the indigent defendant an adequate opportunity to present his claims fairly." *Ross* v. *Moffitt.* "[M]eaningful access" to the courts is the touchstone.

Petitioners contend, however, that this constitutional duty merely obliges States to allow inmate "writ writers" to function. They argue that under *Johnson* v. *Avery, supra,* as long as inmate communications on legal problems are not restricted, there is no further obligation to expend state funds to implement affirmatively the right of access. This argument misreads the cases.

In *Johnson* and *Wolff* v. *McDonnell, supra,* the issue was whether the access rights of ignorant and illiterate inmates were violated without adequate justification. Since these inmates were unable to present their own claims in writing to the courts, we held that their "constitutional right to help," *Johnson* v. *Avery* (WHITE, J., dissenting), required at least allowing assistance from their literate fellows. But in so holding, we did not attempt to set forth the full breadth of the right of access. In *McDonnell,* for example, there was already an adequate law library in the prison. The case was thus decided against a backdrop of availability of legal information to those inmates capable of using it. And in *Johnson,* although the petitioner originally requested lawbooks, the Court did not reach the question, as it invalidated the regulation because of its effect on illiterate inmates. Neither case considered the question we face today and neither is inconsistent with requiring additional measures to assure meaningful access to inmates able to present their own cases.

Moreover, our decisions have consistently required States to shoulder affirmative obligations to assure all prisoners meaningful access to the courts. It is indisputable that indigent inmates must be provided at state expense with paper and pen to draft legal documents, with notarial services to authenticate them, and with stamps to mail them. States must forgo collection of docket fees otherwise payable to the treasury and expend funds for transcripts. State expenditures are necessary to pay lawyers for indigent defendants at trial, *Gideon* v. *Wainwright* (1963); *Argersinger* v. *Hamlin* (1972), and in appeals as of right, *Douglas* v. *California.* This is not to say that economic factors may not be considered, for example, in choosing the methods used to provide meaningful access. But the cost of protecting a constitutional right cannot justify its total denial. Thus, neither the availability of jailhouse lawyers nor the necessity for affirmative state action is dispositive of respondents' claims. The inquiry is rather whether law libraries or other forms of legal assistance are needed to give prisoners a reasonably adequate opportunity to present claimed violations of fundamental constitutional rights to the courts.

B. Although it is essentially true, as petitioners argue, that a habeas corpus petition or civil rights complaint need only set forth facts giving rise to the cause of action, but see, Fed. Rules Civ. Proc. 8 (a)(1), (3), it hardly follows that a law library or other legal assistance is not essential to frame such documents. It would verge on incompetence for a lawyer to file an initial pleading without researching such issues as jurisdiction, venue, standing, exhaustion of remedies, proper parties plaintiff and defendant, and types of relief available. Most importantly, of course, a lawyer must know what the law is in order to determine whether a colorable claim exists, and if so, what facts are necessary to state a cause of action.

If a lawyer must perform such preliminary research, it is no less vital for a *pro se* prisoner. Indeed, despite the "less stringent standards" by which a *pro se* pleading is judged, *Haines* v. *Kerner* (1972), it is often more important that a prisoner complaint set forth a nonfrivolous claim meeting all procedural prerequisites, since the court may pass on the complaint's sufficiency before allowing filing *in forma pauperis* and may dismiss the case if it is deemed frivolous. See 28 U.S.C. § 1915. Moreover, if the State files a response to a *pro se* pleading, it will undoubtedly contain seemingly authoritative citations. Without a library, an inmate will be unable to rebut the State's argument. It is not enough to answer that the court will evaluate the facts pleaded in light of the relevant law. Even the most dedicated trial judges are bound to overlook meritorious cases without the benefit of an adversary presentation. *Gardner* v. *California* (1969). In fact, one of the consolidated cases here was initially dismissed by the same judge who later ruled for respondents, possibly because *Younger* v. *Gilmore* was not cited.

We reject the State's claim that inmates are "ill-equipped to use" "the tools of the trade of the legal profession," making libraries useless in assuring meaningful access. In the first place, the claim is inconsistent with the State's representations on its LEAA grant application, and with its argument that access is adequately protected by allowing inmates to help each other with legal problems. More importantly, this Court's experience indicates that *pro se* petitioners are capable of using lawbooks to file cases raising claims that are serious and legitimate even if ultimately unsuccessful. Finally, we note that if petitioners had any doubts about the efficacy of libraries, the District Court's initial decision left them free to choose another means of assuring access.

It is also argued that libraries or other forms of legal assistance are unnecessary to assure meaningful access in light of the Court's decision in *Ross* v. *Moffitt*. That case held that the right of prisoners to "an adequate opportunity to present [their] claims fairly," did not require appointment of counsel to file petitions for discretionary review in state courts or in this Court. *Moffitt*'s rationale, however, supports the result we reach here. The decision in *Moffitt* noted that a court addressing a discretionary review petition is not primarily concerned with the correctness of the judgment below. Rather, review is generally granted only if a case raises an issue of significant public interest or jurisprudential importance or conflicts with controlling precedent. *Moffitt* held that *pro se* applicants can present their claims adequately for appellate courts to decide whether these criteria are met because they have already had counsel for their initial appeals as of right. They are thus likely to have appellate briefs previously written on their behalf, trial transcripts, and often intermediate appellate court opinions to use in preparing petitions for further review.

By contrast in this case, we are concerned in large part with original actions seeking new trials, release from confinement, or vindication of fundamental civil rights. Rather than presenting claims that have been passed on by two courts, they frequently raise heretofore unlitigated issues. As this Court has "constantly emphasized," habeas corpus and civil rights actions are of "fundamental importance . . . in our constitutional scheme" because they directly protect our most valued rights. *Johnson* v. *Avery, Wolff* v. *McDonnell.* While applications for discretionary review need only apprise an appellate court of a case's possible relevance to the development of the law, the prisoner petitions here are the first line of defense against constitutional violations. The need for new legal research or advice to make a meaningful initial presentation to a trial court in such a case is far greater than is required to file an adequate petition for discretionary review.

We hold, therefore, that the fundamental constitutional right of access to the courts requires prison authorities to assist inmates in the preparation and filing of meaningful legal papers by providing prisoners with adequate law libraries or adequate assistance from persons trained in the law.

C. Our holding today is, of course, a reaffirmation of the result reached in *Younger* v. *Gilmore.* While *Gilmore* is not a necessary element in the preceding analysis, its precedential weight strongly reinforces our decision. The substantive question presented in *Gilmore* was: "Does a state have an affirmative federal constitutional duty to furnish prison inmates with extensive law libraries or, alternatively, to provide inmates with professional or quasi-professional legal assistance?" This Court explicitly decided that question when it affirmed the judgment of the District Court in reliance on *Johnson* v. *Avery.* Cf. this Court's Rule 15 (c). The affirmative answer was given unanimously after full briefing and oral argument. *Gilmore* has been relied upon without question in our subsequent decisions. *Cruz* v. *Hauck* (1971) (vacating and remanding for reconsideration in light of *Gilmore* a decision that legal materials need not be furnished to county jail inmates); *Cruz* v. *Beto* (1972) (*Gilmore* cited approvingly in support of inmates' right of access to the courts); *Chaffin* v. *Stynchcombe* (1973) (*Gilmore* cited approvingly as a decision "removing roadblocks and disincentives to appeal"). Most recently, in *Wolff* v. *McDonnell,* despite differences over other issues in the case, the Court unanimously reaffirmed that *Gilmore* requires prison officials "to provide indigent inmates with access to a reasonably adequate law library for preparation of legal actions."

Experience under the *Gilmore* decision suggests no reason to depart from it. Most States and the Federal Government have made impressive efforts to fulfill *Gilmore*'s mandate by establishing law libraries, prison legal-assistance programs, or combinations of both. Correctional administrators have supported the programs and acknowledged their value. Resources and support including substantial funding from LEAA have come from many national organizations.

It should be noted that while adequate law libraries are one constitutionally acceptable method to assure meaningful access to the courts, our decision here, as in *Gilmore,* does not foreclose alternative means to achieve that goal. Nearly half the States and the District of Columbia provide some degree of professional or quasi-professional legal assistance to prisoners. Such programs take many imaginative forms and may have a number of advantages over libraries alone. Among the alternatives are the training of inmates as paralegal assistants to work under lawyers' supervision, the use of paraprofessionals and law students, either as volunteers or in formal clinical programs, the organization of volunteer attorneys through bar associations or other groups, the hiring of lawyers on a part-time consultant basis, and the use of full-time staff attorneys, working either in new prison legal assistance organizations or as part of public defender or legal services offices. Legal services plans not only result in more efficient and skillful handling of prisoner cases, but also avoid the disciplinary problems associated with writ writers, see *Johnson* v. *Avery, Procunier* v. *Martinez* (1974). Independent legal advisors can mediate or resolve administratively many prisoner complaints that would otherwise burden the courts, and can convince inmates that other grievances against the prison or the legal system are ill-founded, thereby facilitating rehabilitation by assuring the inmate that he has not been treated unfairly. It has been estimated that as few as 500 full-time lawyers would be needed to serve the legal needs of the entire national prison population. Nevertheless, a legal access program need not include any particular element we have discussed, and we encourage local experimentation. Any plan, however, must be evaluated as a whole to ascertain its compliance with constitutional standards.

III

Finally, petitioners urge us to reverse the decision below because federal courts should not "sit as co-administrators of state prisons," and because the District Court "exceeded its powers when it puts [*sic*] itself in the place of the [prison] administrators." While we have recognized that judicial restraint is often appropriate in prisoners' rights cases, we have also repeatedly held that this policy "cannot encompass any failure to take cognizance of valid constitutional claims." *Procunier* v. *Martinez.*

Petitioners' hyperbolic claim is particularly inappropriate in this case, for the courts below scrupulously respected the limits on their role. The District Court initially held only that petitioners had violated the "fundamental constitutional guarantee," of access to the courts. It did not thereupon thrust itself into prison administration. Rather, it ordered petitioners themselves to devise a remedy for the violation, strongly suggesting that it would prefer a plan providing trained legal advisors. Petitioners chose to establish law libraries, however, and their plan was approved with only minimal changes over the strong objections of respondents. Prison administrators thus exercised wide discretion within the bounds of constitutional requirements in this case.

The judgment is

Affirmed.

GLEN BURTON AKE, PETITIONER
versus
OKLAHOMA

Argued Nov. 7, 1984
Decided Feb. 26, 1985

Defendant was convicted before the District Court, Canadian County, James D. Bednar, J., of two counts of murder in the first degree and two counts of shooting with intent to kill, and he appealed. The Oklahoma Court of Criminal Appeals, affirmed, and certiorari was granted. The Supreme Court, Justice Marshall, held that when a defendant has made a preliminary showing that his sanity at the time of the offense is likely to be a significant factor at trial, due process requires that a State provide access to a psychiatrist's assistance on this issue, if a defendant cannot otherwise afford one.

Reversed and remanded.

Justice MARSHALL delivered the opinion of the Court.

The issue in this case is whether the Constitution requires that an indigent defendant have access to the psychiatric examination and assistance necessary to prepare an effective defense based on his mental condition, when his sanity at the time of the offense is seriously in question.

Late in 1979, Glen Burton Ake was arrested and charged with murdering a couple and wounding their two children. He was arraigned in the District Court for Canadian County, Okla., in February 1980. His behavior at arraignment, and in other prearraignment incidents at the jail, was so bizarre that the trial judge, *sua sponte,* ordered him to be examined by a psychiatrist "for the purpose of advising with the Court as to his impressions of whether the Defendant may need an extended period of mental observation." The examining psychiatrist reported: "At times Ake appears to be frankly delusional. . . . He claims to be the 'sword of vengeance' of the Lord and that he will sit at the left hand

of God in heaven." He diagnosed Ake as a probable paranoid schizo-
phrenic and recommended a prolonged psychiatric evaluation to determine whether Ake was competent to stand trial.

In March, Ake was committed to a state hospital to be examined
with respect to his "present sanity," *i.e.*, his competency to stand trial.
On April 10, less than six months after the incidents for which Ake was
indicted, the chief forensic psychiatrist at the state hospital informed
the Court that Ake was not competent to stand trial. The Court then
held a competency hearing, at which a psychiatrist testified:

> "Ake is a psychotic . . . his psychiatric diagnosis was that of para-
> noid schizophrenia—chronic, with exacerbation, that is with cur-
> rent upset, and that in addition . . . he is dangerous. . . . Be-
> cause of the severity of his mental illness and because of the
> intensities of his rage, his poor control, his delusions, he requires a
> maximum security facility within—I believe—the State Psychiatric
> Hospital system."

The Court found Ake to be a "mentally ill person in need of care
and treatment" and incompetent to stand trial, and ordered him committed to the state mental hospital.

Six weeks later, the chief forensic psychiatrist informed the Court
that Ake had become competent to stand trial. At the time, Ake was
receiving 200 milligrams of Thorazine, an antipsychotic drug, three
times daily, and the psychiatrist indicated that, if Ake continued to
receive that dosage, his condition would remain stable. The State then
resumed proceedings against Ake.

At a pretrial conference in June, Ake's attorney informed the Court
that his client would raise an insanity defense. To enable him to prepare and present such a defense adequately, the attorney stated, a
psychiatrist would have to examine Ake with respect to his mental
condition at the time of the offense. During Ake's 3-month stay at the
state hospital, no inquiry had been made into his sanity at the time of
the offense, and, as an indigent, Ake could not afford to pay for a
psychiatrist. Counsel asked the Court either to arrange to have a psychiatrist perform the examination, or to provide funds to allow the
defense to arrange one. The trial judge rejected counsel's argument
that the Federal Constitution requires that an indigent defendant receive the assistance of a psychiatrist when that assistance is necessary to
the defense, and he denied the motion for a psychiatric evaluation at

state expense on the basis of this Court's decision in *United States ex rel. Smith* v. *Baldi* (1953).

Ake was tried for two counts of murder in the first degree, a crime punishable by death in Oklahoma, and for two counts of shooting with intent to kill. At the guild phase of trial, his sole defense was insanity. Although defense counsel called to the stand and questioned each of the psychiatrists who had examined Ake at the state hospital, none testified about his mental state at the time of the offense because none had examined him on that point. The prosecution, in turn, asked each of these psychiatrists whether he had performed or seen the results of any examination diagnosing Ake's mental state at the time of the offense, and each doctor replied that he had not. *As a result, there was no expert testimony for either side on Ake's sanity at the time of the offense.* The jurors were then instructed that Ake could be found not guilty by reason of insanity if he did not have the ability to distinguish right from wrong at the time of the alleged offense. They were further told that Ake was to be presumed sane at the time of the crime unless *he* presented evidence sufficient to raise a reasonable doubt about his sanity at that time. If he raised such a doubt in their minds, the jurors were informed, the burden of proof shifted to the State to prove sanity beyond a reasonable doubt. The jury rejected Ake's insanity defense and returned a verdict of guilty on all counts.

At the sentencing proceeding, the State asked for the death penalty. No new evidence was presented. The prosecutor relied significantly on the testimony of the state psychiatrists who had examined Ake, and who had testified at the guilt phase that Ake was dangerous to society, to establish the likelihood of his future dangerous behavior. Ake had no expert witness to rebut this testimony or to introduce on his behalf evidence in mitigation of his punishment. The jury sentenced Ake to death on each of the two murder counts, and to 500 years' imprisonment on each of the two counts of shooting with intent to kill.

On appeal to the Oklahoma Court of Criminal Appeals, Ake argued that, as an indigent defendant, he should have been provided the services of a court-appointed psychiatrist. The Court rejected this argument, observing: "We have held numerous times that, the unique nature of capital cases notwithstanding, the State does not have the responsibility of providing such services to indigents charged with capital crimes." Finding no error in Ake's other claims, the Court affirmed the convictions and sentences. We granted certiorari (1984).

We hold that when a defendant has made a preliminary showing that his sanity at the time of the offense is likely to be a significant factor at trial, the Constitution requires that a State provide access to a psychiatrist's assistance on this issue if the defendant cannot otherwise afford one. Accordingly, we reverse.

I

Initially, we must address our jurisdiction to review this case. After ruling on the merits of Ake's claim, the Oklahoma court observed that in his motion for a new trial Ake had not repeated his request for a psychiatrist and that the claim was thereby waived. The Court cited *Hawkins* v. *State* (1977), for this proposition. The State argued in its brief to this Court that the Court's holding on this issue therefore rested on an adequate and independent state ground and ought not be reviewed. Despite the Court's state-law ruling, we conclude that the state court's judgment does not rest on an independent state ground and that our jurisdiction is therefore properly exercised.

The Oklahoma waiver rule does not apply to fundamental trial error. See *Hawkins* v. *State.* Under Oklahoma law, and as the State conceded at oral argument, federal constitutional errors are "fundamental." Thus, the State has made application of the procedural bar depend on an antecedent ruling on federal law, that is, on the determination of whether federal constitutional error has been committed. Before applying the waiver doctrine to a constitutional question, the state court must rule, either explicitly or implicitly, on the merits of the constitutional question.

As we have indicated in the past, when resolution of the state procedural law question depends on a federal constitutional ruling, the state-law prong of the Court's holding is not independent of federal law, and our jurisdiction is not precluded. See *Herb* v. *Pitcairn* (1945) ("We are not permitted to render an advisory opinion, and if the same judgment would be rendered by the state court after we corrected its views of Federal laws, our review could amount to nothing more than an advisory opinion"); *Enterprise Irrigation District* v. *Farmers Mutual Canal Co.* (1917). ("But where the non-Federal ground is so interwoven with the other as not to be an independent matter, or is not of sufficient breadth to sustain the judgment without any decision of the other, our jurisdiction is plain.") In such a case, the federal-law holding is integral to the state court's disposition of the matter, and our ruling on the issue is no respect advisory. In this case, the additional holding of the state court —that the constitutional challenge presented here was waived—depends on the Court's federal-law ruling and consequently does not present an independent state ground for the decision rendered. We therefore turn to a consideration of the merits of Ake's claim.

II

This Court has long recognized that when a State brings its judicial power to bear on an indigent defendant in a criminal proceeding, it must take steps to assure that the defendant has a fair opportunity to present his defense. This elementary principle, grounded in significant part on the Fourteenth Amendment's due process guarantee of fundamental fairness, derives from the belief that justice cannot be equal where, simply as a result of his poverty, a defendant is denied the opportunity to participate meaningfully in a judicial proceeding in which his liberty is at stake. In recognition of this right, this Court held almost 30 years ago that once a State offers to criminal defendants the opportunity to appeal their cases, it must provide a trial transcript, to an indigent defendant if the transcript is necessary to a decision on the merits of the appeal. *Griffin* v. *Illinois* (1956). Since then, this Court has held that an indigent defendant may not be required to pay a fee before filing a notice of appeal of his conviction, *Burns* v. *Ohio* (1959), that an indigent defendant is entitled to the assistance of counsel at trial, *Gideon* v. *Wainwright* (1963), and on his first direct appeal as of right, *Douglas* v. *California* (1963), and that such assistance must be effective. See *Evitts* v. *Lucey* (1985). Indeed, in *Little* v. *Streater* (1981), we extended this principle of meaningful participation to a "quasi-criminal" proceeding and held that, in a paternity action, the State cannot deny the putative father blood grouping tests, if he cannot otherwise afford them.

Meaningful access to justice has been the consistent theme of these cases. We recognized long ago that mere access to the courthouse doors does not by itself assure a proper functioning of the adversary process, and that a criminal trial is fundamentally unfair if the State proceeds against an indigent defendant without making certain that he has access to the raw materials integral to the building of an effective defense. Thus, while the Court has not held that a State must purchase for the indigent defendant all the assistance that his wealthier counterpart might buy, see *Ross* v. *Moffitt* (1974), it has often reaffirmed that fundamental fairness entitles indigent defendants to "an adequate opportunity to present their claims fairly within the adversary system." To implement this principle, we have focused on identifying the "basic tools of an adequate defense or appeal," *Britt* v. *North Carolina* (1971), and we have required that such tools be provided to those defendants who cannot afford to pay for them.

To say that these basic tools must be provided is, of course, merely to begin our inquiry. In this case we must decide whether, and under what conditions, the participation of a psychiatrist is important enough to preparation of a defense to require the State to provide an indigent defendant with access to competent psychiatric assistance in preparing the defense. Three factors are relevant to this determination. The first is the private interest that will be affected by the action of the State. The second is the governmental interest that will be affected if the safeguard is to be provided. The third is the probable value of the additional or substitute procedural safeguards that are sought, and the risk of an erroneous deprivation of the affected interest if those safeguards are not provided. See *Little* v. *Streater.* We turn, then, to apply this standard to the issue before us.

A

The private interest in the accuracy of a criminal proceeding that places an individual's life or liberty at risk is almost uniquely compelling. Indeed, the host of safeguards fashioned by this Court over the years to diminish the risk of erroneous conviction stands as a testament to that concern. The interest of the individual in the outcome of the State's effort to overcome the presumption of innocence is obvious and weighs heavily in our analysis.

We consider, next, the interest of the State. Oklahoma asserts that to provide Ake with psychiatric assistance on the record before us would result in a staggering burden to the State. We are unpersuaded by this assertion. Many States, as well as the Federal Government, currently make psychiatric assistance available to indigent defendants, and they have not found the financial burden so great as to preclude this assistance. This is especially so when the obligation of the State is limited to provision of one competent psychiatrist, as it is in many States, and as we limit the right we recognize today. At the same time, it is difficult to identify any interest of the State, other than that in its economy, that weighs against recognition of this right. The State's interest in prevailing at trial—unlike that of a private litigant—is necessarily tempered by in its interest in the fair and accurate adjudication of criminal cases. Thus, also unlike a private litigant a State may not legitimately assert an interest in maintenance of a strategic advantage over the defense, if the result of that advantage is to cast a pall on the accuracy of the verdict obtained. We therefore conclude that the governmental interest in denying Ake the assistance of a psychiatrist is not substantial, in light of the compelling interest of both the State and the individual in accurate dispositions.

Last, we inquire into the probable value of the psychiatric assistance sought, and the risk of error in the proceeding if such assistance is not offered. We begin by considering the pivotal role that psychiatry has come to play in criminal proceedings. More than 40 States, as well as the Federal Government, have decided either through legislation or judicial decision that indigent defendants are entitled, under certain circumstances, to the assistance of a psychiatrist's expertise. For example, in subsection (e) of the Criminal Justice Act, 18 U.S.C. § 3006A, Congress has provided that indigent defendants shall receive the assistance of all experts "necessary for an adequate defense." Numerous state statutes guarantee reimbursement for expert services under a like standard. And in many States that have not assured access to psychiatrists through the legislative process, state courts have interpreted the State or Federal Constitution to require that psychiatric assistance be provided to indigent defendants when necessary for an adequate defense, or when insanity is at issue.

These statutes and court decisions reflect a reality that we recognize today, namely, that when the State has made the defendant's mental condition relevant to his criminal culpability and to the punishment he might suffer, the assistance of a psychiatrist may well be crucial to the defendant's ability to marshal his defense. In this role, psychiatrists gather facts, through professional examination, interviews, and elsewhere, that they will share with the judge or jury; they analyze the information gathered and from it draw plausible conclusions about the defendant's mental condition, and about the effects of any disorder on behavior; and they offer opinions about how the defendant's mental condition might have affected his behavior at the time in question. They know the probative questions to ask of the opposing party's psychiatrists and how to interpret their answers. Unlike lay witnesses, who can merely describe symptoms they believe might be relevant to the defendant's mental state, psychiatrists can identify the "elusive and often deceptive" symptoms of insanity, *Solesbee* v. *Balkcom* (1950), and tell the jury why their observations are relevant. Further, where permitted by evidentiary rules, psychiatrists can translate a medical diagnosis into language that will assist the trier of fact, and therefore offer evidence in a form that has meaning for the task at hand. Through this process of investigation, interpretation, and testimony, psychiatrists ideally assist lay jurors, who generally have no training in psychiatric matters, to make a sensible and educated determination about the mental condition of the defendant at the time of the offense.

Psychiatry is not, however, an exact science, and psychiatrists disagree widely and frequently on what constitutes mental illness, on the appropriate diagnosis to be attached to given behavior and symptoms, on cure and treatment, and on likelihood of future dangerousness. Perhaps because there often is no single, accurate psychiatric conclusion on legal insanity on a given case, juries remain the primary factfinders on this issue, and they must resolve differences in opinion within the psychiatric profession on the basis of the evidence offered by each party. When jurors make this determination about issues that inevitably are complex and foreign, the testimony of psychiatrists can be crucial and "a virtual necessity if an insanity plea is to have any chance of success." By organizing a defendant's mental history, examination results and behavior, and other information, interpreting it in light of their expertise, and then laying out their investigative and analytic process to the jury, the psychiatrists for each party enable the jury to make its most accurate determination of the truth on the issue before them. It is for this reason that States rely on psychiatrists as examiners, consultants, and witnesses, and that private individuals do as well, when they can afford to do so. In so saying, we neither approve nor disapprove the widespread reliance on psychiatrists but instead recognize the unfairness of a contrary holding in light of the evolving practice.

The foregoing leads inexorably to the conclusion that, without the assistance of a psychiatrist to conduct a professional examination on issues relevant to the defense, to help determine whether the insanity defense is viable, to present testimony, and to assist in preparing the cross-examination of a State's psychiatric witnesses, the risk of an inaccurate resolution of sanity issues is extremely high. With such assistance, the defendant is fairly able to present at least enough information to the jury, in a meaningful manner, as to permit it to make a sensible determination.

A defendant's mental condition is not necessarily at issue in every criminal proceeding, however, and it is unlikely that psychiatric assistance of the kind we have described would be of probable value in cases where it is not. The risk of error from denial of such assistance, as well as its probable value, is most predictably at its height when the defendant's mental condition is seriously in question. When the defendant is able to make an (*ex parte*) threshold showing to the trial court that his sanity is likely to be a significant factor in his defense, the need for the assistance of a psychiatrist is readily apparent. It is in such cases that a defense may be devastated by the absence of a psychiatric examination and testimony; with such assistance, the defendant might have a reasonable chance of success. In such a circumstance, where the potential accuracy of the jury's determination is so dramatically enhanced, and where the interest of the individual and the State in an accurate proceeding are substantial, the State's interest in its fisc must yield.

We therefore hold that when a defendant demonstrates to the trial judge that his sanity at the time of the offense is to be a significant factor at trial, the State must, at a minimum, assure the defendant access to a competent psychiatrist who will conduct an appropriate examination and assist in evaluation, preparation, and presentation of the defense. This is not to say, of course, that the indigent defendant has a constitutional right to choose a psychiatrist of his personal liking or to receive funds to hire his own. Our concern is that the indigent defendant have access to a competent psychiatrist for the purpose we have discussed, and as in the case of the provision of counsel we leave to the State the decision on how to implement this right.

B

Ake also was denied the means of presenting evidence to rebut the State's evidence of his future dangerousness. The foregoing discussion compels a similar conclusion in the context of a capital sentencing proceeding, when the State presents psychiatric evidence of the defendant's future dangerousness. We have repeatedly recognized the defendant's compelling interest in fair adjudication at the sentencing phase of a capital case. The State, too, has a profound interest in assuring that its ultimate sanction is not erroneously imposed, and we do not see why monetary considerations should be more persuasive in this context than at trial. The variable on which we must focus is, therefore, the probable value that the assistance of a psychiatrist will have in this area, and the risk attendant on its absence.

This Court has upheld the practice in many States of placing before the jury psychiatric testimony on the question of future dangerousness, see *Barefoot* v. *Estelle* (1983), at least where the defendant has had access to an expert of his own. In so holding, the Court relied, in part, on the assumption that the factfinder would have before it both the views of the prosecutor's psychiatrists and the "opposing views of the defendant's doctors" and would therefore be competent to "uncover, recognize, and take due account of . . . shortcomings" in predictions on this point. Without a psychiatrist's assistance, the defendant cannot offer a well-informed expert's opposing view, and thereby loses a significant opportunity to raise in the jurors' minds questions about the State's proof of an aggravating factor. In such a circumstance, where the consequence of error is so great, the relevance of responsive psychiatric testimony so evident, and the burden on the State so slim, due process requires access to a psychiatric examination on relevant issues, to the testimony of the psychiatrist, and to assistance in preparation at the sentencing phase.

C

The trial court in this case believed that our decision in *United States ex rel. Smith* v. *Baldi* (1953) absolved it completely of the obligation to provide access to a psychiatrist. For two reasons, we disagree. First, neither *Smith,* nor *McGarty* v. *O'Brien,* to which the majority cited in *Smith,* even suggested that the Constitution does not require any psychiatric examination or assistance whatsoever. Quite to the contrary, the record in *Smith* demonstrated that neutral psychiatrists in fact had examined the defendant as to his sanity and had testified on that subject at trial, and it was on that basis that the Court found no additional assistance was necessary. Similarly, in *McGarty,* the defendant had been examined by two psychiatrists who were not beholden to the prosecution. We therefore reject the State's contention that *Smith* supports the broad proposition that "[t]here is presently no constitutional right to have a psychiatric examination of a defendant's sanity at the time of the offense." At most it supports the proposition that there is no constitutional right to more psychiatric assistance than the defendant in *Smith* had received.

In any event, our disagreement with the State's reliance on *Smith* is more fundamental. That case was decided at a time when indigent defendants in state courts had no constitutional rights to even the presence of counsel. Our recognition since then of elemental constitutional rights, each of which has enhanced the ability of an indigent defendant to attain a fair hearing, has signaled our increased commitment to assuring meaningful access to the judicial process. Also, neither trial practice nor legislative treatment of the role of insanity in the criminal process sits paralyzed simply because this Court has once addressed them, and we would surely be remiss to ignore the extraordinarily enhanced role of psychiatry in criminal law today. Shifts in all these areas since the time of *Smith* convince us that the opinion in that case was addressed to altogether different variables, and that we are not limited by it in considering whether fundamental fairness requires a different result.

III

We turn now to apply these standards to the facts of this case. On the record before us, it is clear that Ake's mental state at the time of the offense was a substantial factor in his defense, and that the trial court was on notice of that fact when the request for a court-appointed psychiatrist was made. For one, Ake's sole defense was that of insanity. Second, Ake's behavior at arraignment, just four months after the offense, was so bizarre as to prompt the trial judge, *(sua sponte),* to have him examined for competency. Third, a state psychiatrist shortly thereafter found Ake to be incompetent to stand trial, and suggested that he be committed. Fourth, when he was found to be competent six weeks later, it was only on the condition that he be sedated with large doses of Thorazine three times a day, during the trial. Fifth, the psychiatrists who examined Ake for competency described to the trial court the severity of Ake's mental illness less than six months after the offense in question, and suggested that this mental illness might have begun many years earlier. Finally, Oklahoma recognizes a defense of insanity, under which the initial burden of producing evidence falls on the defendant. Taken together, these factors make clear that the question of Ake's sanity was likely to be a significant factor in his defense.

In addition, Ake's future dangerousness was a significant factor at the sentencing phase. The state psychiatrist who treated Ake at the state mental hospital testified at the guilt phase that, because of his mental illness, Ake posed a threat of continuing criminal violence. This testimony raised the issue of Ake's future dangerousness, which is an aggravating factor under Oklahoma's capital sentencing scheme, Okla. Stat., Tit. 21, and on which the prosecutor relied at sentencing. We therefore conclude that Ake also was entitled to the assistance of a psychiatrist on this issue and that the denial of that assistance deprived him of due process.

Accordingly, we reverse and remand for a new trial.

It is so ordered.

VILLAGE OF BELLE TERRE ET AL., APPELLANTS,
versus
BRUCE BORAAS ET AL.

No. 73-191

Argued February 19, 20, 1974
Decided April 1, 1974

A New York village ordinance restricted land use to one-family dwellings, defining the word "family" to mean one or more persons related by blood, adoption, or marriage, or not more than two unrelated persons, living and cooking together as a single housekeeping unit and expressly excluding from the term lodging, boarding, fraternity, or multiple-dwelling houses. After the owners of a house in the village, who had leased it to six unrelated college students, were cited for violating the ordinance, this action was brought to have the ordinance declared unconstitutional as violative of equal protection and the rights of association, travel, and privacy. The District Court held the ordinance constitutional, and the Court of Appeals reversed. Held:

1. Economic and social legislation with respect to which the legislature has drawn lines in the exercise of its discretion, will be upheld if it is "reasonable, not arbitrary," and bears "a state objective," *Reed* v. *Reed,* and here the ordinance—which is not aimed at transients and involves no procedural disparity inflicted on some but not on others or deprivation of any "fundamental" right—meets that constitutional standard and must be upheld as valid land-use legislation addressed to family needs. *Berman* v. *Parker.*

2. The fact that the named tenant appellees have vacated the house does not moot this case as the challenged ordinance continues to affect the value of the property.

Reversed.

Mr. Justice MARSHALL, dissenting.

THE OPINIONS / 407

This case draws into question the constitutionality of a zoning ordinance of the incorporated village of Belle Terre, New York, which prohibits groups of more than two unrelated persons, as distinguished from groups consisting of any number of persons related by blood, adoption, or marriage, from occupying a residence within the confines of the township. Lessor-appellees, the two owners of a Belle Terre residence, and three unrelated student tenants challenged the ordinance on the ground that it establishes a classification between households of related and unrelated individuals, which deprives them of equal protection of the laws. In my view, the disputed classification burdens the students' fundamental rights of association and privacy guaranteed by the First and Fourteenth Amendments. Because the application of strict equal protection scrutiny is therefore required, I am at odds with my Brethren's conclusion that the ordinance may be sustained on a showing that it bears a rational relationship to the accomplishment of legitimate governmental objectives.

I am in full agreement with the majority that zoning is a complex and important function of the State. It may indeed be the most essential function performed by local government, for it is one of the primary means by which we protect that sometimes difficult to define concept of quality of life. I therefore continue to adhere to the principle of *Village of Euclid* v. *Ambler Realty Co.,* that deference should be given to governmental judgments concerning proper land-use allocation. That deference is a principle which has served this Court well and which is necessary for the continued development of effective zoning and land-use control mechanisms. Had the owners alone brought this suit alleging that the restrictive ordinance deprived them of their property or was an irrational legislative classification, I would agree that the ordinance would have to be sustained. Our role is not and should not be to sit as a zoning board of appeals.

I would also agree with the majority that local zoning authorities may properly act in furtherance of the objectives asserted to be served by the ordinance at issue here: restricting uncontrolled growth, solving traffic problems, keeping rental costs at a reasonable level, and making the community attractive to families. The police power which provides the justification for zoning is not narrowly confined. See *Berman* v. *Parker.* And, it is appropriate that we afford zoning authorities considerable latitude in choosing the means by which to implement such purposes. But deference does not mean abdication. This Court has an obligation to ensure that zoning ordinances, even when adopted in furtherance of such legitimate aims, do not infringe upon fundamental constitutional rights.

When separate but equal was still accepted constitutional dogma, this Court struck down a racially restrictive zoning ordinance. *Buchanan* v. *Warley.* I am sure the Court would not be hesitant to invalidate that ordinance today. The lower federal courts have considered procedural aspects of zoning, and acted to ensure that land-use controls are not used as a means of confining minorities and the poor to the ghettos of our central cities. These are limited but necessary intrusions on the discretion of zoning authorities. By the same token, I think it clear that the First Amendment provides some limitation on zoning laws. It is inconceivable to me that we would allow the exercise of the zoning power to burden First Amendment freedoms, as by ordinances that restrict occupancy to individuals adhering to particular religious, political, or scientific beliefs. Zoning officials properly concern themselves with the uses of land—with, for example, the number and kind of dwellings to be constructed in a certain neighborhood or the number of persons who can reside in those dwellings. But zoning authorities cannot validly consider who those persons are, what they believe, or how they choose to live, whether they are Negro or white, Catholic or Jew, Republican or Democrat, married or unmarried.

My disagreement with the Court today is based upon my view that the ordinance in this case unnecessarily burdens appellees' First Amendment freedom of association and their constitutionally guaranteed right to privacy. Our decisions establish that the First and Fourteenth Amendments protect the freedom to choose one's associates. *NAACP* v. *Button.* Constitutional protection is extended, not only to modes of association that are political in the usual sense, but also to those that pertain to the social and economic benefit of the members. The selection of one's living companions involves similar choices as to the emotional, social, or economic benefits to be derived from alternative living arrangements.

The freedom of association is often inextricably entwined with the constitutionally guaranteed right of privacy. The right to "establish a home" is an essential part of the liberty guaranteed by the Fourteenth Amendment. *Meyer* v. *Nebraska.* And the Constitution secures to an individual a freedom "to satisfy his intellectual and emotional needs in the privacy of his own home." *Stanley* v. *Georgia.* Constitutionally protected privacy is, in Mr. Justice Brandeis's words, "as against the Government, the right to be let alone . . . the right most valued by civilized man." *Olmstead* v. *United States.* The choice of household companions—of whether a person's "intellectual and emotional needs" are best met by living with family, friends, professional associates, or others—involves deeply personal considerations as to the kind and quality of intimate relationships within the home. That decision surely falls within the ambit of the right to privacy protected by the Constitution. See *Roe* v. *Wade.*

The instant ordinance discriminates on the basis of just such a personal lifestyle choice as to household companions. It permits any number of persons related by blood or marriage, be it two or twenty, to live in a single household, but it limits to two the number of unrelated persons bound by profession, love, friendship, religious or political affiliation, or mere economics who can occupy a single home. Belle Terre imposes upon those who deviate from the community norm in their choice of living companions significantly greater restrictions than are applied to residential groups who are related by blood or marriage, and compose the established order within the community. The village has, in effect, acted to fence out those individuals whose choice of lifestyle differs from that of its current residents.

This is not a case where the Court is being asked to nullify a township's sincere efforts to maintain its residential character by preventing the operation of rooming houses, fraternity houses, or other commercial or high-density residential uses. Unquestionably, a town is free to restrict such uses. Moreover, as a general proposition, I see no constitutional infirmity in a town's limiting the density of use in residential areas by zoning regulations which do not discriminate on the basis of constitutionally suspect criteria. This ordinance, however, limits the density of occupancy of only those homes occupied by unrelated persons. It thus reaches beyond control of the use of land or the density of population, and undertakes to regulate the way people choose to associate with each other within the privacy of their own homes.

It is no answer to say, as does the majority that associational interests are not infringed because Belle Terre residents may entertain whomever they choose. Only last Term Mr. Justice Douglas indicated in concurrence that he saw the right of association protected by the First Amendment as involving far more than the right to entertain visitors. He found that right infringed by a restriction on food stamp assistance, penalizing households of "unrelated persons." As Mr. Justice Douglas there said, freedom of association encompasses the "right to invite the stranger into one's home" not only for "entertainment" but to join the household as well. *United States Department of Agriculture* v. *Moreno.* I am still persuaded that the choice of those who will form one's household implicates constitutionally protected rights.

Because I believe that this zoning ordinance creates a classification which impinges upon fundamental personal rights, it can withstand constitutional scrutiny only upon a clear showing that the burden imposed is necessary to protect a compelling and substantial governmental interest. *Shapiro* v. *Thompson.* And, once it be determined that a burden has been placed upon a constitutional right, the onus of demonstrating that no less intrusive means will adequately protect the compelling state interest and that the challenged statute is sufficiently narrowly drawn, is upon the party seeking to justify the burden. See *Memorial Hospital* v. *Maricopa County.*

A variety of justifications have been proffered in support of the village's ordinance. It is claimed that the ordinance controls population density, prevents noise, traffic and parking problems, and preserves the rent structure of the community and its attractiveness to families. As I noted earlier, these are all legitimate and substantial interests of government. But I think it clear that the means chosen to accomplish these purposes are both overinclusive and underinclusive, and that the asserted goals could be as effectively achieved by means of an ordinance that did not discriminate on the basis of constitutionally protected choices of lifestyle. The ordinance imposes no restriction whatsoever on the number of persons who may live in a house, as long as they are related by marital or sanguinary bonds—presumably no matter how distant their relationship. Nor does the ordinance restrict the number of income earners who may contribute to rent in such a household, or the number of automobiles that may be maintained by its occupants. In that sense the ordinance is underinclusive. On the other hand, the statute restricts the number of unrelated persons who may live in a home to no more than two. It would therefore prevent three unrelated people from occupying a dwelling even if among them they had but one income and no vehicles. While an extended family of a dozen or more might live in a small bungalow, three elderly and retired persons could not occupy the large manor house next door. Thus the statute is also grossly overinclusive to accomplish its intended purposes.

There are some 220 residences in Belle Terre occupied by about 700 persons. The density is therefore just above three per household. The village is justifiably concerned with density of population and the related problems of noise, traffic, and the like. It could deal with those problems by limiting each household to a specified number of adults, two or three perhaps, without limitation on the number of dependent children. The burden of such an ordinance would fall equally upon all segments of the community. It would surely be better tailored to the goals asserted by the village than the ordinance before us today, for it would more realistically restrict population density and growth and their attendant environmental costs. Various other statutory mechanisms also suggest themselves as solutions to Belle Terre's problems—rent control, limits on the number of vehicles per household, and so forth, but, of course, such schemes are matters of legislative judgment and not for this Court. Appellants also refer to the necessity of maintaining the family character of the village. There is not a shred of evidence in the record indicating that if Belle Terre permitted a limited number of unrelated persons to live together, the residential, familial character of the community would be fundamentally affected.

By limiting unrelated households to two persons while placing no limitation on households of related individuals, the village has embarked upon its commendable course in a constitutionally faulty vessel. Cf. *Marshall* v. *United States*. I would find the challenged ordinance unconstitutional. But I would not ask the village to abandon its goal of providing quiet streets, little traffic, and a pleasant and reasonably priced environment in which families might raise their children. Rather, I would commend the village to continue to pursue those purposes but by means of more carefully drawn and even-handed legislation.

I respectfully dissent.

KELLEY, COMMISSIONER, SUFFOLK COUNTY POLICE DEPARTMENT
versus
JOHNSON

Argued December 8, 1975
Decided April 5, 1976

A county regulation limiting the length of county policemen's hair *held* not to violate any right guaranteed respondent policeman by the Fourteenth Amendment.

(a) Respondent sought the protection of the Fourteenth Amendment, not as an ordinary citizen, but as a law enforcement employee of the county, a subdivision of the State, and this distinction is one of considerable significance since a State has wider latitude and notably different interests in imposing restrictive regulations on its employees than it does in regulating the citizenry at large.

(b) Choice of organization, dress, and equipment for law enforcement personnel is entitled to the same sort of presumption of legislative validity as are state choices to promote other aims within the cognizance of the State's police power. Thus, the question is not whether the State can "establish" a "genuine public need" for the specific regulation, but whether respondent can demonstrate that there is no rational connection between the regulation, based as it is on the county's method of organizing its police force, and the promotion of safety of persons and property.

(c) Whether a state or local government's choice to have its police uniformed reflects a desire to make police officers readily recognizable to the public or to foster the esprit de corps that similarity of garb and appearance may inculcate within the police force itself, the justification for the hair-style regulation is sufficiently rational to defeat respondent's claim based on the liberty guarantee of the Fourteenth Amendment.

* * *

REHNQUIST, J., delivered the opinion of the Court, in which BURGER, C. J., and STEWART, WHITE, BLACKMUN, and POWELL, JJ., joined. POWELL, J., filed a concurring opinion. MARSHALL, J., filed a dissenting opinion, in which BRENNAN, J., joined. STEVENS, J., took no part in the consideration or decision of the case.

MR. JUSTICE MARSHALL, with whom MR. JUSTICE BRENNAN joins, dissenting.

The Court today upholds the constitutionality of Suffolk County's regulation limiting the length of a policeman's hair. While the Court only assumes for purposes of its opinion that "the citizenry at large has some sort of 'liberty' interest within the Fourteenth Amendment in matters of personal appearance . . . ," I think it clear that the Fourteenth Amendment does indeed protect against comprehensive regulation of what citizens may or may not wear. And I find that the rationales offered by the Court to justify the regulation in this case are insufficient to demonstrate its constitutionality. Accordingly, I respectfully dissent.

I

As the Court recognizes, the Fourteenth Amendment's guarantee against the deprivation of liberty "protects substantive aspects of liberty against unconstitutional restrictions by the State." And we have observed that "[l]iberty under law extends to the full range of conduct which the individual is free to pursue." *Bolling* v. *Sharpe* (1954). *Poe* v. *Ullman* (1961) (Harlan, J., dissenting). It seems to me manifest that that "full range of conduct" must encompass one's interest in dressing according to his own taste. An individual's personal appearance may reflect, sustain, and nourish his personality and may well be used as a means of expressing his attitude and lifestyle. In taking control over a citizen's personal appearance, the government forces him to sacrifice substantial elements of his integrity and identity as well. To say that the liberty guarantee of the Fourteenth Amendment does not encompass matters of personal appearance would be fundamentally inconsistent with the values of privacy, self-identity, autonomy, and personal integrity that I have always assumed the Constitution was designed to protect. See *Roe* v. *Wade* (1973); *Stanley* v. *Georgia* (1969); *Griswold* v.

Connecticut (1965); *Olmstead* v. *United States* (1928) (Brandeis, J., dissenting).

If little can be found in past cases of this Court or indeed in the Nation's history on the specific issue of a citizen's right to choose his own personal appearance, it is only because the right has been so clear as to be beyond question. When the right has been mentioned, its existence has simply been taken for granted. For instance, the assumption that the right exists is reflected in the 1789 congressional debates over which guarantees should be explicitly articulated in the Bill of Rights. There was considerable debate over whether the right of assembly should be expressly mentioned. Congressman Benson of New York argued that its inclusion was necessary to assure that the right would not be infringed by the government. In response, Congressman Sedgwick of Massachusetts indicated:

> "If the committee were governed by that general principle . . . they might have declared that *a man should have a right to wear his hat if he pleased* . . . but [I] would ask the gentleman whether he thought it necessary to enter these trifles in a declaration of rights, *in a Government where none of them were intended to be infringed."*

Thus, while they did not include it in the Bill of Rights, Sedgwick and his colleagues clearly believed there to be a right in one's personal appearance. And, while they may have regarded the right as a trifle as long as it was honored, they clearly would not have so regarded it if it were infringed.

This Court, too, has taken as an axiom that there is a right in one's personal appearance. Indeed, in 1958 we used the existence of that right as support for our recognition of the right to travel:

> "The right to travel is a part of the 'liberty' of which the citizen cannot be deprived without due process of law under the Fifth Amendment. . . . *It may be as close to the heart of the individual as the choice of what he eats, or wears, or reads."* Kent v. Dulles (1958).

To my mind, the right in one's personal appearance is inextricably bound up with the historically recognized right of "every individual to the possession and control of his own person," *Union Pacific R. Co.* v. *Botsford* (1891), and, perhaps even more fundamentally, with "the right to be let alone—the most comprehensive of rights and the right most valued by civilized men." *Olmstead* v. *United States* (Brandeis, J., dissenting). In an increasingly crowded society in which it is already extremely difficult to maintain one's identity and personal integrity, it would be distressing, to say the least, if the government could regulate our personal appearance unconfined by any constitutional strictures whatsoever.

II

Acting on its assumption that the Fourteenth Amendment does encompass a right in one's personal appearance, the Court justifies the challenged hair-length regulation on the grounds that such regulations may "be based on a desire to make police officers readily recognizable to the members of the public, or a desire for the esprit de corps which such similarity is felt to inculcate within the police force itself." While fully accepting the aims of "identifiability" and maintenance of esprit de corps, I find no rational relationship between the challenged regulation and these goals.

As for the first justification offered by the Court, I simply do not see how requiring policemen to maintain hair of under a certain length could rationally be argued to contribute to making them identifiable to the public as policemen. Surely, the fact that a uniformed police officer is wearing his hair below his collar will make him no less identifiable as a policeman. And one cannot easily imagine a plainclothes officer being readily identifiable as such simply because his hair does not extend beneath his collar.

As for the Court's second justification, the fact that it is the president of the Patrolmen's Benevolent Association, in his official capacity, who has challenged the regulation here would seem to indicate that the regulation would if anything, decrease rather than increase the police force's esprit de corps. And even if one accepted the argument that substantial similarity in appearance would increase a force's esprit de corps, I simply do not understand how implementation of this regulation could be expected to create any increment in similarity of appearance among members of a uniformed police force. While the regulation prohibits hair below the ears or the collar and limits the length of sideburns, it allows the maintenance of any type of hairstyle, other than a ponytail. Thus, as long as their hair does not go below their collars, two police officers, one with an "Afro" hairstyle and the other with a crewcut could both be in full compliance with the regulation.

The Court cautions us not to view the hair-length regulation in isolation, but rather to examine it "in the context of the county's chosen mode of organization for its police force." While the Court's caution is well taken, one should also keep in mind, as I fear the Court does not, that what is ultimately under scrutiny is neither the overall structure of the police force nor the uniform and equipment requirements to which its members are subject, but rather the regulation which dictates acceptable hair lengths. The fact that the uniform requirement, for instance, may be rationally related to the goals of increasing police officer "identifiability" and the maintenance of esprit de corps does absolutely nothing to establish the legitimacy of the hair-length regulation. I see no connection between the regulation and the offered rationales and would accordingly affirm the judgment of the Court of Appeals.

THOMAS E. ZABLOCKI, MILWAUKEE
COUNTY CLERK, ETC., APPELLANT,
versus
ROGER C. REDHAIL, ETC.

Argued October 4, 1977
Decided January 18, 1978

Class action was brought challenging Wisconsin statute, which provides that any resident having minor issue (child) not in his custody that he is under obligation to support by any court order or judgment may not marry without court approval, as violative of the equal protection and due process clauses and seeking declaratory and injunctive relief. The Three-Judge District Court, held the statute unconstitutional under the equal protection clause and enjoined its enforcement, and probable jurisdiction was noted. The Supreme Court, Mr. Justice Marshall, held that: (1) since [the] right to marry is of fundamental importance and since statutory classification significantly interfered with exercise of that right, critical examination of state interests advanced in support of classification was required, and (2) since means selected by the state for achieving its interests in providing opportunity to counsel applicants as to necessity of fulfilling prior support obligations and protecting welfare of out-of-custody children unnecessarily impinged on right to marry, statute could not be sustained.

Affirmed.

Mr. Justice MARSHALL delivered the opinion of the Court.

At issue in this case is the constitutionality of a Wisconsin statute, Wis.Stat. §§ 245.-10(1), (4), (5) (1973), which provides that members of a certain class of Wisconsin residents may not marry, within the State or elsewhere, without first obtaining a court order granting permission to marry. The class is defined by the statute to include any "Wisconsin resident having minor issue not in his custody and which he is under obligation to support by any court order or judgment." The statute specifies that court permission cannot be granted unless the marriage applicant submits proof of compliance with the support obligation and, in addition, demonstrates that the children covered by the support order "are not then and are not likely thereafter to become public charges." No marriage license may lawfully be issued in Wisconsin to a person covered by the statute, except upon court order; any marriage entered into without compliance with § 245.10 is declared void; and persons acquiring marriage licenses in violation of the section are subject to criminal penalties.

After being denied a marriage license because of his failure to comply with § 245.10, appellee brought this class action under 42 U.S.C. § 1983, challenging the statute as violative of the Equal Protection and Due Process Clauses of the Fourteenth Amendment and seeking declaratory and injunctive relief. The United States District Court for the Eastern District of Wisconsin held the statute unconstitutional under the Equal Protection Clause and enjoined its enforcement (1976). We noted probable jurisdiction (1977), and we now affirm.

I

Appellee Redhail is a Wisconsin resident who, under the terms of § 245.10, is unable to enter into a lawful marriage in Wisconsin or elsewhere so long as he maintains his Wisconsin residency. The facts, according to the stipulation filed by the parties in the District Court, are as follows. In January 1972, when appellee was a minor and a high school student, a paternity action was instituted against him in Milwaukee County Court, alleging that he was the father of a baby girl born out of wedlock on July 5, 1971. After he appeared and admitted that he was the child's father, the court entered an order on May 12, 1972, adjudging appellee the father and ordering him to pay $109 per month as support for the child until she reached 18 years of age. From May 1972 until August 1974, appellee was unemployed and indigent, and consequently was unable to make any support payments.

On September 27, 1974, appellee filed an application for a marriage license with appellant Zablocki, the County Clerk of Milwaukee County, and a few days later the application was denied on the sole ground that appellee had not obtained a court order granting him permission to marry, as required by § 245.10. Although appellee did not petition a state court thereafter, it is stipulated that he would not have been able to satisfy either of the statutory prerequisites for an order granting permission to marry. First, he had not satisfied his support obligations to his illegitimate child, and as of December 1974 there was an arrearage in excess of $3,700. Second, the child had been a public charge since her birth, receiving benefits under the Aid to Families with Dependent Children program. It is stipulated that the child's benefit payments were such that she would have been a public charge even if appellee had been current in his support payments.

On December 24, 1974, appellee filed his complaint in the District Court, on behalf of himself and the class of all Wisconsin residents who had been refused a marriage license pursuant to § 245.10(1) by one of the county clerks in Wisconsin. Zablocki was named as the defendant, individually and as representative of a class consisting of all county clerks in the State. The complaint alleged, among other things, that appellee and the woman he desired to marry were expecting a child in March 1975 and wished to be lawfully married before that time. The statute was attacked on the grounds that it deprived appellee, and the class he sought to represent of equal protection and due process rights secured by the First, Fifth, Ninth, and Fourteenth Amendments to the United States Constitution.

A three-judge court was convened pursuant to 28 U.S.C. §§ 2281, 2284. Appellee moved for certification of the plaintiff and defendant classes named in his complaint, and by order dated February 20, 1975, the plaintiff class was certified under Fed. Rule Civ. Proc. 23(b)(2). After the parties filed the stipulation of facts, and briefs on the merits, oral argument was heard in the District Court on June 23, 1975, with a representative from the Wisconsin Attorney General's office participating in addition to counsel for the parties.

The three-judge court handed down a unanimous decision on August 31, 1976. The court ruled, first, that it was not required to abstain from decision under the principles set forth in *Huffman* v. *Pursue Ltd.* (1975), and *Younger* v. *Harris* (1971), since there was no pending state-court proceeding that could be frustrated by the declaratory and injunctive relief requested. Second, the court held that the class of all county clerks in Wisconsin was a proper defendant class under Rules 23(a) and (b)(2), and that neither Rule 23 nor due process required prejudgment notice to the members of the plaintiff or the defendant class.

On the merits, the three-judge panel analyzed the challenged statute under the Equal Protection Clause and concluded that "strict scrutiny" was required because the classification created by the statute infringed upon a fundamental right, the right to marry. The court then proceeded to evaluate the interests advanced by the State to justify the statute, and, finding that the classification was not necessary for the achievement of those interests, the court held the statute invalid and enjoined the county clerks from enforcing it.

Appellant brought this direct appeal pursuant to 28 U.S.C. § 1253, claiming that the three-judge court erred in finding §§ 245.10(1), (4), (5) invalid under the Equal Protection Clause. Appellee defends the lower court's equal protection holding and, in the alternative, urges affirmance of the District Court's judgment on the grounds that the statute does not satisfy the requirements of substantive due process. We agree with the District Court that the statute violates the Equal Protection Clause.

II

In evaluating §§ 245.10(1), (4), (5) under the Equal Protection Clause, "we must first determine what burden of justification the classification created thereby must meet, by looking to the nature of the classification and the individual interests affected." *Memorial Hospital* v. *Maricopa County* (1974). Since our past decisions make clear that the right to marry is of fundamental importance, and since the classification at issue here significantly interferes with the exercise of that right, we believe that "critical examination" of the State interests advanced in support of the classification is required. *Massachusetts Board of Retirement* v. *Murgia* (1976); see, *e.g., San Antonio Independent School Dist.* v. *Rodriguez* (1973).

The leading decision of this Court on the right to marry is *Loving* v. *Virginia* (1967). In that case, an interracial couple who had been convicted of violating Virginia's miscegenation laws challenged the statutory scheme on both equal protection and due process grounds. The Court's opinion could have rested solely on the grounds that the statutes discriminated on the basis of race in violation of the Equal Protection Clause. But the Court went on to hold that the laws arbitrarily deprived the couple of a fundamental liberty protected by the Due Process Clause, the freedom to marry. The Court's language on the latter point bears repeating:

"The freedom to marry has long been recognized as one of the vital personal rights essential to the orderly pursuit of happiness by free men.

"Marriage is one of the 'basic civil rights of man,' fundamental to our very existence and survival." Quoting *Skinner* v. *Oklahoma ex rel. Williamson* (1942).

Although *Loving* arose in the context of racial discrimination, prior and subsequent decisions of this Court confirm that the right to marry is of fundamental importance for all individuals. Long ago, in *Maynard* v. *Hill* (1888), the Court characterized marriage as "the most important relation in life," and as "the foundation of the family and of society, without which there would be neither civilization or progress." In *Meyer* v. *Nebraska* (1923), the Court recognized that the right "to marry, establish a home and bring up children" is a central part of the liberty protected by the Due Process Clause, and in *Skinner* v. *Oklahoma* (1942), marriage was described as "fundamental to the very existence and survival of the race."

More recent decisions have established that the right to marry is part of the fundamental "right of privacy" implicit in the Fourteenth Amendment's Due Process Clause. In *Griswold* v. *Connecticut* (1965), the Court observed:

"We deal with a right of privacy older than the Bill of Rights— older than our political parties, older than our school system. Marriage is a coming together for better or for worse, hopefully enduring, and intimate to the degree of being sacred. It is an association that promotes a way of life, not causes; a harmony in living, not political faiths; a bilateral loyalty, not commercial or social projects. Yet it is an association for as noble a purpose as any involved in our prior decisions."

Cases subsequent to *Griswold* and *Loving* have routinely categorized the decision to marry as among the personal decisions protected by the right to privacy. See generally *Whalen* v. *Roe* (1977). For example, last Term in *Carey* v. *Population Services International* (1977), we declared.

"While the outer limits of [the right of personal privacy] have not been marked by the Court, it is clear that among the decisions that an individual may make without unjustified government interference are personal decisions 'relating to marriage, *Loving* v. *Virginia* (1967); procreation, *Skinner* v. *Oklahoma ex rel. Williamson* (1942);

contraception, *Eisenstadt* v. *Baird;* family relationships, *Prince* v. *Massachusetts* (1944); and child rearing and education, *Pierce* v. *Society of Sisters* (1925); *Meyer* v. *Nebraska* (1923).' "

See also *Cleveland Board of Education* v. *LaFleur* (1974) ("This Court has long recognized that freedom of personal choice in matters of marriage and family life is one of the liberties protected by the Due Process Clause of the Fourteenth Amendment"); *Smith* v. *Organization of Foster Families* (1977).

It is not surprising that the decision to marry has been placed on the same level of importance as the decision relating to procreation, childbirth, child rearing, and family relationships. As the facts of this case illustrate, it would make little sense to recognize a right of privacy with respect to other matters of family life and not with respect to the decision to enter the relationship that is the foundation of the family in our society. The woman whom appellee desired to marry had a fundamental right to seek an abortion of their expected child, see *Roe* v. *Wade, supra,* or to bring the child into life to suffer the myriad social, if not economic, disabilities that the status of illegitimacy brings, see *Trimble* v. *Gordon* (1977). Surely, a decision to marry and raise the child in a traditional family setting must receive equivalent protection. And, if appellee's right to procreate means anything at all, it must imply some right to enter the only relationship in which the State of Wisconsin allows sexual relations legally to take place.

By reaffirming the fundamental character of the right to marry, we do not mean to suggest that every state regulation which relates in any way to the incidents of or prerequisites for marriage must be subjected to rigorous scrutiny. To the contrary, reasonable regulations that do not significantly interfere with decisions to enter into the marital relationship may legitimately be imposed. See *Califano* v. *Jobst.* The statutory classification at issue here, however, clearly does not interfere directly and substantially with the right to marry.

Under the challenged statute, no Wisconsin resident in the affected class may marry in Wisconsin or elsewhere without a court order, and marriages contracted in violation of the statute are both void and punishable as criminal offenses. Some of those in the affected class, like appellee, will never be able to obtain the necessary court order, because they either lack the financial means to meet their support obligations or cannot prove that their children will not become public charges. These persons are absolutely prevented from getting married. Many others, able in theory to satisfy the statute's requirements, will be sufficiently burdened by having to do so that they will in effect be coerced into forgoing their right to marry. And even those who can be persuaded to meet the statute's requirements suffer a serious intrusion into their freedom of choice in an area in which we have held such freedom to be fundamental.

III

When a statutory classification significantly interferes with the exercise of a fundamental right, it cannot be upheld unless it is supported by sufficiently important state interests and is closely tailored to effectuate only those interests. See, *e.g., Carey* v. *Population Services International; Memorial Hospital* v. *Maricopa County; San Antonio Independent School Dist.* v. *Rodriguez.* Appellant asserts that two interests are served by the challenged statute: the permission-to-marry proceeding furnishes an opportunity to counsel the applicant as to the necessity of fulfilling his prior support obligations; and the welfare of the out-of-custody children is protected. We may accept for present purposes that these are legitimate and substantial interests, but, since the means selected by the State for achieving these interests unnecessarily impinge on the right to marry, the statute cannot be sustained.

There is evidence that the challenged statute, as originally introduced in the Wisconsin Legislature, was intended merely to establish a mechanism whereby persons with support obligations to children from prior marriages could be counseled before they entered into new marital relationships and incurred further support obligations. Court permission to marry was to be required, but apparently permission was automatically to be granted after counseling was completed. The statute actually enacted, however, does not expressly require or provide for any counseling whatsoever, nor for any automatic granting of permission to marry by the court, and thus it can hardly be justified as a means for ensuring counseling of the persons within its coverage. Even assuming that counseling does take place—a fact as to which there is no evidence in the record—this interest obviously cannot support the withholding of court permission to marry once counseling is completed.

With regard to safeguarding the welfare of the out-of-custody children, appellant's brief does not make clear the connection between the State's interest and the statute's requirements. At argument, appellant's counsel suggested that, since permission to marry cannot be granted unless the applicant shows that he has satisfied his court-determined support obligations to the prior children and that those children will not become public charges, the statute provides incentive for the applicant to make support payments to his children. This "collection device" rationale cannot justify the statute's broad infringement on the right to marry.

First, with respect to individuals who are unable to meet the statutory requirements, the statute merely prevents the applicant from getting married, without delivering any money at all into the hands of the applicant's prior children. More importantly, regardless of the applicant's ability or willingness to meet the statutory requirements, the State already has numerous other means for exacting compliance with support obligations, means that are at least as effective as the instant statute's and yet do not impinge upon the right to marry. Under Wisconsin law, whether the children are from a prior marriage or were born out of wedlock, court-determined support obligations may be enforced directly via wage assignments, civil contempt proceedings, and criminal penalties. And, if the State believes that parents of children out of their custody should be responsible for ensuring that those children do not become public charges, this interest can be achieved by adjusting the criteria used for determining the amounts to be paid under their support orders.

There is also some suggestion that § 245.10 protects the ability of marriage applicants to meet support obligations to prior children by preventing the applicants from incurring new support obligations. But the challenged provisions of § 245.10 are grossly underinclusive with respect to this purpose, since they do not limit in any way new financial commitments by the applicant other than those arising out of the contemplated marriage. The statutory classification is substantially overinclusive as well: Given the possibility that the new spouse will actually better the applicant's financial situation, by contributing income from a job or otherwise, the statute in many cases may prevent affected individuals from improving their ability to satisfy their prior support obligations. And, although it is true that the applicant will incur support obligations to any children born during the contemplated marriage, preventing the marriage may only result in the children being born out of wedlock, as in fact occurred in appellee's case. Since the support obligations is the same whether the child is born in or out of wedlock, the net result of preventing the marriage is simply more illegitimate children.

The statutory classification created by §§ 245.10(1), (4), (5) thus cannot be justified by the interests advanced in support of it. The judgment of the District Court is, accordingly,

Affirmed.

MILLIKEN, GOVERNOR OF MICHIGAN, ET AL.
versus
BRADLEY ET AL.

CERTIORARI TO THE UNITED STATES COURT OF APPEALS
FOR THE SIXTH CIRCUIT

Argued February 27, 1974
Decided July 25, 1974

Respondents brought this class action, alleging that the Detroit public school system is racially segregated as a result of the official policies and actions of petitioner state and city officials, and seeking implementation of a plan to eliminate the segregation and establish a unitary nonracial school system. The District Court, after concluding that various acts by the petitioner Detroit Board of Education had created and perpetuated school segregation in Detroit, and that the acts of the Board, as a subordinate entity of the State, were attributable to the State, ordered the Board to submit Detroit-only desegregation plans. The court also ordered the state officials to submit desegregation plans encompassing the three-county metropolitan area, despite the fact that the 85 outlying school districts in these three counties were not parties to the action and there was no claim that they had committed constitutional violations. Subsequently, outlying school districts were allowed to intervene, but were not permitted to assert any claim or defense on issues previously adjudicated or to reopen any issue previously decided, but were allowed merely to advise the court as to the propriety of a metropolitan plan and to submit any objections, modifications, or alternatives to any such plan. Thereafter, the District Court ruled that it was proper to consider metropolitan plans, that Detroit-only plans submitted by the Board and respondents were inadequate to accomplish desegregation, and that therefore it would seek a solution beyond the limits of the Detroit School District, and concluded that "[s]chool district lines are simply matters of political convenience and may not be used to deny constitutional rights." Without having evidence that the suburban school districts had committed acts of *de jure* segregation, the court appointed a panel to submit a plan for the Detroit schools that would encompass an entire designated desegregation area consisting of 53 of the 85 suburban school districts plus Detroit, and ordered the Detroit Board to acquire at least 295 school buses to provide transportation under an interim plan to be developed for the 1972–1973 school year. The Court of Appeals, affirming in part, held that the record supported the District Court's finding as to the constitutional violations committed by the Detroit Board and the state officials; that therefore the District Court was authorized and required to take effective measures to desegregate the Detroit school system; and that a metropolitan area plan embracing the 53 outlying districts was the only feasible solution and was within the District Court's equity powers. But the court remanded so that all suburban school districts that might be affected by a metropolitan remedy could be made parties and have an opportunity to be heard as to the scope and implementation of such a remedy, and vacated the order as to the bus acquisitions, subject to its reimposition at an appropriate time. *Held:* The relief ordered by the District Court and affirmed by the Court of Appeals was based upon erroneous standards and was unsupported by record evidence that acts of the outlying districts had any impact on the discrimination found to exist in the Detroit schools. A federal court may not impose a multidistrict, area-wide remedy for single-district *de jure* school segregation violations where there is no finding that the other included school districts have failed to operate unitary school systems or have committed acts that effected segregation within the other districts, there is no claim or finding that the school district boundary lines were established with the purpose of fostering racial segregation, and there is no meaningful opportunity for the included neighboring school districts to present evidence or be heard on the propriety of a multidistrict remedy or on the question of constitutional violations by those districts.

(a) The District Court erred in using as a standard the declared objective of development of a metropolitan area plan which, upon implementation, would leave "no school, grade or classroom . . . substantially disproportionate to the overall pupil racial composition" of the metropolitan area as a whole. The clear import of *Swann* v. *Board of Education,* is that desegregation, in the sense of dismantling a dual school system, does not require any particular racial balance.

(b) While boundary lines may be bridged in circumstances where there has been a constitutional violation calling for interdistrict relief, school district lines may not be casually ignored or treated as a mere administrative convenience; substantial local control of public education in this country is a deeply rooted tradition.

(c) The interdistrict remedy could extensively disrupt and alter the structure of public education in Michigan, since that remedy would require, in effect, consolidation of 54 independent school districts historically administered as separate governmental units into a vast new super school district, and, since—entirely apart from the logistical problems attending large-scale transportation of students—the consolidation would generate other problems in the administration, financing, and operation of this new school system.

(d) From the scope of the interdistrict plan itself, absent a complete restructuring of the Michigan school district laws, the District Court would become, first, a *de facto* "legislative authority" to resolve the complex operational problems involved and thereafter a "school superintendent" for the entire area, a task which few, if any, judges are qualified to perform and one which would deprive the people of local control of schools through elected school boards.

(e) Before the boundaries of separate and autonomous school districts may be set aside by consolidating the separate units for remedial purposes or by imposing a cross-district remedy, it must be first shown that there has been a constitutional violation within one district that produces a significant segregative effect in another district; *i.e.,* specifically, it must be shown that racially discriminatory acts of the State or local school districts, or of a single school district have been a substantial cause of interdistrict segregation.

(f) With no showing of significant violation by the 53 outlying school districts and no evidence of any interdistrict violation or effect, the District Court transcended the original theory of the case as framed by the pleadings, and mandated a metropolitan area remedy, the approval of which would impose on the outlying districts, not shown to have committed any constitutional violation, a standard not previously hinted at in any holding of this Court.

(g) Assuming, *arguendo,* that the State was derivatively responsible for Detroit's segregated school conditions, it does not follow that an interdistrict remedy is constitutionally justified or required, since there has been virtually no showing that either the State or any of the 85 outlying districts engaged in any activity that had a cross-district effect.

(h) An isolated instance of a possible segregative effect as between two of the school districts involved would not justify the broad metropolitan-wide remedy contemplated, particularly since that remedy embraced 52 districts having no responsibility for the arrangement and potentially involved 503,000 pupils in addition to Detroit's 276,000 pupils.

Reversed and remanded.

MR. JUSTICE MARSHALL, with whom MR. JUSTICE DOUGLAS, MR. JUSTICE BRENNAN, and MR. JUSTICE WHITE join, dissenting.

In *Brown* v. *Board of Education* (1954), this Court held that segregation of children in public schools on the basis of race deprives minority group children of equal educational opportunities and therefore denies them the equal protection of the laws under the Fourteenth Amendment. This Court recognized then that remedying decades of segregation in public education would not be an easy task. Subsequent events, unfortunately, have seen that prediction bear bitter fruit. But however imbedded old ways, however ingrained old prejudices, this Court has not been diverted from its appointed task of making "a living truth" of our constitutional ideal of equal justice under law. *Cooper* v. *Aaron* (1958).

After 20 years of small, often difficult steps toward that great end, the Court today takes a giant step backward. Notwithstanding a record showing widespread and pervasive racial segregation in the educational system provided by the State of Michigan for children in Detroit, this Court holds that the District Court was powerless to require the State to remedy its constitutional violation in any meaningful fashion. Ironically purporting to base its result on the principle that the scope of the remedy in a desegregation case should be determined by the nature and the extent of the constitutional violation, the Court's answer is to provide no remedy at all for the violation proved in this case, thereby guaranteeing that Negro children in Detroit will receive the same separate and inherently unequal education in the future as they have been unconstitutionally afforded in the past.

I cannot subscribe to this emasculation of our constitutional guarantee of equal protection of the laws and must respectfully dissent. Our precedents, in my view, firmly establish that where, as here, state-imposed segregation has been demonstrated, it becomes the duty of the State to eliminate root and branch all vestiges of racial discrimination and to achieve the greatest possible degree of actual desegregation. I agree with both the District Court and the Court of Appeals that, under the facts of this case, this duty cannot be fulfilled unless the State of Michigan involves outlying metropolitan area school districts in its desegregation remedy. Furthermore, I perceive no basis either in law or in the practicalities of the situation justifying the State's interposition of school district boundaries as absolute barriers to the implementation of an effective desegregation remedy. Under established and frequently used Michigan procedures, school district lines are both flexible and permeable for a wide variety of purposes, and there is no reason why they must now stand in the way of meaningful desegregation relief.

The rights at issue in this case are too fundamental to be abridged on grounds as superficial as those relied on by the majority today. We deal here with the right of all of our children, whatever their race, to an equal start in life and to an equal opportunity to reach their full potential as citizens. Those children who have been denied that right in the past deserve better than to see fences thrown up to deny them that right in the future. Our Nation, I fear, will be ill served by the Court's refusal to remedy separate and unequal education, for unless our children begin to learn together, there is little hope that our people will ever learn to live together.

I

The great irony of the Court's opinion and, in my view, its most serious analytical flaw may be gleaned from its concluding sentence, in which the Court remands for "prompt formulation of a decree directed to eliminating the segregation found to exist in Detroit city schools, a remedy which has been delayed since 1970." The majority, however, seems to have forgotten the District Court's explicit finding that a Detroit-only decree, the only remedy permitted under today's decision, "would not accomplish desegregation."

Nowhere in the Court's opinion does the majority confront, let alone respond to, the District Court's conclusion that a remedy limited to the city of Detroit would not effectively desegregate the Detroit city schools. I, for one, find the District Court's conclusion well supported by the record and its analysis compelled by our prior cases. Before turning to these questions, however, it is best to begin by laying to rest some mischaracterizations in the Court's opinion with respect to the basis for the District Court's decision to impose a metropolitan remedy.

The Court maintains that while the initial focus of this lawsuit was the condition of segregation within the Detroit city schools, the District Court abruptly shifted focus in mid-course and altered its theory of the case. This new theory, in the majority's words, was "equating racial imbalance with a constitutional violation calling for a remedy." As the following review of the District Court's handling of the case demonstrates, however, the majority's characterization is totally inaccurate. Nowhere did the District Court indicate that racial imbalance between school districts in the Detroit metropolitan area or within the Detroit School District constituted a constitutional violation calling for interdistrict relief. The focus of this case was from the beginning, and has remained, the segregated system of education in the Detroit city schools and the steps necessary to cure that condition which offends the Fourteenth Amendment.

The District Court's consideration of this case began with its finding, which the majority accepts, that the State of Michigan, through its instrumentality, the Detroit Board of Education, engaged in widespread purposeful acts of racial segregation in the Detroit School District. Without belaboring the details, it is sufficient to note that the various techniques used in Detroit were typical of methods employed to segregate students by race in areas where no statutory dual system of education has existed. See, *e.g., Keyes* v. *School District No. 1, Denver, Colorado* (1973). Exacerbating the effects of extensive residential segregation between Negroes and whites, the school board consciously drew attendance zones along lines which maximized the segregation of the races in schools as well. Optional attendance zones were created for neighborhoods undergoing racial transition so as to allow whites in these areas to escape integration. Negro students in areas with overcrowded schools were transported past or away from closer white schools with available space to more distant Negro schools. Grade structures and feeder-school patterns were created and maintained in a manner which had the foreseeable and actual effect of keeping Negro and white pupils in separate schools. Schools were also constructed in locations and in sizes which ensured that they would open with predominantly one-race student bodies. In sum, the evidence adduced below showed that Negro children had been intentionally confined to an expanding core of virtually all-Negro schools immediately surrounded by a receding band of all-white schools.

Contrary to the suggestions in the Court's opinion, the basis for affording a desegregation remedy in this case was not some perceived racial imbalance either between schools within a single school district or between independent school districts. What we confront here is "a systematic program of segregation affecting a substantial portion of the students, schools . . . and facilities within the school system. . . ." The constitutional violation found here was not some *de facto* racial imbalance, but rather the purposeful, intentional, massive, *de jure* segregation of the Detroit city schools, which under our decision in *Keyes,* forms "a predicate for a finding of the existence of a dual school system," and justifies "all-out desegregation."

Having found a *de jure* segregated public school system in operation in the city of Detroit, the District Court turned next to consider which officials and agencies should be assigned the affirmative obligation to cure the constitutional violation. The court concluded that responsibility for the segregation in the Detroit city schools rested not only with the Detroit Board of Education, but belonged to the State of Michigan itself and the state defendants in this case—that is, the Governor of Michigan, the Attorney General, the State Board of Education, and the State Superintendent of Public Instruction. While the validity of this conclusion will merit more extensive analysis below, suffice it for now to say that it was based on three considerations. First, the evidence at trial showed that the State itself had taken actions contributing to the segregation within the Detroit schools. Second, since the Detroit Board of Education was an agency of the State of Michigan, its acts of racial discrimination were acts of the State for purposes of the Fourteenth Amendment. Finally, the District Court found that under Michigan law and practice, the system of education was in fact a *state* school system, characterized by relatively little local control and a large degree of centralized state regulation, with respect to both educational policy and the structure and operation of school districts.

Having concluded, then, that the school system in the city of Detroit was a *de jure* segregated system and that the State of Michigan had the affirmative duty to remedy that condition of segregation, the District Court then turned to the difficult task of devising an effective remedy. It bears repeating that the District Court's focus at this stage of the litigation remained what it had been at the beginning—the condition of segregation within the Detroit city schools. As the District Court stated: "From the initial ruling [on segregation] to this day, the basis of the proceedings has been and remains the violation: *de jure* school segregation. . . . The task before this Court, therefore, is now, and . . . has always been, how to desegregate the Detroit public schools."

The District Court first considered three desegregation plans limited to the geographical boundaries of the city of Detroit. All were rejected as ineffective to desegregate the Detroit city schools. Specifically, the District Court determined that the racial composition of the Detroit student body is such that implementation of any Detroit-only plan "would clearly make the entire Detroit public school system racially identifiable as Black" and would "leave many of its schools 75 to 90 per cent Black." The District Court also found that a Detroit-only plan "would change a school system which is now Black and White to one that would be perceived as Black, thereby increasing the flight of Whites from the city and the system, thereby increasing the Black student population." Based on these findings, the District Court reasoned that "relief of segregation in the public schools of the City of Detroit cannot be accomplished within the corporate geographical limits of the city" because a Detroit-only decree "would accentuate the racial identifiability of the district as a Black school system, and would not accomplish desegregation." The District Court therefore concluded that it "must look beyond the limits of the Detroit School District for a solution to the problem of segregation in the Detroit public schools. . . ."

In seeking to define the appropriate scope of that expanded desegregation area, however, the District Court continued to maintain as its sole focus the condition shown to violate the Constitution in this case—the segregation of the Detroit school system. As it stated, the primary question "remains the determination of the area necessary and practicable effectively to eliminate 'root and branch' the effects of state-imposed and supported segregation and to desegregate the Detroit public schools."

There is simply no foundation in the record, then, for the majority's accusation that the only basis for the District Court's order was some desire to achieve a racial balance in the Detroit metropolitan area. In fact, just the contrary is the case. In considering proposed desegregation areas, the District Court had occasion to criticize one of the State's proposals specifically because it had no basis other than its "particular racial ratio" and did not focus on "relevant factors, like eliminating racially identifiable schools [and] accomplishing maximum actual desegregation of the Detroit public schools." Similarly, in rejecting the Detroit School Board's proposed desegregation area, even though it included more all-white districts and therefore achieved a higher white-Negro ratio, the District Court commented:

"There is nothing in the record which suggests that these districts need be included in the desegregation area in order to disestablish the racial identifiability of the Detroit public schools. From the evidence, the primary reason for the Detroit School Board's interest in the inclusion of these school districts is not racial desegregation but to increase the average socio-economic balance of all the schools in the abutting regions and clusters."

The Court also misstates the basis for the District Court's order by suggesting that since the only segregation proved at trial was within the Detroit school system, any relief which extended beyond the jurisdiction of the Detroit Board of Education would be inappropriate because it would impose a remedy on outlying districts "not shown to have committed any constitutional violation." The essential foundation of interdistrict relief in this case was not to correct conditions within outlying districts which themselves engaged in purposeful segregation. Instead, interdistrict relief was seen as a necessary part of any meaningful effort by the State of Michigan to remedy the state-caused segregation within the City of Detroit.

Rather than consider the propriety of interdistrict relief on this basis, however, the Court has conjured up a largely fictional account of what the District Court was attempting to accomplish. With all due respect, the Court, in my view, does a great disservice to the District Judge who labored long and hard with this complex litigation by accusing him of changing horses in midstream and shifting the focus of this case from the pursuit of a remedy for the condition of segregation within the Detroit school system to some unprincipled attempt to impose his own philosophy of racial balance on the entire Detroit metropolitan area. The focus of this case has always been the segregated system of education in the City of Detroit. The District Court determined that interdistrict relief was necessary and appropriate only because it found that the condition of segregation within the Detroit school system could not be cured with a Detroit-only remedy. It is on this theory that the interdistrict relief must stand or fall. Unlike the Court, I perceive my task to be to review the District Court's order for what it is, rather than to criticize it for what it manifestly is not.

II

As the foregoing demonstrates, the District Court's decision to expand its desegregation decree beyond the geographical limits of the City of Detroit rested in large part on its conclusions (A) that the State of Michigan was ultimately responsible for curing the condition of segregation within the Detroit city schools, and (B) that a Detroit-only remedy would not accomplish this task. In my view, both of these conclusions are well supported by the facts of this case and by this Court's precedents.

A

To begin with, the record amply supports the District Court's findings that the State of Michigan, through state officers and state agencies, had engaged in purposeful acts which created or aggravated segregation in the Detroit schools. The State Board of Education, for example, prior to 1962, exercised its authority to supervise local school-site selection in a manner which contributed to segregation. (CA6 1973.) Furthermore, the State's continuing authority, after 1962, to approve school building construction plans had intertwined the State with site-selection decisions of the Detroit Board of Education which had the purpose and effect of maintaining segregation.

The State had also stood in the way of past efforts to desegregate the Detroit city schools. In 1970, for example, the Detroit School Board had begun implementation of its own desegregation plan for its high schools, despite considerable public and official resistance. The State Legislature intervened by enacting Act 48 of the Public Acts of 1970, specifically prohibiting implementation of the desegregation plan and thereby continuing the growing segregation of the Detroit school system. Adequate desegregation of the Detroit system was also hampered by discriminatory restrictions placed by the State on the use of transportation within Detroit. While state aid for transportation was provided by statute for suburban districts, many of which were highly urbanized, aid for intracity transportation was excepted. One of the effects of this restriction was to encourage the construction of small walk-in neighborhood schools in Detroit, thereby lending aid to the intentional policy of creating a school system which reflected, to the greatest extent feasible, extensive residential segregation. Indeed, that one of the purposes of the transportation restriction was to impede desegregation was evidenced when the Michigan Legislature amended the State Transportation Aid Act to cover intracity transportation but expressly prohibited the allocation of funds for cross-busing of students within a school district to achieve racial balance. Cf. *North Carolina State Board of Education* v. *Swann* (1971).

Also significant was the State's involvement during the 1950's in the transportation of Negro high school students from the Carver School District past a closer white high school in the Oak Park District to a more distant Negro high school in the Detroit system. Certainly the District Court's finding that the State Board of Education had knowledge of this action and had given its tacit or express approval was not clearly erroneous. Given the comprehensive statutory powers of the State Board of Education over contractual arrangements between school districts in the enrollment of students on a nonresident tuition basis, including certification of the number of pupils involved in the transfer and the amount of tuition charged, over the review of transportation routes and distances, and over the disbursement of transportation funds, the State Board inevitably knew and understood the significance of this discriminatory act.

Aside from the acts of purposeful segregation committed by the State Legislature and the State Board of Education, the District Court also concluded that the State was responsible for the many intentional acts of segregation committed by the Detroit Board of Education, an agency of the State. The majority is only willing to accept this finding *arguendo*. I have no doubt, however, as to its validity under the Fourteenth Amendment.

"The command of the Fourteenth Amendment," it should be recalled, "is that no 'State' shall deny to any person within its jurisdiction the equal protection of the laws." *Cooper* v. *Aaron* (1958). While a State can act only through "the officers or agents by whom its powers are exerted," *Ex parte Virginia* (1880), actions by an agent or officer of the State are encompassed by the Fourteenth Amendment for, "as he acts in the name and for the State, and is clothed with the State's power, his act is that of the State." See also *Cooper* v. *Aaron, Virginia* v. *Rives* (1880); *Shelley* v. *Kraemer* (1948).

Under Michigan law a "school district is an agency of the State government." *School District of the City of Lansing* v. *State Board of Education* (1962). It is "a legal division of territory, created by the State for educational purposes, to which the State has granted such powers as are deemed necessary to permit the district to function as a State agency." *Detroit Board of Education* v. *Superintendent of Public Instruc-*

tion (1947). Racial discrimination by the school district, an agency of the State, is therefore racial discrimination by the State itself, forbidden by the Fourteenth Amendment. See, *e.g., Pennsylvania* v. *Board of Trusts* (1957).

We recognized only last Term in *Keyes* that it was the State itself which was ultimately responsible for *de jure* acts of segregation committed by a local school board. A deliberate policy of segregation by the local board, we held, amounted to "state-imposed segregation." Wherever a dual school system exists, whether compelled by state statute or created by a local board's systematic program of segregation, "the *State* automatically assumes an affirmative duty 'to effectuate a transition to a racially nondiscriminatory school system' [and] to eliminate from the public schools within their school system 'all vestiges of state-imposed segregation.' "

Vesting responsibility with the State of Michigan for Detroit's segregated schools is particularly appropriate as Michigan, unlike some other States, operates a single statewide system of education rather than several separate and independent local school systems. The majority's emphasis on local governmental control and local autonomy of school districts in Michigan will come as a surprise to those with any familiarity with that State's system of education. School districts are not separate and distinct sovereign entities under Michigan law, but rather are " 'auxiliaries of the State,' " subject to its "absolute power." *Attorney General of Michigan ex rel. Kies* v. *Lowrey* (1905). The courts of the State have repeatedly emphasized that education in Michigan is not a local governmental concern, but a state function.

> "Unlike the delegation of other powers by the legislature to local governments, education is not inherently a part of the local self-government of a municipality. . . . Control of our public school system is a State matter delegated and lodged in the State Legislature by the Constitution. The policy of the State has been to retain control of its school system, to be administered throughout the State under State laws by local State agencies organized with plenary powers to carry out the delegated functions given [them] by the legislature." *School District of the City of Lansing* v. *State Board of Education.*

The Supreme Court of Michigan has noted the deep roots of this policy:

"It has been settled by the Ordinance of 1787, the several Constitutions adopted in this State, by its uniform course of legislation,
and by the decisions of this Court, that education in Michigan is a
matter of State concern, that it is no part of the local self-government of a particular township or municipality. . . . The legislature has always dictated the educational policy of the State." *In re
School District No. 6* (1938).

The State's control over education is reflected in the fact that, contrary to the Court's implication, there is little or no relationship between school districts and local political units. To take the 85 outlying
local school districts in the Detroit metropolitan area as examples, 17
districts lie in two counties, two in three counties. One district serves
five municipalities; other suburban municipalities are fragmented into
as many as six school districts. Nor is there any apparent state policy
with regard to the size of school districts, as they now range from 2,000
to 285,000 students.

Centralized state control manifests itself in practice as well as in
theory. The State controls the financing of education in several ways.
The legislature contributes a substantial portion of most school districts' operating budgets with funds appropriated from the State's General Fund revenues raised through statewide taxation. The State's
power over the purse can be and is in fact used to enforce the State's
powers over local districts. In addition, although local districts obtain
funds through local property taxation, the State has assumed the responsibility to ensure equalized property valuations throughout the
State. The State also establishes standards for teacher certification and
teacher tenure; determines part of the required curriculum; sets the
minimum school term; approves bus routes, equipment, and drivers;
approves textbooks; and establishes procedures for student discipline.
The State Superintendent of Public Instruction and the State Board of
Education have the power to remove local school board members from
office for neglect of their duties.

Most significantly for present purposes, the State has wide-ranging
powers to consolidate and merge school districts, even without the consent of the districts themselves or of the local citizenry. See, *e.g., Attorney General ex rel. Kies* v. *Lowrey* (1902). Indeed, recent years have
witnessed an accelerated program of school district consolidations,
mergers, and annexations, many of which were state imposed. Whereas
the State had 7,362 local districts in 1912, the number had been re-

duced to 1,438 in 1964 and to 738 in 1968. By June 1972, only 608 school districts remained. Furthermore, the State has broad powers to transfer property from one district to another, again without the consent of the local school districts affected by the transfer. See, *e.g., School District of the City of Lansing* v. *State Board of Education, supra; Imlay Township District* v. *State Board of Education* (1960).

Whatever may be the history of public education in other parts of our Nation, it simply flies in the face of reality to say, as does the majority, that in Michigan, "[n]o single tradition in public education is more deeply rooted than local control over the operation of schools. . . ." As the State's Supreme Court has said: "We have repeatedly held that education in this State is not a matter of local concern, but belongs to the State at large." *Collins* v. *City of Detroit* (1917). See also *Sturgis* v. *County of Allegan* (1955); *Van Fleet* v. *Oltman* (1928); *Child Welfare Society of Flint* v. *Kennedy School District* (1922). Indeed, a study prepared for the 1961 Michigan Constitutional Convention noted that the Michigan Constitution's articles on education had resulted in "the establishment of a state system of education in contrast to a series of local school systems." Elementary and Secondary Education and the Michigan Constitution, Michigan Constitutional Convention Studies 1 (1961).

In sum, several factors in this case coalesce to support the District Court's ruling that it was the State of Michigan itself, not simply the Detroit Board of Education, which bore the obligation of curing the condition of segregation within the Detroit city schools. The actions of the State itself directly contributed to Detroit's segregation. Under the Fourteenth Amendment, the State is ultimately responsible for the actions of its local agencies. And, finally, given the structure of Michigan's educational system, Detroit's segregation cannot be viewed as the problem of an independent and separate entity. Michigan operates a single statewide system of education, a substantial part of which was shown to be segregated in this case.

B

What action, then, could the District Court require the State to take in order to cure Detroit's condition of segregation? Our prior cases have not minced words as to what steps responsible officials and agencies must take in order to remedy segregation in the public schools. Not only must distinctions on the basis of race be terminated for the future, but school officials are also "clearly charged with the affirmative duty to take whatever steps might be necessary to convert to a unitary system in which racial discrimination would be eliminated root and branch." *Green* v. *County School Board of New Kent County* (1968). (MD Ala.), aff'd *sub nom. Wallace* v. *United States* (1967). Negro students are not only entitled to neutral nondiscriminatory treatment in the future. They must receive "what *Brown II* promised them: a school system in which all vestiges of enforced racial segregation have been eliminated." *Wright* v. *Council of the City of Emporia* (1972). See also *Swann* v. *Charlotte-Mecklenburg Board of Education* (1971). These remedial standards are fully applicable not only to school districts where a dual system was compelled by statute, but also where, as here, a dual system was the product of purposeful and intentional state action. See *Keyes*.

After examining three plans limited to the city of Detroit, the District Court correctly concluded that none would eliminate root and branch the vestiges of unconstitutional segregation. The plans' effectiveness, of course, had to be evaluated in the context of the District Court's findings as to the extent of segregation in the Detroit city schools. As indicated earlier, the most essential finding was that Negro children in Detroit had been confined by intentional acts of segregation to a growing core of Negro schools surrounded by a receding ring of white schools. Thus, in 1960, of Detroit's 251 regular-attendance schools, 100 were 90% or more white and 71 were 90% or more Negro. In 1970, of Detroit's 282 regular-attendance schools, 69 were 90% or more white and 133 were 90% or more Negro. While in 1960, 68% of all schools were 90% or more one race, by 1970, 71.6% of the schools fell into that category. The growing core of all-Negro schools was further evidenced in total school district population figures. In 1960 the Detroit system had 46% Negro students and 54% white students, but by 1970, 64% of the students were Negro and only 36% were white. This increase in the proportion of Negro students was the highest of any major Northern city.

It was with these figures in the background that the District Court evaluated the adequacy of the three Detroit-only plans submitted by the parties. Plan A, proposed by the Detroit Board of Education, desegregated the high schools and about a fifth of the middle-level schools. It was deemed inadequate, however, because it did not desegregate elementary schools and left the middle-level schools not included in the plan more segregated than ever. Plan C, also proposed by the Detroit Board, was deemed inadequate because it too covered only some grade levels and would leave elementary schools segregated. Plan B, the plaintiffs' plan, though requiring the transportation of 82,000 pupils and the acquisition of 900 school buses, would make little headway in rooting out the vestiges of segregation. To begin with, because of practical limitations, the District Court found that the plan would leave many of the Detroit city schools 75% to 90% Negro. More significantly, the District Court recognized that in the context of a community which historically had a school system marked by rigid *de jure* segregation, the likely effect of a Detroit-only plan would be to "change a school system which is now Black and White to one that would be perceived as Black. . . ." The result of this changed perception, the District Court found, would be to increase the flight of whites from the city to the outlying suburbs, compounding the effects of the present rate of increase in the proportion of Negro students in the Detroit system. Thus, even if a plan were adopted which, at its outset, provided in every school a 65% Negro-35% white racial mix in keeping with the Negro-white proportions of the total student population, such a system would, in short order, devolve into an all-Negro system. The net result would be a continuation of the all-Negro schools which were the hallmarks of Detroit's former dual system of one-race schools.

Under our decisions, it was clearly proper for the District Court to take into account the so-called "white flight" from the city schools which would be forthcoming from any Detroit-only decree. The court's prediction of white flight was well supported by expert testimony based on past experience in other cities undergoing desegregation relief. We ourselves took the possibility of white flight into account in evaluating the effectiveness of a desegregation plan in *Wright, supra,* where we relied on the District Court's finding that if the city of Emporia were allowed to withdraw from the existing system, leaving a system with a higher proportion of Negroes, it " 'may be anticipated that the proportion of whites in county schools may drop as those who can register in private academies'. . . ." One cannot ignore the white-flight problem, for where legally imposed segregation has been established, the District Court has the responsibility to see to it not only that the dual system is terminated at once but also that future events do not serve to perpetuate or re-establish segregation. See *Swann.* See also *Green, Monroe* v. *Board of Comm'rs* (1968).

We held in *Swann, supra,* that where *de jure* segregation is shown, school authorities must make "every effort to achieve the greatest possible degree of actual desegregation." This is the operative standard re-emphasized in *Davis* v. *School Comm'rs of Mobile County* (1971). If these words have any meaning at all, surely it is that school authorities must, to the extent possible, take all practicable steps to ensure that Negro and white children in fact go to school together. This is, in the final analysis, what desegregation of the public schools is all about.

Because of the already high and rapidly increasing percentage of Negro students in the Detroit system, as well as the prospect of white flight, a Detroit-only plan simply has no hope of achieving actual desegregation. Under such a plan white and Negro students will not go to school together. Instead, Negro children will continue to attend all-Negro schools. The very evil that *Brown I* was aimed at will not be cured, but will be perpetuated for the future.

Racially identifiable schools are one of the primary vestiges of state-imposed segregation which an effective desegregation decree must attempt to eliminate. In *Swann, supra,* for example, we held that "[t]he district judge or school authorities . . . will thus necessarily be concerned with the elimination of one-race schools." There is "a presumption," we stated, "against schools that are substantially disproportionate in their racial composition." And in evaluating the effectiveness of desegregation plans in prior cases, we ourselves have considered the extent to which they discontinued racially identifiable schools. See, *e.g., Green* v. *County School Board of New Kent County, supra; Wright* v. *Council of the City of Emporia, supra.* For a principal end of any desegregation remedy is to ensure that it is no longer "possible to identify a 'white school' or a 'Negro school.' " *Swann.* The evil to be remedied in the dismantling of a dual system is the "[r]acial identification of the system's schools." *Green.* The goal is a system without white schools or Negro schools—a system with "just schools." A school authority's remedial plan or a district court's remedial decree is to be judged by its effectiveness in achieving this end. See *Swann.*

We cautioned in *Swann,* of course, that the dismantling of a segregated school system does not mandate any particular racial balance. We also concluded that a remedy under which there would remain a small number of racially identifiable schools was only presumptively inadequate and might be justified. But this is a totally different case. The flaw of a Detroit-only decree is not that it does not reach some ideal degree of racial balance or mixing. It simply does not promise to achieve actual desegregation at all. It is one thing to have a system where a small number of students remain in racially identifiable schools. It is something else entirely to have a system where all students continue to attend such schools.

The continued racial identifiability of the Detroit schools under a Detroit-only remedy is not simply a reflection of their high percentage of Negro students. What is or is not a racially identifiable vestige of *de jure* segregation must necessarily depend on several factors. Cf. *Keyes.* Foremost among these should be the relationship between the schools in question and the neighboring community. For these purposes the city of Detroit and its surrounding suburbs must be viewed as a single community. Detroit is closely connected to its suburbs in many ways, and the metropolitan area is viewed as a single cohesive unit by its residents. About 40% of the residents of the two suburban counties included in the desegregation plan work in Wayne County, in which Detroit is situated. Many residents of the city work in the suburbs. The three counties participate in a wide variety of cooperative governmental ventures on a metropolitan-wide basis, including a metropolitan transit system, park authority, water and sewer system, and council of governments. The Federal Government has classified the tri-county area as a Standard Metropolitan Statistical Area, indicating that it is an area of "economic and social integration." *United States* v. *Connecticut National Bank.*

Under a Detroit-only decree, Detroit's schools will clearly remain racially identifiable in comparison with neighboring schools in the metropolitan community. Schools with 65% and more Negro students will stand in sharp and obvious contrast to schools in neighboring districts with less than 2% Negro enrollment. Negro students will continue to perceive their schools as segregated educational facilities and this perception will only be increased when whites react to a Detroit-only decree by fleeing to the suburbs to avoid integration. School district lines, however innocently drawn, will surely be perceived as fences to separate the races when, under a Detroit-only decree, white parents withdraw their children from the Detroit city schools and move to the suburbs in order to continue them in all-white schools. The message of this action will not escape the Negro children in the city of Detroit. See *Wright.* It will be of scant significance to Negro children who have for years been confined by *de jure* acts of segregation to a growing core of all-Negro schools surrounded by a ring of all-white schools that the new dividing line between the races is the school district boundary.

Nor can it be said that the State is free from any responsibility for the disparity between the racial makeup of Detroit and its surrounding suburbs. The State's creation, through *de jure* acts of segregation, of a growing core of all-Negro schools inevitably acted as a magnet to attract Negroes to the areas served by such schools and to deter them from settling either in other areas of the city or in the suburbs. By the same token, the growing core of all-Negro schools inevitably helped drive whites to other areas of the city or to the suburbs. As we recognized in *Swann*:

> "People gravitate toward school facilities, just as schools are located in response to the needs of people. The location of schools may thus influence the patterns of residential development of a metropolitan area and have important impact on composition of inner-city neighborhoods. . . . [Action taken] to maintain the separation of the races with a minimum departure from the formal principles of 'neighborhood zoning' . . . does more than simply influence the short-run composition of the student body. . . . It may well promote segregated residential patterns which, when combined with 'neighborhood zoning,' further lock the school system into the mold of separation of the races. Upon a proper showing a district court may consider this in fashioning a remedy."

See also *Keyes*. The rippling effects on residential patterns caused by purposeful acts of segregation do not automatically subside at the school district border. With rare exceptions, these effects naturally spread through all the residential neighborhoods within a metropolitan area.

The State must also bear part of the blame for the white flight to the suburbs which would be forthcoming from a Detroit-only decree and would render such a remedy ineffective. Having created a system where whites and Negroes were intentionally kept apart so that they could not become accustomed to learning together, the State is responsible for the fact that many whites will react to the dismantling of that segregated system by attempting to flee to the suburbs. Indeed, by limiting the District Court to a Detroit-only remedy and allowing that flight to the suburbs to succeed, the Court today allows the State to profit from its own wrong and to perpetuate for years to come the separation of the races it achieved in the past by purposeful state action.

The majority asserts, however, that involvement of outlying districts would do violence to the accepted principle that "the nature of the violation determines the scope of the remedy." Not only is the majority's attempt to find in this single phrase the answer to the complex and difficult questions presented in this case hopelessly simplistic, but more important, the Court reads these words in a manner which perverts their obvious meaning. The nature of a violation determines the scope of the remedy simply because the function of any remedy is to cure the violation to which it is addressed. In school segregation cases, as in other equitable causes, a remedy which effectively cures the violation is what is required. See *Green.* No more is necessary, but we can tolerate no less. To read this principle as barring a district court from imposing the only effective remedy for past segregation and remitting the court to a patently ineffective alternative is, in my view, to turn a simple commonsense rule into a cruel and meaningless paradox. Ironically, by ruling out an interdistrict remedy, the only relief which promises to cure segregation in the Detroit public schools, the majority flouts the very principle on which it purports to rely.

Nor should it be of any significance that the suburban school districts were not shown to have themselves taken any direct action to promote segregation of the races. Given the State's broad powers over local school districts, it was well within the State's powers to require those districts surrounding the Detroit school district to participate in a metropolitan remedy. The State's duty should be no different here than in cases where it is shown that certain of a State's voting districts are malapportioned in violation of the Fourteenth Amendment. See *Reynolds* v. *Sims* (1964). Overrepresented electoral districts are required to participate in reapportionment although their only "participation" in the violation was to do nothing about it. Similarly, electoral districts which themselves meet representation standards must frequently be redrawn as part of a remedy for other over- and under-inclusive districts. No finding of fault on the part of each electoral district and no finding of a discriminatory effect on each district is a prerequisite to its involvement in the constitutionally required remedy. By the same logic, no finding of fault on the part of the suburban school districts in this case and no finding of a discriminatory effect on each district should be a prerequisite to their involvement in the constitutionally required remedy.

It is the State, after all, which bears the responsibility under *Brown* of affording a nondiscriminatory system of education. The State, of course, is ordinarily free to choose any decentralized framework for education it wishes, so long as it fulfills that Fourteenth Amendment obligation. But the State should no more be allowed to hide behind its delegation and compartmentalization of school districts to avoid its constitutional obligations to its children than it could hide behind its political subdivisions to avoid its obligations to its voters. *Reynolds* v. *Sims.*

It is a hollow remedy indeed where "after supposed 'desegregation' the schools remained segregated in fact." *Hobson* v. *Hansen.* We must do better than " 'substitute . . . one segregated school system for another segregated school system.' " *Wright.* To suggest, as does the majority, that a Detroit-only plan somehow remedies the effects of *de jure* segregation of the races is, in my view, to make a solemn mockery of *Brown I*'s holding that separate educational facilities are inherently unequal and of *Swann*'s unequivocal mandate that the answer to *de jure* segregation is the greatest possible degree of actual desegregation.

III

One final set of problems remains to be considered. We recognized in *Brown II,* and have re-emphasized ever since, that in fashioning relief in desegregation cases, "the courts will be guided by equitable principles. Traditionally, equity has been characterized by a practical flexibility in shaping its remedies and by a facility for adjusting and reconciling public and private needs." *Brown II.*

Though not resting its holding on this point, the majority suggests that various equitable considerations militate against interdistrict relief. The Court, for example, refers to financing and administrative problems, the logistical problems attending large-scale transportation of students, and the prospect of the District Court's becoming a *"de facto* 'legislative authority' " and " 'school superintendent' for the entire area." The entangling web of problems woven by the Court, however, appears on further consideration to be constructed of the flimsiest of threads.

I deal first with the last of the problems posed by the Court—the specter of the District Court *qua* "school superintendent" and "legislative authority"—for analysis of this problem helps put the other issues in proper perspective. Our cases, of course, make clear that the initial responsibility for devising an adequate desegregation plan belongs with school authorities, not with the District Court. The court's primary role is to review the adequacy of the school authorities' efforts and to substitute its own plan only if and to the extent they default. See *Swann.* Contrary to the majority's suggestions, the District Judge in this case consistently adhered to these procedures and there is every indication that he would have continued to do so. After finding *de jure* segregation the court ordered the parties to submit proposed Detroit-only plans. The State defendants were also ordered to submit a proposed metropolitan plan extending beyond Detroit's boundaries. As the District Court stated, "the State defendants . . . bear the initial burden of coming forward with a proposal that promises to work." The State defendants defaulted in this obligation, however. Rather than submit a complete plan, the State Board of Education submitted six proposals, none of which was in fact a desegregation plan. It was only upon this default that the District Court began to take steps to develop its own plan. Even then the District Court maximized school authority participation by appointing a panel representing both plaintiffs and defendants to develop a plan. Furthermore, the District Court still left the State defendants the initial responsibility for developing both interim and final financial and administrative arrangements to implement interdistrict relief. *Id.,* at 104a–105a. The Court of Appeals further protected the interests of local school authorities by ensuring that the outlying suburban districts could fully participate in the proceedings to develop a metropolitan remedy.

These processes have not been allowed to run their course. No final desegregation plan has been proposed by the panel of experts, let alone approved by the District Court. We do not know in any detail how many students will be transported to effect a metropolitan remedy, and we do not know how long or how far they will have to travel. No recommendations have yet been submitted by the State defendants on financial and administrative arrangements. In sum, the practicality of a final metropolitan plan is simply not before us at the present time. Since the State and the panel of experts have not yet had an opportunity to come up with a workable remedy, there is no foundation for the majority's suggestion of the impracticality of interdistrict relief. Furthermore, there is no basis whatever for assuming that the District Court will inevitably be forced to assume the role of legislature or school superintendent. Were we to hold that it was its constitutional duty to do so, there is every indication that the State of Michigan would fulfill its obligation and develop a plan which is workable, administrable, financially sound, and, most important, in the best interest of quality education for all of the children in the Detroit metropolitan area.

Since the Court chooses, however, to speculate on the feasibility of a metropolitan plan, I feel constrained to comment on the problem areas it has targeted. To begin with, the majority's questions concerning the practicality of consolidation of school districts need not give us pause. The State clearly has the power, under existing law, to effect a consolidation if it is ultimately determined that this offers the best prospect for a workable and stable desegregation plan. And given the 1,000 or so consolidations of school districts which have taken place in the past, it is hard to believe that the State has not already devised means of solving most, if not all, of the practical problems which the Court suggests consolidation would entail.

Furthermore, the majority ignores long-established Michigan procedures under which school districts may enter into contractual agreements to educate their pupils in other districts using state or local funds to finance nonresident education. Such agreements could form an easily administrable framework for interdistrict relief short of outright consolidation of the school districts. The District Court found that interdistrict procedures like these were frequently used to provide special educational services for handicapped children, and extensive statutory provision is also made for their use in vocational education. Surely if school districts are willing to engage in interdistrict programs to help those unfortunate children crippled by physical or mental handicaps, school districts can be required to participate in an interdistrict program to help those children in the city of Detroit whose educations and very futures have been crippled by purposeful state segregation.

Although the majority gives this last matter only fleeting reference, it is plain that one of the basic emotional and legal issues underlying these cases concerns the propriety of transportation of students to achieve desegregation. While others may have retreated from its standards, see, *e.g., Keyes* (POWELL, J., concurring in part and dissenting in part), I continue to adhere to the guidelines set forth in *Swann* on this issue. And though no final desegregation plan is presently before us, to the extent the outline of such a plan is now visible, it is clear that the transportation it would entail will be fully consistent with these guidelines.

First of all, the metropolitan plan would not involve the busing of substantially more students than already ride buses. The District Court found that, statewide, 35%–40% of all students already arrive at school on a bus. In those school districts in the tri-county Detroit metropolitan area eligible for state reimbursement of transportation costs, 42%–52% of all students rode buses to school. In the tri-county areas as a whole, approximately 300,000 pupils arrived at school on some type of bus, with about 60,000 of these apparently using regular public transit. In comparison, the desegregation plan, according to its present rough outline, would involve the transportation of 310,000 students, about 40% of the population within the desegregation area.

With respect to distance and amount of time traveled, 17 of the outlying school districts involved in the plan are contiguous to the Detroit district. The rest are all within 8 miles of the Detroit city limits. The trial court, in defining the desegregation area, placed a ceiling of 40 minutes one way on the amount of travel time, and many students will obviously travel for far shorter periods. As to distance, the average statewide bus trip is 8 1/2 miles one way, and in some parts of the tri-county area, students already travel for one and a quarter hours or more each way. In sum, with regard to both the number of students transported and the time and distances involved, the outlined desegregation plan "compares favorably with the transportation plan previously operated. . . ." *Swann.*

As far as economics are concerned, a metropolitan remedy would actually be more sensible than a Detroit-only remedy. Because of prior transportation aid restrictions Detroit largely relied on public transport, at student expense, for those students who lived too far away to walk to school. Since no inventory of school buses existed, a Detroit-only plan was estimated to require the purchase of 900 buses to effectuate the necessary transportation. The tri-county area, in contrast, already has an inventory of 1,800 buses, many of which are now underutilized. Since increased utilization of the existing inventory can take up much of the increase in transportation involved in the interdistrict remedy, the District Court found that only 350 additional buses would probably be needed, almost two-thirds fewer than a Detroit-only remedy. Other features of an interdistrict remedy bespeak its practicality, such as the possibility of pairing up Negro schools near Detroit's boundary with nearby white schools on the other side of the present school district line.

Some disruption, of course, is the inevitable product of any desegregation decree, whether it operates within one district or on an interdistrict basis. As we said in *Swann,* however:

"Absent a constitutional violation there would be no basis for judicially ordering assignment of students on a racial basis. All things being equal, with no history of discrimination, it might well be desirable to assign pupils to schools nearest their homes. But all things are not equal in a system that has been deliberately constructed and maintained to enforce racial segregation. The remedy for such segregation may be administratively awkward, inconvenient, and even bizarre in some situations and may impose burdens on some; but all awkwardness and inconvenience cannot be avoided. . . ."

Desegregation is not and was never expected to be an easy task. Racial attitudes ingrained in our Nation's childhood and adolescence are not quickly thrown aside in its middle years. But just as the inconvenience of some cannot be allowed to stand in the way of the rights of others, so public opposition, no matter how strident, cannot be permitted to divert this Court from the enforcement of the constitutional principles at issue in this case. Today's holding, I fear, is more a reflection of a perceived public mood that we have gone far enough in enforcing the Constitution's guarantee of equal justice than it is the product of neutral principles of law. In the short run, it may seem to be the easier course to allow our great metropolitan areas to be divided up each into two cities—one white, the other black—but it is a course, I predict, our people will ultimately regret. I dissent.

CITY OF RICHMOND
versus
J. A. CROSON CO.

APPEAL FROM THE UNITED STATES COURT OF APPEALS
FOR THE FOURTH CIRCUIT

Argued October 5, 1988
Decided January 23, 1989

Appellant city adopted a Minority Business Utilization Plan (Plan) requiring prime contractors awarded city construction contracts to subcontract at least 30% of the dollar amount of each contract to one or more "Minority Business Enterprises" (MBE's), which the Plan defined to include a business from anywhere in the country at least 51% of which is owned and controlled by black, Spanish-speaking, Oriental, Indian, Eskimo, or Aleut citizens. Although the Plan declared that it was "remedial" in nature, it was adopted after a public hearing at which no direct evidence was presented that the city had discriminated on the basis of race in letting contracts or that its prime contractors had discriminated against minority subcontractors. The evidence that was introduced included: a statistical study indicating that, although the city's population was 50% black, only 0.67% of its prime construction contracts had been awarded to minority businesses in recent years; figures establishing that a variety of local contractors' associations had virtually no MBE members; the city's counsel's conclusion that the Plan was constitutional under *Fullilove* v. *Klutznick,* and the statements of Plan proponents indicating that there had been widespread racial discrimination in the local, state, and national construction industries. Pursuant to the Plan, the city adopted rules requiring individualized consideration of each bid or request for a waiver of the 30% set-aside, and providing that a waiver could be granted only upon proof that sufficient qualified MBE's were unavailable or unwilling to participate.

After appellee construction company, the sole bidder on a city contract, was denied a waiver and lost its contract, it brought suit under 42 U. S. C. § 1983, alleging that the Plan was unconstitutional under the Fourteenth Amendment's Equal Protection Clause. The Federal District Court upheld the Plan in all respects, and the Court of Appeals affirmed, applying a test derived from the principal opinion in *Fullilove, supra,* which accorded great deference to Congress's findings of past societal discrimination in holding that a 10% minority set-aside for certain federal construction grants did not violate the equal protection component of the Fifth Amendment. However, on appellee's petition for certiorari in this case, this Court vacated and remanded for further consideration in light of its intervening decision in *Wygant* v. *Jackson Board of Education,* in which the plurality applied a strict scrutiny standard in holding that a race-based layoff program agreed to by a school board and the local teachers' union violated the Fourteenth Amendment's Equal Protection Clause. On remand, the Court of Appeals held that the city's Plan violated both prongs of strict scrutiny, in that (1) the Plan was not justified by a compelling governmental interest, since the record revealed no prior discrimination by the city itself in awarding contracts, and (2) the 30% set-aside was not narrowly tailored to accomplish a remedial purpose.

Held: The judgment is affirmed.

JUSTICE O'CONNOR delivered the opinion of the Court with respect to Parts I, III-B, and IV, concluding that:

1. The city has failed to demonstrate a compelling governmental interest justifying the Plan, since the factual predicate supporting the Plan does not establish the type of identified past discrimination in the city's construction industry that would authorize race-based relief under the Fourteenth Amendment's Equal Protection Clause.

(a) A generalized assertion that there has been past discrimination in the entire construction industry cannot justify the use of an unyielding racial quota, since it provides no guidance for the city's legislative body to determine the precise scope of the injury it seeks to remedy and would allow race-based decisionmaking essentially limitless in scope and duration. The city's argument that it is attempting to remedy various forms of past societal discrimination that are alleged to be responsible for the small number of minority entrepreneurs in the local contracting industry fails, since the city also lists a host of nonracial factors which would seem to face a member of any racial group seeking to establish a new business enterprise, such as deficiencies in working capital, inability to meet bonding requirements, unfamiliarity with bidding procedures, and disability caused by an inadequate track record.

(b) None of the "facts" cited by the city or relied on by the District Court, singly or together, provide a basis for a prima facie case of a constitutional or statutory violation by *anyone* in the city's construction industry. The fact that the Plan declares itself to be "remedial" is insufficient, since the mere recitation of a "benign" or legitimate purpose for a racial classification is entitled to little or no weight. Similarly, the views of Plan proponents as to past and present discrimination in the industry are highly conclusory and of little probative value. Reliance on the disparity between the number of prime contracts awarded to minority businesses and the city's minority population is also misplaced, since the proper statistical evaluation would compare the percentage of MBE's in the relevant market that are qualified to undertake city subcontracting work with the percentage of total city construction dollars that are presently awarded to minority subcontractors, neither of which is known to the city. The fact that MBE membership in local contractors' associations was extremely low is also not probative absent some link to the number of MBE's eligible for membership, since there are numerous explanations for the dearth of minority participation, including past societal discrimination in education and economic opportunities as well as both black and white career and entrepreneurial choices. Congress's finding in connection with the set-aside approved in *Fullilove* that there had been nationwide discrimination in the construction industry also has extremely limited probative value, since, by including a waiver procedure in the national program, Congress explicitly recognized that the scope of the problem would vary from market area to market area. In any event, Congress was acting pursuant to its unique enforcement powers under § 5 of the Fourteenth Amendment.

(c) The "evidence" relied upon by JUSTICE MARSHALL's dissent—the city's history of school desegregation and numerous congressional reports—does little to define the scope of any injury to minority contractors in the city or the necessary remedy, and could justify a preference of any size or duration. Moreover, JUSTICE MARSHALL's suggestion that discrimination findings may be "shared" from jurisdiction to jurisdiction is unprecedented and contrary to this Court's decisions.

(d) Since there is *absolutely no evidence* of past discrimination against Spanish-speaking, Oriental, Indian, Eskimo, or Aleut persons in any aspect of the city's construction industry, the Plan's random inclusion of those groups strongly impugns the city's claim of remedial motivation.

2. The Plan is not narrowly tailored to remedy the effects of prior discrimination, since it entitles a black, Hispanic, or Oriental entrepreneur from anywhere in the country to an absolute preference over other citizens based solely on their race. Although many of the barriers to minority participation in the construction industry relied upon by the city to justify the Plan appear to be race neutral, there is no evidence that the city considered using alternative, race-neutral means to increase minority participation in city contracting. Moreover, the Plan's rigid 30% quota rests upon the completely unrealistic assumption that minorities will choose to enter construction in lockstep proportion to their representation in the local population. Unlike the program upheld in *Fullilove,* the Plan's waiver system focuses upon the availability of MBE's, and does not inquire whether the particular MBE seeking a racial preference has suffered from the effects of past discrimination by the city or prime contractors. Given the fact that the city must already consider bids and waivers on a case-by-case basis, the city's only interest in maintaining a quota system rather than investigating the need for remedial action in particular cases would seem to be simply administrative convenience, which, standing alone, cannot justify the use of a suspect classification under equal protection strict scrutiny.

JUSTICE O'CONNOR, joined by THE CHIEF JUSTICE and JUSTICE WHITE, concluded in Part II that if the city could identify past discrimination in the local construction industry with the particularity required by the Equal Protection Clause, it would have the power to adopt race-based legislation designed to eradicate the effects of that discrimination. The principal opinion in *Fullilove* cannot be read to relieve the city of the necessity of making the specific findings of discrimination required by the Clause, since the congressional finding of past discrimination relied on in that case was made pursuant to Congress's unique power under § 5 of the Amendment to enforce, and therefore to identify and redress violations of, the Amendment's provisions. Conversely, § 1 of the Amendment, which includes the Equal Protection Clause, is an explicit constraint upon the power of States and political subdivisions, which must undertake any remedial efforts in accordance with the dictates of that section. However, the Court of Appeals erred to the extent that it followed by rote the *Wygant* plurality's ruling that the Equal Protection Clause requires a showing of prior discrimination by the governmental unit involved, since that ruling was made in the context of a race-based policy that affected the particular public employer's own work force, whereas this case involves a state entity which has specific state-law authority to address discriminatory practices within local commerce under its jurisdiction.

JUSTICE O'CONNOR, joined by THE CHIEF JUSTICE, JUSTICE WHITE, and JUSTICE KENNEDY, concluded in Parts III–A and V that:

1. Since the Plan denies certain citizens the opportunity to compete for a fixed percentage of public contracts based solely on their race, *Wygant's* strict scrutiny standard of review must be applied, which requires a firm evidentiary basis for concluding that the underrepresentation of minorities is a product of past discrimination. Application of that standard, which is not dependent on the race of those burdened or benefited by the racial classification, assures that the city is pursuing a remedial goal important enough to warrant use of a highly suspect tool and that the means chosen "fit" this compelling goal so closely that there is little or no possibility that the motive for the classification was illegitimate racial prejudice or stereotype. The relaxed standard of review proposed by JUSTICE MARSHALL's dissent does not provide a means for determining that a racial classification is in fact "designed to further remedial goals," since it accepts the remedial nature of the classification before examination of the factual basis for the classification's enactment and the nexus between its scope and that factual basis. Even if the level of equal protection scrutiny could be said to vary according to the ability of different groups to defend their interests in the representative process, heightened scrutiny would still be appropriate in the circumstances of this case, since blacks comprise approximately 50% of the city's population and hold five of nine seats on the city council, thereby raising the concern that the political majority may have acted to disadvantage a minority based on unwarranted assumptions or incomplete facts.

2. Even in the absence of evidence of discrimination in the local construction industry, the city has at its disposal an array of race-neutral devices to increase the accessibility of city contracting opportunities to small entrepreneurs of all races who have suffered the effects of past societal discrimination, including simplification of bidding procedures, relaxation of bonding requirements, training, financial aid, elimination or modification of formal barriers caused by bureaucratic inertia, and the prohibition of discrimination in the provision of credit or bonding by local suppliers and banks.

Justice Stevens, although agreeing that the Plan cannot be justified as a remedy for past discrimination, concluded that the Fourteenth Amendment does not limit permissible racial classifications to those that remedy past wrongs, but requires that race-based governmental decisions be evaluated primarily by studying their probable impact on the future.

(a) Disregarding the past history of racial injustice, there is not even an arguable basis for suggesting that the race of a subcontractor or contractor on city projects should have any relevance to his or her access to the market. Although race is not always irrelevant to sound governmental decisionmaking, the city makes no claim that the public interest in the efficient performance of its construction contracts will be served by granting a preference to minority-business enterprises.

(b) Legislative bodies such as the city council, which are primarily policymaking entities that promulgate rules to govern future conduct, raise valid constitutional concerns when they use the political process to punish or characterize past conduct of private citizens. Courts, on the other hand, are well equipped to identify past wrongdoers and to fashion remedies that will create the conditions that presumably would have existed had no wrong been committed, and should have the same broad discretion in racial discrimination cases that chancellors enjoy in other areas of the law to fashion remedies against persons who have been proved guilty of violations of law.

(c) Rather than engaging in debate over the proper standard of review to apply in affirmative-action litigation, it is more constructive to try to identify the characteristics of the advantaged and disadvantaged classes that may justify their disparate treatment. Here, instead of carefully identifying those characteristics, the city has merely engaged in the type of stereotypical analysis that is the hallmark of Equal Protection Clause violations. The class of persons benefited by the Plan is not limited to victims of past discrimination by white contractors in the city, but encompasses persons who have never been in business in the city, minority contractors who may have themselves been guilty of discrimination against other minority group members, and firms that have prospered notwithstanding discriminatory treatment. Similarly, although the Plan unquestionably disadvantages some white contractors who are guilty of past discrimination against blacks, it also punishes some who discriminated only before it was forbidden by law and some who have never discriminated against anyone.

Justice Kennedy concluded that the Fourteenth Amendment

ought not to be interpreted to reduce a State's power to eradicate racial discrimination and its effects in both the public and private sectors, or its absolute duty to do so where those wrongs were caused intentionally by the State itself, except where there is a conflict with federal law or where, as here, a state remedy itself violates equal protection. Although a rule striking down all racial preferences which are not necessary remedies to victims of unlawful discrimination would serve important structural goals by eliminating the necessity for courts to pass on each such preference that is enacted, that rule would be a significant break with this Court's precedents that require a case-by-case test, and need not be adopted. Rather, it may be assumed that the principle of race neutrality found in the Equal Protection Clause will be vindicated by the less absolute strict scrutiny standard, the application of which demonstrates that the city's Plan is not a remedy but is itself an unconstitutional preference.

JUSTICE SCALIA, agreeing that strict scrutiny must be applied to all governmental racial classifications, concluded that:

1. The Fourteenth Amendment prohibits state and local governments from discriminating on the basis of race in order to undo the effects of past discrimination, except in one circumstance: where that is necessary to eliminate their own maintenance of a system of unlawful racial classification. Moreover, the State's remedial power in that instance extends no further than the scope of the constitutional violation, and does not encompass the continuing effects of a discriminatory system once the system itself has been eliminated.

2. The State remains free to undo the effects of past discrimination in permissible ways that do not involve classification by race—for example, by according a contracting preference to small or new businesses or to actual victims of discrimination who can be identified. In the latter instance, the classification would not be based on race but on the fact that the victims were wronged.

O'CONNOR, J., announced the judgment of the Court and delivered the opinion of the Court with respect to Parts I, III–B, and IV, in which REHNQUIST, C. J., and WHITE, STEVENS, and KENNEDY, J.J., joined, an opinion with respect to Part II, in which REHNQUIST, C. J., and WHITE, J., joined, and an opinion with respect to Parts III–A and V, in which REHNQUIST, C. J., and WHITE and KENNEDY, JJ., joined. STEVENS, J., and KENNEDY, J. filed opinions concurring in part and concurring in the judgment. SCALIA, J., filed an opinion concurring in the judgment. MAR-

SHALL, J., filed a dissenting opinion, in which BRENNAN and BLACKMUN, JJ., joined. BLACKMUN, J., filed a dissenting opinion, in which BRENNAN, J., joined.

JUSTICE MARSHALL, with whom JUSTICE BRENNAN and JUSTICE BLACK-MUN join, dissenting.

It is a welcome symbol of racial progress when the former capital of the Confederacy acts forthrightly to confront the effects of racial discrimination in its midst. In my view, nothing in the Constitution can be construed to prevent Richmond, Virginia, from allocating a portion of its contracting dollars for businesses owned or controlled by members of minority groups. Indeed, Richmond's set-aside program is indistinguishable in all meaningful respects from—and in fact was patterned upon—the federal set-aside plan which this Court upheld in *Fullilove* v. *Klutznick* (1980).

A majority of this Court holds today, however, that the Equal Protection Clause of the Fourteenth Amendment blocks Richmond's initiative. The essence of the majority's position is that Richmond has failed to catalog adequate findings to prove that past discrimination has impeded minorities from joining or participating fully in Richmond's construction contracting industry. I find deep irony in second-guessing Richmond's judgment on this point. As much as any municipality in the United States, Richmond knows what racial discrimination is; a century of decisions by this and other federal courts has richly documented the city's disgraceful history of public and private racial discrimination. In any event, the Richmond City Council *has* supported its determination that minorities have been wrongly excluded from local construction contracting. Its proof includes statistics showing that minority-owned businesses have received virtually no city contracting dollars and rarely if ever belonged to area trade associations; testimony by municipal officials that discrimination has been widespread in the local construction industry; and the same exhaustive and widely publicized federal studies relied on in *Fullilove,* studies which showed that pervasive discrimination in the Nation's tight-knit construction industry had operated to exclude minorities from public contracting. These are precisely the types of statistical and testimonial evidence which, until today, this Court had credited in cases approving of race-conscious measures designed to remedy past discrimination.

More fundamentally, today's decision marks a deliberate and giant step backward in this Court's affirmative-action jurisprudence. Cynical of one municipality's attempt to redress the effects of past racial discrimination in a particular industry, the majority launches a grapeshot attack on race-conscious remedies in general. The majority's unnecessary pronouncements will inevitably discourage or prevent governmental entities, particularly States and localities, from acting to rectify the scourge of past discrimination. This is the harsh reality of the majority's decision, but it is not the Constitution's command.

I

As an initial matter, the majority takes an exceedingly myopic view of the factual predicate on which the Richmond City Council relied when it passed the Minority Business Utilization Plan. The majority analyzes Richmond's initiative as if it were based solely upon the facts about local construction and contracting practices adduced during the city council session at which the measure was enacted. In so doing, the majority downplays the fact that the city council had before it a rich trove of evidence that discrimination in the Nation's construction industry had seriously impaired the competitive position of businesses owned or controlled by members of minority groups. It is only against this backdrop of documented national discrimination, however, that the local evidence adduced by Richmond can be properly understood. The majority's refusal to recognize that Richmond has proved itself no exception to the dismaying pattern of national exclusion which Congress so painstakingly identified infects its entire analysis of this case.

Six years before Richmond acted, Congress passed, and the President signed, the Public Works Employment Act of 1977, (Act), a measure which appropriated $4 billion in federal grants to state and local governments for use in public works projects. Section 103(f)(2) of the Act was a minority business set-aside provision. It required state or local grantees to use 10% of their federal grants to procure services or supplies from businesses owned or controlled by members of statutorily identified minority groups, absent an administrative waiver. In 1980, in *Fullilove,* this Court upheld the validity of this federal set-aside. Chief Justice Burger's principal opinion noted the importance of overcoming those "criteria, methods, or practices thought by Congress to have the effect of defeating, or substantially impairing, access by the minority business community to public funds made available by congressional appropriations." *Fullilove.* Finding the set-aside provision properly tailored to this goal, the Chief Justice concluded that the program was valid under either strict or intermediate scrutiny.

The congressional program upheld in *Fullilove* was based upon an array of congressional studies which documented the powerful influence of racially exclusionary practices in the business world. A 1975 Report by the House Committee on Small Business concluded:

"The effects of past inequities stemming from racial prejudice have not remained in the past. The Congress has recognized the reality that past discriminatory practices have, to some degree, adversely affected our present economic system.

"While minority persons comprise about 16 percent of the Nation's population, of the 13 million businesses in the United States, only 382,000, or approximately 3.0 percent, are owned by minority individuals. The most recent data from the Department of Commerce also indicates that the gross receipts of all businesses in this country totals about $2,540.8 billion, and of this amount only $16.6 billion, or about 0.65 percent was realized by minority business concerns.

"These statistics are not the result of random chance. *The presumption must be made that past discriminatory systems have resulted in present economic inequities.*" H. R. Rep. No. 94–468, pp. 1–2 (1975) (quoted in *Fullilove, supra,* at 465) (opinion of Burger, C. J.).

A 1977 Report by the same Committee concluded:

"[O]ver the years, there has developed a business system which has traditionally excluded measurable minority participation. In the past more than the present, this system of conducting business transactions overtly precluded minority input. Currently, we more often encounter a business system which is racially neutral on its face, but because of past overt social and economic discrimination is presently operating, in effect, to perpetuate these past inequities. Minorities, until recently, have not participated to any measurable extent, in our total business system generally, or in the construction industry in particular." H. R. Rep. No. 94–1791, (1977), summarizing H. R. Rep. No. 94–468, (1976) (quoted in *Fullilove*).

Congress further found that minorities seeking initial public contracting assignments often faced immense entry barriers which did not confront experienced nonminority contractors. A report submitted to Congress in 1975 by the United States Commission on Civil Rights, for example, described the way in which fledgling minority-owned businesses were hampered by "deficiencies in working capital, inability to meet bonding requirements, disabilities caused by an inadequate 'track record,' lack of awareness of bidding opportunities, unfamiliarity with bidding procedures, preselection before the formal advertising process, and the exercise of discretion by government procurement officers to disfavor minority businesses." *Fullilove* (summarizing United States Comm'n on Civil Rights, Minorities and Women as Government Contractors (May 1975)).

Thus, as of 1977, there was "abundant evidence" in the public domain "that minority businesses ha[d] been denied effective participation in public contracting opportunities by procurement practices that perpetuated the effects of prior discrimination." *Fullilove.* Significantly, this evidence demonstrated that discrimination had prevented existing or nascent minority-owned businesses from obtaining not only federal contracting assignments, but state and local ones as well. See *Fullilove.*

The members of the Richmond City Council were well aware of these exhaustive congressional findings, a point the majority, tellingly, elides. The transcript of the session at which the council enacted the local set-aside initiative contains numerous references to the 6-year-old congressional set-aside program, to the evidence of nationwide discrimination barriers described above, and to the *Fullilove* decision itself. (Remarks of City Attorney William H. Hefty); (remarks of Councilmember William J. Leidinger); (remarks of minority community task force president Freddie Ray); (remarks of Councilmember Henry L. Marsh III); (remarks of City Manager Manuel Deese).

The city council's members also heard testimony that, although minority groups made up half of the city's population, only 0.67% of the $24.6 million which Richmond had dispensed in construction contracts during the five years ending in March 1983 had gone to minority-owned prime contractors. *Id.,* at 43 (remarks of Councilmember Henry W. Richardson). They heard testimony that the major Richmond area construction trade associations had virtually no minorities among their hundreds of members. Finally, they heard testimony from city officials as to the exclusionary history of the local construction industry. As the District Court noted, not a single person who testified before the city council denied that discrimination in Richmond's construction industry had been widespread. Civ. Action No. 84–0021 (ED Va., Dec. 3, 1984).

So long as one views Richmond's local evidence of discrimination against the backdrop of systematic nationwide racial discrimination which Congress had so painstakingly identified in this very industry, this case is readily resolved.

II

"Agreement upon a means for applying the Equal Protection Clause to an affirmative-action program has eluded this Court every time the issue has come before us." *Wygant* v. *Jackson Bd. of Education* (1986) (MARSHALL, J., dissenting). My view has long been that race-conscious classifications designed to further remedial goals "must serve important governmental objectives and must be substantially related to achievement of those objectives" in order to withstand constitutional scrutiny. *University of California Regents* v. *Bakke* (1978) (joint opinion of BRENNAN, WHITE, MARSHALL, and BLACKMUN, JJ.); see also *Wygant* (MARSHALL, J., dissenting); *Fullilove* (MARSHALL, J., concurring in judgment). Analyzed in terms of this two-pronged standard, Richmond's set-aside, like the federal program on which it was modeled, is "plainly constitutional." *Fullilove,* (MARSHALL, J., concurring in judgment).

A

1

Turning first to the governmental interest inquiry, Richmond has two powerful interests in setting aside a portion of public contracting funds for minority-owned enterprises. The first is the city's interest in eradicating the effects of past racial discrimination. It is far too late in the day to doubt that remedying such discrimination is a compelling, let alone an important, interest. In *Fullilove,* six Members of this Court deemed this interest sufficient to support a race-conscious set-aside program governing federal contract procurement. The decision, in holding that the federal set-aside provision satisfied the Equal Protection Clause under any level of scrutiny, recognized that the measure sought to remove "barriers to competitive access which had their roots in racial and ethnic discrimination, and which continue today, even absent any intentional discrimination or unlawful conduct." Indeed, we have repeatedly reaffirmed the government's interest in breaking down barriers erected by past racial discrimination, in cases involving access to public education, *McDaniel* v. *Barresi* (1971); *University of California*

Regents v. *Bakke,* employment, *United States* v. *Paradise* (1987) (Powell, J., concurring), and valuable government contracts, *Fullilove* (opinion of Burger, C. J.); (Powell, J., concurring); (MARSHALL, J., concurring in judgment).

Richmond has a second compelling interest in setting aside, where possible, a portion of its contracting dollars. That interest is the prospective one of preventing the city's own spending decisions from reinforcing and perpetuating the exclusionary effects of past discrimination. See *Fullilove,* (noting Congress's conclusion that "the subcontracting practices of prime contractors could perpetuate the prevailing impaired access by minority businesses to public contracting opportunities"); (Powell, J., concurring).

The majority pays only lipservice to this additional governmental interest. But our decisions have often emphasized the danger of the government tacitly adopting, encouraging, or furthering racial discrimination even by its own routine operations. In *Shelley* v. *Kraemer* (1948), this Court recognized this interest as a constitutional command, holding unanimously that the Equal Protection Clause forbids courts to enforce racially restrictive covenants even where such covenants satisfied all requirements of state law and where the State harbored no discriminatory intent. Similarly, in *Norwood* v. *Harrison* (1973), we invalidated a program in which a State purchased textbooks and loaned them to students in public and private schools, including private schools with racially discriminatory policies. We stated that the Constitution requires a State "to steer clear, not only of operating the old dual system of racially segregated schools, but also of giving significant aid to institutions that practice racial or other invidious discrimination." See also *Gilmore* v. *City of Montgomery* (1974) (upholding federal-court order forbidding city to allow private segregated schools which allegedly discriminated on the basis of race to use public parks).

The majority is wrong to trivialize the continuing impact of government acceptance or use of private institutions or structures once wrought by discrimination. When government channels all its contracting funds to a white-dominated community of established contractors whose racial homogeneity is the product of private discrimination, it does more than place its *imprimatur* on the practices which forged and which continue to define that community. It also provides a measurable boost to those economic entities that have thrived within it, while denying important economic benefits to those entities which, but for prior discrimination, might well be better qualified to receive valuable government contracts. In my view, the interest in ensuring that the government does not reflect and reinforce prior private discrimination in dispensing public contracts is every bit as strong as the interest in eliminating private discrimination—an interest which this Court has repeatedly deemed compelling. See, *e.g., New York State Club Assn.* v. *New York City* (1988); *Board of Directors of Rotary Int'l* v. *Rotary Club of Duarte* (1987); *Roberts* v. *United States Jaycees* (1984); *Bob Jones University* v. *United States* (1983); *Runyon* v. *McCrary* (1976). The more government bestows its rewards on those persons or businesses that were positioned to thrive during a period of private racial discrimination, the tighter the deadhand grip of prior discrimination becomes on the present and future. Cities like Richmond may not be constitutionally required to adopt set-aside plans. But see *North Carolina State Bd. of Education* v. *Swann* (1971) (Constitution may require consideration of race in remedying state-sponsored school segregation); *McDaniel* (same, and stating that "[a]ny other approach would freeze the status quo that is the very target of all desegregation processes"). But there can be no doubt that when Richmond acted affirmatively to stem the perpetuation of patterns of discrimination through its own decision-making, it served an interest of the highest order.

2

The remaining question with respect to the "governmental interest" prong of equal protection analysis is whether Richmond has proffered satisfactory proof of past racial discrimination to support its twin interests in remediation and in governmental nonperpetuation. Although the Members of this Court have differed on the appropriate standard of review for race-conscious remedial measures, see *United States* v. *Paradise* (plurality opinion); *Sheet Metal Workers* v. *EEOC* (1986) (plurality opinion), we have always regarded this factual inquiry as a practical one. Thus, the Court has eschewed rigid tests which require the provision of particular species of evidence, statistical or otherwise. At the same time we have required that government adduce evidence that, taken as a whole, is sufficient to support its claimed interest and to dispel the natural concern that it acted out of mere "paternalistic stereotyping, not on a careful consideration of modern social conditions." *Fullilove* v. *Klutznick* (MARSHALL, J., concurring in judgment).

The separate opinions issued in *Wygant* v. *Jackson Bd. of Education,* a case involving a school board's race-conscious layoff provision, reflect this shared understanding. Justice Powell's opinion for a plurality of four Justices stated that "the trial court must make a factual determination that the employer had a strong basis in evidence for its conclusion that remedial action was necessary." JUSTICE O'CONNOR's separate concurrence required "a firm basis for concluding that remedial action was appropriate." The dissenting opinion I authored, joined by JUSTICES BRENNAN and BLACKMUN, required a government body to present a "legitimate factual predicate" and a reviewing court to "genuinely consider the circumstances of the provision at issue." Finally, JUSTICE STEVENS' separate dissent sought and found "a rational and unquestionably legitimate basis" for the school board's action. Our unwillingness to go beyond these generalized standards to require specific types of proof in all circumstances reflects, in my view, an understanding that discrimination takes a myriad of "ingenious and pervasive forms." *University of California Regents* v. *Bakke* (separate opinion of MARSHALL, J.).

The varied body of evidence on which Richmond relied provides a "strong," "firm," and "unquestionably legitimate" basis upon which the city council could determine that the effects of past racial discrimination warranted a remedial and prophylactic governmental response. As I have noted, Richmond acted against a backdrop of congressional and Executive Branch studies which demonstrated with such force the nationwide pervasiveness of prior discrimination that Congress presumed that " 'present economic inequities' " in construction contracting resulted from " 'past discriminatory systems.' " (Quoting H. R. Rep. No. 94–468, (1975).) The city's local evidence confirmed that Richmond's construction industry did not deviate from this pernicious national pattern. The fact that just 0.67% of public construction expenditures over the previous five years had gone to minority-owned prime contractors, despite the city's racially mixed population, strongly suggests that construction contracting in the area was rife with "present economic inequities." To the extent this enormous disparity did not itself demonstrate that discrimination had occurred, the descriptive testimony of Richmond's elected and appointed leaders drew the necessary link between the pitifully small presence of minorities in construction contracting and past exclusionary practices. That *no one* who testified challenged this depiction of widespread racial discrimination in area construction contracting lent significant weight to these accounts. The fact that area trade associations had virtually no minority members dramatized the extent of present inequities and suggested the lasting power of past discriminatory systems. In sum, to suggest that the facts on which Rich-

466 / Thurgood Marshall

mond has relied do not provide a sound basis for its finding of past racial discrimination simply blinks credibility.

Richmond's reliance on localized, industry-specific findings is a far cry from the reliance on generalized "societal discrimination" which the majority decries as a basis for remedial action. But characterizing the plight of Richmond's minority contractors as mere "societal discrimination" is not the only respect in which the majority's critique shows an unwillingness to come to grips with why construction-contracting in Richmond is essentially a whites-only enterprise. The majority also takes the disingenuous approach of disaggregating Richmond's local evidence, attacking it piecemeal, and thereby concluding that no *single* piece of evidence adduced by the city, "standing alone," suffices to prove past discrimination. But items of evidence do not, of course, "stan[d] alone" or exist in alien juxtaposition; they necessarily work together, reinforcing or contradicting each other.

In any event, the majority's criticisms of individual items of Richmond's evidence rest on flimsy foundations. The majority states, for example, that reliance on the disparity between the share of city contracts awarded to minority firms (0.67%) and the minority population of Richmond (approximately 50%) is "misplaced." It is true that, when the factual predicate needed to be proved is one of *present* discrimination, we have generally credited statistical contrasts between the racial composition of a work force and the general population as proving discrimination only where this contrast revealed "gross statistical disparities." *Hazelwood School Dist.* v. *United States,* see also *Teamsters* v. *United States* (1977). But this principle does not impugn Richmond's statistical contrast, for two reasons. First, considering how minuscule the share of Richmond public construction contracting dollars received by minority-owned businesses is, it is hardly unreasonable to conclude that this case involves a "gross statistical disparit[y]." *Hazelwood School Dist.* There are roughly equal numbers of minorities and nonminorities in Richmond—yet minority-owned businesses receive *one-seventy-fifth* the public contracting funds that other businesses receive. See *Teamsters,* ("[F]ine tuning of the statistics could not have obscured the glaring absence of minority [bus] drivers. . . . [T]he company's inability to rebut the inference of discrimination came not from a misuse of statistics but from 'the inexorable zero' ").

Second, and more fundamentally, where the issue is not present discrimination but rather whether *past* discrimination has resulted in the *continuing exclusion* of minorities from an historically tight-knit industry, a contrast between population and work force is entirely appropriate to help gauge the degree of the exclusion. In *Johnson* v. *Transportation Agency, Santa Clara County,* JUSTICE O'CONNOR specifically observed that, when it is alleged that discrimination has prevented blacks from "obtaining th[e] experience" needed to qualify for a position, the "relevant comparison" is not to the percentage of blacks in the pool of qualified candidates, but to "the total percentage of blacks in the labor force." See also *Steelworkers* v. *Weber* (1979); *Teamsters.* This contrast is especially illuminating in cases like this, where a main avenue of introduction into the work force—here, membership in the trade associations whose members presumably train apprentices and help them procure subcontracting assignments—is itself grossly dominated by nonminorities. The majority's assertion that the city "does not even know how many MBE's in the relevant market are qualified," is thus entirely beside the point. If Richmond indeed has a monochromatic contracting community—a conclusion reached by the District Court—this most likely reflects the lingering power of past exclusionary practices. Certainly this is the explanation Congress has found persuasive at the national level. See *Fullilove.* The city's requirement that prime public contractors set aside 30% of their subcontracting assignments for minority-owned enterprises, subject to the ordinance's provision for waivers where minority-owned enterprises are unavailable or unwilling to participate, is designed precisely to ease minority contractors into the industry.

The majority's perfunctory dismissal of the testimony of Richmond's appointed and elected leaders is also deeply disturbing. These officials —including councilmembers, a former mayor, and the present city manager—asserted that race discrimination in area contracting had been widespread, and that the set-aside ordinance was a sincere and necessary attempt to eradicate the effects of this discrimination. The majority, however, states that where racial classifications are concerned, "simple legislative assurances of good intention cannot suffice." It similarly discounts as minimally probative the city council's designation of its set-aside plan as remedial. "[B]lind judicial deference to legislative or executive pronouncements," the majority explains, "has no place in equal protection analysis."

No one, of course, advocates "blind judicial deference" to the findings of the city council or the testimony of city leaders. The majority's suggestion that wholesale deference is what Richmond seeks is a classic straw-man argument. But the majority's trivialization of the testimony of Richmond's leaders is dismaying in a far more serious respect. By disregarding the testimony of local leaders and the judgment of local government, the majority does violence to the very principles of comity within our federal system which this Court has long championed. Local officials, by virtue of their proximity to, and their expertise with, local affairs, are exceptionally well qualified to make determinations of public good "within their respective spheres of authority." *Hawaii Housing Authority* v. *Midkiff* (1984); see also *FERC* v. *Mississippi* (1982) (O'CONNOR, J., concurring in judgment in part and dissenting in part). The majority, however, leaves any traces of comity behind in its head-long rush to strike down Richmond's race-conscious measure.

Had the majority paused for a moment on the facts of the Richmond experience, it would have discovered that the city's leadership is deeply familiar with what racial discrimination is. The members of the Richmond City Council have spent long years witnessing multifarious acts of discrimination, including, but not limited to, the deliberate diminution of black residents' voting rights, resistance to school desegregation, and publicly sanctioned housing discrimination. Numerous decisions of federal courts chronicle this disgraceful recent history. In *Richmond* v. *United States,* (1975), for example, this Court denounced Richmond's decision to annex part of an adjacent county at a time when the city's black population was nearing 50% because it was "infected by the impermissible purpose of denying the right to vote based on race through perpetuating white majority power to exclude Negroes from office." (BRENNAN, J., dissenting) (describing Richmond's "flagrantly discriminatory purpose . . . to avert a transfer of political control to what was fast becoming a black-population majority.")

In *Bradley* v. *School Bd. of Richmond* (CA4 1972), aff'd by an equally divided Court, (1973), the Court of Appeals for the Fourth Circuit, sitting en banc, reviewed in the context of a school desegregation case Richmond's long history of inadequate compliance with *Brown* v. *Board of Education* (1954), and the cases implementing its holding. The dissenting judge elaborated:

> "The sordid history of Virginia's, and Richmond's attempts to circumvent, defeat, and nullify the holding of *Brown I* has been recorded in the opinions of this and other courts, and need not be repeated in detail here. It suffices to say that there was massive resistance and every state resource, including the services of the legal officers of the State, the services of private counsel (costing

THE OPINIONS / 469

the State hundreds of thousands of dollars), the State police, and the power and prestige of the Governor, was employed to defeat *Brown I.* In Richmond, as has been mentioned, not even freedom of choice became actually effective until 1966, *twelve years after the decision of Brown I."*

The Court of Appeals majority in *Bradley* used equally pungent words in describing public and private housing discrimination in Richmond. Though rejecting the black plaintiffs' request that it consolidate Richmond's school district with those of two neighboring counties, the majority nonetheless agreed with the plaintiffs' assertion that "within the City of Richmond there has been state (also federal) action tending to perpetuate apartheid of the races in ghetto patterns throughout the city."

When the legislatures and leaders of cities with histories of pervasive discrimination testify that past discrimination has infected one of their industries, armchair cynicism like that exercised by the majority has no place. It may well be that "the autonomy of a State is an essential component of federalism," *Garcia* v. *San Antonio Metropolitan Transit Authority* (1985) (O'CONNOR, J., dissenting), and that "each State is sovereign within its own domain, governing its citizens and providing for their general welfare," *FERC* v. *Mississippi* (O'CONNOR, J., dissenting), but apparently this is not the case when federal judges, with nothing but their impressions to go on, choose to disbelieve the explanations of these local governments and officials. Disbelief is particularly inappropriate here in light of the fact that appellee Croson, which had the burden of proving unconstitutionality at trial, *Wygant* has *at no point* come forward with *any* direct evidence that the city council's motives were anything other than sincere.

Finally, I vehemently disagree with the majority's dismissal of the congressional and Executive Branch findings noted in *Fullilove* as having "extremely limited" probative value in this case. The majority concedes that Congress established nothing less than a "presumption" that minority contracting firms have been disadvantaged by prior discrimination. The majority, inexplicably, would forbid Richmond to "share" in this information, and permit only Congress to take note of these ample findings. In thus requiring that Richmond's local evidence be severed from the context in which it was prepared, the majority would require cities seeking to eradicate the effects of past discrimination within their borders to reinvent the evidentiary wheel and engage in unnecessarily duplicative, costly, and time-consuming factfinding.

No principle of federalism or of federal power, however, forbids a state or local government from drawing upon a nationally relevant historical record prepared by the Federal Government. See *Renton* v. *Playtime Theatres, Inc.* (1986) (city is "entitled to rely on the experiences of Seattle and other cities" in enacting an adult theater ordinance, as the First Amendment "does not require a city . . . to conduct new studies or produce evidence independent of that already generated by other cities, so long as whatever evidence the cities relies upon is reasonably believed to be relevant to the problem that the city addresses"); see also *Steelworkers* v. *Weber* ("Judicial findings of exclusion from crafts on racial grounds are so numerous as to make such exclusion a proper subject for judicial notice"); cf. *Wygant* (MARSHALL, J., dissenting) ("No race-conscious provision that purports to serve a remedial purpose can be fairly assessed in a vacuum"). Of course, Richmond could have built an even more compendious record of past discrimination, one including additional stark statistics and additional individual accounts of past discrimination. But nothing in the Fourteenth Amendment imposes such onerous documentary obligations upon States and localities once the reality of past discrimination is apparent.

B

In my judgment, Richmond's set-aside plan also comports with the second prong of the equal protection inquiry, for it is substantially related to the interests it seeks to serve in remedying past discrimination and in ensuring that municipal contract procurement does not perpetuate that discrimination. The most striking aspect of the city's ordinance is the similarity it bears to the "appropriately limited" federal set-aside provision upheld in *Fullilove*. Like the federal provision, Richmond's is limited to five years in duration, and was not renewed when it came up for reconsideration in 1988. Like the federal provision, Richmond's contains a waiver provision freeing from its subcontracting requirements those nonminority firms that demonstrate that they cannot comply with its provisions. Like the federal provision, Richmond's has a minimal impact on innocent third parties. While the measure affects 30% of *public* contracting dollars, that translates to only 3% of overall Richmond area contracting. (Recounting federal census figures on construction in Richmond); see *Fullilove,* (burden shouldered by nonminority firms is "relatively light" compared to "overall construction contracting opportunities").

Finally, like the federal provision, Richmond's does not interfere with any vested right of a contractor to a particular contract; instead it operates entirely prospectively. Richmond's initiative affects only future economic arrangements and imposes only a diffuse burden on nonminority competitors—here, businesses owned or controlled by nonminorities which seek subcontracting work on public construction projects. The plurality in *Wygant* emphasized the importance of not disrupting the settled and legitimate expectations of innocent parties. "While hiring goals impose a diffuse burden, often foreclosing only one of several opportunities, layoffs impose the entire burden of achieving racial equality on particular individuals, often resulting in serious disruption of their lives. That burden is too intrusive." *Wygant,* see *Steelworkers* v. *Weber.*

These factors, far from "justify[ing] a preference of any size or duration," are precisely the factors to which this Court looked in *Fullilove.* The majority takes issue, however, with two aspects of Richmond's tailoring: the city's refusal to explore the use of race-neutral measures to increase minority business participation in contracting, and the selection of a 30% set-aside figure. The majority's first criticism is flawed in two respects. First, the majority overlooks the fact that since 1975, Richmond has barred both discrimination by the city in awarding public contracts and discrimination by public contractors. The virtual absence of minority businesses from the city's contracting rolls, indicated by the fact that such businesses have received less than 1% of public contracting dollars, strongly suggests that this ban has not succeeded in redressing the impact of past discrimination or in preventing city contract procurement from reinforcing racial homogeneity. Second, the majority's suggestion that Richmond should have first undertaken such race-neutral measures as a program of city financing for small firms, ignores the fact that such measures, while theoretically appealing, have been discredited by Congress as ineffectual in eradicating the effects of past discrimination in this very industry. For this reason, this Court in *Fullilove* refused to fault Congress for not undertaking race-neutral measures as precursors to its race-conscious set-aside. See *Fullilove* (noting inadequacy of previous measures designed to give experience to minority businesses); ("By the time Congress enacted [the federal set-aside] in 1977, it knew that other remedies had failed to ameliorate the effects of racial discrimination in the construction industry"). The Equal Protection Clause does not require Richmond to retrace Congress's steps when Congress has found that those steps lead nowhere. Given the well-exposed limitations of race-neutral measures, it was thus appropriate for a municipality like Richmond to conclude that, in the words of JUSTICE BLACKMUN, "[i]n order to get beyond racism, we must first take account of race. There is no other way." *University of California Regents* v. *Bakke.*

As for Richmond's 30% target, the majority states that this figure "cannot be said to be narrowly tailored to any goal, except perhaps outright racial balancing." The majority ignores two important facts. First, the set-aside measure affects only 3% of overall city contracting; thus, any imprecision in tailoring has far less impact than the majority suggests. But more important, the majority ignores the fact that Richmond's 30% figure was patterned directly on the *Fullilove* precedent. Congress's 10% figure fell "roughly halfway between the present percentage of minority contractors and the percentage of minority group members in the Nation." *Fullilove.* The Richmond City Council's 30% figure similarly falls roughly halfway between the present percentage of Richmond-based minority contractors (almost zero) and the percentage of minorities in Richmond (50%). In faulting Richmond for not presenting a different explanation for its choice of a set-aside figure, the majority honors *Fullilove* only in the breach.

III

I would ordinarily end my analysis at this point and conclude that Richmond's ordinance satisfies both the governmental interest and substantial relationship prongs of our Equal Protection Clause analysis. However, I am compelled to add more, for the majority has gone beyond the facts of this case to announce a set of principles which unnecessarily restricts the power of governmental entities to take race-conscious measures to redress the effects of prior discrimination.

A

Today, for the first time, a majority of this Court has adopted strict scrutiny as its standard of Equal Protection Clause review of race-conscious remedial measures. (SCALIA, J., concurring in judgment.) This is an unwelcome development. A profound difference separates governmental actions that themselves are racist, and governmental actions that seek to remedy the effects of prior racism or to prevent neutral governmental activity from perpetuating the effects of such racism. See, *e.g., Wygant* v. *Jackson Bd. of Education* (1986) (MARSHALL, J., dissenting); *Fullilove* (MARSHALL, J., concurring in judgment); *University of California Regents* v. *Bakke* (1978) (joint opinion of BRENNAN, WHITE, MARSHALL, and BLACKMUN, JJ.).

Racial classifications "drawn on the presumption that one race is inferior to another or because they put the weight of government behind racial hatred and separatism" warrant the strictest judicial scrutiny because of the very irrelevance of these rationales. By contrast, racial classifications drawn for the purpose of remedying the effects of discrimination that itself was race based have a highly pertinent basis: the tragic and indelible fact that discrimination against blacks and other racial minorities in this Nation has pervaded our Nation's history and continues to scar our society. As I stated in *Fullilove:* "Because the consideration of race is relevant to remedying the continuing effects of past racial discrimination, and because governmental programs employing racial classifications for remedial purposes can be crafted to avoid stigmatization . . . such programs should not be subjected to conventional 'strict scrutiny'—scrutiny that is strict in theory, but fatal in fact." *Fullilove.*

In concluding that remedial classifications warrant no different standard of review under the Constitution than the most brutal and repugnant forms of state-sponsored racism, a majority of this Court signals that it regards racial discrimination as largely a phenomenon of the past, and that government bodies need no longer preoccupy themselves with rectifying racial injustice. I, however, do not believe this Nation is anywhere close to eradicating racial discrimination or its vestiges. In constitutionalizing its wishful thinking, the majority today does a grave disservice not only to those victims of past and present racial discrimination in this Nation whom government has sought to assist, but also to this Court's long tradition of approaching issues of race with the utmost sensitivity.

B

I am also troubled by the majority's assertion that, even if it did not believe generally in strict scrutiny of race-based remedial measures, "the circumstances of this case" require this Court to look upon the Richmond City Council's measure with the strictest scrutiny. The sole such circumstance which the majority cites, however, is the fact that blacks in Richmond are a "dominant racial grou[p]" in the city. In support of this characterization of dominance, the majority observes that "blacks comprise approximately 50% of the population of the city of Richmond" and that "[f]ive of the nine seats on the city council are held by blacks."

While I agree that the numerical and political supremacy of a given racial group is a factor bearing upon the level of scrutiny to be applied, this Court has never held that numerical inferiority, standing alone, makes a racial group "suspect" and thus entitled to strict scrutiny review. Rather, we have identified *other* "traditional indicia of suspectness": whether a group has been "saddled with such disabilities, or subjected to such a history of purposeful unequal treatment, or relegated to such a position of political powerlessness as to command extraordinary protection from the majoritarian political process." *San Antonio Independent School Dist.* v. *Rodriguez* (1973).

It cannot seriously be suggested that nonminorities in Richmond have any "history of purposeful unequal treatment." Nor is there any indication that they have any of the disabilities that have characteristically afflicted those groups this Court has deemed suspect. Indeed, the numerical and political dominance of nonminorities within the State of Virginia and the Nation as a whole provides an enormous political check against the "simple racial politics" at the municipal level which the majority fears. If the majority really believes that groups like Richmond's nonminorities, which comprise approximately half the population but which are outnumbered even marginally in political fora, are deserving of suspect class status for these reasons alone, this Court's decisions denying suspect status to women, see *Craig* v. *Boren* (1976), and to persons with below-average incomes, see *San Antonio Independent School Dist.,* stand on extremely shaky ground. See *Castaneda* v. *Partida* (1977) (MARSHALL, J., concurring).

In my view, the "circumstances of this case" underscore the importance of *not* subjecting to a strict scrutiny straitjacket the increasing number of cities which have recently come under minority leadership and are eager to rectify, or at least prevent the perpetuation of, past racial discrimination. In many cases, these cities will be the ones with the most in the way of prior discrimination to rectify. Richmond's leaders had just witnessed decades of publicly sanctioned racial discrimination in virtually all walks of life—discrimination amply documented in the decisions of the federal judiciary. This history of "purposefully unequal treatment" forced upon minorities, not imposed by them, should raise an inference that minorities in Richmond had much to remedy—and that the 1983 set-aside was undertaken with sincere remedial goals in mind, not "simple racial politics."

Richmond's own recent political history underscores the facile nature of the majority's assumption that elected officials' voting decisions are based on the color of their skins. In recent years, white and black councilmembers in Richmond have increasingly joined hands on controversial matters. When the Richmond City Council elected a black man mayor in 1982, for example, his victory was won with the support of the city council's four white members. The vote on the set-aside plan a year later also was not purely along racial lines. Of the four white councilmembers, one voted for the measure and another abstained. The majority's view that remedial measures undertaken by municipalities with black leadership must face a stiffer test of Equal Protection Clause scrutiny than remedial measures undertaken by municipalities with white leadership implies a lack of political maturity on the part of this Nation's elected minority officials that is totally unwarranted. Such insulting judgments have no place in constitutional jurisprudence.

C

Today's decision, finally, is particularly noteworthy for the daunting standard it imposes upon States and localities contemplating the use of race-conscious measures to eradicate the present effects of prior discrimination and prevent its perpetuation. The majority restricts the use of such measures to situations in which a State or locality can put forth "a prima facie case of a constitutional or statutory violation." In so doing, the majority calls into question the validity of the business set-asides which dozens of municipalities across this Nation have adopted on the authority of *Fullilove.*

Nothing in the Constitution or in the prior decisions of this Court supports limiting state authority to confront the effects of past discrimination to those situations in which a prima facie case of a constitutional or statutory violation can be made out. By its very terms, the majority's standard effectively cedes control of a large component of the content of that constitutional provision to Congress and to state legislatures. If an antecedent Virginia or Richmond law had defined as unlawful the award to nonminorities of an overwhelming share of a city's contracting dollars, for example, Richmond's subsequent set-aside initiative would then satisfy the majority's standard. But without such a law, the initiative might not withstand constitutional scrutiny. The meaning of "equal protection of the laws" thus turns on the happenstance of whether a state or local body has previously defined illegal discrimination. Indeed, given that racially discriminatory cities may be the ones least likely to have tough antidiscrimination laws on their books, the majority's constitutional incorporation of state and local statutes has the perverse effect of inhibiting those States or localities with the worst records of official racism from taking remedial action.

Similar flaws would inhere in the majority's standard even if it incorporated only federal antidiscrimination statutes. If Congress tomorrow dramatically expanded Title VII of the Civil Rights Act of 1964—or alternatively, if it repealed that legislation altogether—the meaning of equal protection would change precipitously along with it. Whatever the Framers of the Fourteenth Amendment had in mind in 1868, it certainly was not that the content of their Amendment would turn on the amendments to or the evolving interpretations of a federal statute passed nearly a century later.

To the degree that this parsimonious standard is grounded on a view that either § 1 or § 5 of the Fourteenth Amendment substantially disempowered States and localities from remedying past racial discrimination, the majority is seriously mistaken. With respect, first, to § 5, our precedents have never suggested that this provision—or, for that matter, its companion federal-empowerment provisions in the Thirteenth and Fifteenth Amendments—was meant to pre-empt or limit state police power to undertake race-conscious remedial measures. To the contrary, in *Katzenbach* v. *Morgan* (1966), we held that § 5 "is a *positive* grant of legislative power authorizing Congress to exercise its discretion in determining whether and what legislation is needed to secure the guarantees of the Fourteenth Amendment." *South Carolina* v. *Katzenbach* (1966) (interpreting similar provision of the Fifteenth Amendment to empower Congress to "implemen[t] the rights created" by its passage); see also *City of Rome* v. *United States* (1980). Indeed, we have held that Congress has this authority even where no constitutional violation has been found. See *Katzenbach* (upholding Voting Rights Act provision nullifying state English literacy requirement we had previously upheld against Equal Protection Clause challenge). Certainly *Fullilove* did not view § 5 either as limiting the traditionally broad police powers of the States to fight discrimination, or as mandating a zero-sum game in which state power wanes as federal power waxes. On the contrary, the *Fullilove* plurality invoked § 5 only because it provided specific and certain authorization for the Federal Government's attempt to impose a race-conscious condition on the dispensation of federal funds by state and local grantees. See *Fullilove*, (basing decision on § 5 because "[i]n certain contexts, there are limitations on the reach of the Commerce Power").

As for § 1, it is too late in the day to assert seriously that the Equal Protection Clause prohibits States—or for that matter, the Federal Government, to whom the equal protection guarantee has largely been applied, see *Bolling* v. *Sharpe* (1954)—from enacting race-conscious remedies. Our cases in the areas of school desegregation, voting rights, and affirmative action have demonstrated time and again that race is constitutionally germane, precisely because race remains dismayingly relevant in American life.

In adopting its prima facie standard for States and localities, the majority closes its eyes to this constitutional history and social reality. So, too, does JUSTICE SCALIA. He would further limit consideration of race to those cases in which States find it "necessary to eliminate their own maintenance of a system of unlawful racial classification"—a "distinction" which, he states, "explains our school desegregation cases." (SCALIA, J., concurring in judgment.) But this Court's remedy-stage school desegregation decisions cannot so conveniently be cordoned off. These decisions (like those involving voting rights and affirmative action) stand for the same broad principles of equal protection which Richmond seeks to vindicate in this case: all persons have equal worth, and it is permissible, given a sufficient factual predicate and appropriate tailoring, for government to take account of race to eradicate the present effects of race-based subjugation denying that basic equality. JUSTICE SCALIA's artful distinction allows him to avoid having to repudiate "our school desegregation cases," but, like the arbitrary limitation on race-conscious relief adopted by the majority, his approach "would freeze the status quo that is the very target" of the remedial actions of States and localities. *McDaniel* v. *Barresi;* see also *Board of Education* v. *Swann* (striking down State's flat prohibition on assignment of pupils on basis of race as impeding an "effective remedy"); *United Jewish Organizations* v. *Carey* (1977) (upholding New York's use of racial criteria in drawing district lines so as to comply with § 5 of the Voting Rights Act).

The fact is that Congress's concern in passing the Reconstruction Amendments, and particularly their congressional authorization provisions, was that States would *not* adequately respond to racial violence or discrimination against newly freed slaves. To interpret any aspect of these Amendments as proscribing state remedial responses to these very problems turns the Amendments on their heads. As four Justices, of whom I was one, stated in *University of California Regents* v. *Bakke:*

> "[There is] no reason to conclude that the States cannot voluntarily accomplish under § 1 of the Fourteenth Amendment what Congress under § 5 of the Fourteenth Amendment validly may authorize or compel either the States or private persons to do. A contrary position would conflict with the traditional understanding recognizing the competence of the States to initiate measures consistent with federal policy in the absence of congressional preemption of the subject matter. *Nothing whatever in the legislative history of either the Fourteenth Amendment or the Civil Rights Acts even remotely suggests that the States are foreclosed from furthering the fundamental purpose of equal opportunity to which the Amendment and those Acts are addressed.* Indeed, voluntary initiatives by the States to achieve the national goal of equal opportunity have been recognized to be essential to its attainment. 'To use the Fourteenth Amendment as a sword against such State power would stultify that Amendment.' *Railway Mail Assn.* v. *Corsi* (Frankfurter, J., concurring)."

In short, there is simply no credible evidence that the Framers of the Fourteenth Amendment sought "to transfer the security and protection of all the civil rights . . . from the States to the Federal Government." The *Slaughter-House Cases* (1873). The three Reconstruction Amendments undeniably "worked a dramatic change in the balance between congressional and state power," they forbade state-sanctioned slavery, forbade the state-sanctioned denial of the right to vote, and (until the content of the Equal Protection Clause was substantially applied to the Federal Government through the Due Process Clause of the Fifth Amendment) uniquely forbade States from denying equal protection. The Amendments also specifically empowered the Federal Government to combat discrimination at a time when the breadth of federal power under the Constitution was less apparent than it is today. But nothing in the Amendments themselves, or in our long history of interpreting or applying those momentous charters, suggests that States, exercising their police power, are in any way constitutionally inhibited from working alongside the Federal Government in the fight against discrimination and its effects.

IV

The majority today sounds a full-scale retreat from the Court's long-standing solicitude to race-conscious remedial efforts "directed toward deliverance of the century-old promise of equality of economic opportunity." *Fullilove.* The new and restrictive tests it applies scuttle one city's effort to surmount its discriminatory past, and imperil those of dozens more localities. I, however, profoundly disagree with the cramped vision of the Equal Protection Clause which the majority offers today and with its application of that vision to Richmond, Virginia's, laudable set-aside plan. The battle against pernicious racial discrimination or its effects is nowhere near won. I must dissent.

Appendix

1	Ake v. Oklahoma 470 U.S. 68 (1985)
2	Akins v. Texas 325 U.S. 398 (1945)
3	Alberts v. California 354 U.S. 476 (1957)
4	Amalgamated Food Employees Local 590 v. Logan Valley Plaza, 391 U.S. 308 (1968)
5	Amos v. United States 255 v. 313 (1921)
6	Anderson v. Alabama 366 U.S. 208 (1961)
7	Arkansas Writers' Project, Inc. v. Ragland 481 U.S. 221 (1987)
8	Arnett v. Kennedy 416 U.S. 134 (1974)
9	Associated Press v. United States 326 U.S. 1 (1945)
10	Attorney General of Michigan ex rel Kies v Lowrey 199 U.S. 233 (1905)
11	Austin v. Michigan Chamber of Commerce 110 S. Ct. 1391 (1990)
12	Badders v. United States 240 U.S. 391 (1916)
13	Barefoot v. Estelle 463 U.S. 880 (1983)
14	Barrows v. Jackson 346 U.S. 249 (1953)
15	Beal v. Doe 432 U.S. 438 (1977)
16	Belle Terre v. Boraas 416 U.S. 1 (1973)
17	Belton v. Gebhart 87 A. 2d 862 (1952)
18	Berman v. Parker 348 U.S. 26 (1954)
19	Betts v. Brady 316 U.S. 455 (1942)
20	Board of Directors of Rotary Int'l v. Rotary Club of Duarte 481 U.S. 537 (1987)
21	Board of Education v. Allen 392 U.S. 236 (1968)
22	Board of Regents v. Roth 408 U.S. 564 (1972)
23	Bob Jones University v. United States 461 U.S. 574 (1983)
24	Bob-Lo Excursion Co. v. Michigan 333 U.S. 28 (1948)
25	Bolling v. Sharpe 347 U.S. 497 (1954)
26	Bounds v. Smith 430 U.S. 817 (1977)
27	Boynton v. Virginia 364 U.S. 454 (1960)
28	Bradley v. School Board of Richmond 402 F. 2d 1058 (1960)
29	Brewer v. Williams 430 U.S. 387 (1977)
30	Briggs v. Elliot 342 U.S. 350 (1952)
31	Britt v. North Carolina 404 U.S. 226 (1971)
32	Browder v. Gayle 142 F. Supp. 707 (1956)
33	Brown v. Board of Education (Brown II) 349 U.S. 294 (1955)
34	Brown v. Board of Education 347 U.S. 483 (1954)
35	Brown v. Louisiana 383 U.S. 131 (1966)
36	Brown v. Mississippi 297 U.S. 278 (1936)
37	Buchanan v. Warley 245 U.S. 60 (1917)
38	Buckley v. Valeo 424 U.S. 1 (1976)
39	Bumper v. North Carolina 391 U.S. 543 (1968)

40	Burns v. Ohio 360 U.S. 252 (1959)
41	Burns v. Ohio 360 U.S. 252 (1959)
42	Bush v. Orleans Parish School Board 364 U.S. 506 (1960)
43	Cable News Network, Inc. v. Noriega 111 S. Ct. 451 (1990)
44	Califano v. Jobst 434 U.S. 47 (1977)
45	California's Bankers Assoc. v. Schultz 416 U.S. 24 (1974)
46	Carey v. Population Services International 431 U.S. 678 (1977)
47	Carter v. United States 252 F. 2d 608 (1957)
48	Castanada v. Partida 430 U.S. 482 (1977)
49	Chambers v. Florida 309 U.S. 227 (1940)
50	Child Welfare Society of Flint v. Kennedy School District 189 N.W. 1002 (1922)
51	Citizens to Preserve Overton Park v. Volpe 401 U.S. 402 (1971)
52	City of Cleburne, Texas v. Cleburne Living Center 473 U.S. 432 (1985)
53	City of Richmond v. Deans 281 U.S. 704 (1930)
54	City of Rome v. United States 446 U.S. 156 (1980)
55	Clark v. Community for Creative Non-Violence 468 U.S. 288 (1984)
56	Collins v. City of Detroit 161 N.W. 905 (1917)
57	Cooper v. Aaron 358 U.S. 1 (1958)
58	Corrigan v. Buckley 271 U.S. 323 (1926)
59	Cox Broadcasting Corp. v. Cohn 420 U.S. 469 (1975)
60	Craig v. Boren 429 U.S. 190 (1976)
61	Cruz v. Beto 405 U.S. 319 (1972)
62	Cupp v. Murphy 412 U.S. 291 (1973)
63	D.H. Overmyer Co., Inc. v. Frick Co. 405 U.S. 174 (1972)
64	Dandridge v. Williams 397 U.S. 471 (1970)
65	Davis v. County School Board 103 F. Supp 337
66	Davis v. Schnell 81 F. Supp. 872 (S.D. Alabama 1949) Affirmed 336 U.S. 933 (1949)
67	Davis v. School Commissioners of Mobile County 402 U.S. 33 (1971)
68	Detroit Board of Education v. Superintendent of Public Instruction 29 N.W. 2d 902 (1947)
69	Doe v. Sarasota-Bradenton Florida Television Co., Inc. 436 So. 2d 328 (1983)
70	Douglas v. California 372 U.S. 353 (1963)
71	Dunn v. Blumstein 405 U.S. 330 (1972)
72	Durham v. United States 214 F. 2d 862 (1954)
73	Eisenstadt v. Baird 405 U.S. 438 (1972)
74	Enterprise Irrigation District v. Farmers Mutual Canal Corp. 243 U.S. 157 (1917)
75	Evitts v. Lucey 469 U.S. 387 (1985)
76	Ex parte Hull 312 U.S. 546 (1941)
77	Ex parte Virginia 100 U.S. 339 (1879)
78	Fare v. Michael C. 442 U.S. 707 (1979)
79	Faubus v. Aaron 361 U.S. 197 (1959)
80	FERC v. Mississippi 456 U.S. 742 (1982)
81	Fisher v. Hurst 333 U.S. 147 (1948)
82	Flagg Bros. Inc. v. Brooks 436 U.S. 149 (1978)
83	Flemming v. South Carolina Electric and Gas Co. 224 F. 2d 752 (1956)
84	Florida ex rel. Hawkins v. Board of Control 350 U.S. 979 (1956)
85	Florida Star v. B.J.F. 491 U.S. 524 (1989)
86	Florida v. Bostick 111 S. Ct. 2382 (1991)
87	Food Employees v. Logan Valley Plaza 391 U.S. 308 (1968)
88	Ford v. Wainwright 477 U.S. 399 (1986)
89	University of North Carolina v. Frasier 350 U.S. 979 (1956)
90	Fuentes v. Shevin 407 U.S. 67 (1972)
91	Fullilove v. Klutznick 448 U.S. 448 (1980)
92	Furman v. Georgia 408 U.S. 238 (1972)
93	Garcia v. San Antonio Metropolitan Transit Authority 469 U.S. 528 (1985)
94	Gardner v. California 393 U.S. 367 (1969)
95	Garner v. Louisiana 368 U.S. 157 (1961)

96	Garrison v. Louisiana 379 U.S. 64 (1964)
97	Gertz v. Robert Welch Inc. 418 U.S. 323 (1974)
98	Gideon v. Wainwright 372 U.S. 335 (1963)
99	Gillette v. United States 401 U.S. 437 (1971)
100	Gilmore v. City of Montgomery 417 U.S. 556 (1974)
101	Ginsberg v. New York 390 U.S. 629 (1968)
102	Globe Newspaper Co. v. Superior Court 457 U.S. 596 (1982)
103	Gong Lum v. Rice 275 U.S. 78 (1927)
104	Gray v. University of Tennessee 342 U.S. 517 (1952)
105	Grayned v. City of Rockford 408 U.S. 104 (1971)
106	Green v. County School Board of New Kent County 391 U.S. 436 (1968)
107	Greer v. Spock 424 U.S. 828 (1976)
108	Gregg v. Georgia 428 U.S. 153 (1976)
109	Griffin v. Illinois 351 U.S. 12 (1956)
110	Griswold v. Connecticut 381 U.S. 479 (1965)
111	Guinn v. United States 238 U.S. 347 (1915)
112	H.L. v. Matheson 450 U.S. 398 (1981)
113	Haines v. Kerner 404 U.S. 519 (1972)
114	Hall v. De Cuir 95 U.S. 485 (1878)
115	Hansberry v. Lee 311 U.S. 32 (1940)
116	Harmon v. Tyler 273 U.S. 668 (1927)
117	Harris v. McRae 448 U.S. 297 (1980)
118	Harrison v. NAACP 360 U.S. 167 (1959)
119	Harryman v. Estelle 616 F. 2d 870 (1980)
120	Hawaii Housing Authority v. Midkiff 467 U.S. 229 (1984)
121	Hawkins v. State 569 P. 2d 4990 (1977)
122	Haynes v. Washington 373 U.S. 503 (1963)
123	Hazelwood School District v. United States 433 U.S. 299 (1977)
124	Herb v. Pitcairn 324 U.S. 117 (1945)
125	Hill v. Texas 316 U.S. 400 (1942)
126	Hobson v. Hansen 269 F. supp 401 (1967)
127	Hodgson v. Minnesota 110 S. Ct. 2926 (1990)
128	Hollenbaugh v. Carnegie Free Library 439 U.S. 1052 (1978)
129	Hollins v. Oklahoma 295 U.S. 394 (1935)
130	Holmes v. Atlanta 191 U.S. 879 (1955)
131	Howard v. Fleming 101 U.S. 126 (1903)
132	Hudgens v. NLRB 424 U.S. 507 (1976)
133	Huffman v. Pursue, Ltd. 420 U.S. 592 (1975)
134	Humphrey v. Smith 336 U.S. 695 (1949)
135	Hurd v. Hodge 334 U.S. 24 (1948)
136	Illinois v. Perkins 110 S. Ct. 2394 (1990)
137	Imlay Township District v. State Board of Education 102 N.W. 2d 720 (1960)
138	In re Kemmler 136 U.S. 436 (1890)
139	Jackson v. Metropolitan Edison Co. 419 U.S. 345 (1974)
140	Jacobellis v. Ohio 378 U.S. 184 (1964)
141	James v. Valtierra 402 U.S. 137 (1971)
142	Jefferson v. Hackney 406 U.S. 535 (1972)
143	Johnson v. Avery 393 U.S. 483 (1969)
144	Joseph Burstyn, Inc. v. Wilson 343 U.S. 495 (1952)
145	Kadrmas v. Dickinson Public Schools 487 U.S. 450 (1988)
146	Katzenback v. Morgan 384 U.S. 641 (1966)
147	Kelley v. Johnson 425 U.S. 238 (1976)
148	Kent v. Dulles 357 U.S. 116 (1958)
149	Keyes v. School District No. 1, Denver, Co. 413 U.S. 189 (1973)
150	Kingsley International Pictures Corp v. Regents 360 U.S. 684 (1959)
151	Kulko v. Superior Court 436 U.S. 84 (1978)
152	Landmark Communications, Inc. v. Virginia 435 U.S. 829 (1978)

209	Newberry v. United States 256 U.S. 232 (1921)
210	Nixon v. Herndon 273 U.S. 536 (1927)
211	Norris v. Alabama 294 U.S. 587 (1935)
212	North Carolina State Board of Education v. Swann 402 U.S. 43 (1971)
213	O'Neil v. Vermont 144 U.S. 323 (1892)
214	Oklahoma Publishing Co. v. District Court 430 U.S. 308 (1977)
215	Oliver v. United States 466 U.S. 170 (1984)
216	Olmstead v. United States 277 U.S. 438 (1928)
217	Oregon v. Bradshaw 462 U.S. 1039 (1983)
218	Orozco v. Texas 394 U.S. 324 (1969)
219	Patton v. Mississippi 332 U.S. 463 (1947)
220	Payne v. Tennessee 111 S. Ct. 2597 (1991)
221	Pennsylvania v. Board of Trusts 353 U.S. 230 (1957)
222	Pennsylvania v. Muniz 110 S. Ct. 2638 (1990)
223	Personnel Administrator of Massachusetts v. Feeney 442 U.S. 256 (1979)
224	Purvear v. Massachusetts, 5 Wall. 475 (1867)
225	Peters v. Kiff 407 U.S. 493 (1972)
226	Pickering v. Board of Education 391 U.S. 563 (1968)
227	Pierce v. Society of Sisters 268 U.S. 510 (1925)
228	Plessy v. Ferguson 163 U.S. 537 (1896)
229	Plyer v. Doe, 457 U.S. 202 (1982)
230	Poe v. Ullman 367 U.S. 497 (1961)
231	Police Department v. Mosley 408 U.S. 92 (1972)
232	Powell v. Texas 392 U.S. 514 (1968)
233	Powers v. Ohio 111 S. Ct 1364 (1991)
234	Press Enterprise Co. v. Superior Court of California 464 U.S. 501 (1984)
235	Prince v. Massachusetts 321 U.S. 158 (1944)
236	Procunier v. Martinez 416 U.S. 396 (1974)
237	Prune Yard Shopping Center v. Robins 447 U.S. 74 (1980)
238	Railway Mail Association v. Corsi 326 U.S. 88 (1945)
239	Rankin v. McPherson 483 U.S. 378 (1987)
240	Rawlings v. Kentucky 448 U.S. 98 (1980)
241	Redrup v. New York 386 U.S. 767 (1967)
242	Reynolds v. Sims 377 U.S. 533 (1964)
243	Rhode Island v. Innis 446 U.S. 291 (1980)
244	Rice v. Elmore 165 F.2d 387 (1947)
245	Richmond v. J.A. Croson Co. 488 U.S. 469 (1989)
246	Roberts v. United States Jaycees 468 U.S. 609 (1984)
247	Robinson v. California 370 U.S. 660 (1962)
248	Rochin v. California 342 U.S. 165 (1952)
249	Roe v. Wade 410 U.S. 113 (1973)
250	Rosenbloom v. Metromedia, Inc. 403 U.S. 29 (1971)
251	Ross v. Moffitt 417 U.S. 600 (1974)
252	Roth v. United States 354 U.S. 476 (1957)
253	Roth v. United States 354 U.S. 476 (1957)
254	Runyon v. McCrary 427 U.S. 160 (1976)
255	Rushen v. Spain 464 U.S. 114 (1983)
256	Sabbath v. United States 391 U.S. 585 (1968)
257	San Antonio Independent School District v. Rodriguez 411 U.S. 1 (1973)
258	Schlesinger v. Reservists Committee 418 U.S. 208 (1974)
259	School District of the City of Lansing v. State Board of Education 116 N.W. 2d 866 (1962)
260	Shaffer v. Heitner 433 U.S. 186 (1977)
261	Shapiro v. Thompson 394 U.S. 618 (1969)
262	Sheet Metal Workers v. EEOC 478 U.S. 421 (1986)
263	Shelley v. Kraemer 334 U.S. 1 (1948)
264	Silverthorne Lumber v. United States 251 U.S. 385 (1920)

Glossary

1) *Affirmative Action*
   Legislation or other efforts taken in behalf of groups, such as racial minorities, to compensate for past discrimination against that group. Such action includes setting aside a certain number of slots for members of the group for admission to a medical school, as in the Bakke case.

2) *certiori*
   The discretionary method used by the Supreme Court to decide which cases it wishes to hear on appeal from the lower courts.

3) *common law*
   Judge-made law which has developed over the years through decisions in individual cases.

4) *Due Process*
   The due process clauses prohibit the United States (Fifth Amendment) and the States (Fourteenth Amendment) from depriving a person of life, liberty or property unfairly. Initially, due process was solely concerned with fair procedure, for example, ensuring that a person was given a hearing before the government regulated the action of the legislative and judicial branches of government. Over time, the Supreme Court held that due process also restricted what laws legislatures could pass, called "substantive due process." It is this more controversial use of due process that was used to strike down laws prohibiting contraceptive use and abortions.

5) *Equal Protection*
   That part of the Fourteenth Amendment which prohibits the states from discriminating against individuals. Originally intended to prohibit discrimination against Blacks, it has been interrupted to prohibit discrimination against other groups, including discrimination on the basis of sex, alienage and illegitimacy. There is no Equal Protection Clause in the Fifth Amendment, which applies to the United States, but Court decisions have held that the Fifth Amendment effectively incorporates equal protection concepts.

6) *Fundamental Right*
   A constitutional right of the individual which is given great protection under the Due Process and Equal Protection Clauses. When a law restricts a fundamental right, the law is usually declared unconstitutional by the courts. Examples of fundamental rights are the right to vote and the right to marry.

7) *negligence per se*
   Automatic negligence, usually for violation of a statute or ordinance.

8) *Sliding scale approach*
   This is the methodology which Marshall uses in analyzing equal protection cases. On one side of the scale, he would weigh the importance of the individual's interest involved plus the "suspectness" of the classification; on the other side, he would put the State's interest. If the individual's side of the balance outweighed the State's interest, the law would be unconstitutional. This approach rejects the three tiered approach used by the majority of the Court. Although Marshall's approach has never been accepted by the Court, the Court's adoption of the intermediate standard in the mid-seventies and the Court's use of the rational basis test to protect the mentally

retarded in the *City of Cleburne* case are indications that the Court at least partially accepts the validity of the sliding scale approach.

9) *Standing*

The ability of a litigant to raise a legal claim in court.

10) *stare decisis*

The judicial practice of following earlier decisions, called precedent, when deciding the case before the court.

11) *Strict scrutiny, intermediate scrutiny, rational basis*

The three different approaches used by the Court in analyzing equal protection cases. Strict scrutiny is used when the case involves fundamental rights or suspect classifications: the law will be held unconstitutional unless the government has a compelling reason for the law and use of the suspect class or fundamental right is necessary to achieve that purpose. It is virtually impossible for the State to meet those requirements.

Intermediate scrutiny is used for "quasi-suspect" classifications, mainly in analyzing discrimination on the basis of gender. For such a law to survive a constitutional attack, the State's purpose for classification on the basis of sex must be important, and the use of such a classification must be substantially related to achieving that purpose. Although most of the time laws which use sex-based classifications are held unconstitutional, the Court is willing to uphold these laws than those in which strict scrutiny is used.

The rational basis test is used for those classifications which do not involve suspect or quasi-suspect classes. That is, of course, the great majority of legislative classifications. When the classification is legitimate and the classification is rationally related to that purpose. In practice, the use of the rational basis test means that the law will be automatically upheld with minimal, if any, judicial scrutiny.

12) *sua sponte*

Refers to the practice of a court to take some action on its own initiative, without being asked to by the parties.

13) *Suspect Classification*

The description given by the Court to legislation which discriminates against certain groups, such as racial minorities, women and aliens. When the State makes use of such a classification, the Court usually holds the law violative of equal protection.

14) *Taking of Property*

The clause of the Fifth Amendment which prohibits an individual's private property from being taken by the government for public purposes, unless the person is fairly compensated for the property.

Index

A

Aaron et al. v. *Faubus, Governor of Arkansas,* 126
Abernathy, Ralph, 134
abortion rights, 205, 237–239, 419
    minors and, 14, 238–239
Abraham, Henry J., 138–139
access to courts, 19, 184, 212–213, 224, 382–390
    standing and, 81, 217–218, 226
Adams v. *Williams,* 240–241
administrative agencies, 233
affirmative action, 156, 170–171, 183, 208, 258–261, 448–476
Africa, 22, 139, 145, 153, 177–178
Aid to Families with Dependent Children (AFDC), 209–210, 213–214, 256, 416
Air Force, U.S., 113, 116
Ake v. *Oklahoma,* 21, 224, 391–402
Akins v. *Texas,* 66
Alabama, 53, 67, 120, 121–122, 127–129, 131–132, 134, 136, 141, 162–163, 191–193, 364
Alabama, University of, 121–122, 162–163
Alaska, 379
Alberts v. *California,* 278
alcohol and drug testing, 183, 242–244
alcoholics, incarceration of, 206, 336–350, 359
Allen, Florence, 164
Allred, James, 50
Amalgamated Food Employees Union Local 590 v. *Logan Valley Plaza, Inc.,* 16, 17
American Baptist Convention on Christian Social Progress, 128
American Bar Association Journal, 173
American Civil Liberties Union, 63, 96

American Council of Human Rights, 96
American Fund for Public Service, 30, 39
Anderson v. *Alabama,* 132
Anti-Defamation League of B'nai B'rith, 128
appearance, privacy rights and, 235, 409–413
Arizona, 251, 379
Arkansas, 36, 270
    desegregation and, 14, 110, 122–126, 152–153
Arkansas Writers' Project, Inc. v. *Ragland,* 270
Armed Forces Reserves, 217
Army, U.S., 57, 113–119, 150
Arnett v. *Kennedy,* 233
arrest warrants, 245, 247–248
Associated Press v. *United States,* 298–299
association, *see* freedom of association
Attorney General of Michigan ex rel. Kies v. *Lowrey,* 434, 435
Austin v. *Michigan Chamber of Commerce,* 211
Azikiwe, Nnamdi, 145

B

Bagley, United States v., 221n
Bail Reform Act (1984), 226–227
Baker v. *Carr,* 206
Baltimore, Md., 21, 22–24, 27–31, 133, 143, 146, 173, 176
banking records, 249
bankruptcy fees, 180–181, 212–213
Barrows v. *Jackson,* 79–81
Bates, Daisy, 152

R

S

Z